Politics and Development of Contemporary China

Series Editors
Kevin G. Cai
University of Waterloo
Renison University College
Waterloo, ON, Canada

Pan Guang
Shanghai Center for International Studies
Shanghai Academy of Social Sciences
Shanghai, China

Daniel C. Lynch
University of Southern California
School of International Relations
Los Angeles, CA, USA

As China's power grows, the search has begun in earnest for what superpower status will mean for the People's Republic of China as a nation as well as the impact of its new-found influence on the Asia-Pacific region and the global international order at large. By providing a venue for exciting and ground-breaking titles, the aim of this series is to explore the domestic and international implications of China's rise and transformation through a number of key areas including politics, development and foreign policy. The series will also give a strong voice to non-western perspectives on China's rise in order to provide a forum that connects and compares the views of academics from both the east and west reflecting the truly international nature of the discipline.

More information about this series at
http://www.palgrave.com/gp/series/14541

Wei-chin Lee
Editor

Taiwan's Political Re-Alignment and Diplomatic Challenges

palgrave
macmillan

Editor
Wei-chin Lee
Department of Politics and International Affairs
Wake Forest University
Winston-Salem, NC, USA

Politics and Development of Contemporary China
ISBN 978-3-319-77124-3   ISBN 978-3-319-77125-0   (eBook)
https://doi.org/10.1007/978-3-319-77125-0

Library of Congress Control Number: 2018935940

© The Editor(s) (if applicable) and The Author(s) 2019
This work is subject to copyright. All rights are solely and exclusively licensed by the Publisher, whether the whole or part of the material is concerned, specifically the rights of translation, reprinting, reuse of illustrations, recitation, broadcasting, reproduction on microfilms or in any other physical way, and transmission or information storage and retrieval, electronic adaptation, computer software, or by similar or dissimilar methodology now known or hereafter developed.
The use of general descriptive names, registered names, trademarks, service marks, etc. in this publication does not imply, even in the absence of a specific statement, that such names are exempt from the relevant protective laws and regulations and therefore free for general use.
The publisher, the authors, and the editors are safe to assume that the advice and information in this book are believed to be true and accurate at the date of publication. Neither the publisher nor the authors or the editors give a warranty, express or implied, with respect to the material contained herein or for any errors or omissions that may have been made. The publisher remains neutral with regard to jurisdictional claims in published maps and institutional affiliations.

Cover design by Laura de Grasse

Printed on acid-free paper

This Palgrave Macmillan imprint is published by the registered company Springer International Publishing AG part of Springer Nature.
The registered company address is: Gewerbestrasse 11, 6330 Cham, Switzerland

ACKNOWLEDGMENTS

This book grew, in large part, from an international conference on "Taiwan in the Realm of East Asia" at Wake Forest University, Oct. 21–23, 2016. The grant awarded by the Taipei Economic and Cultural Representative Office (TECRO) in Washington, D.C., was essential in the arrangement and logistics of the conference as well as the preparation of the book project. Wake Forest University's Office of Associate Provost for Global Affairs headed by Dr. Kline Harrison also co-sponsored the conference. As the conference organizer and the editor of the volume, I would like to express my sincere gratitude for their generous support and encouragement for scholarly exchanges and knowledge advancement on the study of Taiwanese politics. Meanwhile, in any collaborative effort for an edited volume, chapter contributors are the heart and soul of the work. Without their substantial contribution and solid commitment, it would be impossible to materialize the initial project idea. I would like to thank them each and all for their tremendous support, intellectual contribution, and extraordinary patience throughout the entire process.

Numerous people assisted the execution of this project. Special recognition and thanks go to the TECRO staffs administering the grant, Gloria Kuo initially and then Michael Chen, for their unwavering guidance and support. Emily Young offered her valuable editorial service with dedication and enthusiasm. We all are deeply indebted to her work. Dr. Katy Harriger, the department chair; Elide Vargas, the administrative coordinator; and colleagues of the Department of Politics and International Affairs at Wake Forest University provided assistance in many ways to ensure a successful conference. Last, but not least, the editors at Palgrave Macmillan naturally deserve our thanks for their patience during the long process of this project execution and their diligent work in taking care of every step of this book publication. In particular, Dr. Kevin G. Cai, co-editor of the series of *Politics and Development of Contemporary China,* introduced me to the series, and Alina Yurova, editor for Regional Politics and Development Studies, gave treasured suggestions to navigate the process of publication. All these wonderful people involved made this project an enjoyable and rewarding experience.

Contents

1 The Turn of Fortune: Realignment in Taiwan's Domestic
  Politics and Diplomacy 1
  Wei-chin Lee

Part I Democracy and New Political Landscape 31

2 The Quality of Democracy in Taiwan 33
  Bruce J. Dickson

3 Taiwan's General Elections of 2016 49
  John Fuh-sheng Hsieh

4 The Rise of the New Power Party in Taiwan's 2016
  Legislative Election: Reality and Challenges 71
  Ian Tsung-yen Chen and Da-chi Liao

5 Party's Issue Competence and Electoral Decisions
  in Taiwan's 2012 and 2016 Presidential Elections 97
  Ching-hsin Yu and T. Y. Wang

Part II The China Factor and Taiwan's Cross-Strait Dilemma — 117

6 A Comparative Study of the China Factor in Taiwan and Hong Kong Elections — 119
Karl Ho, Stan Hok-wui Wong, Harold D. Clarke, and Kuan-Chen Lee

7 Consensus Found and Consensus Lost: Taiwan's 2016 Election, the "1992 Consensus," and Cross-Strait Relations — 145
Wei-chin Lee

8 The DPP Ascendancy and Cross-Strait Relations — 177
Yu-Shan Wu

Part III Taiwan's International Way-out — 207

9 American Policy Toward Taiwan-China Relations in the Twenty-First Century — 209
Robert Sutter

10 Rethinking US Security Commitment to Taiwan — 245
Yuan-kang Wang

11 Beyond Diplomacy: The Political Economy of Taiwan's Relations with Southeast Asia — 271
Samuel C. Y. Ku

12 The Japan-Taiwan Relationship Under the Tsai Ing-wen Administration — 297
Madoka Fukuda

Index — 323

Notes on Contributors

Ian Tsung-yen Chen is Assistant Professor in the Institute of Political Science at National Sun Yat-sen University, Taiwan.

Harold D. Clarke is Ashbel Smith Professor in the School of Economic, Political and Policy Sciences at the University of Texas at Dallas, USA.

Bruce J. Dickson is Professor of Political Science and International Affairs, Chair of the Department of Political Science, and Director of the Sigur Center for Asian Studies at George Washington University, USA.

Madoka Fukuda is Professor in the Department of Global Politics, Faculty of Law at Hosei University, Japan.

Karl Ho is Clinical Associate Professor in the School of Economic, Political and Policy Science at the University of Texas at Dallas, USA.

John Fuh-sheng Hsieh is Professor in the Department of Political Science at the University of South Carolina, USA.

Samuel C. Y. Ku is Professor at the Department of International Affairs and Vice President of International Affairs at Wenzao Ursuline University of Languages, Taiwan.

Kuan-Chen Lee is Postdoctoral Fellow at National Taiwan University, Taiwan.

Wei-chin Lee is Professor in the Department of Politics and International Affairs at Wake Forest University, USA.

Da-chi Liao is Professor in the Institute of Political Science at National Sun Yat-sen University, Taiwan.

Robert Sutter is Professor of International Affairs at George Washington University, USA.

T. Y. Wang is Professor and Chair in the Department of Politics and Government at Illinois State University, USA.

Yuan-kang Wang is Associate Professor in the Department of Political Science at Western Michigan University, USA.

Stan Hok-wui Wong is Assistant Professor in the Department of Applied Social Sciences at the Hong Kong Polytechnic University, Hong Kong.

Yu-Shan Wu is Academician, Distinguished Research Fellow at the Institute of Political Science, Academia Sinica, and Professor in the Department of Political Science at National Taiwan University (NTU), Taiwan.

Ching-hsin Yu is Researcher in the Election Study Center at National Chengchi University, Taiwan.

List of Figures

Fig. 2.1	BTI indicators for Taiwan, 2006–2016	43
Fig. 2.2	V-Dem indicators for Taiwan, 1990–2016	44
Fig. 2.3	EIU overall democracy scores for Taiwan, 2006–2016	45
Fig. 3.1	Turnout rates in presidential elections (Source: Central Election Commission, various years)	52
Fig. 4.1	Policy position of Taiwan's political parties (Source: 2016 iVoter project: http://ivoter.tw/)	83
Fig. 6.1	Economic integration: Better, same, or worse for economy? Taiwan and Hong Kong	134
Fig. 6.2	Hong Konger and Chinese identities, 1997–2016 (Source: Public Opinion Programme, The University of Hong Kong (https://www.hkupop.hku.hk/english/popexpress/ethnic/eidentity/poll/datatables.html)	135
Fig. 8.1	Ideological positions of KMT, DPP, and CCP	180
Fig. 8.2	Presidential approval rating: Chen vs Tsai (Source: TVBS opinion polls, http://www.tvbs.com.tw/poll-center, compiled by author)	188
Fig. 8.3	Identity stances and possibility of G moment	193

LIST OF TABLES

Table 3.1	Logistic regression for voting participation, 2016	57
Table 3.2a	Logistic regression for voting for Eric Chu (KMT) in the presidential election	62
Table 3.2b	Logistic regression for voting for the KMT candidates in the Legislative Yuan election (single-member districts and aboriginal districts only)	63
Table 4.1	Representative deficit and position mismatch	78
Table 4.2	Three parties' supporter attitudes toward national statehood	84
Table 4.3	Free trade will benefit Taiwan economically	85
Table 4.4	Dissatisfaction with incumbent and opposition parties	87
Table 4.5	Four groups of NPP supporters	88
Table 4.6	Three parties supporters' education levels	89
Table 5.1	Descriptions of variables	103
Table 5.2	Binary logit of vote choice (KMT = 1; DPP = 0)	106
Table 6.1	"Third Force" new voters in 2016 Hong Kong and Taiwan elections	136

CHAPTER 1

The Turn of Fortune: Realignment in Taiwan's Domestic Politics and Diplomacy

Wei-chin Lee

When Taiwan's President Ma Ying-jeou of the Nationalist Party (Kuomintang, KMT) won the 2008 presidential election, his supporters were exuberant about the end of the turbulent years of the Democratic Progress Party's (DPP) President Chen Shui-bian's era of governance. In 2012, Ma received another solid electoral confirmation for one more term of the presidency. Even so, Ma encountered frequent challenges and criticism of his governance style and policies. Public frustration and fury led to a few large-scale social movements and a devastating loss for Ma's ruling party in the island-wide local elections in November 2014. The KMT's stumbling defeat in the mid-term elections signaled the DPP's muscly surge in subsequent elections. In 2016, the DPP's stunning upset victory in the presidential race and its substantial gain in legislative seats placed the DPP in full control of both the legislative and executive branches of governance. Taiwan completed its third regime turnover since its democratic transition in the late 1980s during the "third wave" of the global trend of democracy.[1]

W.-c. Lee (✉)
Department of Politics and International Affairs, Wake Forest University, Winston-Salem, NC, USA

© The Author(s) 2019
W.-c. Lee (ed.), *Taiwan's Political Re-Alignment and Diplomatic Challenges*, Politics and Development of Contemporary China, https://doi.org/10.1007/978-3-319-77125-0_1

Even with the glow of electoral victory and a new mandate to govern, the Tsai administration has encountered the daunting task of fulfilling multiple campaign pledges. President Tsai has attempted to soothe past social and political tensions, has navigated through the tedious business of legislating, has reached possible deals with various opposition parties and interest groups with divergent demands, and has reversed Ma's rapprochement policy toward China as expected. Tsai's strategic alternation is leaning toward the US and Japan to counterbalance China's security pressure. Being anxious to demonstrate the new government's sincerity in fulfilling the electoral mandate, President Tsai has launched a variety of controversial policy changes with her party's dominant legislative muscle.

The regime change is assuredly a critical turning point for Taiwan. For instance, in July 2016, against the common presumption of innocence until proven guilty, the government passed a law inferring that all KMT property is ill-gotten and subject to seizure by an authorized government committee with the power to assess and judge whether each and every KMT property is legitimately acquired and legally owned. The burden of proof resides on the KMT.[2] In December 2016, the legislature amended Taiwan's Labor Standards Act for a five-workday week without careful and thorough deliberation of the policy feasibility and economic impact on Taiwan's global market competition. This followed the government effort to legalize marriage equality rights for all, especially the lesbian, gay, bisexual, transgender, and queer (LGBTQ) community, and ignited an uproar from opponents with stronger religious convictions. Some opponents had been long-term dedicated DPP supporters. Fortunately, Taiwan's grand justices of the Constitutional Court timely stepped in to deliver a landmark ruling in favor of LGBTQ rights in May 2017, which took the heat off of the DPP. Then in late June 2017, the DPP-dominated parliament engaged in a nasty battle for the reduction of pension benefits for teachers and civil servants amid constant street protests and partisan squabbles, including the unexpected disruption of the opening ceremony of the 29th Summer Universiade Game in August 2017. Even so, the Tsai government still faces the daunting tasks of pension reform for military personnel and labor. It will dearly cost the DPP's political capital to navigate these two segments. The military service pension reform issue pierces the heart of Taiwan's civil-military relations—a crucial element embedded in Taiwan's defense against China's threat. Workers' pension reform may shake up the DPP's support base in elections.

Finally, on August 15, 2017, a massive island-wide power blackout triggered by a technician's blunder at a gas-fired power plant led to public anger, policy scrutiny, and renewed doubt about Tsai's campaign pledge to replace nuclear energy and coal-generated energy with renewable energy and other low-carbon sources. The outage became a test of the Tsai government's credibility for which she swore that there would be no power shortage and electricity fee increase under her administration. Taiwan's power woes may also become a serious drawback for the island's bid for foreign investments and may cause an exodus of domestic factories to seek sufficient and stable power supply abroad.

On the diplomatic front, Tsai's refusal to honor Ma's pledge of the "1992 Consensus" ("One China" with separate interpretations) toward China has thrown cross-Strait relations in limbo. China not only has suspended the functionality of all official channels of bilateral interactions but also has dramatically reduced the number of Chinese tourists in Taiwan. Meanwhile, China has gradually squeezed Taiwan's international space and diplomatic endeavors. In response, Tsai has strategically swung close to the US in order to secure and strengthen Taiwan's national security, a move that has uncalculatedly proceeded to a stage of unpredictability with the temperamental Trump presidency overseeing US foreign policy. Without a clear gauge of the US approach to cross-Strait relations and their unequivocal commitment to Taiwan, Tsai has encountered an increasingly powerful China under Xi Jinping, who has repeatedly signaled China's iron will in maintaining territorial integrity, including over Taiwan and the South China Sea. Xi recently asserted that China has the "resolve, confidence, and ability" to crush any attempt at Taiwan independence by stating in his 19th Party Congress in October 2017, "We will never allow anyone, any organization, or any party, at any time or in any form, to separate any part of Chinese territory from China."[3]

In sum, the landslide victory in both the executive and legislative branches apparently convinced the DPP government that its multifaceted reform agendas and reversal of her predecessor's stance on the cross-Strait policy would receive broad public support. However, unintended consequences and mishaps have occurred to disrupt their fulfillment of campaign agendas in Tsai's first year of governance. Notwithstanding, the 2016 elections signified a major party realignment in Taiwan's political terrain. It represents a game changer for its significant impact on Taiwan's domestic developments as well as external relations. Even so, the tenure and departure of the Ma government has not ended Taiwan's political fissures, which are caused partially by hate-fueled national identity polarization and partially by the inherent complexity and contortion of Taiwan's institutional design and operation. The good thing about a democracy is that the majority was able to choose to offer the DPP the political authority to govern, but whatever ill-will and problems existed prior to 2016 continue to afflict Taiwan's politics.

Causes, Context, and Consequences of Taiwan's Political Realignment in 2016

This is exactly what this volume aims to investigate and evaluate: the causes, context, and consequences of Taiwan's political realignment and their ramifications on domestic politics and external relations in the wake of the 2016 elections. Indeed, each country's democratic transition has its unique sources for democratic ferment and liberal inspiration, its own pace of cracking open the old regime's tight control, and the emergence of the new institutional design. Subsequent consolidation of a democracy requires a move beyond democratic forms and procedures into solid substance by fair and free periodic elections and the vitality of civil society and public internalization of the core idea that democracy is "the only game in town," as Linz and Stepan have stated.[4] Likewise, Amartya Sen has pointed out, "While democracy is not yet universally practiced, nor indeed uniformly accepted, in the general climate of world opinion, democratic governance has now achieved the status of being taken to be generally right."[5]

Certainly, no one would doubt the claim that democracy in Taiwan is surely the game in town. Yet, Taiwan's political endeavor in consolidation has been both tenacious and tumultuous. The conceptual definition and measurement of democratic consolidation have generated numerous scholarly debates and intellectual inquiries for disciplinary communication and policy learning.[6] Bruce Dickson thinks it is time for us to evaluate the quality of Taiwan's democracy in a long-term span and broad scale. Dickson starts with a reflective exploration of the rise and decline of Taiwanese parties, the complexity and oddity of Taiwan's semi-presidential system in implementation, and institutional gridlock between the executive and legislative branches. He even probes the procedural requirements for partisan coordination and consensual building in the legislature, as well as exploring the merits and drawbacks of the change of a single, non-transferable vote (SNTV) system to a two-vote system, with one for an individual candidate and the other for party preference in the national legislature. All these problems are compounded with politicians' aggravated brandishing of ethno-nationalism for sensational electoral mobilization and political capital accumulation. Unsurprisingly, parties and politicians are concerned about self-interest rather than the collective welfare in political gameplay. The unwillingness to mediate for a compromising deal sometimes results in stalemates or institutional sclerosis on urgent policy matters. Even so, Dickson's qualitative analysis pairs with quantitative indices of democracy as measured by the Bertelsmann Transformation Index (BTI), the Varieties of Democracy (V-Dem) database, and the Economist Intelligence Unit (EIU). Like some other democracies, Taiwan's predicament in democratic consolidation is "neither unique nor severe," in Dickson's words. In a broad comparison, the quality of Taiwan's democracy remains positive and promising. Improvements of some institutional matters, like the addition of a requirement for a runoff in the presidential election to ensure more than 50 percent support for the winning candidate, would strengthen the political legitimacy of presidents in governance. Regrettably, Taiwan's national identity dispute has long been embedded in various policy debates, and harsh partisan competition has made it difficult to reach a middle ground for dispute resolution.

Zooming in on the 2016 elections, John Hsieh dissects the electoral results and deciphers what the voters want by plowing through the large-scale post-election 2016 Taiwan Election and Democratization Studies (TEDS) survey. Based on the single-member district (SMD) plurality, known as the "first-past-the-post" system, Taiwan's presidential race is likely to follow Duverger's Law by converging to the top two candidates. On the contrary, the mixed-member majoritarian (MMM) system—a combination of the SMD plurality system for individual districts and the party-list Proportional Representation (PR)—dictates the Legislative Yuan election. The SMD plurality provides the winning party with a disproportional advantage in seats as projected by the "cube law" regarding the ratio between vote shares and seat shares.[7] The PR segment of the election in party shares yield benefits to smaller parties. The 2016 legislative election gave the DPP a 2.45 ratio of seat shares in contrast to the KMT's, a big bonus of legislative control higher than the 1.58 ratio projected by the cubic law. Thus, in light of a relatively lower turnout rate of 66.3 percent in 2016 as compared to the 74.4 percent of the 2012 elections, Hsieh probes what was in the voter's mind through his logistic regression models. Among the four policy areas—economic development, national sovereignty, cross-Strait relations, and social welfare—an unexpected finding is that the voters apparently did not consider the cross-Strait issue and social welfare as significant as other two policy issues. It is no wonder why the KMT's usual campaign agenda on cross-Strait relations did not significantly register voters' attention. A bigger surprise is that the public did not put too much stock in social welfare as a key variable in voting decisions. After all, Taiwan's tumultuous 2014 Sunflower Movement had explicitly and boisterously demanded better wages and socio-economic equality. Perhaps, with multiple issues in mind, the rational voter simply followed party identification to navigate noisy and confusing agendas by giving the DPP and the Tsai government an opportunity to govern.

Other than the DPP claiming the presidency and the national legislature, the 2016 elections witnessed the soaring popularity of the New Power Party (NPP), which captured five seats in the national legislature and became a noticeable player in national politics. The awesome performance of the NPP, the "new kid on the block," in the 2016 elections hence deserves an in-depth scrutiny to examine Taiwan's political realignment. Ian Tsung-yen Chen and Da-chi Liao answer this calling and painstakingly conduct a detailed analysis to reveal why the NPP could claim the third-largest party position in Taiwan's national legislature. Some analysts even speculate the potential of the NPP to become the largest opposition party by eventually edging out the old-fashioned KMT. Chen and Liao investigate the NPP's emergence, ascension, acceleration, and future trajectory by exploring four factors—the electoral system, the party's ideological stand, the bases of its supporters, and its organizational strategy.

Taiwan's implementation of a Mixed-Member-Majoritarian (MMM) system, including two-thirds Single-Member-District (SMD) system, tends to lean toward a two-party system. Since the KMT's vote shares had been in steady decline from 52.4 percent to 32.8 percent during the period of 2008–2016, the NPP was ready to ride the trend to embrace those who were disappointed by KMT governance. On ideological grounds, the NPP proclaimed itself a left-wing party fighting for domestic social equality and justice and seeking Taiwan's independence. Most of their supporters harbor a strong sense of discontent that Taiwanese parties have failed to represent their interests and policy preferences. In this case, the NPP's interactive style of social media communication as well as a non-rigid and multi-centric approach to leadership and organizational strategy appealed to those whose party affiliation and commitment is feeble and thin.

By combining both qualitative and quantitative analysis with rich data and evidence, Chen and Liao detail the nuances, intrigues, and contradictions of the NPP saga. For example, although NPP supporters stressed the importance of the domestic economy and generational equality, more than 66 percent of them firmly believe that free trade is essential to Taiwan's economic growth. Moreover, while the NPP gives a public image of "pro-independence," most of its supporters tend to consider that Taiwan has been an independent country called the Republic of China (ROC). In NPP supporters' view, the primary task should be to materialize Taiwan's "normalcy" as a sovereign actor equivalent to other countries in the international society rather than rushing for independence. In this case, NPP supporters' frustration, derived from their frustration with the "representative deficit" in Taiwan's usual KMT-DPP binary choice, had drawn them closer to the NPP in Taiwan's party politics. Nevertheless, should the NPP bundle and fumble in policy decisions, the alarming effect of "position mismatch"—the gap between the party's official policy position and its supporters' policy expectations—might make its supporters drift away from the NPP and thereby diminish the NPP's likelihood to become a formidable party in Taiwan's political arena.

Other than electoral system and contextual constraints, Taiwanese parties have long learned how to explore and exploit electoral advantages of certain political issues, as examined in the contribution by Ching-hsin Yu and T.Y. Wang. In other words, each party has persistently claimed or "owned" specific issues to champion and maximize its electoral campaign advantage or cultivate a sense of legitimacy in governance. It follows, then, that the shift in public perception of a party's competence in propagating and professing a specific policy can predict the fate of the party in the election. Certainly, this involves each party's narrative as well as their persuasive capability to defuse and diminish the opposing party's issue ownership. As a result, a study of issue ownership in the 2016 elections gives a glimpse of what voters perceived and wanted and whether the party successfully captured and capitalized public support. Yu and Wang chose to focus on the 2012 and 2016 elections for a comparison of issue ownership in the exploration of cross-Strait relations, economic development, social welfare, and Taiwan's sovereignty guardianship. The authors found that voters' electoral calculus in the 2012 presidential election considered that both parties and candidates are capable of handling most issues except the matter of cross-Strait relations, on which the KMT had a pivotal advantage in management. However, the 2016 presidential election witnessed an alteration of public sentiment. The DPP shrewdly neutralized the KMT's issue leverage on multiple fronts, including the KMT's presumed advantage on cross-Strait relations. In the meantime, the DPP branded itself as a capable and competent party to safeguard Taiwan's sovereignty, boost economic development, and promote social welfare. The DPP turned the tables and consequently achieved a sizable victory. Surely, the lingering puzzle is whether or not the Tsai government is truly able to break new ground under its pledge of "maintaining the status quo" in its cross-Strait relations. With China's insistence on the "1992 Consensus" and reluctance to reciprocate Taiwan's new policy, Yu and Wang caution that the DPP's issue "ownership" of cross-Strait relations could become only a temporary "lease" on the issue. This foretells the significance of the China factor in Taiwan's political development with Taiwan's heavy reliance on the China market for trade balance.

The validity and limitation of the trade peace theory is an enduring issue in intellectual inquiry. Alesina and others have submitted that closer economic transactions as part of the globalization process can be an impetus for separatism for a smaller state, rather than a catalyst for political integration with a strong counterpart. Stated differently, "trade liberalization and average country size are inversely related." And "...as the process of economic 'globalization' will progress, political separatism will continue to be alive and well."[8] While the recent Brexit issue could offer plausible support for their assertion, Karl Ho and his co-authors chose to conduct a comparative study of Taiwan and Hong Kong in dealing with China's extraordinary effort in expanding and deepening economic transactions with either entity. The purpose is to fulfill China's grand vision of political integration of Taiwan and Hong Kong. By scrutinizing the immense data from the Taiwan Election and Democratization Study (TEDS) and the Hong Kong Election Study (HKES), Ho et al. investigate public opinions on the impact of economic integration in an asymmetric relationship between two smaller economies—Taiwan and Hong Kong—and their monumental and mighty counterpart, China. Despite their political regime disparities, Taiwan and Hong Kong both experienced colonialism and now practice a market economy and maintain a strong connection to the West, not to mention their cultural affinity and language roots. Separately, each has an increasingly high level of trade volume with China. In order to bring them closer to China for future political integration, the Chinese government offered generous and concessional trade deals to each through the Closer Economic Partnership Arrangement (CEPA) in 2003 to boost Hong Kong's ailing economy and the Economic Cooperation Framework Agreement (ECFA) in 2010 to accelerate and expand cross-Strait trade. Nonetheless, the growth of bilateral trade by leaps and bounds has not accelerated the speed of political integration. In fact, getting closer economically simply prompted Taiwan and Hong Kong to drift away politically for fear of being sucked into higher dependency on China to a point of no return. In Taiwan's case, for example, the expectation that Taiwan's economic and social actors could be catalysts for China's positive changes through cross-Strait interactions appeared to lose its political appeal in the 2010s.[9] Public fear of unwanted political influence has reverberated to heightened levels of indigenous identity, large-scale social movements, and powerful testimony of anti-China sentiment in electoral results in both Taiwan and Hong Kong. Various surveys indicate vividly the declining affiliation with Chinese identity. Young voters cast doubt on the wisdom of economic integration with China.

Here, both Taiwan and Hong Kong encounter a dilemma. Regardless of Hong Kong people's preference, China's geographic proximity, economic influence, and the presence of the People's Liberation Army make any supposition of Hong Kong's political autonomy only an unrealistic illusion. Taiwan's fate is more promising than that of Hong Kong. After all, the Taiwanese people have viable venues to channel their views to influence policy choices and to unseat the incumbent in democratic elections. While the Taiwanese people might not be interested in political integration, the Taiwanese business community finds it hard to resist the appeal of resources and profitability of the China market. In Taiwan's case, the China market is too close for comfort and too far to lose. Taiwanese leaders have desperately looked for policy guidelines to resist China's repeated urge for political integration, but at the same time maintain a healthy and profitable economic relationship with China. So far, the golden guideline remains elusive. The 1992 Consensus is the preferred policy by the Ma government to manage cross-Strait interactions. However, the 2016 electoral campaign and its consequences have summed up optimistic spirit of the time in the society. As Tsai proudly proclaimed during her campaign, China would have no other choice but to follow Taiwan's turn to the DPP's move for accommodation.

Thus, the DPP and the Tsai government have attempted to ride and capture the passion and aspiration of their electoral supporters, who believed that the Tsai government would provide Taiwan with a much better deal in cross-Strait relations without falling into China's economic trap for political integration. As the DPP's presidential candidate, Tsai proposed a simple "status quo maintenance" to supersede "the 1992 Consensus" in administering cross-Strait relations.

The status quo claim is easy to appeal to the public, though Tsai never specifically elaborated the contour and context of the term "status quo." In Tsai's view, the term seemed ambiguous and broad subject to various interpretations. Still, it fed the multitudes of campaign inquires. It served to soften the opponent's attack on the DPP's Achilles heel—the perception of the DPP's incompetency in cross-Strait relations. Indeed, should one consider the status quo as the circumstance constructed under the premise of President Ma's "no unification, no independence, and no use of force," the wording of status quo seems self-explanatory and signals the DPP's moderate move toward the center and away from the party's passionate desire for Taiwan independence in the past. Broadly speaking, the status quo understanding could be in dynamic motion and subject to interpretation and reconfiguration. With the DPP's electoral victory in 2016, the Tsai government could now stretch or compress a favorable definition of the status quo as it sees fit to the newly minted electoral mandate.

As Wei-chin Lee points out in his chapter on the 1992 Consensus, the interpretation of the status quo has been subject to shifting political circumstances, evolving public sentiment, and identity constructs in Taiwanese society. The growing devotees of Taiwanese identity may gradually configure a socio-political climate foreshadowing a natural tendency toward independence from China. Along with the change of electoral generations, the increase in Taiwanese identifiers has been a perpetual trend, particularly among the younger generation. Stated differently, the conceptual interpretation of the status quo has to take into account the temporal and spatial dimension of Taiwan's political development. In the DPP's calculation, the subtlety of identity constructs, if cultivated skillfully, may progress and translate into demands for hardened boundaries in the state-building process to accomplish its pro-independence vision.

Thus, the 2016 elections not only indicated an unbearable disaster for the KMT but also announced a severe blow to the 1992 Consensus, a consensus based on a mutual understanding to "agree to disagree" on the meaning of "China," either the People's Republic of China or the Republic of China in Taiwan. The DPP chose to challenge the validity and utility of such a consensus. The challenging task for the Tsai government is to find a mutually acceptable framework to conduct cross-Strait interactions. Since the DPP has endlessly criticized Ma's rapprochement policy toward

China, it becomes interesting to see how Tsai's status quo proposition could push the boundaries beyond Ma's discursive markers for ample agreeable space to continue meaningful cross-Strait relations.

Yu-Shan Wu has taken up the baton in his spectacular research to ponder the DPP's pathway in cross-Strait relations. Wu delineates an electoral cycle theory in association with Taiwan's China policy. Weighing the public sentiment and social atmosphere at the moment, political parties and leaders would consider the adoption of a *median* or *galvanizing* approach during elections in order achieve an electoral victory. When the party feels confident of capturing the majority of median voters' interests, it typically shifts its position to the ideological center. However, when a party sees a bi-modal distribution of public opinion, it tends to embrace a galvanizing approach to boost electoral momentum for the cohesion and consolidation of its support base. During the relative calm interval of general elections, which lacks the necessity of electoral mobilization, parties are usually realistic and sensible in policymaking and implementation. Based on the framework of the electoral cycle theory, Wu has thus plotted an ideological spectrum of Taiwanese parties' China policies in various temporal periods and issue positions from "one China, one Taiwan," "two Chinas," to "one China," with intriguing variations in each broad category.

By examining former DPP President Chen Shui-bian's shifts in his China policy from a series of median to realistic to galvanizing approaches, Wu contemplates whether President Tsai would follow a similar path. He reasons that the KMT's devastating defeat in the 2016 elections and the loss of its party assets after the regime change have paralyzed the KMT so severely that it will not be of any meaningful challenge to the Tsai government in the immediate future. Instated, Tsai's challengers will likely emerge from the pan-green camp, Premier Lai Ching-te, a rising star within the party, and Taipei Mayor Ko Wen-je, who has a strong political inclination toward the DPP, though Ko is not a DPP member. As long as President Tsai's approval rating does not plunge unsatisfactorily low, and the opponents remain weak, it is safe to presume that President Tsai would keep a realistic approach toward China without much ideological baggage.

So far, one fundamental difference between the KMT and the DPP has centered on the China policy with incessant implications for Taiwan's overall national security and economic sustainability. The KMT insists on the necessity and priority of peaceful co-existence with a friendly China as a primary and preliminary condition for Taiwan's overall strategy toward others abroad. This is not to deny that the Ma government of the KMT fully understood the gravity of the US in Taiwan's national security. Any of Ma's policy initiatives toward China understandably tried to avoid contradicting Washington's China policy and sought the US endorsement as much as possible. In comparison, the DPP's national security and foreign policy logic has placed high hopes on its closer relations with Japan, the US, and other Western countries as a check on China's unification threat and to facilitate Taiwan's sustainability and expansion of international space. Consequently, the Tsai government's policy reverses her predecessor's calculation by betting on the US and Japan for regional and international endeavors and keeping a passive and unprovocative profile toward China.

Against this backdrop, Robert Sutter presents a succinct and valuable layout of American policy toward Taiwan-China relations in recent years. By plowing through the US policy, Sutter illuminates the ups and downs of US-Taiwan relations in association with the US-China dyadic interplay. While President Chen Shui-bian's contentious "beacon-fire or torching diplomacy" (*fenghuo waijiao*) to antagonize China led to Washington's heavy barrage of Taiwan as a troublemaker, the successive Ma government reverted to rapprochement, called "pragmatic diplomacy" (*Wushi waijiao*), to reassure and accommodate China without causing any skirmish with US foreign policy. The reduction of cross-Strait tension naturally put the Obama administration at ease. The Taiwan issue was then no longer a topic seriously aggravating Beijing. Should Taiwan become a contentious issue, Beijing might pressure the US to make concessions on the Taiwan issue as a trade-off to get China's reciprocal endorsement of US interests in critical global security issues. Even so, when the US launched its "pivoting" or "rebalancing" policy in 2011 to counterbalance China's influence in the East Asian region, Taiwan quietly offered its assistance to the US regional security layout. However, Taiwan's dedicated effort in the assistance of US security interests still failed to gain US support and endorsement either in the initial Trans-Pacific Partnership (TPP) negotiation or in substantial arms transfers.[10] The clear message is that in an asymmetric dyad, Taiwan as a weak partner would have to accommodate as much as possible to secure US protection against China's threat. On the other hand, like any major power, the US prioritizes its own interest above Taiwan's interest in global strategic calculation and has no urgency to reciprocate equivalently to its weaker partner. Furthermore, as Sutter cautions, under the current Trump administration's volatile policymaking style, the Taiwan issue remains a primary concern among policy analysts in US policy. After all, in any US-China grand bargain, Taiwan could be a convenient bargaining chip for coercion, compromise, and concession.

Indeed, the interplay between Taiwan and the US has been a conventional illustration of alliance politics. In a formal or quasi-formal alliance framework, one predominant concern for the weaker state is a rooted fear of abandonment by its stronger counterpart at the critical moment of military strife with its security adversary. However, a stronger state foresees a possibility of involvement in a serious confrontation with another major power for fulfilling its security commitment to its weaker ally, even if the military confrontation provoked by its weaker associate might not serve the strong party's best interest. Consequently, if the regional and global security circumstance or the ally's identity has changed, it is imperative for the strong state to reconfigure its strategic vision and policy to meet the new challenge. China's powerful ascent in economic and military power has made it impossible for the US to neglect and negate China's critical role in US global policies.

Therefore, Sutter's reflective scrutiny of US policy toward Taiwan in a historical span fits perfectly with Yuan-kang Wang's critical and systematic examination of some US policy analysts' recent call for "abandoning Taiwan" for accommodating the changing circumstance of China's rise to satisfy US global challenges. Wang's inquisitive analysis questions the realistic utility and wisdom of such proclamations to serve the best interests of the US. The logic of "abandoning Taiwan" by those proponents rests on the necessity of accommodation to mitigate any likelihood of war with China for a peaceful power transition. In their view, the only issue on which the US could confront China's huge military establishment is the cross-Strait issue, considering China's core mission of unifying Taiwan for territorial integrity and Taiwan's resistance to the unification pressure for its own independent statehood. The solution, as accommodationists have proposed, is to end the US quasi-alliance with Taiwan by repealing or significantly undercutting US security obligations stipulated in the 1979 Taiwan Relations Act.

Following the rationale of offensive realism, Wang points out some flaws in accommodationists' main arguments. In Wang's scrutiny, the cause for US-China tensions resides not on an issue-specific factor, for example, the Taiwan issue, but rather on the spectacle of the "Thucydides Trap" inherent in the structural transition of the international anarchy, because China's rapid upward trajectory in global politics inevitably prompts the current hegemon's anxiety, suspicion, and fear of being overtaken by a rising power.[11] Although China has repeatedly cited its sutra of peaceful rise, Wang cautions that the accommodationists' optimistic view of China's rise as not seriously "competitive and dangerous"[12] fails to gauge China's aspiration to be a proud and powerful country without peer competitors in world politics. Such a divine ambition or manifest destiny embedded in its historical past and ingrained by the recent century of imperial humiliation is surely more profound than the Taiwan issue. Moreover, the suggestion of "abandoning Taiwan" gives the international audience an impression of unilateral concession toward Beijing. It undercuts US alliance cohesion and credibility, erodes Taiwan's democratic commitment, disregards Taiwan's geographic nexus in Chinese strategic thinkers' Mahanian logic and grammar for China's navel development and deployment, and unsettles the well-conceived US strategy of deterrence and reassurance on cross-Strait relations and regional stability.[13] Besides, numerous historical episodes have evidenced that Taiwan's security essence is not merely figurative and ideologically oriented but also substantial and a geo-strategic imperative for China, as Wachman has keenly expounded before.[14]

Naturally, other than the dependence on US assistance, Taiwan has to find a way to expand its international space. Repeating and revising a Southbound Policy toward Southeast Asia launched by former Presidents Lee Teng-hui and Chen Shui-bian separately in 1994 and 2003, the Tsai government hopes to tap into the thriving political economy of Southeast Asia by encouraging and assisting younger Taiwanese entrepreneur talents to strengthen multifaceted relations with Southeast Asian countries. Policies in the so-called "people-centered" initiative include the approval of low-interest loans and investment requests, generous delivery of humanitarian disaster relief, pursuits of trade deals, encouragement of people-to-people exchanges through visa waiver programs, and the establishment of an extensive advocacy network with Southeast Asian NGOs.[15] The purpose is to diminish Taiwan's heavy dependence on the China market and to divert Taiwan's investment load to Southeast Asia. The emphasis on economic strategy can also indirectly stretch Taiwan's diplomatic goal in international space expansion and coalition building of Southeast Asian states to mitigate China's influential expansion in the region through its grand "One Belt, One Road" strategy.[16]

As a seasoned Southeast Asian specialist, Samuel C. Y. Ku's Chap. 11 examines the promises and limitations of Taiwan's relations with the Southeast Asian region, which has emerged to be Taiwan's second-largest trading partner after the China market in the recent decade. The surge of its regional economic vitality has given members of the Association for Southeast Asian Nations (ASEAN) a key role to play in proposing and participating in multiple free trade agreements and regional blocs, such as its own Regional Comprehensive Economic Partnership (RCEP) and the formerly US-directed Trans-Pacific Partnership (TPP). By establishing close linkages with states in the region, Taiwan expects to enlist their support and assistance in advancing economic and trade advantages, because the region could serve as a springboard to other markets for Taiwan's market expansion. Even so, China's commanding presence and influence remain a formidable barrier for most Southeast Asian countries to move ahead their relations with Taiwan boldly without fear of China's pressures and retaliations.

Here, Taiwan encounters the abiding question between politics and trade in international relations. Is trade advancement capable of overcoming political obstacles, as liberal interdependence proponents have claimed? Will Taiwan be able to acquire sufficient commitments from ASEAN members to facilitate Taiwan's "New Southbound Policy" by overcoming China's pressures? Furthermore, are Taiwan's diplomatic endeavors and economic statecraft in the region compelling enough to entice and secure ASEAN members' sincere endorsement of Taiwan's participation in the RCEP or any trade agreement? Regrettably, in all permutations of Taiwan's exploration of trade deals, it is surely an uphill battle for Taiwan's quest for trade deals without China's tacit nod.

Aside from Southeast Asia, Japan has been another prong of Taiwan's diplomatic ventures in light of Japan's crucial strategic role to the national security and economic wellbeing of Taiwan. Madoka Fukuda deftly recounts that Taiwan's relationship with Japan during the Ma government has witnessed a combination of consonance and dissonance. On the positive side, the Ma government reached a fishery agreement in 2013 after a 17-year marathon negotiation. Yet, Taiwan-Japan relations have been hampered by disagreements on the territorial sovereignty over the Diaoyu/Senkaku islands in the East China Sea, maritime rights of the Okinotori Reef, the ban of Japanese foods from areas affected by the Fukushima nuclear disaster, and divergent historical discourses of the Sino-Japanese war, 1937–1945. Still, Ma strived to alter his "anti-Japan" image by cultivating a Japan-Taiwan "special partnership" beginning in 2009 in multiple dimensions to promote political and diplomatic dialogues and increase exchanges in trade, culture, and tourism. Nevertheless, the mutual distrust between the Abe administration and the Ma government inhibited further breakthroughs on bilateral relations.

On the contrary, it was no secret that Japanese Prime Minister Abe has found the Tsai government more acceptable than her predecessor. Abe publicly congratulated Tsai's electoral victory and warmly welcomed her ascension to the presidency, hoping for a reversion of Ma's unfriendly policy toward Japan. As a goodwill gesture to Japan's demands, the Tsai government quickly reciprocated that Taiwan had no "specific position" on the qualification of the island status of Okinotori Reef and tacitly accepted Japan's proposition. The Tsai government has also muted its response on the disputed "dashed line" claim in the South China Sea in correspondence to Japan's claims. The DPP government has even expressed its desire to lift the ban on Japanese food from Fukushima and its surrounding prefectures. When announced, these policies instantly spurred public rebuffs and policy controversies in Taiwan. The public criticism for ignoring health safety soon elicited the government response to prolong the food ban lift indefinitely. The explicit refusal to safeguard Taiwan's fishing rights and territorial claims in some thorny maritime disputes with Japan has made the public doubt the DPP's frequent assertion of "Taiwan first."

The biggest disappointment happened when the International Arbitral Tribunal's decision in 2016 severely affected Taiwan's rights over the South China Sea. It declared all islands, including the Taiwan-controlled Taiping Island, as "rocks" in accordance with the Law of the Sea. Hence, they no longer qualified for claims of exclusive economic zones. In contrast to the Tsai government's tacit acceptance of Japan's bold claim of the Okinotori Reef's justification of an exclusive economic zone, the Tribunal's decision gave Taiwanese media and policy analysts a distinctive case of the Tsai government's inconsistency in its treatment of Japan's Okinotori Reef versus its handling of Taiwan's own South China Sea claim. Mounting pressure finally made the government reject the court's merit publicly.[17] Taiwan's official denouncement of the court ruling is certainly in direct opposition to the interest and position of the US and Japan in the South China Sea.

It is a natural tendency for the Tsai government to show an exuberant spirit in building up strong ties with Japan because of both the DPP elite's sentimental fondness for Japan due to Japan's colonial past in Taiwan and their strategic calculation to rely on Japan against China's threat. Even so, Madoka Fukuda's adroit analysis submits that China is still a crucial factor in any advancement of the current Taiwan-Japanese relationship. Japan's market sensitivity and vulnerability to China's pressures has made Japan reluctant to substantially raise the official level of Taiwan-Japan relations. Interestingly, the major breakthrough of accomplishing a Taiwan-Japanese fishery agreement occurred during the Ma era, when both Taiwan and China were under the framework of the 1992 Consensus. There is no doubt that the Taiwan-Japan bilateral relationship will progress steadily in pace and scope during the Tsai era. It will be interesting to see whether both can reach major accomplishments even though cross-Strait relations remain stalled.

Different Regimes, Similar Challenges

While Taiwan's 2016 elections signified a major benchmark in the island's political development, there is no doubt that the present is a continuation of the past in evolution, innovation, and modification. It is impossible to cover and examine all aspects of Taiwanese politics in recent years, but all authors of these chapters have endeavored to bring to the fore the similarities and differences, the continuities and changes, and the essential and accidental features of Taiwanese politics. A survey of works in this volume would show several distinctive features of Taiwan's politics in association with the 2016 elections.

First, similar to most party politics in democracies, the DPP took every opportunity to pressure and bitterly oppose most of the KMT's policies prior to the 2016 elections. The DPP adopted an "anti-government and anti-establishment" populist stand mixed with rosy campaign policy visions that garner support from civil society groups and the public to "take back" the state. However, the peril for the ruling party elites is that they soon realize that the "jig is up" after they over-promised during the campaign and now face the embarrassments of under-delivery on their pledges. That is why the Tsai government has had to scale back or reverse some of its overly dramatized and unrealistic campaign pledges, such as the labor law revision to regulate the labor workday limit and an overblown energy supply blueprint vowing sufficient power supply for industrial and residential necessities. The impracticability of the DPP's revised labor law in 2016 and an unexpected island-wide power shortage in 2017 have greatly consumed and costed the DPP political capital, its image of governability, and its credibility in honoring its campaign assertions.

This has been a recurrent pattern in Taiwan's party politics with candidates and parties making bloated campaign promises and then failing to fulfill them. Their goal is to have a catchall platform to entice multi-class support, though the all-inclusive agendas may result in incompatible policies bundled together and disappointed downturns of quixotic promises to loyal supporters.[18] Along with the impact of institutional design, the 2016 regime change appears to repeat the tones and tunes of previous elections in electoral strategy, party politics, and political mobilization as fully analyzed in chapters by Dickson (Chap. 2), Hsieh (Chap. 3), and Chen and Liao (Chap. 4). Unsurprisingly, the 2016 elections have meshed with a strong wave of populism in social movements since the 2014 Sunflower Movement. The DPP's ability to capitalize on the populist sentiment derived from the Sunflower Movement offered a winning edge in the manipulation of issue ownership and campaign dialogues as indicated in the Chap. 5 by Yu and Wang. Of course, it would be interesting to see how long the rapid growth of "virtual" civil society during the Sunflower Movement as Bennett and Segerberg have called the "logic of connective action" will be a solid base for the DPP regime in coming years.[19]

Second, Taiwan's democratic transition and consolidation has witnessed a persistent display of identity politics corresponding with the diminution and demise of a China-based social construct and the permeation and progression of a Taiwan-centered identity. The employment of identity politics has been the DPP's attempt to "denaturalize" previous beliefs constructed by the KMT. Meanwhile, the DPP "sensitizes and publicizes" new social constructs and norms to increment the justification of its legitimacy in governance at home and abroad. Consequently, through all these years in repetitive elections, "Love Taiwan" has become an omnipresent code of political correctness and a mesmerizing term for political mobilization in campaign dialogues.[20] The aftereffect is a strenuous push of "Chineseness" into "Otherization" owing to the discursive ascension of a younger electorate's belief in a Taiwan-based social construct concurrent with the withering away of the old guardians of the China-centered construct. The holders of the China-centered social construct are increasingly losing their audiences in Taiwan's public sphere.

Such a paradigm shift in identity construct simultaneously proceeded in education, communication, and socialization. This has given electoral and policy advantages to parties, like the DPP, in public appeal. With the assistance of cyber commentaries, policy provocation, and whiffs of campaign sensationalism, parties and political activists have constantly saturated the public realm with identity anxiety over potential social anguish and economic distress evoked by the China factor. By so frantically "rejecting China," Taiwan's policy debates have tended to oversimplify the topic by focusing on the China factor and pushing "*other* themes, problems, and arguments below the threshold of attention and, thereby, withholding them from opinion-formation" in a balanced and reasonable manner.[21] In this case, the yearning for an independent statehood in separation from China has become a somewhat treacherous game indeed. By portraying China as an antagonistic, arrogant, and bossy counterpart, any policy critic can easily sensationalize and simplify any policy, including those remotely linked to China, along the identity boundary of pro- or anti-China, leaving no room for judicious appraisal of policies. Put simply, policy acceptance and support is thus subject to the identity affiliation and ideological belief of its policy initiator and executor rather than to its policy merits and feasibility.

Vivid examples are the extradition of Taiwanese nationals by some African or Southeast Asian countries in 2016 and 2017. Following the extradition process, host countries decided to send some Taiwanese criminals to China. Prior to the regime change in May 2016, the then opposition DPP legislators piercingly criticized the ruling KMT government for its betrayal of Taiwanese dignity as well as its incompetency in safeguarding Taiwan's sovereign jurisdiction over its own nationals. Frankly speaking, the DPP's accusation neglected the strength of legal justification and political feasibility of a Taiwanese request in such cases of competitive jurisdictions in international law. However, the DPP legislators' political attitudes swiftly shifted after the Tsai government assumed power. Realizing the difficulty in extraditing Taiwanese criminal suspects back home, the DPP legislators' finger pointing and feisty allegations soon dissipated in the wake of regime change in May 2016. Since then, similar cases seldom have attracted the ruling party's legislative concerns at all. In brief, when the issue involves identity politics relevant to China, political mudslinging usually takes precedence over any meaningful problem solving. Reasoned dialogue is rarely given sufficient time and space in policy deliberation.

Third, the polarization of identity naturally has become a key variable in Taiwan's economic interactions with China, which has occupied a significant share of Taiwan's external trade and investment. The conventional claim is that economic interactions could pave the way for peace and stability across borders. After all, business entrepreneurs and trading groups would seek ways to advance policies friendly and favorable to the maximization of material benefits through interaction. All economic actors involved would try to persuade and compel their governments not to adopt policies to harm business benefits, at the very least. As Moravcsik elaborates, "the state is not an actor but a representative institution constantly subject to capture and recapture, construction and reconstruction by coalitions of social actors."[22] The expectation of mutual benefits in economic transactions would prompt business constituencies and sectorial coalitions to lobby the government to advance and facilitate economic transactions. As the logic goes, reciprocal economic interactions spill over to inter-societal transactions and generate multiplying effects on the people in attitudes and perceptions of the masses. That is, the "give and take" norm in trade has a stalling, if not pacifying, effect to minimize the likelihood of dyadic conflicts. Nevertheless, it is difficult to ascertain exactly the damping or amplifying effect of economic linkage on the potentiality of military conflicts. It is an ongoing inquiry and an unsettling debate about the virtues and vices of trade in association with interstate conflicts.[23]

States have no problem in collaboration with friendly partners and close allies. However, states would stay cautious and extremely calculative in trading with adversaries for concerns about national security, as Karl Ho and his co-authors testify.[24] Particularly in the case of cross-Strait relations, China has never abandoned its goal of unification with Taiwan. The Taiwanese public has been fully aware of China's unification ambitions and, hence, persistently has resisted it. Still, the cross-Strait relationship is a key issue of public concern. Yu-Shan Wu's findings in his Chap. 8 demonstrate that electoral sensation, strenuous party competition, and swing of approval ratings could drive the leader to flaunt assertiveness toward China as a politically expedient means of poll boosting. Therefore, there is a strong level of economic interdependence across the Strait, but both sides have been politically drifting apart in their visions of future unification.

Thus, one enduring task for Taiwan remains how to achieve a normal and acceptable balance between Taiwan's political autonomy and its sustainable economy. Despite Ma's effort in maintaining cross-Strait peace, progress, and prosperity, opponents sharply criticized his economic engagement policy along with his peace initiative toward China, and they unforgivingly ridiculed his undertakings as "selling out Taiwan." One chilling effect has been that opponents are quick to demonize any initiative and deliberation of cross-Strait economic initiatives. Any substantial acceleration of cross-Strait economic transactions in capital mobility, technology flow, financial networking, and labor complementarity would signify threats to Taiwan's autonomy and national security in the view of opponents, including the DPP. Gradually in such a climate, the China market or anything touching on China becomes a taboo, a non-existent subject, as well as a political liability in contemporary Taiwanese politics. Hypocritically, Taiwan's weighty dependence on the China market makes the "de-link with China" option or "deceleration of Taiwan's trade relations with China" a daunting task to execute. Regardless of how the Tsai government plans to proceed, the conventional assumption that economic transactions will facilitate and accelerate political cooperation requires additional qualifications in Taiwan's cross-Strait relations.

One option seeking to bypass the China market is the Tsai government's New Southbound Policy to mitigate Taiwan's dependence and to ward off any potential political risks of China's employment of economic transactions as a wedge for its political agendas on Taiwan. Understandably, the replacement of the China market with the one in Southeast Asia might not be easily made, and the market niche and reconfiguration might not be compatible in value and volume to China's. Given a lapse of time, it would be interesting to evaluate the substitution effect on Taiwan's overall economic growth during the Tsai era in comparison with the limited achievements of two similar Southbound Policies during the presidencies of Lee Teng-hui and Chen Shui-bian.

Another alternative that has been pursued by the Taiwanese government is to seek various regional trade arrangements to join for multiple benefits. These trade deals could grant Taiwan an opportunity to mitigate its over-dependence on the China market. They also fulfill Taiwan's quest for meaningful representation and contribution in international institutions. Finally, trade deals would offer the government justifications and opportunities of internalization of international obligations. Deals could trigger economic reforms either on the elimination of "on border" trade barriers or re-calibration "within border" economic policies and rules in multiple areas, such as intellectual property rights, financial liberalization, and overall industrial upgrades for standard compliance.

Because some economic sectors would benefit greatly from those deals even as others may not, the government will need to navigate Taiwan's noisy, populist, and loathsome political atmosphere, which has been full of self-righteous know-it-all media commentators and self-aggravating politicians and pundits of various ideological convictions and identity affiliations. During the 2016 elections, the DPP addressed issues of social and economic equality for vote solicitation and presented an image of economic nationalism. Even though there is no major trade agreement currently on the horizon for Taiwan due to the "China factor," it is still beneficial for the Tsai government to focus on economic growth. One major job for the DPP government is to tone down or reverse its rhetoric of economic nationalism for the advancement and promotion of Taiwan's export-oriented economy.

Fourth, after 2016 the new regime apparently has chosen to cool cross-Strait relations by adopting a broadly defined "status quo maintenance" policy to replace the "1992 Consensus" as elaborated in Wei-chin Lee's Chap. 7. Additionally, the government has decided to put stock in the US, Japan, and the Southeast Asian region both as international levers to ward off China's pressure and threats and as a response to domestic audiences who dislike the former regime's tilt toward China as Robert Sutter, Madoka Fukuda, and Samuel Ku analyze. The DPP government is convinced that Taiwan's aspiration for independence surely needs endorsement and assistance from major powers. The question is to what extent Taiwan should lean on their support. Indeed, Taiwan has relied on the security support of the US since 1949. Under the asymmetric framework of this security alignment, their bilateral interactions of the past were a mix of competitive and complementary interests with each having their own perspectives and priorities.[25] Therefore, it is not surprising to learn of US internal debates about the option of "abandoning Taiwan" for a close and cordial US-China relationship, as elaborated in Yuan-kang Wang's Chap. 10. After all, the primacy of self-interests might dictate the US to sidestep Taiwan's interest request, if necessary, as the Melian Dialogue remarks, "the strong do what they can and the weak suffer what they must."[26] Consequently, it is a constant guessing game regarding the US commitment to Taiwan's security against China's threats, with all parties' full awareness of the accelerating cost for the US to balance China for Taiwan's sake. Similarly, anxiety and fear of direct confrontation with China has also made Japan cautious in challenging China on Taiwan's account. Overall, the Tsai government's policy of leaning toward the US or Japan has its benefits, doubts, and costs.

An ironic feature is that when the US is in cordial and harmonious relations with China, Taiwan might recede into a less significant factor in US strategic consideration. On the other hand, when both are in a mode of confrontation, the US might urge Taiwan to join its united front against China to boost the US policy stance. Such a collaborative policy imposed on Taiwan is not necessarily in the best interest of Taiwan domestically and internationally, as past disputes in the South China Sea and the East China Sea have evidenced.[27] In fact, the "US first" approach applies generally to most US administrations, including the Obama era that has often proclaimed noble ideas of deliberative, liberalist, and transparent foreign policymaking in dealing with Taiwan.[28]

Finally, in any analysis of Taiwan's domestic politics, national security, and foreign policy, cross-Strait relations remain an inescapable variable for consideration. Different from her predecessor's commitment to the 1992 Consensus ("One China" with different interpretations), Tsai's proposition of "status quo maintenance" has not revealed concrete details in practice. Even so, a glimpse of her policies since 2016 shows several pillars of her cross-Strait thinking. First, she has adopted an inactive policy of "let the situation evolve" on its own course without any urgency on her part to re-open and boost official channels of communication. In fact, Beijing's decision in suspending official channels of communication fits well in her first pillar of "status quo maintenance," with a concealed intent to drift away from China. When the detachment from China becomes a normality at home and abroad, "China" would gradually recede into a rhetorical reference point in conversation and policy analysis. Such a disengagement from China also corresponds to the DPP government's subtlety in advancing the social deconstruction of "Chineseness" in official documents, textbook writings, and political discourses. Unlike President Chen Shui-bian's active, bold, and top-down act in reducing, revising, and removing the substance and influence of a "China-centered" social construct, President Tsai's social construct move proceeds in a piecemeal, subtle, and bottom-up approach. The DPP government would encourage or condone any civil society organization in agenda setting and issue framing, including the jettisoning of national symbols and references to the ROC in official or unofficial settings in an implied favoritism toward Taiwan independence. When confronted, the government would simply employ freedom of expression and transitional justice as convenient shields to defend its position.

The concern is that as intentional obliteration of all contents and references related to the ROC or China compounded with calculated neglect of symbols, logos, and motifs as the DPP intentionally propagated, the Tsai regime may encounter a political limbo of state identity. Domestically, the gap of identity polarization between parties and supporters would persist and may obstruct normal political operation. Internationally, the "ROC" increasingly loses its representative and utilitarian value, while the preferred nomenclature of "Taiwan" appears to have no realistic prospects to replace the ROC, owing to China's powerful obstruction in the international society.

One sure thing is that the dynamics of "status quo maintenance" is indeed a way to bide time for the domestic shift tilting toward pro-independence. The DPP appears to bet its hope on the annual accession of younger generations of *"Tianran du"* (naturally born to be pro-independence advocates) in electoral campaigns to mold and shape a socio-political context as evolving over time for an amicable trajectory toward its independence vision fulfilled by Taiwan's democratic process.[29] Stated differently, Taiwan has a profound sense of incompleteness of not being a "normal" state like other sovereign states in national title, flag, and international participation.[30] The DPP government's "status quo maintenance" policy embedded in Taiwanese nationalist sentiment seems to be a temporal and contingent option for the pursuit of Taiwan's "normalcy." Of course, the existence of Taiwanese identity does not automatically lead to a quest for independence. However, the continuous push and electoral propagation of the uniqueness and sacredness of Taiwanese *different-ness* in identity from China might eventually cross the line to adamantly demand a clear-cut *separate-ness,* legally and politically, from China as a non-negotiable manifest destiny for Taiwan.[31] Should both sides decline to conciliate for a compromising solution, cross-Strait clashes in the coming years could be a possibility as the DPP may choose to lift the veil of ambiguity under "the 1992 Consensus" and precipitate China to move forward with straightforward demands for an unequivocal response.

The 2016 regime change in Taiwan affects the political process as well as social discourse. Concurrently, one can conceive that China travels a similar course, as President Xi Jinping consolidates his power, and a new generation of leaders emerges after the 19th Party Congress. Both sides, understandably, have a major stake domestically and internationally in keeping cross-Strait economic transactions and political dialogues manageable. The difficulty for China is how to penalize the DPP government without creating collateral damage for the Taiwanese people. However, like the unfortunate possibility inherent in the game of "chicken," each side's anticipation of the other side's eventual swerving tends to mistakenly stiffen one's own resolve to not yield at all prior to the final collision.

NOTES

1. Samuel P. Huntington, *The Third Wave: Democratization in the Late Twentieth Century* (Norman: University of Oklahoma Press, 1991). Fukuyama, Francis, *The Origins of Political Order: From Prehuman Times to the French Revolution* (New York: Farrar, Strauss and Giroux, 2012).
2. "From Riches to Rags: Taiwan's Kuomintang party is Broke and Adrift," *The Economist*, Dec. 15, 2016, www.economist.com/news/asia/21711925-new-law-has-allowed-government-freeze-its-assets-leaving-it-unable-pay-staff-taiwans. Accessed Oct. 15, 2017.
3. Edward White, "Xi Jinping Talks Tough on Taiwan 'Separatists'," *Financial Times*, Oct. 18, 2017, www.ft.com/content/0093e84d-da46-36a8-a6db-28f311c2b2c1. Accessed Nov. 5, 2017.
4. Juan J. Linz and Alfred C. Stepan, *Problems of Democratic Transition and Consolidation* (Baltimore, MD: Johns Hopkins University Press, 1996), 5. Also see Thomas Carothers, "The End of the Transition Paradigm," *Journal of Democracy* 13, no. 1 (January 2002): 7.
5. Amartya Sen, "Democracy as a Universal Value," *Journal of Democracy* 10, no. 3 (1999): 5.
6. For definitional controversy, see Andre Schedler, "*Concepts of Democratic Consolidation*," paper presented at the 20th International Congress of the Latin American Studies Association, Guadalajara, Mexico. Vienna: Institute for Advanced Studies, 1997. lasa.international.pitt.edu/LASA97/schedler.pdf. Accessed Nov. 5, 2017. Mark J. Gasiorowski and Timothy J. Power, "The Structural Determinants of Democratic Consolidation: Evidence from the Third World," *Comparative Political Studies* 31, no. 6 (1998): 740–771.
7. Rein Taagepera, "Seats and Votes: A Generalization of the Cube Law of Elections," *Social Science Research* 2, no. 3 (1973): 257–275. Rein Taagepera, "Reformulating the Cube Law for Proportional Representation Elections," *American Political Science Review* 80, no. 2 (June 1986): 489–504. Tse-min Lin and Feng-yu Lee, "The Spatial Organization of Elections and the Cube Law," *Issues and Studies* 45, no. 2 (2009): 61–98.
8. Alberto Alesina, Enrico Spolaore, and Romain Wacziarg, "Economic Integration and Political Disintegration," *American Economic Review* 90, no. 50 (2000): 1293–94.

9. Yun-han Chu, "The Taiwan Factor," *Journal of Democracy* 23, no. 1 (2012): 42–56.
10. T. J. Cheng and Wei-chin Lee, "Wrestling over the Trans-Pacific Partnership (TPP): US Strategic Interests, China's Responses, and Taiwan's Membership Options," in *The Trans-Pacific Partnership and the Path to Free Trade in the Asia-Pacific*, ed. Peter Chow (Cheltenham, UK; Northampton, MA: Edward Elgar, 2016), 49–77.
11. Graham Allison, *Destined for War: Can America and China Escape Thucydides's Trap* (Boston: Houghton Mifflin Harcourt, 2017). Also see Ronald L. Tammen, *Power Transitions: Strategies for the 21st Century* (Washington, DC: CQ Press, 2000). A.F.K. Organski, *World Politics* (New York: Knopf, 1958).
12. Charles Glaser, "Will China's Rise Lead to War? Why Realism Does not Mean Pessimism," *Foreign Affairs* 90, no. 2 (March/April 2011): 81.
13. Toshi Yoshihara and James R. Holmes, *Red Star over the Pacific: China's Rise and the Challenges to US Maritimes Strategy* (Annapolis, MD: Naval Institute Press, 2010).
14. Alan M. Wachman, *Why Taiwan? Geostrategic Rationales for China's Territorial Integrity* (Redwood City, CA: Stanford University Press, 2007). David Gitter, "How Chinese analysts Understand Taiwan's Geostrategic Significance," *The Diplomat*, March 11, 2016, thediplomat.com/2016/03/how-chinese-analysts-understand-taiwans-geostrategic-significance/. Accessed Oct. 3, 2017.
15. Jane Rickards, "Taiwan Looks Southward," *Taiwan Business TOPICS*, American Chamber of Commerce, May 11, 2017, topics.amcham.com.tw/2017/05/taiwan-looks-southward/. Accessed Nov. 5, 2017.
16. Peter Ferdinand, "Westward Ho—the China Dream and 'One Belt, One Road': Chinese Foreign Policy under Xi Jinping," *International Affairs* 92, no. 4 (2016): 941–957.
17. Wei-chin Lee, "Taiwan, the South China Sea Dispute, and the 2016 Arbitration Decision," *Journal of Chinese Political Science* 22, no. 2 (2017): 229–250; Anne Hsiao-An Hsiao, "The South China Sea Arbitration and Taiwan's Claim: Legal and Political Implications," *Journal of Chinse Political Science* 22, no. 2 (2017): 221–228.
18. Luis Roniger, "Modern Populism in Latin America," *Oxford Bibliographies*, August 26, 2013, http://www.oxfordbibliographies.com/view/document/obo-9780199766581/obo-9780199766581-0130.xml. Accessed April 2, 2017. Dwayne Woods, "The Many Faces of Populism: Diverse But not Disparate," in *The Many Faces of Populism: Current Perspectives*, ed. Daywane Woods and Barbara Wejnert (Bingley, UK: Emerald Pub., 2014), 1–26.

19. W. Lance Bennett and Alexandra Segerberg, *The Logic of Connective Action: Digital Media and the Personalization of Contentious Politics* (Cambridge: Cambridge University Press, 2013). Mark R. Beissinger, "'Conventional' and 'Virtual' Civil Societies in Autocratic Regimes," *Comparative Politics* 49 no. 3 (2017): 351–371.
20. David Armstrong, Theo Farrell and Helene Lambert, *International Law and International Relations* (New York: Cambridge University Press, 2012), 104–110.
21. Jűrgen Habermas, *Legitimation Crisis,* trans. Thomas McCarthy (Cambridge, UK: Polity Press, 1988), 70.
22. Andrew Moravcsik, "Taking Preferences Seriously: A Liberal Theory of International Politics," *International Organization* 51, no. 4 (1997): 518.
23. Katherine Barbieri, "Economic Interdependence: A Path to Peace or a Source of Interstate Conflict," *Journal of Peace Research* 33, no. 1 (1996): 29–49.
24. Joanne Gowa, *Allies, Adversaries, and International Trade* (Princeton, NJ: Princeton University Press, 1994), 6. A brief piece of this claim can be found in Joanne Gowa and Edward D. Mansfield, "Power Politics and International Trade," in *Contending Perspectives in International Political Economy,* ed. Nikolaos Zahariadis (Fort Worth, TX: Harcourt Brace, 1999), 79–87.
25. Nancy Bernkopf Tucker, *Strait Talk: United States-Taiwan Relations and the Crisis with China* (Harvard University Press, 2011).
26. Thucydides, *The History of the Peloponnesian War,* Book 5, Chapter 17 (The Melian Dialogue), trans. Richard Crawley, Project Gutenberg, May 1, 2009 [EBook #7142], Last Updated: February 7, 2013, www.gutenberg.org/ebooks/7142.
27. Wei-chin Lee, "A Quartet in Disharmony: Taiwan, Japan, China, and the US in the Diaoyu(tai)/Senkaku Islands Dispute in the 2010s," *American Journal of Chinese Studies* 21 (June 2014): 95–109. Wei-chin Lee, "Taiwan, the South China Sea Dispute, and the 2016 Arbitration Decision," *Journal of Chinese Political Science* 22, no. 2 (2017): 229–250.
28. Fred Kaplan, "Obama's Way," *Foreign Affairs* 95, no. 1 (Jan/Feb. 2016): 46–63.
29. For a study of the relationship between development and context by developmental psychologists, please see Robert Cohen and Alexander W. Siegel, "A Context for Context: Toward an Analysis of Context and Development," in *Context and Development,* eds. Robert Cohen and Alexander W. Siegel (Hillsdale, NJ: Lawrence Erlbaum Associates, Pub., 1991), 3–23.
30. Michael J. Green, "Future Visions of Asian Security: The Five Rings," *Asian Policy* no. 3 (2007): 21.

31. Wei-chin Lee, "Taiwan's Cultural Reconstruction Movement: Identity Politics and Collective Action since 2000," *Issues and Studies* 41, no. 1 (March 2005): 1–51; Alastair Iain Johnston, "Beijing's Security Behavior in the Asia-Pacific: Is China a Dissatisfied Power?" in *Rethinking Security in East Asia: Identity, Power, and Efficiency*, ed. J. J. Suh, Peter J. Katzenstein, and Allen Carson (Stanford, CA: Stanford University Press, 2004), 65. See Richard Bush, "Taiwan Faces China; Attraction and Repulsion," in *Power Shift*, ed. David Shambaugh (Berkeley, CA: University of California Press, 2005), 180.

BIBLIOGRAPHY

Alesina, Alberto, Enrico Spolaore, and Romain Wacziarg. 2000. Economic Integration and Political Disintegration. *American Economic Review* 90 (50): 1293–1294.
Allison, Graham. 2017. *Destined for War: Can America and China Escape Thucydides's Trap*. Boston: Houghton Mifflin Harcourt.
Armstrong, David, Theo Farrell, and Helene Lambert. 2012. *International Law and International Relations*, 104–110. New York: Cambridge University Press.
Barbieri, Katherine. 1996. Economic Interdependence: A Path to Peace of a Source of Interstate Conflict. *Journal of Peace Research* 33 (1): 29–49.
Beissinger, Mark R. 2017. 'Conventional' and 'Virtual' Civil Societies in Autocratic Regimes. *Comparative Politics* 49 (3): 351–371.
Bennett, W. Lance, and Alexandra Segerberg. 2013. *The Logic of Connective Action: Digital Media and the Personalization of Contentious Politics*. Cambridge: Cambridge University Press.
Bush, Richard. 2005. Taiwan Faces China; Attraction and Repulsion. In *Power Shift*, ed. David Shambaugh, 170–186. Berkeley: University of California Press.
Carothers, Thomas. 2002. The End of the Transition Paradigm. *Journal of Democracy* 13 (1, January): 5–21.
Cheng, T.J., and Wei-chin Lee. 2016. Wrestling Over the Trans-Pacific Partnership (TPP): US Strategic Interests, China's Responses, and Taiwan's Membership Options. In *The Trans-Pacific Partnership and the Path to Free Trade in the Asia-Pacific*, ed. Peter Chow, 49–77. Cheltenham/Northampton: Edward Elgar.
Chu, Yun-han. 2012. The Taiwan Factor. *Journal of Democracy* 23 (1): 42–56.
Cohen, Robert, and Alexander W. Siegel. 1991. A Context for Context: Toward an Analysis of Context and Development. In *Context and Development*, ed. Robert Cohen and Alexander W. Siegel, 3–23. Hillsdale: Lawrence Erlbaum Associates, Pub.
Ferdinand, Peter. 2016. Westward Ho—The China Dream and 'One Belt, One Road': Chinese Foreign Policy Under Xi Jinping. *International Affairs* 92 (4): 941–957.

Fukuyama, Francis. 2012. *The Origins of Political Order: From Prehuman Times to the French Revolution*. New York: Farrar, Strauss and Giroux.

Gasiorowski, Mark J., and Timothy J. Power. 1998. The Structural Determinants of Democratic Consolidation: Evidence from the Third World. *Comparative Political Studies* 31 (6): 740–771.

Gitter, David. 2016. How Chinese Analysts Understand Taiwan's Geostrategic Significance. *The Diplomat*, March 11. thediplomat.com/2016/03/how-chinese-analysts-understand-taiwans-geostrategic-significance/. Accessed 3 Oct 2017.

Glaser, Charles. 2011. Will China's Rise Lead to War? Why Realism Does Not Mean Pessimism. *Foreign Affairs* 90 (2, March/April): 80–91.

Gowa, Joanne. 1994. *Allies, Adversaries, and International Trade*. Princeton: Princeton University Press.

Gowa, Joanne, and Edward D. Mansfield. 1999. Power Politics and International Trade. In *Contending Perspectives in International Political Economy*, ed. Nikolaos Zahariadis, 79–87. Fort Worth: Harcourt Brace.

Green, Michael J. 2007. Future Visions of Asian Security: The Five Rings. *Asian Policy* 3: 19–24.

Habermas, Jűrgen. 1988. *Legitimation Crisis*. Trans. Thomas McCarthy. Cambridge: Polity Press.

Hsiao, Anne Hsiao-An. 2017. The South China Sea Arbitration and Taiwan's Claim: Legal and Political Implications. *Journal of Chinese Political Science* 22 (2): 221–228.

Huntington, Samuel P. 1991. *The Third Wave: Democratization in the Late Twentieth Century*. Norman: University of Oklahoma Press.

Johnston, Alastair Iain. 2004. Beijing's Security Behavior in the Asia-Pacific: Is China a Dissatisfied Power? In *Rethinking Security in East Asia: Identity, Power, and Efficiency*, ed. J.J. Suh, Peter J. Katzenstein, and Allen Carson, 34–73. Stanford: Stanford University Press.

Kaplan, Fred. 2016. Obama's Way. *Foreign Affairs* 95 (1, January/February): 46–63.

Lee, Wei-chin. 2005. Taiwan's Cultural Reconstruction Movement: Identity Politics and Collective Action Since 2000. *Issues and Studies* 41 (1, March): 1–51.

———. 2014. A Quartet in Disharmony: Taiwan, Japan, China, and the US in the Diaoyu(tai)/Senkaku Islands Dispute in the 2010s. *American Journal of Chinese Studies* 21 (June): 95–109.

———. 2017. Taiwan, the South China Sea Dispute, and the 2016 Arbitration Decision. *Journal of Chinese Political Science* 22 (2): 229–250.

Lin, Tse-min, and Feng-yu Lee. 2009. The Spatial Organization of Elections and the Cube Law. *Issues and Studies* 45 (2): 61–98.

Linz, Juan J., and Alfred C. Stepan. 1996. *Problems of Democratic Transition and Consolidation*. Baltimore: Johns Hopkins University Press.

Moravcsik, Andrew. 1997. Taking Preferences Seriously: A Liberal Theory of International Politics. *International Organization* 51 (4): 513–553.

Organski, A.F.K. 1958. *World Politics*. New York: Knopf.

Rickards, Jane. 2017. Taiwan Looks Southward. *Taiwan Business TOPICS*, American Chamber of Commerce, May 11. topics.amcham.com.tw/2017/05/taiwan-looks-southward/. Accessed 5 Nov 2017.

Roniger, Luis. 2013. Modern Populism in Latin America. *Oxford Bibliographies*, August 26. http://www.oxfordbibliographies.com/view/document/obo-9780199766581/obo-9780199766581-0130.xml. Accessed 2 Apr 2017.

Schedler, Andre. 1997. *Concepts of Democratic Consolidation*. Paper Presented at the 20th International Congress of the Latin American Studies Association, Guadalajara, Mexico. Vienna: Institute for Advanced Studies, lasa.international. pitt.edu/LASA97/schedler.pdf. Accessed 5 Nov 2017.

Sen, Amartya. 1999. Democracy as a Universal Value. *Journal of Democracy* 10 (3): 3–17.

Taagepera, Rein. 1973. Seats and Votes: A Generalization of the Cube Law of Elections. *Social Science Research* 2 (3): 257–275.

———. 1986. Reformulating the Cube Law for Proportional Representation Elections. *American Political Science Review* 80 (2, June): 489–504.

Tammen, Ronald L. 2000. *Power Transitions: Strategies for the 21st Century*. Washington, DC: CQ Press.

The Economists. 2016. From Riches to Rags: Taiwan's Kuomintang Party Is Broke and Adrift, December 15. www.economist.com/news/asia/21711925-new-law-has-allowed-government-freeze-its-assets-leaving-it-unable-pay-staff-taiwans. Accessed 15 Oct 2017.

Thucydides. 2009. *The History of the Peloponnesian War*, Book 5, Chapter 17 (The Melian Dialogue). Trans. Richard Crawley. Project Gutenberg, May 1 [EBook #7142]. www.gutenberg.org/ebooks/7142. Accessed 2 Nov 2017.

Tucker, Nancy Bernkopf. 2011. *Strait Talk: United States-Taiwan Relations and the Crisis with China*. Cambridge: Harvard University Press.

Wachman, Alan M. 2007. *Why Taiwan? Geostrategic Rationales for China's Territorial Integrity*. Redwood City: Stanford University Press.

White, Edward. 2017. Xi Jinping Talks Tough on Taiwan 'Separatists'. *Financial Times*, October 18. www.ft.com/content/0093e84d-da46-36a8-a6db-28f311c2b2c1. Accessed 5 Nov 2017.

Woods, Dwayne. 2014. The Many Faces of Populism: Diverse But Not Disparate. In *The Many Faces of Populism: Current Perspectives*, ed. Daywane Woods and Barbara Wejnert, 1–26. Bingley: Emerald Pub.

Yoshihara, Toshi, and James R. Holmes. 2010. *Red Star Over the Pacific: China's Rise and the Challenges to US Maritimes Strategy*. Annapolis: Naval Institute Press.

PART I

Democracy and New Political Landscape

CHAPTER 2

The Quality of Democracy in Taiwan

Bruce J. Dickson

Most studies agree that Taiwan has a consolidated democracy. But while the level of democracy has been fairly constant for the past 20 years, the quality of democracy has varied considerably. This chapter examines the quality of democracy in Taiwan through a variety of indicators, analyzes the institutional sources of decline in the quality of democracy, and identifies the challenges facing the Tsai administration.

CONSOLIDATING TAIWAN'S DEMOCRACY

There should be no question that Taiwan has become a consolidated democracy. Its gradual, peaceful, and successful democratization has been thoroughly studied, and its key turning points are well-known:

- The 1986 lifting of martial law by the ruling Nationalist Party (Kuomintang, or KMT), and the formation of Democratic Progressive Party (DPP);
- In 1992, the first direct elections for all Legislative Yuan (LY) seats;
- In 1996, the first competitive presidential election;

B. J. Dickson (✉)
George Washington University, Washington, DC, USA

© The Author(s) 2019
W.-c. Lee (ed.), *Taiwan's Political Re-Alignment and Diplomatic Challenges*, Politics and Development of Contemporary China, https://doi.org/10.1007/978-3-319-77125-0_2

- In 2000, the DPP's Chen Shui-bian presidential election win and the first loss of presidential office by the KMT; a period of divided government with the DPP holding the presidency and the KMT (alone or with coalition partners) controlling the LY;
- The 2008 presidential election win by the KMT's Ma Ying-jeou, fulfilling Huntington's two-turnover rule; the end of divided government;
- In 2016, the DPP's Tsai Ing-wen's presidential election win; and the DPP's first time to win a majority in the LY.

These benchmarks of Taiwan's democratization are reflected in the best-known indices of regime types. The Polity IV dataset shows a steady rise in the level of democracy after 1986 and a perfect ten since 2003. Similarly, the Freedom House index has classified Taiwan as "free" since 1996, although the more specific scores for political rights and civil liberties have fluctuated during those years. The political rights score varied according to several well-known developments. For example, it improved to 1 (the highest possible score on a 1–7 scale) in 2005, due to electoral and constitutional reforms, declined to 2 over corruption allegations during Chen Shui-bian's second term as president, and improved again to 1 because of enforcement of corruption laws after Chen left office. Since 2009, Taiwan's political rights score has held steady at 1. At the same time, Taiwan's civil liberties score declined from 1 to 2 due to insufficient protection of criminal defendants' rights, including corruption cases. The civil liberties score also was a response to restrictions on the political activities of scholars at public universities. In 2017, Taiwan's civil liberties score also rose to 1 following improvements in press independence and academic freedoms.

Even though there is little dispute about whether or not Taiwan qualifies as a democracy, the quality of Taiwan's democracy remains an ongoing problem. This concern about the quality of democracy in Taiwan is representative of a broader trend in the comparative study of democracy and democratization. As the "Third Wave" of democratization waned in the 1990s, scholarly attention turned from transitions to consolidation with a particular focus on the quality of democracy around the world.[1] A country can have stable democratic institutions and still have subpar performance from those institutions. Identifying and measuring the key indicators of democratic governance has become a growth industry, with numerous projects providing different datasets on issues of democratic institutions and governance. The most used databases include the Varieties of Democracy (V-Dem), the Bertelsmann Transformation Index (BTI), and the Economist Intelligence Unit (EIU). In addition, the World Bank includes Taiwan in its Global Governance Indicators. These different indices are discussed later in the chapter. They do not always agree on either levels or trends in the quality of democracy in Taiwan, but provide helpful insights that put Taiwan in comparative perspective.

In Taiwan's case, assessing the quality of democracy begins with the party system and institutional relationships. Above these factors is ethnic identity, which overlays most aspects of politics in Taiwan.

THE PARTY SYSTEM

A core aspect of a democratic political system is the regular election of officials. Elections alone do not define democracy; even authoritarian regimes can have elections,[2] but it is nearly impossible to envision a democracy without elections. But the quality of democracy is also determined by what happens in between elections. In between elections, elected officials debate policies and attempt to find a resolution that can gain majority support. Democratic governance is improved by the parties' willingness to negotiate compromises on key issues. In Taiwan, partisan polarization makes compromise difficult. The DPP and KMT have not been willing to compromise on many key policy issues, often leading to gridlock and an inability of the Legislative Yuan to pass even budget bills in a timely fashion.[3]

Party polarization was very prominent in the early years of democratization, but moderated in later years. The KMT co-opted most of the DPP's positions on domestic public policy issues in order to get more votes. Whereas the DPP first distinguished itself with a focus on domestic issues, like social and distributional justice, clean government, and the environment, the KMT over time adopted similar positions on these issues. A study by Dafydd Fell found that the KMT and DPP were well differentiated on many social welfare positions, corruption, and cross-Strait issues between 1991 and 2004, but the degree of differentiation moderated even during that time span. According to Fell, this is a sign of a maturing democracy.[4]

The DPP lost ownership of the corruption issue during Chen's second term and his imprisonment afterwards. Part of the DPP's appeal to voters—and Chen in particular—was the promise of clean government after decades of KMT rule. But the criminal investigations of Chen, his officials, and his cronies damaged the DPP's clean reputation and its ability to use political corruption as a campaign tool. These investigations may have been politically motivated, but they nevertheless took their toll on the DPP. Ma was elected with a clean image in 2008, and that was one of the factors that made him appealing to voters after Chen's two terms as president.

Ethnic identity underlies this partisan rivalry. The DPP has a predominantly Taiwanese ethnic identity, whereas the KMT has traditionally had a more mainlander orientation, even though this segment of the population has been steadily shrinking. Their allies have similar ethnic identities: the Taiwan Solidarity Union (TSU) and the New Power Party (NPP) have a Taiwanese identity (and explicitly pro-independence platforms), and the New Party and People First Party (PFP) have a more overt mainlander identity than even the KMT.

This ethnic identity has been one of the obstacles to compromise and a contributor to gridlock in the LY. Even discussion of economic reform quickly turns to discussion of cross-Strait relations[5] which is the main symbol of ethnic identity. The KMT has traditionally sought improved relations with China to improve Taiwan's economy, but the DPP has been wary of relying too much on the Chinese economy as an engine of growth for Taiwan's economy.

On a broader scale, the parties' ethnic identities shape not only specific policy positions but also visions of Taiwan's current and future identity. When Chen Shui-bian was president, his clear preference for Taiwanese independence not only complicated his relationship with China and the US but also made compromise with the KMT difficult. According to Dankwart Rustow, consensus on national identity is the only prerequisite for a transition to democracy.[6] That is clearly overstating the case: Taiwan is definitely a successful case of democratization despite the lack of consensus on national identity, but Rustow's insight helps explain the partisan polarization in Taiwan. If parties cannot agree on national identity, it is hard to agree on much else.

There is one potential advantage within this partisan polarization: the parties are more polarized than public opinion. DPP and KMT supporters have different policy positions, but the distance between these positions is not as wide as between the parties' platforms.[7] When either party strays too far from the center on cross-Strait relations, the public punishes them. When the DPP has pushed its independence platform too hard, it tends to lose elections; in contrast, it has typically done better when it has focused on domestic issues like social and distributional justice, corruption, and the environment. The KMT also learned most recently that the public does not approve of deviating from the status quo on cross-Strait issues. Even though Ma Ying-jeou was re-elected in 2012 with almost 52 percent of the vote, and the KMT had 56.6 percent of the seats in the LY (the broader pan-Blue coalition controlled 59.3 percent of the LY seats), when Ma signed the Economic Cooperation Framework Agreement and tried to get the Cross-Strait Service Trade Agreement through the LY without debate, the reaction was swift. The 2014 Sunflower Movement brought the government to a halt, as students occupied the LY for several weeks and for a brief time also occupied the Executive Yuan. In local elections later in 2014, the KMT took heavy losses, a precursor to its massive defeat in the presidential and legislative elections in 2016.

The smaller parties (TSU, NPP, New Party, PFP) do not attract broad popular support, in part because of their strong ethnic identity, which only appeals to small segments of the voters. While party insiders may be determined to assert their parties' traditional ethnic identities, voters tend to be more moderate, preferring the status quo to a departure in either direction. When parties move from this central equilibrium, voters and protestors object.

Ethnic identity has also been the source of KMT fragmentation. The New Party and People First Party (PFP) were created when mainlander leaders in the KMT left the party because they thought Lee Teng-hui was trying to loosen its predominantly mainlander reputation and its commitment to reunification in particular. In contrast, the TSU emerged out of the KMT after Lee Teng-hui was forced to resign his post as party chairman in 2001, and he and his supporters created a new party that had a strong Taiwanese identity and perspective. Each of these splinter parties was able to gain only a small share of the votes in most elections, in part because of their emphasis on ethnic identity.

After its devastating loss in the 2016 elections, the KMT faces major questions concerning its future. Now that it no longer holds the presidency or a majority in the LY, it will struggle to regain popular support. If it had lost only the presidential election, it could blame Tsai Ing-wen's appeal or the chaos of the KMT's nomination process, in which its original candidate withdrew just a few months before the election. But the loss of the KMT's LY majority also signals that the public has lost confidence in the KMT and its policies. Its cross-Strait policy and mainlander identity are increasingly out of step with public opinion. Now that the vast majority of the electorate has a Taiwanese (but still status quo) orientation, what is the KMT's base? Who does it represent now? Will it be able to identify appealing candidates in upcoming elections? All these questions must be resolved if the KMT is to have a political future.

Although ethnic identity has been the most salient political cleavage in Taiwan, its importance is likely to diminish over time. As more and more of Taiwan's population—and especially young people—identify as Taiwanese, and less and less as Chinese, appealing to voters with a mainlander orientation will not be an effective electoral strategy. Attitudinal change, inter-marriage, and other social trends have caused the sharp divide between mainlanders and Taiwanese to lose its edge. With fewer and fewer voters identifying as Chinese, ethnic identity may linger as a symbolic cleavage while losing its significance for electoral and legislative outcomes.

Semi-presidential System

Taiwan's semi-presidential system also influences the quality of democracy. In Taiwan, the president appoints the prime minister. Because this appointment does not require legislative approval, the president's nominee does not need majority support in order to attain or remain in office. The LY can take a vote of no confidence in the prime minister, but a no confidence vote would allow the president to call new LY elections. The risk of losing seats in new LY elections has so far deterred legislators from attempting a vote of no confidence. There was a possibility of such a maneuver during the Chen administration when the KMT controlled a majority in the LY (either alone or with coalition partners), but this has not been a realistic possibility since. Even the rivalry between Ma and LY President Wang Jin-pyng was not intense enough to warrant a no confidence vote on Ma's prime minister.

The rationale for these features of Taiwan's semi-presidential system is not readily apparent, but their continuation is largely due to path-dependent forces. There are benefits to whichever party controls the presidency, and that will make it difficult to change. Even when in opposition, parties hope to regain the presidency and the institutional benefits that come with it. As a result, neither party has had an incentive to change the semi-presidential system while they are in the presidential office.

DIVIDED GOVERNMENT

Divided government is a problem for many democratic countries. When the executive and legislative branches are controlled by different parties or coalitions, finding a consensus with majority support can be extremely difficult. The result is typically gridlock that prevents progress on even pressing policy issues. This gridlock in turn influences public opinion against the institutions and politicians that the public blames for doing nothing.

Divided government in its classic sense (i.e., one party controls the executive branch and another party controls the legislature) was on full display during the Chen administration. Annual budget bills were a prominent source of gridlock. Although the LY does not have the authority to increase the government's budget requests, it can cut parts of the budget or engage in other stalling tactics to delay passage of the budget. During the eight years of Chen's presidency, when the DPP never had a majority in the LY, the KMT and its allies increasingly used the budget approval process to stymie Chen's initiatives.[8] Moreover, the tactics of budget cuts, blockages of government-sponsored bills, and passage of budget resolutions that limited how the government could spend its budget increased in frequency.

Although the Chen years were the only years of divided government in this traditional sense, other aspects of Taiwan's executive-legislative arrangements have also prevented effective governance. First, institutional features inhibit a true checks-and-balances system. On the one hand, the LY has weak oversight of the president and Executive Yuan. In the absence of stronger oversight, the LY uses stalling tactics, such as calling cabinet officials to report to it. On the other hand, the president has no veto power over LY votes. If the LY votes to cut the president's proposed budget or passes a resolution to limit the government's discretion on spending its budget, the president cannot issue a veto. In these opposing ways, the power of one branch is enhanced over the other, but the net result does not improve the quality of governance in Taiwan.

A second aspect of executive-legislative arrangements is more political. Although Ma Ying-jeou had a strong mandate upon his landslide election in 2008 (and a smaller mandate in 2012 due to a much smaller margin of victory) and sizeable KMT majorities in the LY, he was not always able to get his legislative agenda through the LY. He failed to include veteran KMT leaders in his policy-making circle and therefore did not get their buy-in before decisions were made. More to the point, the personal rivalry between Ma and LY President Wang Jin-pyng prevented better cooperation between the president's office and the LY. Having the same party control both the presidency and the LY should have created smooth sailing for a KMT agenda, but political calculations got in the way.

As Tsai Ing-wen began her term as president, she hoped to avoid some of these mistakes. She chose to remain DPP chair while serving as president and supported DPP veteran Su Chia-chyuan (her running mate in 2012) as LY president.[9] A key test for her presidency will be whether or not she will be more successful getting her legislative and reform agendas through the LY.

LY POLITICS

In addition to the aspects of divided government noted above, another source of LY gridlock has been the institutional features within the LY itself. Decisions to allow bills to come up for a vote are typically made in a closed-door caucus with representatives from each party in the LY. In an unusual procedure, each party in the LY has the ability to block a bill from advancing. This introduces too many veto players into the legislative process. As Su Chi described it, being elected to the LY makes you a member of the LY, but you can only be an actual legislator if you are in the caucus because the caucus is where the key decisions are made.[10] The LY committee system also includes co-chairs from the minority party, which in principle could improve coordination and the opportunity for consensus but in practice often means that bills get stalled. Beginning in 2016, caucus meetings are now televised and transcripted, which will add to their transparency, but may also lead to grandstanding.

In order for Tsai Ing-wen to get her agenda through the LY, the DPP will need to reform the LY's institutional practices and also get more cooperation from the president of the LY. Remaining as DPP chair and having an ally, Su Chia-chyuan, as LY president, may be helpful, but at least during the early years of her administration she did not attempt the kinds of legislative reforms that would address the potential for stalemate.

ELECTORAL AND CONSTITUTIONAL REFORM

At the beginning of the democratic era, Taiwan had a Japanese-style election system, in which each voter had a single, non-transferable vote (SNTV), but each election district elected multiple representatives. As a result, candidates could get elected with as little as 15–20 percent of the vote (depending on the number of representatives in that district). This led to complicated campaign strategies in which parties had to both maximize their total share of the vote and distribute those votes among several candidates so that as many as possible would get past the winning threshold. This was not a proportional representation system, but did allow more parties to get seats in the LY than would have been the case under a strict "first past the post system." It also led to sometimes large discrepancies between the parties' share of the votes and the percentages of seats they actually received in the LY.

A new electoral law was enacted in 2005 that replaced the SNTV system with a two-vote system. Each voter casts two ballots, one for individual candidates and the other for a party. The new law also shrunk the size of the LY by half to 113 seats. Of these seats, 73 (roughly two-thirds) are determined by the winners of single-member district elections, 34 are determined by party list proportional representation (PR) with a 5 percent minimum threshold, and 6 are given to aborigines. The immediate consequence of this new law was a reduction in the number of parties in the LY. However, the discrepancy between the share of the votes and the share of the seats continued. In 2008 and 2012, the KMT received more seats than its share of the vote, and in 2016, the DPP benefited from the same discrepancy. It won 45 percent of the single-district votes and 44 percent of the PR votes, but ended up with 60 percent of the LY seats. Whether by intention or not, the new election system has the result of boosting the seats controlled by the majority party, disadvantaging the other, and reducing the opportunities for smaller parties to gain representation. As DPP chair, Tsai supported adopting a German-style electoral system to make the results more representative as recently as 2014. Once the DPP controlled both the presidential office and the LY, this proposal was abandoned.[11] Once again, parties support reforms that benefit their short-term interests, even if they have long-term costs.

On balance, Taiwan's current electoral system is not perfect but follows the international trend of a mixed voting system. The single-member districts provide the accountability that is a strength of a plurality voting system, and the seats allotted by proportional representation allow more than two parties, and therefore their supporters, to be represented. The five percent threshold is the international standard for PR systems and strikes a balance between disenfranchisement and party fragmentation. If the threshold is higher, it disenfranchises too much of the electorate; if lower, it allows too many parties with limited appeal, and thereby makes it difficult to achieve a stable majority.

One element missing from Taiwan's electoral system is a requirement for a runoff election when no one wins more than 50 percent of the vote in a presidential election. Such a reform would prevent a president with less than a majority of electoral support from taking office. This would have occurred in 2000, when Chen Shui-bian won with less than 40 percent of the total. In other elections, the winner of the presidential election has always won a majority of the votes (although most pan-Blue voters believe Chen's re-election in 2004, in which he won with 50.1 percent of the vote, was fraudulent). But to protect against a future president being elected without the support of a majority of Taiwan's voters, a constitutional provision for a runoff election would be advantageous.

Assessment

Although these qualitative assessments portray a political system with tremendous problems, the main indices of the quality of democracy are not so gloomy. For instance, the Bertelsmann Transformation Index (BTI) evaluates the political and economic status of 129 countries (not including established democracies in the West and Japan). In the 2016 index, Taiwan ranks third in its democracy status, first for market economy status, and first for its overall status index (the average of democracy and market economy status). By comparison, South Korea ranks 13th, 8th, and 11th for democracy, market economy, and overall status, respectively. In this index, Taiwan's democracy looks quite good. At the same time, the BTI's annual reports reflect some of the structural problems identified above. In particular, the relatively low scores for "party system" and "performance of democratic institutions" reflect the impact of ethnic identity and gridlock that characterize Taiwan's politics (see Fig. 2.1).

The Varieties of Democracy (V-Dem) database gives a less positive portrayal of Taiwan's political institutions. Most relevant here are those for parties, the executive, and the legislature. V-Dem uses multiple indicators to look at each category and scores them on a −5 to 5 scale. This presents

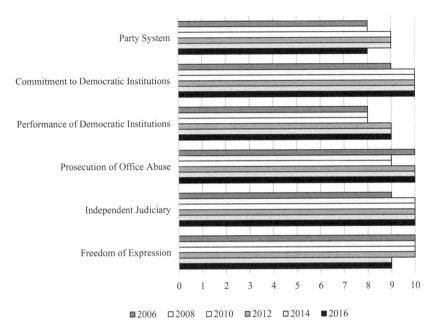

Fig. 2.1 BTI indicators for Taiwan, 2006–2016

a somewhat confusing picture, but two trends are apparent (see Fig. 2.2). First, Taiwan does not come close to a perfect 5 score on any of the indicators, in contrast to the BTI. This is partly because V-Dem includes Western liberal democracies, whereas BTI does not. Second, on most indicators, there is a curvilinear trend over time, with declines after the mid-2000s and a slight uptick in the most recent year (2016). This up-down-up pattern is especially apparent for the distinctiveness of party platforms (see panel 1 in Fig. 2.2) and legislative investigations and executive oversight (panel 3).

The Economist Intelligence Unit (EIU) evaluates Taiwan as a "flawed democracy." The EIU gives Taiwan an overall score of 7.79 out of a possible 10, ranking it 34th globally, below the Czech Republic and India and above Chile and Belgium. It gets relatively high marks for electoral process and pluralism (9.58), civil liberties (9.41), and functioning of government (8.21), but much lower scores for political participation (6.11) and political culture (5.63). Whereas V-Dem shows negative curvilinear trends for most qualities of democracy (see Fig. 2.3), the EIU's overall score for the

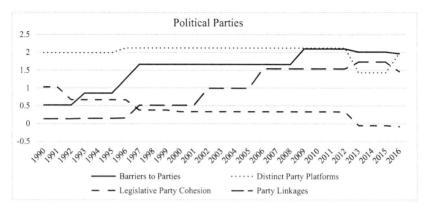
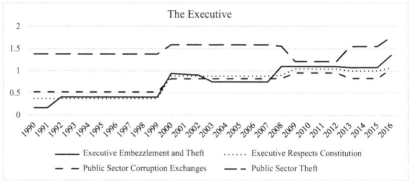
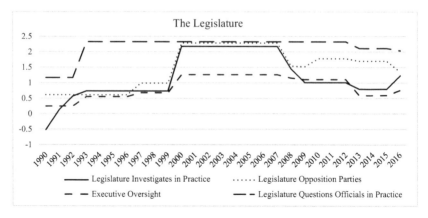

Fig. 2.2 V-Dem indicators for Taiwan, 1990–2016

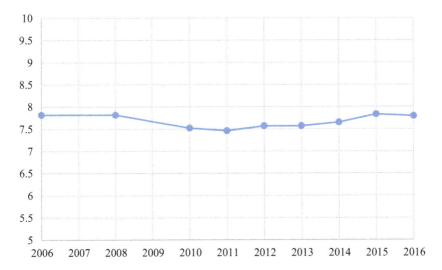

Fig. 2.3 EIU overall democracy scores for Taiwan, 2006–2016

quality of democracy shows only a slight decline in the late 2000s and an upward trajectory in more recent years (see Fig. 2.3), resulting in a relatively constant overall score during these ten years.

In short, the various indices for the quality of democracy in Taiwan identify problematic areas. But from a broader comparative perspective, the problems Taiwan's democracy is facing are neither unique nor particularly severe. The challenge for the political system more generally and the Tsai administration in particular is to address the problems identified above in order to improve the quality of Taiwan's democracy in the years ahead.

Conclusion

While there is little question that Taiwan's political system is appropriately classified as a consolidated democracy, questions persist about the quality of its democracy and what can be done about it. Many of the core issues—especially party polarization and gridlock—are influenced in different ways by the ethnic identity issues that overlay most policy and political issues. For that reason, it may be difficult to fully resolve them.

At the same time, we must recognize that many of the problems that Taiwan's democracy faces are structural problems common to many democracies. Compared to a hypothetical gold standard of democratic government, Taiwan's democracy leaves much to be desired. That is why a comparative perspective, as offered by available indices of the quality of democracy, is helpful. Taiwan's parties have not yet shown they are fully capable of addressing the serious economic, social, and security issues facing their country, but they are problems that many other democracies have not been able to resolve. As Schmitter and Karl note, democracy does not automatically lead to efficient government, good governance, or healthy economies.[12] In that regard, Taiwan is in good company. That may not offer much consolation, but the reality of democracy rarely matches the promise of democratization.

NOTES

1. Larry Diamond and Leonardo Morlino, eds., *Assessing the Quality of Democracy* (Baltimore: Johns Hopkins University Press, 2005).
2. Jennifer Gandhi and Ellen Lust-Okar, "Elections under Authoritarianism," *Annual Review of Political Science* 12 (2009): 403–422; Steven Levitsky and Lucan Way, *Competitive Authoritarianism: Hybrid Regimes after the Cold War* (New York: Cambridge University Press, 2010).
3. Shiow-duan Hawang, "Executive-Legislative Relations Under Divided Government," in *Taiwan's Democracy Challenged: The Chen Shui-bian Years*, ed. Yun-han Chu, Larry Diamond, and Kharis Templeman (Boulder, CO: Lynne Rienner Publishers, 2016), 123–144.
4. Dafydd Fell, *Party Politics in Taiwan: Party Change and the Democratic Evolution of Taiwan, 1991–2004* (London: Routledge, 2005); see also his later studies: "The Polarization of Taiwan's Party Competition in the DPP Era," in *Taiwan's Democracy: Economic and Political Challenges*, ed. Robert Ash, John W. Garver, and Penelope Prime (London: Routledge, 2013), 75–98; and "Taiwan's party system in the Ma Ying-jeou Era," in *Political Changes in Taiwan under Ma Ying-jeou: Partisan Conflict, Policy Choices, External Constraints and Security Challenges*, ed. Jean-Pierre Cabestan and Jacques deLisle (New York: Routledge, 2014), 37–59.
5. Shelley Rigger, "Political Parties and Identity Politics in Taiwan," in *New Challenges for Maturing Democracies in Korea and Taiwan*, ed. Larry Diamond and Shin Gi-wook (Stanford, CA: Stanford University Press, 2014), 106–132.
6. Dankwart A. Rustow, "*Transitions to Democracy*: Toward a Dynamic Model," *Comparative Politics* 2:3 (April 1970): 337–63.

7. Eric Chen-hua Yu, "Partisanship and Public Opinion," in *Taiwan's Democracy Challenged: The Chen Shui-bian Years*, ed. Yun-han Chu, Larry Diamond, and Kharis Templeman (Boulder, CO: Lynne Rienner Publishers, 2016), 73–94.
8. Hawang, "Executive-Legislative Relations Under Divided Government," 123–144.
9. Jessica Drun and Fa-Shen Vincent Wang, "DPP-Dominated Taiwanese Legislature Begins Session," *China Brief* 16:3 (2016), accessed DATE?, https://jamestown.org/program/dpp-dominated-taiwanese-legislature-begins-session/.
10. Su Chi, "An Overview of Taiwan's Legislative Yuan: Procedures and Practices" (presentation at Brookings Institution on *Taiwan's Legislative Yuan: Oversight or Overreach?*, Washington, DC, June 23, 2014). https://www.brookings.edu/wp-content/uploads/2014/06/23_taiwan_legislative_yuan_corrected.pdf.
11. Timothy Rich, "Have Efforts to Reform Taiwan's Electoral System Stalled?," *Taiwan Sentinel*, January 19, 2017, accessed February 7, 2017, https://sentinel.tw/reform-tw-electoral-stalled/.
12. Philippe C. Schmitter and Terry Lynn Karl, "What Democracy Is…and Is Not," *Journal of Democracy* 2.1 (Summer 1991): 75–88.

BIBLIOGRAPHY

Chi, Su. 2014. An Overview of Taiwan's Legislative Yuan: Procedures and Practices. Presentation at Brookings Institution on *Taiwan's Legislative Yuan: Oversight or Overreach?* Washington, DC, June 23. https://www.brookings.edu/wp-content/uploads/2014/06/23_taiwan_legislative_yuan_corrected.pdf.

Diamond, Larry, and Leonardo Morlino, eds. 2005. *Assessing the Quality of Democracy*. Baltimore: Johns Hopkins University Press.

Drun, Jessica, and Fa-Shen Vincent Wang. 2016. DPP-Dominated Taiwanese Legislature Begins Session. *China Brief* 16 (3). Accessed https://jamestown.org/program/dpp-dominated-taiwanese-legislature-begins-session/.

Fell, Dafydd. 2005. *Party Politics in Taiwan: Party Change and the Democratic Evolution of Taiwan, 1991–2004*. London: Routledge.

———. 2013. The Polarization of Taiwan's Party Competition in the DPP Era. In *Taiwan's Democracy: Economic and Political Challenges*, ed. Robert Ash, John W. Garver, and Penelope Prime, 75–98. London: Routledge.

———. 2014. Taiwan's Party System in the Ma Ying-jeou Era. In *Political Changes in Taiwan Under Ma Ying-jeou: Partisan Conflict, Policy Choices, External Constraints and Security Challenges*, ed. Jean-Pierre Cabestan and Jacques de Lisle, 37–59. New York: Routledge.

Gandhi, Jennifer, and Ellen Lust-Okar. 2009. Elections Under Authoritarianism. *Annual Review of Political Science* 12: 403–422.

Hawang, Shiow-duan. 2016. Executive-Legislative Relations Under Divided Government. In *Taiwan's Democracy Challenged: The Chen Shui-bian Years*, ed. Yun-han Chu, Larry Diamond, and Kharis Templeman, 123–144. Boulder: Lynne Rienner Publishers.

Levitsky, Steven, and Lucan Way. 2010. *Competitive Authoritarianism: Hybrid Regimes After the Cold War*. New York: Cambridge University Press.

Rich, Timothy. 2017. Have Efforts to Reform Taiwan's Electoral System Stalled? *Taiwan Sentinel*, January 19. https://sentinel.tw/reform-tw-electoral-stalled/. Accessed 7 Feb 2017.

Rigger, Shelley. 2014. Political Parties and Identity Politics in Taiwan. In *New Challenges for Maturing Democracies in Korea and Taiwan*, ed. Larry Diamond and Shin Gi-wook, 106–132. Stanford: Stanford University Press.

Rustow, Dankwart A. 1970. Transitions to Democracy: Toward a Dynamic Model. *Comparative Politics* 2 (3, April): 337–363.

Schmitter, Philippe C., and Terry Lynn Karl. 1991. What Democracy Is…and Is Not. *Journal of Democracy* 2 (1, Summer): 75–88.

Yu, Eric Chen-hua. 2016. Partisanship and Public Opinion. In *Taiwan's Democracy Challenged: The Chen Shui-bian Years*, ed. Yun-han Chu, Larry Diamond, and Kharis Templeman, 73–94. Boulder: Lynne Rienner Publishers.

CHAPTER 3

Taiwan's General Elections of 2016

John Fuh-sheng Hsieh

INTRODUCTION

On January 16, 2016, voters in Taiwan went to the polls to elect their president and members of the Legislative Yuan (Parliament). As it turned out, the opposition Democratic Progressive Party (DPP) won a landslide victory in both presidential and parliamentary races. The DPP's Tsai Ing-wen defeated Eric Chu of the ruling Kuomintang (KMT or Nationalist Party) and James Soong of the People First Party (PFP) in the presidential election. Tsai garnered 56.1 percent of the popular vote, the highest for any DPP candidate in previous elections. Equally importantly, the DPP was also able to win 68 out of 113 seats (or 60.2 percent) in the Legislative Yuan election, with 44.6 and 44.1 percent of the vote in the districts (mostly single-member districts, plus two three-member districts reserved for the indigenous people) and the proportional representation (PR) part of the election, respectively. This was the first time for the DPP to win an outright majority in Taiwan's national legislature. In contrast, the old ruling KMT was able to win a mere 31 percent of the vote in the presidential race and 38.9 and 26.9 percent of the vote in the two portions of the

---

J. F.-s. Hsieh (✉)
Department of Political Science, University of South Carolina, Columbia, SC, USA

© The Author(s) 2019
W.-c. Lee (ed.), *Taiwan's Political Re-Alignment and Diplomatic Challenges*, Politics and Development of Contemporary China, https://doi.org/10.1007/978-3-319-77125-0_3

legislative election. To a certain extent, the 2016 elections signaled a potential partisan realignment, which may affect Taiwan's party politics for many years to come.[1] So what happened in this election cycle? What are the factors that brought about such a sea change in Taiwan politics? The purpose of this chapter is to investigate these questions by taking a close look at the elections on the basis of the data provided by a large-scale post-election survey, the 2016 Taiwan Election and Democratization Studies (TEDS) survey.[2]

ELECTORAL SYSTEMS

The electoral method used for the presidential race is the single-member district (SMD) plurality, also known as the first-past-the-post system, with the candidate (or more precisely the ticket with presidential and vice-presidential candidates) who earns more votes than others, not necessarily a majority of the vote, winning the election.

The expectation of such a system is that the vote will converge to the top two candidates (or parties). This is dubbed Duverger's Law.[3] And this is indeed what has happened most of the time in the previous presidential elections. With the exception of the election in 2000 and partially in 1996, the vote has been concentrated in the top two candidates. In the 2016 election, an old face in presidential elections, James Soong, entered the race once again and was able to capture 12.8 percent of the vote, a good showing for a third-party candidate; however, his totals were not enough to tilt the balance.[4]

For the Legislative Yuan election, the electoral system is mixed-member majoritarian (MMM) system composed of two parts: 73 out of 113 seats (or 64.6 percent) are elected by SMD plurality system and 34 (or 30.1 percent) by party-list PR. In addition, six seats are reserved for the indigenous people, elected from two three-member districts with the old single nontransferable vote (SNTV) system.[5]

As can be expected, the SMD plurality system facilitates two-party competition while PR and SNTV provide more room for third parties.[6] Indeed, the votes for third parties have dwindled after the electoral system changed from the old SNTV to the new MMM system in 2008. However, in 2016, several third parties, notably the newly formed New Power Party (NPP) and the PFP, were able to pick up some votes and seats.[7] But the two largest parties, the DPP and the KMT, together were still able to gain gigantic shares in terms of both votes and seats.

In general, given the preponderance of the SMDs under the new MMM system, it can be expected that the two large parties, particularly the largest one, would be in an advantageous position vis-à-vis other political parties. Yet, the PR portion of the election and, to a smaller extent, the two three-member indigenous districts with SNTV may give the small parties some chances of winning seats as long as they are able to win a certain percentage of the vote.

Election Results

The election results were not very surprising for the presidential race given the polls released prior to the election,[8] but the margin of victory for the DPP's seat share in the Legislative Yuan election took many by surprise. In the presidential race, the DPP's Tsai Ing-wen easily defeated the KMT's Eric Chu and the PFP's James Soong as described earlier. In the legislative election, the DPP won over 60 percent of the seats with about 44 percent of the vote, enjoying a huge bonus while the KMT was unable to hold onto one-third of the seats with 38.9 and 26.9 percent of the vote in the district and PR parts of the election, respectively. This is, to some extent, understandable given the so-called cube law regarding the SMD plurality elections, which indicates that in such elections, the ratio of seat shares of the two major parties is the cube of the ratio of their vote shares.[9] That is, the advantage of the largest party in vote share under such an electoral rule will be significantly accentuated in seat share. In the SMD part of the Legislative Yuan election of 2016, the ratio of vote shares between the DPP and the KMT was 45.1:38.7 (not including indigenous districts), so the cube of it is 1.58. However, the actual ratio of seat shares between the two parties was 2.45 (67.1: 27.4), which shows that the DPP enjoyed a far larger bonus than predicted by the cube law, indicating that the DPP won many seats with small margins.

The election results were certainly significant in many different ways. Fundamentally, this ended eight years of KMT rule. Moreover, for the first time, the DPP was able to win not only the presidency but also an outright majority of parliamentary seats, rendering it in total control of the government. It is also noteworthy that the NPP, a very young party, was able to capture five seats in the Legislative Yuan election, surpassing the PFP as the third largest parliamentary party. It is allied with the DPP and is able to attract a lot of support from young voters on the island.[10]

Of course, the DPP has a different policy agenda as compared to that of the KMT. Domestically, it appeals to socioeconomic justice, and internationally, it distrusts China, and many of its supporters favor an independent Taiwan permanently separated from China.[11]

It is also interesting to note that the results of the 2016 elections may signal a long-term shift in the relative political fortunes of the two parties or between the Pan-KMT camp (including the KMT, PFP, and the New Party) and the Pan-DPP camp (including the DPP, NPP, and Taiwan Solidarity Union). That is, the Pan-KMT camp used to be the larger of the two camps, but the 2016 elections may signify that it is changing, and a party realignment may be occurring in Taiwan.[12]

In addition to the drastic change in political fortunes between the two major parties (or the two major camps), the 2016 elections were also marked by low turnout rate. It is true that there has been a downward trend for turnout rates in presidential elections, but the turnout drop in 2016 was significant, down from 74.4 percent in 2012 to merely 66.3 percent, the lowest ever recorded for presidential elections in Taiwan (see Fig. 3.1).

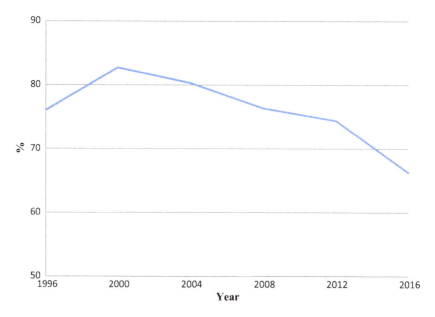

Fig. 3.1 Turnout rates in presidential elections (Source: Central Election Commission, various years)

In the following discussion, I will use survey data to explore the possible reasons for the low turnout and the factors contributing to voters' vote choices in the elections. But before doing so, let me say a few words about the political situation prior to the 2016 elections, which may provide some clues about voting turnout and vote choices.

ROAD TO ELECTIONS

During the eight years of KMT rule, President Ma Ying-jeou and his team had a difficult time in governing the nation as reflected in public opinion polls. Almost from the outset, Ma's approval ratings were never very high. According to many polls, his approval rating during his first term in office (2008–2012) seldom exceeded 40 percent, while during his second term (2012–2016), it hovered around 20 percent or less most of the time.[13]

Ma's low approval had a lot to do with the performance of his administration. From low economic growth figures to poor disaster relief operations to a series of cooking oil scandals, all these events added to the impression that his administration was incompetent and was unable to get things done as they should be. Even his policy toward China, which had increased the interactions and stabilized the situation across the Taiwan Strait, was seen by many as leaning too much toward China.

Ma's extremely low approval ratings indicate that he not only infuriated many opposition party supporters but also angered a lot of people in his own base. One example of this was the military and civil servants who had often been seen as the KMT's staunch supporters. Yet, his government hastily decided to cut off the benefits for retired government employees. The result was the withdrawal of support for the KMT from those retirees. During the election, many of them chose to stay home in protest.

Added to these problems was the division within the KMT. Although the party controlled both the presidency and the Legislative Yuan, the bills preferred by the Ma administration were often blocked in the legislative process, thus creating tensions between the president and the speaker of the Legislative Yuan, Wang Jin-pyng. The tension surfaced in September 2013, when Ma accused Wang of influence peddling in a judicial case involving a heavyweight DPP legislator. Soon afterwards, the KMT revoked Wang's party membership. Since Wang was elected to the Legislative Yuan by PR, a revocation of party membership would disqualify him from sitting in Parliament. As a consequence, he sought an injunction from the court to bar the KMT from nullifying his party membership. In the end, he succeeded, and the tension between Ma and Wang continued.

The schism within the KMT inadvertently provided a political opportunity for a large-scale student movement.[14] On March 18, 2014, protesting the hasty passage of a bill on the service trade agreement with China at the Home Affairs Committee of the Legislative Yuan, students accused the KMT of mishandling the procedure and occupied the Legislative Yuan for over three weeks. It was dubbed the Sunflower Student Movement.

The Sunflower Movement reflected the fear among many Taiwanese that too much dependence on the Chinese market might not only damage Taiwan's economy but also hurt Taiwan's security given that Taiwan's economy might be held hostage by China. To a certain extent, the reason that the students were able to stay in the parliamentary building for such a long time was related to the tension between the Ma administration and the Legislative Yuan. On the one hand, the administration did not want to send the police in to disperse the students, arguing that it was the turf of the national legislature; and on the other hand, Speaker Wang refrained from doing much, too, until the last moment.

The effect of the Sunflower Student Movement was enormous. The public grievances against the Ma administration intensified, resulting in the significant loss of the KMT in important local elections later that year. The whole atmosphere turned against the KMT, and eventually, the KMT was defeated in the 2016 national elections as well.

On the other side, the DPP, after losses in the 2008 and 2012 elections, was able to make a steady comeback. When Tsai Ing-wen assumed leadership of the party and prepared for the presidential run, she and her team started to make it known that she and the DPP would not seek to change the status quo in the cross-Strait relations once in power, thus alleviating the fear of many in Taiwan as well as overseas, notably in Washington, that a future DPP government might take drastic action to destabilize the situation in the Asia-Pacific region. Such a move by Tsai and her party proved to be very effective in presenting the DPP as a stabilizing force, rather than a troublemaker that the previous DPP administration was often portrayed to be.

Why Vote?

As noted earlier, the turnout was low in the 2016 elections. However, still about two-thirds of the voters turned out to vote. According to the Downsian logic, a voter may turn out to vote because the candidates (or parties) are different. That is, there must be utility differences between the winning of one candidate (or party) and the winning of another. However, each voter casts only one vote, which is one out of very many, so the chances that his or her single vote may change the election result (i.e., making one candidate or party, rather than the other, the winner) are almost nil. Thus, a rational voter should abstain.[15]

Of course, a lot of voters still go to the polling booth. Then, how could we explain their motivations? One explanation suggested by William H. Riker and Peter C. Ordeshook is that, in addition to the instrumental thinking (i.e., the party or candidate differential, the chances of affecting election results, and the cost of going to the polling booth), voters may also value what they called a "D term," referring to things like a sense of civic duty, an affirmation of one's partisan preference, and so on.[16] Yet, even if it may be true that voters turn out to vote out of a concern for civic duty or to express their preference for one party (or one candidate) or the other, we still cannot rule out completely the instrumental thinking voters may go through. When voters believe competition is close or when the parties (or candidates) are indeed very different, for instance, they are more likely to turn out to vote.[17]

In the context of Taiwan's 2016 elections, we can hypothesize that the low turnout might have resulted from the expectation that the DPP would win easily, or that the various parties were not that different as a result of the DPP's moderation of its position on cross-Strait relations, or the feeling of being betrayed by their party among lots of KMT supporters. Many voters may have still gone to the polling booth because they saw it as the duty of the citizens or as an opportunity to show one's partisan preference. Along with the cost of voting, these factors might or might not have driven voters to the polling booth.

Unfortunately, not all of these variables are available for study in the 2016 TEDS survey. However, we can still get some ideas about voters' calculus of voting. For instance, in the survey, the respondents were asked to pick a score between one and five, with one standing for the opinion that "no matter whom voters vote for, the situation will be similar" and five for the opinion that "the situation will be different if different people are elected." This measures candidate (or party) differential. Although the situation referred to in the question is too broad, it is still worthwhile using it to check whether voters' decision to turn out to vote would be affected by a general concern about the effect of elections. I will thus include this variable in one of the two logistic regression models of turnout.

There are also a set of four questions tapping into respondents' attitudes toward the KMT and DPP with regard to four specific policy areas: cross-Strait relations, economic development, social welfare, and the protection of national sovereignty. The respondents were asked whether the KMT or the DPP is a lot better, somewhat better, or about the same in handling these policy areas. Although these questions deal only with the two major parties, it would not distort the overall election picture too much since these two together capture most of the votes in Taiwan's elections. I will include these four variables in another regression model. To analyze the effect of these four variables on voters' decisions to go to the polling booth, I recode each of them into three categories: a score of two for "a lot of differences between the two parties," a score of one for "some differences," and a score of zero for "about the same."

Several other variables are incorporated in both regression models. One is civic duty, with a score of one standing for the statement that voting is a duty, and a zero otherwise. In addition to rational choice theory, another important school of thought on political participation stresses the importance of socioeconomic status (SES), a combined measure of such factors as education, income, and occupation. And it is maintained that individuals with high SES are more likely to participate in politics, including going to the polling booth.[18] Such a proposition is not necessarily incompatible with the rational choice theory of voting. For instance, it can be argued that education may bring about a greater sense of civic duty and so on. Here, I incorporate education in both regression models as a proxy for SES. Several demographic variables such as ethnicity, gender, and age are also included in the models.

Table 3.1 shows the two logistic regression models for turnout. In the first model, it can be seen that the variables voting matters, voting as civic duty, education, and age are all significant, showing that the rational choice account and SES do explain why voters turned out to vote in the context of Taiwan's 2016 elections.

In the second model, the results are, to a certain extent, similar. Of the four policy areas, two, economic development and national sovereignty, turn out to be significant, but not the other two, cross-Strait relations and

Table 3.1 Logistic regression for voting participation, 2016

Variable	Model 1		Model 2	
	B	S.E.	B	S.E.
Intercept	−1.921**	0.430	−1.425**	0.402
Voting matters	0.263**	0.055		
Difference cross-Strait			0.203	0.129
Difference economy			0.268*	0.158
Difference welfare			−0.032	0.157
Difference sovereignty			0.297**	0.137
Voting as civic duty	1.396**	0.155	1.433**	0.153
Better educated	0.149**	0.071	0.115	0.070
Minnan Taiwanese	0.093	0.194	0.023	0.190
Mainlanders	−0.121	0.304	−0.204	0.301
Female	0.141	0.153	0.232	0.151
Older	0.453**	0.071	0.455**	0.069
Number of cases	1592		1676	
Nagelkerke R^2	0.217		0.225	

Source: 2016 Taiwan Election and Democratization Studies (TEDS) Survey
The reference category is non-voting
*indicates $p < 0.10$
**indicates $p < 0.05$

social welfare. This is a little surprising since cross-Strait relations were seen as the dominant issue in Taiwan politics, and social welfare was one of the major issues raised by the Sunflower Student Movement. The reason that cross-Strait relations were not the driving force in 2016 might have something to do with the moderation of the DPP's position on the issue. And a lot of talks about low wages for the young in the Sunflower Movement might not be a welfare issue after all, but rather an issue concerning economic development broadly defined.

In the second model, civic duty and age are significant, similar to the regression results of the first model. However, that education is no longer significant is a little surprising; however, it is on the borderline of significance, so it is still something we should take into account in the discussion of voting turnout.

In sum, even with the limitations of the data, we can see that voters in Taiwan do calculate about going to the polling booth. Though we are unable to know why fewer people turned out to vote in 2016 than in other years, we can speculate that it may have had something to do with the expectation that the DPP was going to win easily or the grievances on the part of many KMT supporters who felt that they had been betrayed by their party.[19] But we cannot verify these assertions with the data we have. Interestingly, the regression results which show that cross-Strait relations were no longer significant may indicate that the differences between the two major parties were not as great as in the past as perceived by many voters in this election.

Vote Choice

So, after voters decide to go to the polling booth, the next question is: which candidates or parties are they going to vote for? Obviously, there are many factors that may affect voters' vote choices. According to the Downsian logic, a voter votes for a candidate or party if the candidate or party, when in office, will provide him or her with higher utility income than the other candidate or party will. However, the only concrete information the voter may possess at the time of choosing a candidate or party is the performance of the incumbent. The voter may thus use that piece of information to project what the incumbent will do if reelected. The voter will also speculate what the challenger would have done in office in the previous term and use it to project what the challenger would do in the coming term.[20] This is prospective voting embedded in retrospective evaluations.

Yet, given that information is costly, a voter may not be able to obtain enough information to cast an "informed" vote, so he or she may rely upon some shortcuts to simplify his or her voting decision.[21] One of such shortcuts is partisanship, which is, in Morris Fiorina's words, "a running tally of retrospective evaluations of party promises and performance."[22] That is, a voter may rely upon party identification to make his or her choice as a substitute for an "informed" vote.[23]

At the time of Taiwan's 2016 elections, the incumbent President, Ma Ying-jeou, had already served two terms and was thus ineligible for reelection. However, his party did enter both presidential and legislative races, and voters might have held it accountable for what had been done during President Ma's terms. Thus, for practical purposes, President Ma's party, the KMT, could be treated as the incumbent. Or, to a large extent, the elections could be seen as a referendum on the Ma administration's performance in office.

As mentioned earlier, Ma and his administration's approval rating, particularly in his second term, had been consistently low. One area people complained about was the economy. Yet, it should be noted that when President Ma assumed office in 2008, there was a global financial crisis. Given that Taiwan's economy is highly dependent on trade, it is not surprising that Taiwan was hit hard by the crisis. Although Taiwan's economy recovered in 2010 with a double-digit growth rate, economic growth soon slowed down again and remained sluggish throughout Ma's terms in office.

In addition, many Taiwanese, particularly the young, had been dissatisfied with low wages and unaffordable housing throughout Ma's tenure. And Ma's attempt at facilitating closer economic ties with China did not bring back substantive benefits to folks at home as promised and, in a way, intensified the fear that too much dependence on the Chinese market might bring about the possibility that Taiwanese businesses might be held hostage by China, thus jeopardizing Taiwan's security. Such concerns loomed large in the Sunflower Student Movement and fueled anti-KMT sentiment in the electorate.

Additionally, many incidents plagued the Ma administration. For example, clumsy government rescue efforts following Typhoon Morakot in August 2009 were strongly criticized and hurt Ma and his administration's approval significantly. Another example was a series of scandals involving food safety, which added to the public perception that the government was unable to get things done correctly.

The Ma administration's trouble in the electorate was not confined to those who supported the opposition. Even among Pan-KMT supporters, many felt that they had been mistreated by the KMT government. The proposed pension reform for government employees, for instance, alienated many of those who might be affected by such a policy—and who happened to be strong KMT supporters.

Ironically, even though the KMT commanded a parliamentary majority during Ma's tenure, intraparty divisions brought about gridlock in the legislative process, intensifying the dissatisfaction with the KMT government. And the factional infighting between the president and the speaker of the Legislative Yuan increased distrust and disdain for the KMT government among the general public.

Thus, the 2016 elections reflected the public sentiments toward Ma and his administration's performance in various policy areas. In addition to these specific policies, Taiwanese society has also been divided on some very broad issues which serve as the basis for the formation of major political groupings. Scholars call these broad issues cleavages (e.g., class, religion, post-materialism, etc.) that underpin party configuration in society.[24] Unlike most of the Western democracies where class and religion often play a significant role in sustaining party competition,[25] in the case of Taiwan, the single most important cleavage that pits the KMT (or Pan-KMT camp) against the DPP (or Pan-DPP camp) is national identity.[26]

National identity refers to the various possible future political associations between China and Taiwan: the unification of China and Taiwan; an independent Taiwan to be separated from China permanently; or the status quo which denotes de facto, but not de jure, independence. This is a hotly contested issue on the island. The KMT or the Pan-KMT camp prefers the status quo leaning somewhat toward unification while the DPP or the Pan-DPP camp traditionally leans toward independence. However, the DPP has toned down its rhetoric lately by claiming that Taiwan has already been independent, and its current name is the Republic of China (ROC). During the election campaigns for the 2016 elections, the DPP's presidential candidate, Tsai Ing-wen, went even further by assuring the domestic public as well as the international community that a future DPP government would maintain the status quo.

For a long time, the KMT was seen as the status quo party since the status quo was very much defined by the KMT as it symbolized the name of the country, the constitution, the national flag, the national anthem, and so on. However, in mid-2015, Hung Hsiu-chu who later became the KMT's presidential candidate threw out the idea of "One China with the same interpretation," seemingly deviating from the party's original position of "One China with different interpretations," and giving the impression that she would move the party toward the unification end of the political spectrum—in contrast to Tsai Ing-wen's effort to champion the status quo. Hung's move took the party leadership by surprise and finally led to her ouster. She was replaced by Eric Chu to represent the KMT in the presidential race. This blunder undoubtedly damaged the KMT's image. It hurt the party not only in the presidential race but also in the legislative election held simultaneously.

Quite unfortunately for the KMT, several incidents (e.g., cooking oil scandals, an event involving a Taiwanese singer Chou Tzu-yu, etc.) that took place prior to polling day further eroded the electorate's confidence in the KMT. The election result showed the public's dissatisfaction with the KMT, and the DPP won a landslide victory at the polls.

The TEDS survey provides some clues to these observations. But as in the discussion of voting turnout, not all variables are available in the survey. We cannot ascertain, for instance, the effect of such factors as low turnout, change of presidential candidate at the last moment, and so forth on the votes received by the KMT.[27]

With such limitations in mind, this section proceeds as follows. I will run four binary logistic regression models, two for the presidential race and the other two for the legislative election. The reasons I turn to binary, instead of multinomial, logistic regression are that the number of cases for the third-party candidates in the survey is small for both presidential and legislative elections and that my main interest in this study is the changing political fortunes of the two major political parties. It should be noted that there is one complication with regard to the Legislative Yuan election; that is, each voter can cast two votes, one for the candidate in an SMD or a three-member indigenous district and the other for a party list in the PR portion of the election. This study focuses on the votes in the districts—in both SMDs and indigenous districts—mainly because the seats reserved for the districts account for the lion's share (almost 70 percent) of the total seats available in the election.

For the independent variables, I will include two broad issues, national identity and public services (a proxy for the class issue), which may potentially be the cleavages underpinning the party configuration in Taiwan. Both are measured in the same way. On the national identity issue, the respondents were asked to pick a score between zero and ten, with zero standing for independence and ten for unification. On public services, the respondents were asked to choose a score between zero (cutting taxes and services) and ten (increasing taxes and services). To be consistent with the coding of most of the other variables (from left to right ideologically as commonly known), I reverse the coding of the services issue so that zero stands for increasing taxes and services (the position of the traditional left) and ten for cutting taxes and services (the position of the right).

Also included in the models are two performance variables representing voters' retrospective evaluations of the economic situation. The respondents were asked whether the overall economic situation of the country or their personal economic condition was better off, worse off, or about the same as compared to the situation a year ago. In economic voting literature, the two are often dubbed as sociotropic voting and pocketbook voting, respectively.[28] I do not include the two prospective evaluations comparing the situation of today to that of a year from now in the models, because there is an endogeneity problem as a result of the fact that this is a post-election survey and respondents might "rationalize" their prospective evaluations given their vote choices.

As noted earlier, national identity has been identified as the most important factor affecting voters' partisan attachments. That is, the two are closed intertwined. Thus, I set up a different model by replacing national identity with partisanship. Besides, several demographic variables are included in the models. These include ethnicity, gender, age, and education.

Tables 3.2a and 3.2b report the results of the logistic regression models. As can be expected, the national identity issue matters in both presidential and legislative elections, so does retrospective evaluation of the national economy. It confirms our hypotheses that the cleavage structure,

Table 3.2a Logistic regression for voting for Eric Chu (KMT) in the presidential election

Variable	Model 1		Model 2	
	B	S.E.	B	S.E.
Intercept	−3.550**	0.728	−1.484*	0.811
Unification	0.362**	0.097		
Less welfare	−0.001	0.036	−0.023	0.056
Retrospective sociotropic	0.717**	0.124	0.428**	0.196
Retrospective pocketbook	0.090	0.141	0.107	0.218
KMT			3.653**	0.308
DPP			−2.959**	0.455
Minnan Taiwanese	−0.770	0.600	−1.726**	0.514
Mainlanders	−1.044	1.749	−3.796*	1.974
Minnan × unification	0.063	0.110	0.383**	0.081
Mainlanders × unification	0.452	0.336	0.933**	0.381
Female	0.099	0.166	−0.069	0.260
Older	0.310**	0.076	0.177	0.122
Better educated	0.186**	0.075	−0.011	0.120
Number of cases	968		974	
Nagelkerke R^2	0.360		0.779	

Source: 2016 Taiwan Election and Democratization Studies (TEDS) Survey
The reference category is Tsai Ing-wen (DPP)
*indicates p < 0.10
**indicates p < 0.05

Table 3.2b Logistic regression for voting for the KMT candidates in the Legislative Yuan election (single-member districts and aboriginal districts only)

Variable	Model 1		Model 2	
	B	S.E.	B	S.E.
Intercept	−2.324**	0.643	−0.791	0.632
Unification	0.278**	0.081		
Less welfare	−0.015	0.033	−0.032	0.041
Retrospective sociotropic	0.822**	0.117	0.552**	0.144
Retrospective pocketbook	0.077	0.135	0.095	0.168
KMT			2.452**	0.263
DPP			−1.855**	0.237
Minnan Taiwanese	−0.700	0.488	−1.273**	0.366
Mainlanders	−2.459	2.385	−5.057*	2.683
Minnan × unification	0.023	0.092	0.204**	0.056
Mainlanders × unification	0.664	0.462	1.086**	0.521
Female	0.134	0.158	−0.066	0.199
Older	0.215**	0.073	0.127	0.095
Better educated	0.256**	0.073	0.224**	0.094
Number of cases	904		910	
Nagelkerke R^2	0.324		0.620	

Source: 2016 Taiwan Election and Democratization Studies (TEDS) Survey
The reference category is DPP
*indicates p < 0.10
**indicates p < 0.05

referring essentially to the national identity issue but not the public services issue, conditions voters' vote choices. Those who lean toward unification are more likely to support the KMT. And when national identity is replaced by the two dummy variables, KMT and DPP, it shows clearly that partisanship is a significant factor too. Indeed, given the encompassing nature of the notion of partisanship, it is not surprising that the models with partisan attachments have overall higher explanatory power than the models without. Besides, performance matters. Voters' retrospective assessments of the national economic situation, not personal economic condition, have a significant effect on vote choices. Those who feel that the economy has gotten better are more likely than those who do not to turn to the KMT. Ethnicity, age, and education are significant in some models, and gender is, in general, not significant.

These results show that the 2016 elections in Taiwan did reflect voters' evaluations of the KMT government's performance while in office, and the long-term cleavage in the society continues to shape the politics on the island. The TEDS survey data do give us some clues, but not the whole picture, of the electoral process in Taiwan.

CONCLUSION

The 2016 general elections were undoubtedly a milestone in Taiwan's political history. The ruling KMT, after having won two consecutive elections in 2008 and 2012, was defeated by the DPP a few years later. It was a landslide victory for the DPP. It was not only able to win the presidency but also, for the first time in history, an outright majority in the Legislative Yuan. This surely represents a sea change in Taiwanese politics.

The victory of the DPP over the KMT at the polls in 2016 represents not only the short-term shift of electoral dynamics between the two parties (or the two political camps) but also, very likely, the long-term shift of political fortunes between the two.[29] For a long time, the KMT, being seen as the status quo party, was able to command a large base in the electorate. Given that a majority or close to a majority of the population supports the status quo, the Pan-KMT camp in which the KMT plays a dominant role was the larger of the two major political groupings. Although in the early days, the distribution of voters on the national identity issue had been quite similar across different age groups, in recent polls, the young are moving en masse toward independence.[30] If the trend continues, it will be more and more difficult for the KMT or the Pan-KMT camp to regain its earlier strength in the electorate. This is, of course, good news for the DPP or the Pan-DPP camp. Taiwan politics is, indeed, undergoing some significant changes now.

NOTES

1. See John Fuh-sheng Hsieh, "Taiwan's 2016 Elections: Critical Elections?," *American Journal of Chinese Studies* 23, no. 1 (April 2016): 9–23.
2. The TEDS surveys were conducted by a consortium of academic researchers from various institutions in Taiwan, sponsored by the Ministry of Science and Technology (formerly National Science Council). Professor Chi Huang has been the coordinator of these surveys since 2000.

3. See William H. Riker, "The Two-Party System and Duverger's Law: An Essay on the History of Political Science," *American Political Science Review* 76, no. 4 (December 1982): 753–66. See also Maurice Duverger, *Political Parties: Their Organization and Activity in the Modern State*, trans. Barbara North and Robert North (London: Methuen, 1954).
4. In the 2000 election, James Soong, a KMT-turned independent, lost the race by a small margin. He later formed his own party, the PFP.
5. The SNTV system is one in which a voter can cast only one vote for a candidate in a multimember district. It was used in the Legislative Yuan elections prior to the constitutional reform of 2005. For a comparison between the old and new systems, see John Fuh-sheng Hsieh, "The Origins and Consequences of Electoral Reform in Taiwan," *Issues & Studies* 45, no. 2 (June 2009): 1–22.
6. Ibid. See also Gary W. Cox, *Making Votes Count: Strategic Coordination in the World's Electoral Systems* (Cambridge: Cambridge University Press, 1997).
7. The NPP was able to capture 2.9 and 6.1 percent of the vote with three and two seats in the SMD and PR portions of the election, respectively. The PFP won 6.5 percent of the vote and three seats in the PR part.
8. According to Taiwan's Election and Recall Laws, no polls can be released ten days prior to polling day.
9. The cube law is based essentially upon the British experience. See Rein Taagepera and Matthew Soberg Shugart, *Seats and Votes: The Effects and Determinants of Electoral Systems* (New Haven, Conn.: Yale University Press, 1989).
10. Dafydd Fell, "Small parties in Taiwan's 2016 National Elections: A Limited Breakthrough?" *American Journal of Chinese Studies* 23, no. 1 (April 2016): 41–58.
11. For issues separating the two parties, see John Fuh-sheng Hsieh and Emerson M.S. Niou, "Issue Voting in the Republic of China on Taiwan's 1992 Legislative Yuan Election," *International Political Science Review* 17, no. 1 (January 1996): 13–27; John Fuh-sheng Hsieh and Emerson M.S. Niou, "Salient Issues in Taiwan's Electoral Politics," *Electoral Studies* 15, no. 2 (May 1996): 219–235; and Tse-min Lin, Yun-han Chu, and Melvin J. Hinich, "Conflict Displacement and Regime Transition in Taiwan: A Spatial Analysis," *World Politics* 48, no. 4 (July 1996): 453–481.
12. Hsieh, "Taiwan's 2016 Elections."
13. See, for example, the Taiwan Indicators Survey Research polls at http://www.tisr.com.tw/?p=6745.
14. On political opportunities and social movements, see, for example, Charles Tilly and Sidney Tarrow, *Contentious Politics*, 2nd ed. (Oxford: Oxford University Press, 2015).

15. Anthony Downs, *An Economic Theory of Democracy* (New York: Harper & Row, 1957).
16. William H. Riker and Peter C. Ordeshook, "A Theory of the Calculus of Voting," *American Political Science Review* 62, no. 1 (March 1968): 25–42. See also John H. Aldrich, "Rational Choice and Turnout," *American Journal of Political Science* 37, no. 1 (Feb., 1993): 246–278.
17. See the argument about cross-national differences in Mark N. Franklin, "The Dynamics of Electoral Participation," in *Comparing Democracies 2: New Challenges in the Study of Elections and Voting*, eds. Lawrence LeDuc, Richard G. Niemi, and Pippa Norris (Thousand Oaks, Calif.: Sage, 2002), 148–168.
18. There is a huge literature on the effect of SES on voting. See, for example, Sidney Verba and Norman H. Nie, *Participation in America: Political Democracy and Social Equality* (New York: Harper & Row, 1972).
19. The 2016 TEDS data show that 12.8 percent of KMT supporters, as compared to 8.8 percent of DPP supporters, did not turn out to vote. However, it is hard to interpret this result. First, the turnout rate in the survey is about 18 percent higher than the actual turnout rate, rendering the interpretation difficult. (This is a common problem for election surveys since many respondents may overstate their intention to turn out to vote.) Second, it is likely that some long-time KMT supporters were so disappointed in the party that they refused to support it—at least for now—and did not tell the interviewers that they were KMT supporters.
20. Downs, *An Economic Theory of Democracy*.
21. Ibid.
22. Morris P. Fiorina, *Retrospective Voting in American National Elections* (New Haven, Conn.: Yale University Press, 1981), 84.
23. Interestingly, it seems that rational choice theory of vote choice comes to resemble the Michigan School by including partisanship. However, the two are still different. For the Michigan School, party identification is a long-term *affectional* attachment with a party, which voters may have acquired in the socialization process and is at the core of their voting decisions. For the Michigan School of voting, see Angus Campbell, Philip E. Converse, Warren E. Miller, and Donald E. Stokes, *The American Voter* (New York: John Wiley, 1960), and Michael S. Lewis-Beck, William G. Jacoby, Helmut Norpoth, and Herbert F. Weisberg, *The American Voter Revisited* (Ann Arbor, Mich.: University of Michigan Press, 2008).
24. For a classical treatment of social cleavages, see Seymour M. Lipset and Stein Rokkan, "Cleavage Structures, Party Systems and Voter Alignments: An Introduction," in *Party Systems and Voter Alignments: Cross-National Perspectives, ed.* Seymour M. Lipset and Stein Rokkan (New York: The Free Press, 1967), 1–64. For the emergence of such a new cleavage as

post-materialisms, see Ronald Inglehart, *The Silent Revolution: Changing Values and Political Styles among Western Publics* (Princeton, N.J.: Princeton University Press, 1977), and *Culture Shift in Advanced Industrial Society* (Princeton, N.J.: Princeton University Press, 1990).
25. Arend Lijphart, *Patterns of Democracy: Government Forms and Performance in Thirty-Six Countries* (New Haven, Conn.: Yale University Press, 1999), 78–89.
26. John Fuh-sheng Hsieh, "Ethnicity, National Identity, and Domestic Politics in Taiwan," *Journal of Asian Studies* 40, no. 1–2 (April 2005): 13–28.
27. That low turnout cost the KMT some votes seems to be true given the low turnout in many of the KMT's traditional strongholds. But the TEDS data are not appropriate to examine this effect. See the explanation in fn. 18.
28. There is a huge literature on economic voting. See, for example, Michael B. MacKuen, Robert S. Erikson, and James A. Stimson, "Peasants or Bankers? The American Electorate and the U.S. Economy," *American Political Science Review* 86, no. 3 (September 1972): 597–611; Wouter van der Brug, Cees van der EijK, and Mark Franklin, *The Economy and the Vote: Economic Conditions and Elections in Fifteen Countries* (Cambridge: Cambridge University Press, 2007); and Raymond M. Duch and Randolph T. Stevenson, *The Economic Vote: How Political and Economic Institutions Condition Election Results* (Cambridge: Cambridge University Press, 2008). On the case of Taiwan, see John Fuh-sheng Hsieh, Dean Lacy, and Emerson M.S. Niou, "Retrospective and Prospective Voting in a One-Party-Dominant Democracy: Taiwan's 1996 Presidential Election," *Public Choice* 97, no. 3 (December 1998): 383–99.
29. Hsieh, "Taiwan's 2016 Elections."
30. Ibid.

BIBLIOGRAPHY

Aldrich, John H. 1993. Rational Choice and Turnout. *American Journal of Political Science* 37: 246–278.
Campbell, Angus, Philip E. Converse, Warren E. Miller, and Donald E. Stokes. 1960. *The American Voter*. New York: John Wiley.
Cox, Gary W. 1997. *Making Votes Count: Strategic Coordination in the World's Electoral Systems*. Cambridge: Cambridge University Press.
Downs, Anthony. 1957. *An Economic Theory of Democracy*. New York: Harper & Row.
Duch, Raymond M., and Randolph T. Stevenson. 2008. *The Economic Vote: How Political and Economic Institutions Condition Election Results*. Cambridge: Cambridge University Press.

Duverger, Maurice. 1954. *Political Parties: Their Organization and Activity in the Modern State*. Trans. Barbara North and Robert North. London: Methuen.
Fell, Dafydd. 2016. Small Parties in Taiwan's 2016 National Elections: A Limited Breakthrough? *American Journal of Chinese Studies* 23: 41–58.
Fiorina, Morris P. 1981. *Retrospective Voting in American National Elections*. New Haven: Yale University Press.
Franklin, Mark N. 2002. The Dynamics of Electoral Participation. In *Comparing Democracies 2: New Challenges in the Study of Elections and Voting*, ed. Lawrence LeDuc, Richard G. Niemi, and Pippa Norris, 146–168. Thousand Oaks: Sage.
Hsieh, John Fuh-sheng. 2005. Ethnicity, National Identity, and Domestic Politics in Taiwan. *Journal of Asian and Studies* 40: 13–28.
———. 2009. The Origins and Consequences of Electoral Reform in Taiwan. *Issues & Studies* 45: 1–22.
———. 2016. Taiwan's 2016 Elections: Critical Elections? *American Journal of Chinese Studies* 23: 9–23.
Hsieh, John Fuh-sheng, and Emerson M.S. Niou. 1996a. Issue Voting in the Republic of China on Taiwan's 1992 Legislative Yuan Election. *International Political Science Review* 17: 13–27.
———. 1996b. Salient Issues in Taiwan's Electoral Politics. *Electoral Studies* 15: 219–235.
Hsieh, John Fuh-sheng, Dean Lacy, and Emerson M.S. Niou. 1998. Retrospective and Prospective Voting in a One-Party-Dominant Democracy: Taiwan's 1996 Presidential Election. *Public Choice* 97: 383–399.
Inglehart, Ronald. 1977. *The Silent Revolution: Changing Values and Political Styles among Western Publics*. Princeton: Princeton University Press.
———. 1990. *Culture Shift in Advanced Industrial Society*. Princeton: Princeton University Press.
Lewis-Beck, Michael S., William G. Jacoby, Helmut Norpoth, and Herbert F. Weisberg. 2008. *The American Voter Revisited*. Ann Arbor: University of Michigan Press.
Lijphart, Arend. 1999. *Patterns of Democracy: Government Forms and Performance in Thirty-Six Countries*. New Haven: Yale University Press.
Lin, Tse-min, Yun-han Chu, and Melvin J. Hinich. 1996. Conflict Displacement and Regime Transition in Taiwan: A Spatial Analysis. *World Politics* 48: 453–481.
Lipset, Seymour M., and Stein Rokkan. 1967. Cleavage Structures, Party Systems and Voter Alignments: An Introduction. In *Party Systems and Voter Alignments: Cross-National Perspectives*, ed. Seymour M. Lipset and Stein Rokkan, 1–64. New York: The Free Press.
MacKuen, Michael B., Robert S. Erikson, and James A. Stimson. 1972. Peasants or Bankers? The American Electorate and the U.S. Economy. *American Political Science Review* 86: 597–611.

Riker, William H. 1982. The Two-Party System and Duverger's Law: An Essay on the History of Political Science. *American Political Science Review* 76: 753–766.
Riker, William H., and Peter C. Ordeshook. 1968. A Theory of the Calculus of Voting. *American Political Science Review* 62: 25–42.
Taagepera, Rein, and Matthew Soberg Shugart. 1989. *Seats and Votes: The Effects and Determinants of Electoral Systems*. New Haven: Yale University Press.
Tilly, Charles, and Sidney Tarrow. 2015. *Contentious Politics*. 2nd ed. Oxford: Oxford University Press.
Van der Brug, Wouter, Cees van der EijK, and Mark Franklin. 2007. *The Economy and the Vote: Economic Conditions and Elections in Fifteen Countries*. Cambridge: Cambridge University Press.
Verba, Sidney, and Norman H. Nie. 1972. *Participation in America: Political Democracy and Social Equality*. New York: Harper & Row.

CHAPTER 4

The Rise of the New Power Party in Taiwan's 2016 Legislative Election: Reality and Challenges

Ian Tsung-yen Chen and Da-chi Liao

INTRODUCTION

The New Power Party (NPP) is a new political party in Taiwan that was officially established on January 25, 2015. Since its inception, it has been widely popular and supported among the young generation who had participated the Sunflower Student Movement in Taiwan in 2014. The movement broke out after a series of social protests against the Kuomintang (KMT) government's controversial policies, such as forcible land grabbing in Dapu, Miaoli, and the death of the soldier Chung-chiu Hung (洪仲丘). In March 2014, a coalition of students stormed the Legislative Yuan and later the Executive Yuan to fight against the passage of the Cross-Strait Service Trade Agreement (CSSTA) in the Legislative Yuan, which they considered harmful to Taiwan's industries. The Sunflower Student Movement resonated among college students and the young generation.

I. T.-y. Chen • D.-c. Liao (✉)
Institute of Political Science, National Sun Yat-sen University, Kaohsiung, Taiwan

© The Author(s) 2019
W.-c. Lee (ed.), *Taiwan's Political Re-Alignment and Diplomatic Challenges*, Politics and Development of Contemporary China, https://doi.org/10.1007/978-3-319-77125-0_4

Many of the lead figures and participants of this movement now constitute the core of the NPP. For example, the current Executive Chairman Kuo-chang Huang (黃國昌) was one of the main leaders of the movement. He ran for the legislature in a district in New Taipei County and was elected in 2016. The Sunflower Movement has expanded the popularity and momentum of the NPP and has greatly strengthened its political power and potential.

Right after its establishment, the NPP decided to engage in the upcoming national election in January of 2016, which included elections for the Presidency and legislators. The NPP did not nominate a Presidential candidate but had nominated five candidates for the districts and six candidates for the party list. In addition to Kuo-chang Huang, another spotlight candidate was Tzu-yung Hung (洪慈庸), who is the sister of the dead soldier, Chung-chiu Hung. She was running against a local stronghold, who had been elected the legislator of that district since 1999. Nevertheless, Hung beat her with a margin of 8.71 percent. Although the party was still young in its first national election, it won five seats in the Legislative Yuan and, in terms of the number of seats, the NPP became the third-largest political party in Taiwan. In terms of Taiwanese people's party preference, the NPP surpassed the People First Party (PFP) and become the third most preferred party in Taiwan when it was first included in the survey in June 2016.[1] The proportion of people's identification of KMT dropped from 39.5 percent in 2011 to 19.6 percent in 2016, while the DPP's increased from 30.4 percent to 39.6 percent during the same time and the NPP secured 3.8 percent. Another survey showed that the NPP might have become the second most popular political party for people under age 40 in Taiwan.[2]

Within a short time, the NPP has emerged as a powerful political party in Taiwan whose potential no one dares to underestimate. In the NPP's internal meeting, the party envisages that the national election held in 2024 will be a competition between two parties, the Democratic Progressive Party (DPP) and the NPP. The party also aims at becoming the first genuine left-wing party in Taiwan that focuses on social equality and justice.[3] Due to the KMT's low popularity under the Ma Ying-jeou administration from 2008 to 2016, and the returning KMT's party assets to zero, the KMT does not seem likely to regain its political popularity and resources in a short period. In addition, according to a national survey conducted by the Taiwanese Public Opinion Foundation, 51.4 percent of respondents considered the KMT as representative of Mainland China's interests, while only 19.8 percent considered it representative of the interests of Taiwan (You 2016a). The KMT's unpopular pro-China image was widely received, especially by the new generation. The future of a political party will hinge on support from the young generation. Thus, the current situation looks more favorable to the NPP.

Besides the aforementioned socioeconomic events, in 2005 Taiwan passed constitutional amendments that changed the electoral system from the single non-transferable vote (SNTV) in multimember-district to mixed-member majoritarian (MMM) rules for the election of legislators. Approximately 64.6 percent (73/113) of legislators are elected in single-member districts (SMDs), while the rest are elected by proportional representation (Batto and Cox 2016). According to Duverger's law, a single-member district facilitates a two-party system. Given the fact that 64.6 percent of legislators are elected in SMDs, Taiwan's party system may approach a political system comprising two main parties. Smaller parties may be left limited room to compete.

The NPP has recently emerged, and it is too early to make any conclusion regarding the party's future. With limited materials and resources, nevertheless, this chapter asks that given the abovementioned socioeconomic and electoral changes, can the NPP become one of the main political parties in the upcoming future? We analyze the question by identifying four factors, which are electoral, ideological, supportive, and organizational. The electoral factor looks at the effect of the current SMD-dominant electoral system; the ideological factor examines the ideological distance between the NPP and median voters; the supportive factor analyzes the characteristics of NPP supporters and their types for estimating their future voting orientations; and the organizational factor investigates the effect of the NPP's internal organizational features. Initial findings show that all four factors may give rise to political predicaments for the NPP. Its future trajectory will depend on how well can it respond to those challenges.

In the rest of the chapter, section "Literature Review" discusses related literature that leads to the four main factors of our concern and provides a clue for analyzing the NPP's possible future. Section "Four Analytical Factors" presents the main questions that need further analyses. It also discusses our approaches to those questions. Section "Reality and Challenges" provides empirical evidence for detailed analyses. It respectively presents the effect of electoral, ideological, supportive, and organizational factors. Finally, the last section concludes.

LITERATURE REVIEW

The sudden emergence of the NPP results from multi-dimensional changes in Taiwan, which may mainly include the change of the electoral system, socioeconomic situation, and the changing role of information technology and its effects on the political party's organization and management. Below we discuss the socioeconomic change starting by briefing the influence of the current SMD-dominant electoral rule on party system and ideological stances.

In an MMM electoral system favoring a two-party system, a political party should satisfy as many voters as possible to control efficient power. Downs (1957) argues that in a two-party democracy, political parties can be more profitable as they more closely resemble one another in order to appeal to median voters. However, a new party is more likely to emerge successfully if significant changes occur in the distribution of ideological views among voters. Furthermore, such change may result in a critical election that brings about critical party de- or realignment. Burnham (1970, 10) considers that a critical realignment features a short and sharp reorganization of major parties' coalitions; is proceeded by major third-party revolts; and is associated with abnormal stress in the socioeconomic system and ideological polarization. Under this kind of political situation, both strategic and emotional factors can affect voters' preferences. Before realignment happens, partisan dealignment occurs, where voters become less connected to their political parties (Schmitt 2014). Similar to realignment, dealignment results from social and economic discontent, political polarization, parties' failure in satisfying new demands, and old parties' losing their original support. These are all precursors of critical changes that come with social unrest, which can easily polarize partisan voters and raise people's attention to ideological issues. The momentum of realignment may also come from anti-establishment movements, whose goal is to oppose elites who wield political power all the time. It is a political battle between the ruler and the ruled that is always divided by fundamental societal cleavages (Barr 2009). Recent economic slowdown around the world seems to have facilitated anti-establishment movement (Allen 2016). Taiwan seems not to have escaped from such a trend.

The Sunflower Movement played the exact role of articulating the critical socioeconomic change happening in Taiwan, which further polarized the ideological divides. In addition, students' appeal for a transparent monitoring mechanism in dealing with cross-Strait economic relations has been widely received in the society, especially by the young generation. As the DPP behaved rather passively during the movement, the active role NPP's lead figures played in the movement received positive recognition among many people. Such developments might reflect the NPP's receiving wide social support in its party-list proportional representation. According to the public poll right before the election, the NPP received 10.8 percent support after the DPP's 30.4 percent and the KMT's 20.4 percent (Chen 2016). The DPP once worried that the NPP's emergence would carve up their originally safe seats in the proportional representation (Pai and Yao 2016). Therefore, the NPP successfully seized the opportunity to emerge during Taiwan's critical political momentum, which led to possibly a critical election in Taiwan.

Furthermore, the sources of Taiwan's socioeconomic changes over the past few years should be discussed. In advanced industrialized countries, political changes in the electorates' preferences may result from several factors. Here we discuss those most pertinent to Taiwan's situation. The first factor relates to economic factors, which influence the income and lifestyles of the middle and working class. The second factor relates to the growing political sophistication due to the expansion of basic education and the advance of information technology. The third factor relates to the aging of once-dominating political parties and their aging supporters whose initiatives are seen outdated and irrelevant to the new generation. The last factor relates to the change of value in the new generation. Unlike the older generation who has sought to meet their basic economic needs and become materialistic, young people, without the problem of survival in an advanced industrial society, have shifted their attentions to other matters, such as social equality, dignity, and the pursuit of leisure times (Dalton et al. 1984, 15–20).

This generational shift has occurred in Taiwan in the past decade. Even though Taiwan has accelerated its economic relationship with its political foe, Mainland China, the socioeconomic situation in Taiwan has remained stagnate, as indicated by the sluggish growth in income, the decline of national exports, the extremely high housing price, and the widening of the gap between the rich and the poor. At the same time, the ruling party KMT has looked likely to bail the nation out by its pro-China policies, such as the passage of CSSTA. Regardless of whether closer cross-Strait relations would generate positive economic benefits, many Taiwanese people consider over-reliance on China as too dangerous to Taiwan's economy, as well as the country's national security. For the KMT and much of its old generation supporters, materialistic thinking dominates their political maneuvering. However, for those who have been suspicious of China's intention and the young generation that has already considered Taiwan an independent country and confronted with the distressing economic possibility of cross-Strait economic relations going further, a critical change during the 2016 national election was necessary. Such a societal atmosphere rooting for changes has become favorable to the NPP's campaign. As a consequence, could these factors outperform the strategic thinking underpinning Duverger's law that prescribes voters' preference in SMDs and voters' trust with political parties in casting their votes in the party-list PR? Is Taiwan's party system changing? If it is, will that be a short-term dealignment or a long-term phenomenon that gives rise to party realignment? In other words, will that help the emergence of the NPP, and is it possible for the NPP to replace the KMT as the second largest political party in Taiwan?

In addition to the factor of socioeconomic change, the important role of information technology in effectively organizing political movements has given rise to opportunities for the development of newly established political parties, such as Spanish Podemos and the NPP. The logic of connective action shows that political parties dependent on information technology can be more flexible and efficient in party management and organization. They can connect their potential participants and supporters more effectively than traditional parties can. The style of decision-making facilitates a higher degree of direct democracy that features soft and multiple leaders as well as an interactive communicative manner, and focuses less on traditional ideological rivalry (Bennett and Segerberg 2013; Liao et al. 2016b). Technology facilitates the adaptation of direct democracy in managing the party's affairs, which is attractive especially to the new generation. As a result, technological change allows a new party to attract a great number of supporters in a short period. The effects of the changes identified above may have political implications for the NPP, which will be elaborated below.

Four Analytical Factors

With the above discussion in mind, let us now focus on how those changes will lead to the effect of four important factors on the development of the NPP. The first concerns the electoral system. Assuming that after 2005, Taiwan's legislative election would continue as an MMM system for a long period of time, with 64.6 percent to be elected in SMDs in 2024, Taiwan's political system will approach, yet not fully become, a two-party system according to Duverger's law. The question then will be which two parties will stand out? Are we likely to see the replacement of the KMT by the NPP as the second largest political party in Taiwan in the upcoming future? According to the NPP's ambition, it will introduce as many as possible young candidates in the 2018 local elections and the 2020 national elections. By 2024, it will seek to become the second largest political party in Taiwan, only after the DPP. We still have a long way to see the answer, but it seems certain that there is only limited room for small parties; therefore, in order to prevent its dissolution, the NPP must compete for at least the second place.

Second, to become one of the two main parties, ideological distance between the NPP and median voters must be short. In Taiwan's political history, ideological polarization results from national identity and cross-Strait relations, rather than left-right ideological rivalry (Hsiao and Cheng 2014). To investigate ideological distance, one should look at the NPP's and average people's stances on national identity and cross-Strait relations.

Third, regardless of the average people, we also assess how well the NPP can satisfy its current support bases, which we believe will be decisive in sustaining its political momentum. To see a better picture, the key may manifest in the characteristics of NPP supporters and how well its official policy positions can correspond to its supporters'. The NPP grew out of the Sunflower Student Movement, when part of the society expressed its discontent with the KMT's cross-Strait economic policy. However, some also blamed the DPP's hands-off approach. In other words, movement participants to a certain extent pointed their fingers at both the incumbents and the opposition. As a new force that tried to separate themselves from the DPP, the NPP was a symbol of the hope for the young generation. The Sunflower Student Movement, therefore, was not only a social movement but also a fad for some people. Under such background, we argue that in order to examine the NPP's potential and challenges, there is a need to examine NPP supporters in two dimensions.

The first dimension is "representative deficit," which refers to a fact that elected representatives in a liberal democracy can never fully represent everyone's interests or the policy preferences of that democracy in its legislative processes (Liao et al. 2016a). Therefore, those with political power in a democracy will always confront with public discontent regardless of their party affiliation. Recent growing anti-establishment movements echo such a phenomenon. Therefore, if NPP supporters mainly come from those who pointed their finger at the elites controlling political power (such as dissatisfaction with both the KMT and DPP), it might confront the challenge of the representative deficit as it now is also sharing the power pie with five seats in the Legislative Yuan. However, these kinds of supporters may be more fluid since they seemingly have an anti-establishment tendency because of the permanent phenomenon of representative deficit.

The second dimension is that supporters care about how well their issue positions can be matched by the policy stances of the party they support. Here the term "position mismatch" should be taken into account. It refers to the degree of mismatch between a political party's official positions on public policies and its supporters' policy expectations. If the degree of mismatch is high, supporters will be more likely to shift their political support to others when they become more aware of the party's position or when they find another new political party that satisfies their expectations. However, in reality, NPP supporters may come from both dimensions but have a different degree of feeling representative deficit or position mismatch. Table 4.1 categorizes four kinds of NPP supporters below.

With these two dimensions in mind, we consider four groups in the NPP's case, shown in Table 4.1. First, when the representative deficit, indicating that NPP supporters are those with grave discontent toward the former governing forces, and the issue position mismatch between the NPP's and their supporters' are both high, these kinds of supporters may merely be floating voters. This is because those voters often dislike the incumbent government or established power and support the NPP merely as a convenient alternative rather than necessarily agree with the NPP's policy positions. Once the NPP owns political power and its issue position distance from the supporters' increases even more, this kind of voter

Table 4.1 Representative deficit and position mismatch

		Position mismatch	
		High	Low
Representative deficit	High	Floating voter	Picky supporter
	Low	Bandwagoner	Staunch supporter

support becomes more likely to shift. Second, if representative deficit and position mismatch are both low, supporters may be the staunchest and most stable because they vote for the NPP not because of their anger with the former governing forces but because of their agreement with and recognition of the NPP's public policy positions. Third, in cases where the representative deficit is high while position mismatch is low, these NPP voters can be called picky supporters. This is because this group of NPP supporters has a high anti-establishment tendency, even though they have quite low issue position mismatch with that of the NPP. Their further support may heavily depend on the NPP's future policy position and performance. In other words, they would be very picky about whatever the NPP is doing because it is in power and thereby has become part of the establishment. Fourth, if the representative deficit is low while position mismatch is high, then this group of NPP supporters may come from neither political discontent to the former governing forces nor the recognition of the NPP's policy positions. This kind of supporters may be bandwagoners whose supports may result from a phenomenon in the young generation that advocating for the NPP is fashionable and popular.

To examine the characteristics of NPP supporters by the abovementioned two dimensions, we want to know the relationship between voters' supports for the NPP and their dissatisfaction with former governing forces. Did people support the NPP because of the party's political platform or simply because people feel anger or distrust toward the former governing forces? The NPP's emergence may have resulted from people's dissatisfaction with both the KMT and DPP (You 2016b). Support for new political forces based on resentment of the current situation is not stable and can be easily replaced by some new forces emerging in the future.

In examining the issue position mismatch between the NPP and its supporters, we are first interested in the topic of national identity. Most people recognize the NPP as a pro-independence political party. Its first major political figure individually revealed his support for Taiwan independence (Liberty Times 2016); however, the party itself has not officially revealed such a position. According to the party's basic principle regarding national identity, the NPP will promote Taiwan's normalized status as a state.[4] The NPP's position on Taiwan's national identity is similar to the DPP's, and some people consider the NPP even more extremely pro-independence (Chang 2016). Some of its support is also considered as coming from people who were dissatisfied with both the DPP and the

Taiwan Solidarity Union.[5] Therefore, the question of whether or not the NPP's position on national identity will attract enough supporters may be a key to its future development.

Furthermore, the NPP also expects itself to emerge as a left-wing political party that promotes the value of social justice. The party will emphasize securing labors' and farmers' rights.[6] In Taiwan's political history, political cleavage has always occurred over the issues of national identity and cross-Strait relations, and an ideal left-wing party supporting social equality has always been absent (Hsiao and Cheng 2014). Therefore, will the NPP's voice be heard, and will it become a left-wing party in Taiwan? We also need to find out whether the supporters of the NPP come from the working class, which should form the foundation for a left-wing party.

Last, this chapter also assesses the organizational factor that looks at whether the NPP's much-appreciated value of connective action has survived after it has gained a certain level of political power in Taiwan. Specifically, we investigate whether changes exist in the NPP's leadership style, communicative manner, organizational boundary, and the scope of issues emphasized.

To answer the above questions, we use both descriptive and inferential statistics. Taiwan's effective number of political parties in the Legislative Yuan from 1995 to 2016 will be presented. The number will shed light on whether Taiwan's constitutional amendments that change legislative election to MMM will make Taiwan approach a two-party system. To demonstrate ideological distance, we adopt a two-dimensional political spectrum developed by the iVoter project. It shows the distance of the policy stances in cross-Strait relations and the level of government intervention (left-right political position) between the NPP and median voters.[7]

Regarding the supportive factor, we assume that if NPP supporters mainly belong to the category of staunch voters who feel both low representative deficit (not so anti-establishment) and low position mismatch between theirs and the NPP's, then the NPP could have enough potential to occupy the top two seats in Taiwan's party system. If it is not the case, the NPP's future is more difficult to judge now. To examine NPP's potential, we use both probit analysis and chi-square test to identify the characteristics of NPP supporters, which include their approval of the incumbent, attitudes toward economic globalization (left-right orientation), education, and occupation. The analysis will focus on whether these characteristics can sustain their support for the NPP in the future. Then we identify the distribution of NPP supporters among the four groups structured by two dimensions of representative deficits and position mismatch. As for the organizational factor, we analyze how well the NPP can maintain its style of direct democracy by continuing connective, democratic, flexible, and efficient advantages popular among the young generation.

The analytical data comes from the research projects, "Taiwan's Election and Democratization Study" and "Civil Awareness and Multiple Value."[8] The first project was conducted during the national election in early 2016, and the second one was conducted after the election. For both projects, we coded the support for the NPP by examining whether a respondent chose the NPP on the ballot for party-list proportional representation. We recoded those who voted for the NPP as one and zero otherwise. For comparing supports for different parties, we only included respondents that voted for one of the three parties, the DPP, KMT, and NPP.

REALITY AND CHALLENGES

The Electoral Factor

First, let's take a look at whether the 2005 change of electoral system to the MMM system, which included two-thirds SMDs, has influenced Taiwan toward a two-party system. Data shows that regardless of whether we calculate the effective numbers of the party by seats or votes, both indicators drop after the MMM system was introduced in 2005. The average effective numbers of the party by seats before and after 2005 are 2.94 and 2.05. The result corresponds well to Duverger's law. If we look at the effective number by calculating the number of votes, the average before and after are 3.48 and 2.75, which also illustrates that the MMM system in Taiwan is favorable to reducing the number of effective political parties.

If we compare major parties' share of seats and votes, both seats and votes have been more concentrated in the KMT and DPP after the MMM system was introduced in 2005. Both parties controlled 74.7 percent of legislative seats in 2004 and 91.2 percent in 2016. In terms of votes, both the KMT and DPP accounted for 68.6 percent and 77.3 percent in 2004 and 2016, respectively. Such trend also corresponds to Duverger's law. A tentative conclusion can be made that after 2005, Taiwan was heading toward a two-party system due to the change from an SNTV to an MMM voting system. After the national election in 2016, the two largest political parties have been the KMT and DPP, where the KMT was in decline in terms of both shares of seats and votes. After 2005, the KMT's vote shares had declined from 52.4 percent in 2008 to 32.8 percent in 2016. During the same period, its share of legislative seats had dropped from 71.7 percent to 31 percent. At the same time, the DPP has seen a steady rise. Should such trend remain, we are likely to see a two-party system dominated by the DPP and an emerging party to challenge the KMT's position. So far, the NPP and PFP secured several legislative seats, but only the NPP is on the rise, while the PFP has been losing its political base since 2004. According to the survey, "Trends in Core Political Attitudes among Taiwanese," conducted by the Election Study Center of National Chengchi University, the NPP, which was included in the survey for the first time, had surpassed the PFP as the third most preferable political party in Taiwan.[9]

Evidence suggests that the electoral factor will lead Taiwan to approach a two-party democracy. If the KMT continues to diminish, the most likely political party to replace the KMT so far might be the NPP. However, the latter party now remains a small political party. There is a long way to go to prove its potential. Whether it can expand its size might depend on the following three factors discussed.

Ideological Factor

Here we compare supporters' attitudes toward critical ideological issues and evaluate the possible distance from median voters. Probably the most salient ideological cleavages in Taiwan center around national identity, Taiwan's statehood, and China (Hsiao and Cheng 2014).

Figure 4.1 demonstrates the NPP's policy position according to its official attitude toward the degree of government intervention (left-right orientation) and cross-Strait engagement (active or careful).[10] According to iVoter's data, most (median) voters cluster in areas of the first, second, and third quadrants close to the center. The NPP is located at the bottom-left, which represents a high degree of agreement with government intervention (close to left-wing idea) and the support for carefully, not actively, engaging in cross-Strait relations. According to this figure, the NPP, like many other small parties, might still be far away from the median voters, ideologically.

Table 4.2 reports the attitude of three major parties' supporters regarding Taiwan's statehood. When asked their attitude toward Taiwan-China relations, about 7.5 percent of DPP supporters chose the answer "inde-

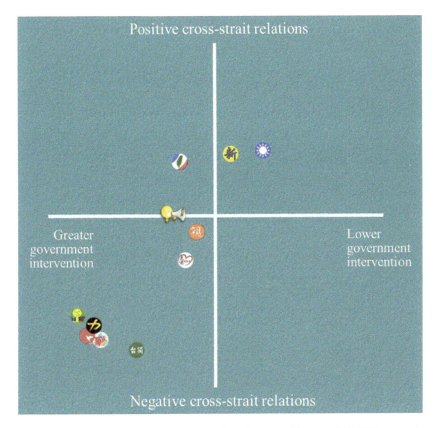

Fig. 4.1 Policy position of Taiwan's political parties (Source: 2016 iVoter project: http://ivoter.tw/)

pendence as soon as possible," while only 4.2 percent of NPP supporters chose the same answer. In addition, 30.1 percent of DPP supporters selected "remain status quo and independence in the future," while 41.1 percent of NPP supporters selected the same option. Although there is a significant difference between the KMT and the other two pan-green parties for Taiwan's independence status, there is no significant difference between the DPP and NPP regarding the status of statehood, albeit supporters of the NPP pragmatically tend to favor the status quo. Regardless of the timing of pursuing independence, 45.3 percent of NPP supporters favor independence, while on average only 28.2 percent of Taiwanese

Table 4.2 Three parties' supporter attitudes toward national statehood

Attitude	KMT(N)	DPP(N)	NPP(N)	Total(N)
Independence	0.8% (2)	7.5% (32)	4.2% (4)	4.9% (38)
↓	5.4% (14)	30.1% (128)	41.1% (39)	23.3% (181)
Status quo	75.5% (194)	56.5% (240)	51.6% (49)	51.6% (483)
↓	16.3% (42)	5.7% (24)	3.2% (3)	8.9% (69)
Unification	2.0% (5)	0.2% (1)	0.0% (0)	0.8% (6)
Total	100% (257)	100% (425)	100% (95)	100% (777)

Source: Civil Awareness and Multiple Value (2016)
Note:
1. Pearson chi2(10) =124.3311; Pr = 0.000
2. The national identity variable has six dimensions, which can be sorted by attitudinal intensity from pro-independence to pro-unification. They include "independence as soon as possible," "remain status quo and independence in the future," "remains status quo forever," "remains status quo and decides later," "remain status quo and unification in the future," and "unification as soon as possible." We combine the third and fourth dimensions as one dimension, "status quo")
3. If we compare only the DPP and NPP, the Pearson chi2(5) = 5.6397; Pr = 0.343. The association is not significant

people favor the same option. To the NPP, Taiwan has already been an independent country named the Republic of China, although not yet a "normal" country that receives worldwide sovereign recognition (Chu 2015). Therefore, the priority should not be pursuing an independent status but to normalize Taiwan's relations with other countries, including China. From this perspective, the NPP probably occupies the longest distance from the views of KMT supporters.

Regarding national identity, respondents of the same survey were asked whether they identified themselves as either Taiwanese, Chinese, or both. The results show that KMT supporters contrast significantly with supporters from the DPP and NPP. About 77.9 percent of DPP's supporting base identified themselves as "Taiwanese" which is the closest to the average Taiwanese people (64.2 percent), followed by the NPP (85.1 percent), in which no one sees him-/herself as Chinese, and the KMT (33.7 percent) that is farthest from the median voters.

Another ideological factor of interest is left versus right. The NPP aims to become a left-wing party that seeks to expand the government's intervention in realizing social equality and justice, which address the problems of distributional and generational inequality. We try to provide some initial survey evidence to see whether or not characteristics of NPP supporters share this perspective, as well as whether or not its supporters agree with left-wing ideas.

Assuming that a left-wing party like the NPP should fight for global and local distributional justice, the party should be distrustful of the economic globalization movement, which might endanger the interests of the poor, workers, and small businesses. Table 4.3 shows the results of three party supporters' attitude to economic globalization. About 82.16 percent of Taiwanese people agree that free trade will help raise Taiwan's national income and increase job opportunities. In the same survey, when respondents were asked whether "free trade will harm Taiwanese companies," about 76.58 percent of respondents disagree with the idea that free trade will harm Taiwanese companies. In general, although Taiwanese people seem to care about domestic social issues, in the global issues, most of them are quite pragmatic and right-wing oriented.

Both DPP and NPP supporters distinguish themselves from the KMT by agreeing that economic globalization will result in social inequity in Taiwan. In such a perspective, the DPP and NPP indeed resemble more left-wing parties. However, the majority of both NPP and DPP supporters, in fact, support free trade. Therefore, the challenge for the NPP will be how a left-wing political party can accommodate the average voters believing in right-wing ideas. That is, how can the NPP adjust their left-wing ideas to Taiwan's situation that relies heavily on international trade? Lots of NPP political figures and young supporters have spoken out against international trade that may harm certain domestic industries or companies. Such gestures might provide them with short-term political momentum. However, if the NPP seeks to attract more median voters, the image of anti-globalization and anti-corporatism may obstruct its development in the long term.

Table 4.3 Free trade will benefit Taiwan economically

Type	KMT(N)	DPP(N)	NPP(N)	Total(N)
Strongly disagree	0.7% (1)	7.0% (15)	7.1% (3)	4.8% (19)
Disagree	6.4% (9)	14.9% (32)	26.2% (11)	13.1% (52)
Agree	36.9% (52)	38.6% (83)	33.3% (14)	37.4% (149)
Strongly agree	56.0% (79)	39.5% (85)	33.3% (14)	44.7% (178)
Total	100% (141)	100% (215)	100% (42)	100% (398)

Source: Civil Awareness and Multiple Value (2016)
Note:
1. Pearson chi2(6) = 25.2805; Pr = 0.000
2. If we compare only the DPP and NPP, the Pearson chi2(3) = 3.2956; Pr = 0.348. The association is not significant

To sum up, the NPP's ideological stances in national identity and left-right politics seem to be the farthest from its supporters when comparing itself, the DPP and the KMT. How the NPP's attitude and policies toward these ideological issues can fit into their beliefs better and become more widely accepted by the average Taiwanese people will be a challenge going forward.

The Supportive Factor

In this part, we investigate the types of NPP supporters, focusing on the interaction of representative deficit and policy position mismatch. Above analysis shows the ideological distance between the NPP and the average Taiwanese person and its supporters, a distance which is especially salient in the policy position of Taiwan's free trade policy. A certain level of position mismatch may exist between the party and its current and prospective supportive base. Regarding the dimension of representative deficit, we look at the major targets that NPP supporters were dissatisfied with. Targets could include the incumbent government, the major opposition political parties, or both. While the incumbent government was responsible for public policy outputs, the opposition was responsible for their inactive behaviors in overseeing the incumbent.

Table 4.4 shows the result of probit analyses that report the association between a person's likelihood of supporting the NPP and voters' attitudes toward the incumbent and the opposition. Model (1) adopts the survey question regarding their satisfaction with Ma Ying-jeou administration for the past three years (2013–2016). The result shows that voters who have a higher degree of dissatisfaction with the Ma administration have a positive association with their probability of supporting the NPP. The result, however, is not statistically significant. In order words, regarding dissatisfaction with the Ma administration, supporters of the NPP are no different from supporters of other political parties. Most voters, regardless of the political parties they support, were dissatisfied with the incumbent.

The association between voters' chances of supporting the NPP and their dissatisfaction with the legislators elected in 2012 is shown in model (2), and models (3) and (4) show their rating of the KMT's leader Li-Luan Chu compared to the DPP's leader Ing-wen Tsai, respectively.[11] Voters who have a higher degree of dissatisfaction with the legislators and lower evaluation of both parties' presidential candidates are more likely to vote for the NPP. The results are all statistically significant. Initial evidence

Table 4.4 Dissatisfaction with incumbent and opposition parties

	(1)	(2)	(3)	(4)
Ma administration	0.014			
	(0.021)			
Legislator (2012)		0.220***		
		(0.023)		
Chu, Li-Luan			−0.027***	
			(0.006)	
Tsai, Ing-Wen				−0.059***
				(0.006)
Observations	5032	3853	5333	5357

Note:
1. Standard errors in parentheses
2. * $p < 0.10$, ** $p < 0.05$, *** $p < 0.01$

suggests that NPP supporters are both dissatisfied with the incumbent KMT and the main opposition DPP. They are not necessarily supporters of Ing-Wen Tsai. Compared with all non-NPP supporters, those giving lower rating scores to the DPP leader are more likely to vote for the NPP. Supporters of the NPP do not seem to be captivated by a political figure's charisma or the old blue-green ideological divide; they care more about the performance of the government, which includes both the executive and legislative branches, as well as the incumbent and the opposition. In other words, NPP supporters are sensitive to the representative deficit or established powers.

Combining both aspects, we provide the distribution of NPP supporters among the four groups structured by the two dimensions of representative deficit and policy position mismatch. We choose questions from the "Civil Awareness and Multiple Value" study to represent the sense of representative deficit, which is the satisfaction with the former major parties' performance in articulating people's opinions. As to the dimension of policy position mismatch, we adopt the question of support for free trade as the key indicator of a left-wing position. The results are shown in Tables 4.5.

Table 4.5 further documents the proportion of NPP supporters by their anti-establishment sentiment as well as their views on free trade. The result shows that a majority of the NPP's supporters may come from a group who frequently feels a representative deficit but also agrees with the trend of globalization, which may contradict the NPP's left-wing approach

Table 4.5 Four groups of NPP supporters

		Free trade	
		Agree (M.H.)	Disagree (M.L.)
Political parties' performance in presenting public opinions	Dissatisfied (R.H.)	48.8% (20)	24.4% (10)
	Satisfied (R.L.)	17.1% (7)	9.8% (4)

Source: Civil Awareness and Multiple Value (2016)
Note: The numbers of respondents are in parentheses
M.H. and M.L. in each parenthesis refer to position mismatch high and low; R.H. and R.L. in the parenthesis refer to representative deficit high and low.

that advocates local distributional justice; therefore, a high degree of position mismatch results. This initial finding may show that many NPP supporters belong to the category of "floating voters," as introduced in Table 4.1. In addition, about one-fourth of NPP voters may belong to the category of "picky voters," who may be easily dissatisfied with the established powers but currently agree with the NPP's left-wing tendencies. Together they constitute almost three-fourths of NPP supporters, which may equal unstable support that could easily shift to some other new substitutes should the political circumstances change. The proportion of bandwagoners (R.L. and M.H.) is not high, as well as the proportion of staunch supporters (R.L. and M.L.).

The floating voter hypothesis can be further supported by looking at supporters' education and occupation. Existing studies indicate that people with higher levels of education and occupation would vote differently on a variety of issues or shift preferences to other political parties if they are dissatisfied with the incumbent (Egerton 2002; Branton 2003). These people also know better about how the balance of power works, as well as the ways to do a cost/benefit analysis of public policies resulting from political processes. Therefore, they are less likely to be hijacked by political ideologies. Instead, they are also more likely to change the political parties they support (Wu and Wang 2003; Chen and Tsai 2010). In other words, partisanship is negatively associated with education and occupation.

As Table 4.6 shows, about 55.38 percent of NPP supporters are highly educated, which are the social elites in Taiwan. The proportion is way above their support for the KMT and DPP. Among NPP supporters, only

Table 4.6 Three parties supporters' education levels

Level	KMT(N)	DPP(N)	NPP(N)	Total(N)
Elementary and below	8.5% (90)	12.0% (189)	2.1% (4)	10.0% (283)
Junior high	7.8% (82)	10.8% (170)	4.1% (8)	9.19% (260)
High	31.9% (336)	30.4% (481)	28.7% (56)	30.9% (873)
Vocational	18.0% (190)	14.4% (228)	9.7% (19)	15.4% (437)
College and above	33.8% (356)	32.5% (513)	55.4% (108)	34.5% (977)
Total	100% (1054)	100% (1581)	100% (195)	100% (2830)

Source: Taiwan's Election and Democratization Study (2016)
Note:
1. Pearson chi2(8) = 69.7804; Pr = 0.000
2. If we compare only the DPP and NPP, the Pearson chi2(4) = 54.3417; Pr = 0.000. The association remains significant

34.87 percent had received high school education or below. The proportion is obviously lower than that of the DPP (53.12 percent) and the KMT (48.12 percent). The NPP seems further away from average voters. Therefore, a higher proportion of NPP supporters are less partisan and are more likely to shift their preferences to other parties when dissatisfied with the NPP. In the same survey, about 45.4 percent of NPP supporters come from low-to-middle white-collar class, the blue-collar class, or farmers, which is the lowest among the three major parties; about 54.6 percent of supporters come from the middle-to-high level white-collar classes, which is the highest percentage among the three parties. Again, these higher educated and more-informed supporters are more likely to float.

The characteristics of NPP supporters suggests that the party is, in fact, supported mainly by social elites that are more likely to shift partisan allegiance rather than middle-to-lower class voters who are supposed to be more loyal politically. If the NPP tries to emerge as a dominating party, the constitution of its supporters might need to change, because at present the NPP is represented more by floating social elites rather than by middle-to-lower class people. In addition, its left-wing approaches need to include more ambitious and popular plans than the DPP's. People from middle-to-lower class constitute the potential target audience with greater allegiance for a left-wing party. So far the NPP has a long and uncertain way to go to become one of the two main parties in Taiwan through a left-wing approach.

Organizational Factor

Last we analyze whether the NPP would be able to maintain its attractive and popular qualitative features, which are close to the idea of direct democracy, if the party becomes a part of the governing force. The connective logic of the NPP features a multi-centric leadership style, an interactive communicative manner, no specific organizational boundary for participation, and a less ideological-centric approach to governing. The NPP may run as a connective political party in form ostensibly; in practice, however, some evidence suggests that the party has deviated from those much-appreciated qualities.

In terms of leadership, the NPP charter stipulates that the decision-making committee is comprised of 15 members coming from 4 working committees' chairs, 4 policy committees' chairs, and 7 board of chairmen. Each committee chair is elected by each committee's members (three to nine members), who are elected by party members. Seven board chairmen are directly elected by the party members. In practice, however, the decision-making power may be controlled by a small core of party elites. The NPP's board of chairmen member Neil Peng (馮光遠) announced his resignation on Facebook with the accusation that his efforts have been harvested by certain NPP members. He further argued that the NPP has become a "national prosperity party," with sarcasm pointed at the concentration of power held by the Executive Chairman Kuo-chang Huang (黃國昌), whose name consists of Mandarin characters for the words "nation" and "prosperous" (Gerber 2017). Our interview also indicates that the "Huang-Chen Regime" forms the real ruling body of the NPP, which Huang refers to Kuo-chang Huang and Chen refers to Huei-ming Chen (陳惠敏) (Liao et al. 2016a, b). Other party members are not actively and effectively participating in the decision-making process.

The NPP's organizational boundary seems to be loose in recruiting members. People can join the party, pay dues online, and undergo a quite easy application process. After joining the party, however, the NPP's communicative manner in practice is neither interactive nor circular. Our other study shows that the communication among each committee and between the committee and the decision-making body remains weak and loose. According to our interviews, party members consider the process quite top-down. Some committees held only a few meetings. The committee cannot make any decisions and must wait for further instruction from the top. The NPP's online system for proposing motion looked quite promising in the beginning, but so far only two motions have been proposed by Chair Huang and passed. Since February 2016, the system has been blocked. It seems harder than expected for NPP members to participate in forming public policies through the party's only institutional communication channel (Liao et al. 2016a, b).

Last, according to the NPP's website, the party mainly focuses on three topics, which consist of "State, Nation, and International," "Constitution and Democratic Constitutional System," and "Social Justice as well as Environment." They include both ideological and common concerns. An NPP party leader also mentioned in its internal meeting that the party is a "left-independence" (左獨) political party. According to online news records, most news reports concerning NPP legislators relate to social issues, such as labor rights, homosexual marriage, physical groups, and military injustice. Ideological matters such as national statehood scarcely put the NPP in the media spotlight (Liao et al. 2016a, b). Judging from these aspects, the NPP's organizational features might deviate from a connective party style, though its several policy positions remain its left-wing ideal. However, the party's current policy stances do not look promising in terms of attracting more supporters in the future.

Conclusion

In the above sections, we have analyzed four factors that we consider important for the NPP's further development. They include electoral, ideological, supportive, and organizational factors. We hope the results shed some light on the likelihood of the NPP's becoming one of the main political parties in Taiwan.

We find that after Taiwan adopted an MMM electoral system that included two-third SMDs in 2005, Taiwan's party system indeed approaches the structure of the two-party system. Currently the KMT confronts political obstacles from various fronts. For example, after the passage of *Act Governing the Handling of Ill-gotten Properties by Political Parties and Their Affiliate Organizations* (政黨及其附隨組織不當取得財產處理條例) in the Legislative Yuan in July 2016, the KMT stands to lose significant financial resources used to facilitate political mobilization and campaigns. The KMT itself as well as its then uncharismatic chairwoman Hsiu-chu Hung (洪秀柱) and their China-friendly policy remain far from the views of the new generation. The current trend looks very unfavorable for the KMT's future and gives the NPP some rooms to emerge. However, the NPP has to accommodate its political positions to the average Taiwanese person in order to expand its support base. The current electoral system seems unfavorable for political parties who rely on radical stances usually adopted by small parties. That is the first challenge for the NPP.

Second, according to Fig. 4.1, the NPP's ideological positions reside in the bottom-left that attracts a small portion of voters. If the NPP wants to expand its voter base, it may need to move up and right and adjust its policy positions accordingly. The DPP's position stands in its way and may constitute a grave challenge. Although the NPP has become the third-largest political party and a formidable opposition voice, it is also considered an ambiguous political ally to the DPP (Sung 2016). If the NPP becomes a version of or a subset of the DPP, then there is no reason for NPP supporters to remain loyal. If the NPP moves downward to represent the most China-bashing party in Taiwan, just like Taiwan Solidarity Union did before, it will not be able to increase its base. That is the second challenge for the NPP's future.

Third, regarding the NPP's existing support base, we find that most NPP supporters resent both the KMT and DPP more than non-NPP supporters. Such feeling or sentiment may come from the permanent phenomenon of representative deficit. Regarding the NPP's policy distance from its supporters, the ambition of becoming a left-wing political party does not seem to correspond well with current supporters, who are not coming from middle-to-lower class people. Instead, most of them are young and well-educated social elites. Evidence further suggests that, in the area of economic globalization the majority of Taiwanese people are right-wing. The NPP's supporters are not exceptional. Current NPP supporters come from the group of floating voters who feel a representative deficit and support free trade that does not match the NPP's left-wing position. The second largest group of NPP supporters are picky voters. They also easily feel a representative deficit and should keep a close eye on what the NPP is doing in the Legislative Yuan, because they consider the NPP to have the same anti-free trade position as they do. Currently, loyal and stable NPP supporters may only account for 5 to 10 percent of the total base. Such a supporting rate does not look promising for the NPP's aspiration to become the second largest party in Taiwan. That is the third challenge for the NPP.

Last, the appraised organizational style by the new internet generation may be losing its popularity. As the NPP's leadership becomes more centralized, a top-down communicative manner is on the rise. The NPP has also started to deviate from its direct democracy promise, which is exactly why supporters voted for the NPP in order to resist the KMT government's indirect and opaque decision-making process. Should such appeal disappear within the NPP's organization, the NPP is likely to lose more supporters. Neil Peng may be the first cascading case. That is the fourth challenge to NPP.

Notes

1. The data and result can be accessed at http://esc.nccu.edu.tw/course/news.php?Sn=165.
2. A survey project, "Civil Awareness and Multiple Value (2016)," showed that among people under forty, 58.6 percent supported the DPP; 21.1 percent supported the NPP; and 20.3 percent supported the KMT.
3. Such an aim was claimed by the NPP in their internal seminar.
4. Please refer to the NPP's basic principal in their official website, which can be accessed at https://www.newpowerparty.tw/pages/%E5%9F%BA%E6%9C%AC%E4%B8%BB%E5%BC%B5.
5. The Taiwan Solidarity Union (TSU) is a pro-Taiwan independence political party in Taiwan. It was founded on August 12, 2001. The party was relatively popular during the early 2000s as it had successfully secured 8.5 percent and 8.3 percent of votes as well as thirteen and twelve seats, respectively, during the legislative elections in 2001 and 2004. However, the party only received 2.5 percent of votes and no seats in the 2016 legislative election.
6. See note 4.
7. iVoter is Taiwan's first voting advice application that was introduced in 2010. Until 2016, 1400 people had completed issue position diagnostic registration. For more information, please visit the website ivoter.tw or see Liao and Chen (2016).
8. The project title is "Taiwan's Election and Democratization Study, 2016–2020(IV): Telephone Interview of the Presidential and Legislative Elections, 2016(TEDS2016-T)." It can be accessed at http://teds.nccu.edu.tw/intro2/super_pages.php?ID=intro11&Sn=117.
9. See note 1.
10. The figure is produced by Dachi Liao's iVoter project, which can be accessed at http://ivoter.tw/.
11. The question was, "from 0 to 10 (0: dislike very much; 10: like very much), how much will you rate Li-Luan Chu and Ing-Wen Tsai?"

BIBLIOGRAPHY

Allen, Katie. 2016. Economic Woes Create Anti-Establishment Movements Around the World. *The Guardian*, November 5. https://www.theguardian.com/business/2016/nov/05/economic-woe-trump-style-movements-created-worldwide. Accessed 9 Jan 2017.

Barr, Robert R. 2009. Populists, Outsiders and Anti-Establishment Politics. *Party Politics* 15: 29–48.

Batto, Nathan F., and Gary W. Cox. 2016. Introduction: Legislature-Centric and Executive-Centric Theories of Party Systems and Faction Systems. In *Mixed-Member Electoral Systems in Constitutional Context*, ed. Nathan F. Batto, Chi Huang, Alexander C. Tan, and Gary W. Cox, 1–22. Ann Arbor: University of Michigan Press.

Bennett, W. Lance, and Alexandra Segerberg. 2013. *The Logic of Connective Action*. New York: Cambridge University Press.

Branton, Regina P. 2003. Examining Individual-Level Voting Behavior on State Ballot Propositions. *Political Research Quarterly* 56: 367–377.

Burnham, Walter D. 1970. *Critical Elections and the Mainsprings of American Politics*. New York: W. W. Norton & Company.

Chang, Kuang-chiu. 2016. Minchintang weilai tsuita te mafan shih shihtai Liliang [New Power Party will be the Biggest Trouble for Democratic Progressive Party]. *Pinguo ribao [Apple Daily]*, March 10. http://www.appledaily.com.tw/realtimenews/article/new/20160310/812930/. Accessed 21 Aug 2016.

Chen, Yu-fu. 2016. Liangan zhengce mindiao: shidai Liliang zhengdangpiao zhichidu 10.8% [Cross-Strait Policy Association's Survey: New Power Party Receives 10.8% Party Support Rate]. *Ziyou Shibao [Liberty Times]*, January 5. http://news.ltn.com.tw/news/politics/breakingnews/1561916. Accessed 21 Aug 2016.

Chen, Kuang-hui, and Chi-lin Tsai. 2010. Xuexiao jiaoyu yu zhengzhi shehuihua: jiaoyu Chengdu yu ziwo rending de guanlianxing [School Education and Political Socialization: Exploring Strength of Association between Education and Self-Identity in Taiwan]. *Taiwan zhengzhi xuekan [Taiwan Political Science Review]* 14: 55–103.

Chu, Pu-ching. 2015. Shidai liliang shoudu biaotai guojia dingwei 'tianrandu shi chuangdang DNA' [New Power Party First Reveals its Position for the Nation, Organic Independence is the Party's DNA]. *Minbao [Taiwan People News]*, July 8. http://www.peoplenews.tw/news/d636485c-1fff-4218-88d7-9afb7f6c4472. Accessed 21 Aug 2016.

Dalton, Russell J., Paul A. Beck, and Scott C. Flangan. 1984. Electoral Change in Advanced Industrial Democracies. In *Electoral Change in Advanced Industrial Democracies: Realignment or Dealignment?* ed. Russell J. Dalton, Paul A. Beck, and Scott C. Flangan, 3–22. Princeton: Princeton University Press.

Downs, Anthony. 1957. *An Economic Theory of Democracy*. New York: Harper & Row.
Duverger, Maurice. 1954. *Political Parties: Their Organization and Activity in the Model State*. New York: Wiley.
Egerton, Muriel. 2002. Political Partisanship, Voting Abstention and Higher Education: Changing Preferences in a British Youth Cohort in the 1990s. *Higher Education Quarterly* 56: 156–177.
Gerber, Abraham. 2017. NPP Lawmakers Shocked by Neil Peng's Resignation. *Taipei Times*, January 10. http://www.taipeitimes.com/News/taiwan/archives/2017/01/10/2003662835. Accessed 16 Jan 2017.
Hsiao, Yi-ching, and Su-feng Cheng. 2014. Citizens' Perceptions of the Left-Right Ideology in Taiwan: Replacing Left-Right Ideology with the Unification—Independence Issue to Measure Taiwan's Party Polarization. *The Taiwanese Political Science Review* 18: 79–138.
Liao, Da-Chi, and Boyu Chen. 2016. Strengthening Democracy: Development of the iVoter Website in Taiwan. In *Political Behavior and Technology: Voting Advice Applications in East Asia*, ed. Da-Chi Liao, Boyu Chen, and Michael Jensen, 67–89. Hampshire: Palgrave Macmillan.
Liao, Da-Chi, Boyu Chen, and Chi-chen Huang. 2013. The Decline of 'Chinese Identity' in Taiwan?!—An Analysis of Survey Data from 1992 to 2012. *East Asia: An International Quarterly* 30: 273–290.
Liao, Da-Chi, Yueh-Ching Chen, San-Yih Hwang, and Shan-Lin Chang. 2016a. *An Assessment of Social Movements' Impact upon Representative Deficit by Two Taiwanese Cases*. Paper presented at the Annual Meeting of American Political Science Association, September.
Liao, Da-Chi, Bo-Jyun Peng, Ian Tsung-Yen Chen, and Jih-Wen Lin. 2016b. *Oligarchical Connective? An Examination of Taiwan New Power Party's Organizational forms and Practice in the Internet age*. Paper presented at the International Workshop on Parties Online Party New Organizational Strategies in 8 Democracies, Kaohsiung, Taiwan, December 14–16.
Liberty Times. 2016. Buyong keyi gaohan Freddy Lim: Taidu shuode hen ziran [No Need to Voice, Freddy Lim: Speaking Taiwan Independence Is Natural]. February 27. http://news.ltn.com.tw/news/politics/breaking-news/1615359. Accessed 15 Aug 2016.
Lin, Wei-feng. 2015. Ludang shemindang zu canzheng lianmeng yu shidai liliang zhenghe poju [Green Party and Social Democratic Party Form an Political Alliance and Broke up with New Power Party]. *Feng chuanmei [Storm Media]*, July 27. www.storm.mg/article/58916. Accessed 20 Aug 2016.
Pai, Chiao-yin and Li-Chiang Yao. 2016. Minjindang bufenqu kong suoshui Liuxi, Cai yingwen jihu: buyao fenpiao buyao peipiao [Democratic Progressive Party's Seats of the Party-list may Reduce 6 seats, Tsai Ing-wen Urges: Don't Separate

or Allocate the Votes]. *Sanli Xinwen [SET TV]*, January 7. http://www.setn.com/News.aspx?NewsID=117066. Accessed 21 Aug 2016.

Schmitt, Hermann. 2014. Partisanship in Nine Western Democracies: Causes and Consequences. In *Political Parties and Partisanship: Social Identity and Individual Attitudes*, ed. John Bartle and Paolo Bellucci, 75–87. London: Routledge.

Sung, Chien-jen. 2016. Shidai liliang: minjindang de tongmengjun Tsai Ing-wen de banjiaoshi [New Power Party: An Ally of Democratic Progressive Party, Tsai Ing-wen's Stepping Stone]. *Lianhebao [United Daily News]*, April 8. http://udn.com/news/story/6844/1616677. Accessed 24 Aug 2016.

Wu, Chung-li, and Hung-chung Wang. 2003. Woguo xuanmin 'fenli zhengfu' xinli renzhi yu wendingdu: yi 2000nian zongtong xuanju yu 2001nian lifa weiyuan xuanju wei li [The Psychological Cognition for Divided Government and Electoral Stability in Taiwan: The Case if the 2000 Presidential and 2001 Legislative Yuan Elections]. *Xuanju yanjiu [Journal of Electoral Studies]* 10: 81–114.

You, Ying-lung. 2016a. Weihe Taiwan zhisheng 16% de ren xihuan Kuomintang [Why only Remain 16% of People that like Kuomintang]. *Feng chuanmei [Storm Media]*, July 30. www.storm.mg/article/147320. Accessed 28 Aug 2016.

———. 2016b. Minjindang zui touting de duishou—shidai liliang [Democratic Progressive Party's Biggest Headache——New Power Party]. *Feng chuanmei [Storm Media]*, August 6. www.storm.mg/article/150490. Accessed 28 Aug 2016.

CHAPTER 5

Party's Issue Competence and Electoral Decisions in Taiwan's 2012 and 2016 Presidential Elections

Ching-hsin Yu and T. Y. Wang

INTRODUCTION

As a nascent democracy, Taiwan has undergone rapid democratization during the past two decades with robust electoral competition between two principal parties: the Nationalist Party (Kuomintang or KMT) and the

---

This chapter was presented at the "Taiwan in the Realm of East Asia" conference at Wake Forest University, North Carolina, USA, October 21–23, 2016. Data analyzed in this chapter are from "Taiwan's Election and Democratization Studies, 2009–2012 (III): the Survey of the Presidential and Legislative Elections, 2012" and "Taiwan's Election and Democratization Study, 2012–2016 (IV): the Survey of the Presidential and Legislative Elections, 2016." The coordinator of the multi-year TEDS project is Professor Chi Huang of National

C.-h. Yu
Election Study Center/Taiwan Institute of Governance and Communication Research, National Chengchi University, Taipei, Taiwan

T. Y. Wang (✉)
Department of Politics and Government, Illinois State University, Normal, IL, USA

© The Author(s) 2019
W.-c. Lee (ed.), *Taiwan's Political Re-Alignment and Diplomatic Challenges*, Politics and Development of Contemporary China, https://doi.org/10.1007/978-3-319-77125-0_5

Democratic Progressive Party (DPP). The formerly authoritarian KMT was beaten at the polls in 2000 and peacefully transferred political power to the DPP at the national level. The KMT returned to power in 2008 in an equally peaceful transition when its opponents lost. In 2016, the DPP regained the presidency with a landslide victory, which marked the third turnover of political power in Taiwan.

As Taiwan transforms itself from a one-party authoritarian state to a vibrant democracy, there is substantial scholarly interest in the country's electoral politics. Researchers generally agree that Taiwan's future relations with China, the key political cleavage in the society which is largely embodied by voters' partisan affiliations, is a major determinant of the island citizens' electoral decisions.[1] Yet, there is little consensus regarding the role that issue ownership and its associated issue competence play in Taiwanese citizens' electoral calculus. Indeed, the importance of issues in politics has long been recognized in scholarly literature. "To speak of politics is to speak of political issues," as Carmines and Stimson indicated almost three decades ago (1989: 3). Candidates thus frequently stress political issues at which the public perceives their affiliated parties as more competent so that they can exploit the party's "issue ownership" to their electoral advantages.[2]

Echoing this literature, research has shown that issue ownership exists in Taiwanese politics as voters perceive each of the two principal parties as more competent in dealing with certain problems of concern.[3] Employing data of two nation-wide surveys collected in Taiwan, this chapter aims to examine the electoral effect of perceived issue competence on the island country's 2012 and 2016 presidential elections.[4]

Issue Ownership and Issue Competence

The theory of issue ownership maintains that specific political parties tend to be perceived by voters as more capable of dealing with certain problems. Voters' assessment of party competence is generally based on a record of policy initiatives, innovations, and accomplishments over a period of time. Once the perception is established, the political party is said to "own" the

---

Chengchi University. More information is available at http://www.tedsnet.org. The authors would like to thank comments from Dr. Hans Stockton and other participants as well as the support from Wake Forest University and the TEDS. The authors are solely responsible for views expressed in the paper.

particular issue(s).[5] In the United States, for instance, the Democratic Party is generally perceived as better at handling social security, civil rights, and matters related to women and minorities. The Republican Party is seen as more capable of maintaining a robust national defense, fighting crimes, and managing inflation and government spending. The relationship between the perceived party competence and issue ownership may reinforce each other, which eventually turns into a party's image that has a certain degree of stability. As such, candidates will strategically emphasize issues that their parties own and avoid issues that may provide advantages to opponents. Through party manifestos and campaign advertisements candidates generally gain the most from issues that they and their parties can claim ownership. It is argued that issue trespassing on an opponent's turf during a campaign is highly risky and should be avoided. Thus, candidates should neglect or maintain an ambiguous position on issues owned by opposing parties and emphasize issues on which their parties are perceived as more competent.[6]

That said, empirical studies have shown that candidates' strategies and skills of persuasion can often transform weaknesses into strengths.[7] Kaufmann, for instance, finds that a candidate's attentiveness to opposing party's issues can minimize the ownership effects if their personal records of accomplishment on these issues warrant it.[8] Bill Clinton's success at neutralizing the Republican advantage on crime-fighting in the 1992 presidential election is a case in point.[9] Thus, candidates may adopt similar campaign strategies as their opponents, including issue trespassing, which sometimes leads to the convergence of issues in campaigns.[10]

These findings also demonstrate that there is considerable variation in the effects that issues have on electoral decisions. Some studies show that issue ownership produces a direct impact on citizens' vote choices,[11] while others present findings with an indirect effect.[12] The differences may be explained by candidate characteristics, personal legislative record, or other contextual factors such as economic hardship and security threat. Indeed, a prolonged economic recession is likely to alienate a party's supporters who may then search for alternative policies or candidates. In times of threat, the public may want strong leadership and reward candidates and parties that are perceived to hold a hawkish position.[13] In the same vein, a party's reputational advantages on issues may diminish due to the poor performance of the ruling party. While Americans traditionally have considered the Republican Party to be more competent in handling national security, President George W. Bush's perceived poor performance on the war in Iraq has substantially reduced the party's reputational advantage on national defense.[14] Such factors may thus provide one party with short-term ownership of a specific issue and exert campaign effects on citizens' electoral choices. Unless the party can seize the opportunity and establish a record of policy initiatives with concrete achievements, the issue ownership will be merely a "lease."[15]

Although more than 30 years have passed since Budge and Farlie published their seminal work in 1983, the study of issue ownership in Taiwan is relatively new. Findings of this limited research show that issue ownership exists in Taiwan, and it exerts effects on the island citizens' political attitudes and behaviors. Due to Beijing's assertive claim of Taiwan's sovereignty, reputational advantage of political parties in Taiwan is largely aligned with the central political cleavage in the society, that is, the island's future relations with China. The two main parties are perceived to take opposite stands on this fundamental cleavage. Because the KMT takes a pro-unification position, it is considered more competent in maintaining a better relationship with the Beijing government and preserving cross-Strait peace and stability. The pro-independence DPP is regarded as more determined to safeguard the island's sovereignty and autonomy but is likely to irk Chinese leaders. The two principal political parties therefore "own" their respective issues along the key political cleavage on the island. In addition, the KMT has also been perceived as more capable of promoting economic development and raising Taiwan's international status. The DPP has the reputational advantage of addressing gender and social welfare issues, promoting environmental protection, and advancing democratic reform. Candidates of both political parties therefore have strategically emphasized issues on which their parties are perceived as stronger. Given the issue ownership of each principal party on the island, empirical research demonstrates that there is a close association between perceived party competence in problems of concern and electoral choices, particularly regarding issues surrounding the key political cleavage on the island.[16]

Interestingly, issue convergence occurred in Taiwan's 1996 and 2008 presidential elections, even though issue trespassing is generally considered a risky endeavor. Because Beijing had begun eight-month long military exercises and missile tests in the wake of the 1996 election to intimidate Taiwanese voters,[17] safeguarding the island's national security was the single most important campaign issue for all political parties. In 2008, the worldwide economic downturn also led competing parties to converge as they offered various policy proposals of revitalizing Taiwan's reeling economy. Both the 1996 and 2008 elections show that issue convergence is a function of the saliency of the issue, which is consistent with prior findings.[18]

The above discussion, therefore, provides a theoretical backdrop for analyzing the effects of perceived issue competence on Taiwanese citizens' electoral decisions in the 2012 and 2016 presidential elections. The following section will provide a brief discussion of the context of the two elections.

Party's Issue Competence in Taiwan

Taiwan's economy was already showing signs of trouble when Ma Ying-jeou of the KMT took office in 2008. To revitalize the failing economy, the Ma administration implemented a series of measures to stabilize the financial system, expand public infrastructure investment, and address unemployment issues.[19] In addition to domestic measures, Ma's economic policies also depended on improving cross-Strait relations to provide an additional economic stimulus. To this end, the newly elected President Ma endorsed "one China with different interpretations," dubbed the "1992 Consensus,"[20] as his commitment to not pursuing the island's de jure independence, which has been the main sticking point between Beijing and Taipei's DPP government, led by Ma's predecessor, former President Chen Shui-bian. This rapprochement approach to cross-Strait relations was thus welcomed by Chinese leaders and praised by Washington as it reduced cross-Strait tension and stabilized the triangular relationship among Beijing, Taipei, and Washington. During Ma's first term as Taiwan's president, a number of cross-Strait agreements were reached, including a landmark trade deal known as the Economic Cooperation Framework Agreement (ECFA), through which China provided significant economic concessions to Taiwan. Ma and his affiliated KMT thus succeeded in securing their long-time reputational advantage on managing cross-Strait relations and promoting economic development. In the three-way race of the 2012 presidential election, Ma easily won reelection by defeating his main opponent, Tsai Ing-wen of the DPP, with a substantial margin, 800,000 votes out of the 13 million votes cast. With the electoral mandate, the Ma administration continued its rapprochement approach toward China in the subsequent four years.

While cross-Strait economic relations expanded rapidly during Ma's tenure as president, Chinese leaders did not relax their tactic of diplomatic isolation and continued to back up their claim on Taiwan with the threat of military force. The prospect of cross-Strait economic integration thus worried many Taiwanese citizens as they feared rapid expansion of economic exchanges would make the island more vulnerable to China's control. Beijing's economic concessions, despite being quite generous, have since been viewed as a sugarcoated ploy to annex Taiwan. The historic Ma-Xi Meeting in November 2015 further consolidated the perception that a KMT-led government would "betray" the Taiwanese people and "sell out" the island country's sovereignty to Beijing. Such discontents may explain the massive protest, known as the Sunflower Movement, against a proposed cross-Strait trade-in-service agreement.[21]

Meanwhile, as trade and tourism with China boomed, the economic reality was grim for many Taiwanese citizens. Big businesses were making profits, but wages were stagnant and economic inequality worsened. Although more jobs were added by 2014, the unemployment rate was higher than that of neighboring countries, particularly among the younger cohort. It hovered around 12–13 percent during Ma's second term. By 2016, many island citizens felt that it was mainly businesses, not ordinary people, that benefited from the expanded cross-Strait economic exchanges.

In this context, the ability to manage cross-Strait relations was clearly an important skill that any candidate must demonstrate for a successful campaign. On the 2016 campaign trail, Tsai of the DPP repeatedly emphasized that she would maintain the status quo if elected. Since public opinion polls had shown that the majority of island citizens opposed any radical political changes, her pledge was consistent with the public's "general will." The pledge also won tacit approval from Washington as it essentially declared that her administration would not pursue formal independence which would certainly invite Beijing's violent response. More importantly, Tsai successfully portrayed the KMT's rapprochement policies as pro-China and pro-unification, arguing that they have deepened Taiwan's economic dependence on China and endangered the island country's independence and autonomy. While Tsai essentially engaged in a risky issue trespassing, she capitalized on voters' discontent with Ma's poor performance and neutralized the KMT's reputational advantage on cross-Strait relations. By vowing to maintain the status quo, Tsai characterized her affiliated DPP as a party that was both determined to defend Taiwan's sovereignty and more competent to manage the island's relations with China.

A series of policy missteps during Ma's second term hurt the KMT's reputation further on issues related to social welfare, on which it did not enjoy an advantage in the first place.[22] These policy initiatives, including permitting a rise in both gas and electricity prices, imposing a capital gains tax on securities transactions, and lifting restrictions on importing US beef products, were perceived as hurting the public's livelihood and encountered fierce public opposition. A series of food safety scandals between 2013 and 2014 also led many to lose confidence in the government's ability to provide a safe and prosperous living environment for its citizens. The Da-pu Incident[23] and the Hung Chung-chiu Incident[24] also tarnished the KMT's image as a party for justice and people's livelihood and augmented substantial popular discontent against the ruling party and its 2016 presidential candidate.[25]

In this context, Table 5.1 presents 2012 and 2016 survey results of voters' perceptions of issue handling differentials in four key areas, revealing a dramatic change of perceived party competence. The data show that the KMT enjoyed considerable advantages on managing cross-Strait rela-

Table 5.1 Descriptions of variables

	2012(%)	2016(%)
Party's Competence in …		
Managing Cross -Strait Relations		
KMT	1121(61.4)	714(42.2)
DPP	212(11.6)	366(21.7)
Others	493(27.0)	610(36.1)
Promoting Economic Development		
KMT	935(51.2)	362(21.4)
DPP	266(14.5)	543(32.1)
Others	625(34.3)	785(46.4)
Advancing Social Welfare		
KMT	514(28.1)	257(15.2)
DPP	452(24.7)	678(40.1)
Others	8619(47.1)	755(44.7)
Defending Taiwan's Sovereignty		
KMT		301(17.8)
DPP		775(45.9)
Others		613(36.3)
N	1826	1690

Data Source: Chu (2012), Huang (2016)

Notes: (1) Percentages are shown in parentheses; (2) *Defending Taiwan's sovereignty* was not included in the 2012 survey

tions and promoting economic development in 2012. While the DPP was perceived capable of dealing with social welfare, it was still lagging behind the KMT by more than 3 percent. The 2016 survey results paint a different picture. The DPP was seen as better able to handle problems related to economic development and social welfare by 11 percent and 25 percent, respectively, over the KMT. While the KMT continued to possess issue advantage on managing cross-Strait relations, its lead was reduced by about 20 percent. The 2016 survey also assesses perceived party competence in defending Taiwan's sovereignty, which was a prominent issue in the 2016 presidential election. The DPP clearly held a solid advantage in this respect. Survey data thus show that the ruling KMT lost ground in all aspects, including those issues of which it had enjoyed ownership for a long time. These perceived changes of issue competence of both parties were rather drastic and significant. In particular, the island citizens' stands on these issues reflect the key political cleavage in the society, that is, Taiwan's future relationship with China. It begs the question if the perceived change in party competence affects Taiwanese citizens' electoral decisions.

Shifting Perception and Vote Choices

To answer the above research question, the aforementioned survey data collected in 2012 and 2016 are employed. As noted earlier, Ma of the then-ruling KMT defeated his main challenger, Tsai of the opposition DPP, in his reelection bid in 2012 and secured a second term in office. In the 2016 election, Tsai won a landslide victory over the KMT candidate, Eric Chu, to become the island country's first female president. To assess citizens' electoral decisions, the dependent variable, *Vote Choice*, is coded dichotomously, with one indicating a vote for the KMT candidate and zero for the DPP candidate.[26] A series of issue competence assessments of the two principal parties are created based on the data presented in Table 5.1, and they are *cross-Strait relations, economic development, social welfare*, and *defending Taiwan's sovereignty*.[27] These four issues are coded one for the perceived party competence of the KMT and the DPP, respectively, and zero otherwise. Finally, because there is a consensus in political science literature that citizens' partisan affiliations and candidate evaluation exert influential effects on their electoral decisions,[28] respondents' *partisan favorability* and *candidate evaluation* are included. They are numerically assessed by zero to ten "feeling thermometers," with zero and ten indicating the lowest and the highest favorability and evaluation, respectively.

To assess the effects of perceived issue ownership on Taiwanese voters' electoral decisions, multivariate analyses are conducted. Statistical results are presented in Table 5.2. Model 1 of the table shows that in the 2012 presidential election all coefficients associated with party competence variables are statistically significant. Compared with respondents with a neutral attitude, those who perceived the KMT as being more capable of managing cross-Strait relations tended to vote for Ma, while those who considered the DPP as competent on this issue were less likely to support Ma. Similar findings can be identified for promoting economic development and advancing social welfare. However, when partisan favorability and candidate evaluation are included in the analysis, as Model 2 shows, only the perceived DPP competence on cross-Strait relations presents a statistically significant effect which bears a negative sign. That is, voters who considered the DPP as being more capable of managing cross-Strait relations tended not to vote for Ma and were more likely to support Tsai. Interestingly, the KMT did not extract any electoral advantages from "owning" the issue. Meanwhile, coefficients of both partisan favorability and candidate evaluation are statistically significant and bear expected signs. As noted earlier, Taiwan's future relation with China is the most important political cleavage on the island. Because the two principal parties are perceived to take opposite positions on this fundamental divide, partisanship and the associated candidate evaluation embody the same electoral division. Thus, issue politics was not as important as partisanship and candidate evaluation in the Taiwan 2012 presidential election, except subjects related to cross-Strait relations.

Models 3 and 4 tell a somewhat different story about Taiwan's 2016 election. Like Model 1, Model 3 shows that perceived issue competence provides candidates with electoral advantages as all associated coefficients are statistically significant with expected signs. However, when voters' partisan affiliations and candidate preferences are included in the analysis, coefficients associated with the KMT's ability to manage cross-Strait relations, advance social welfare, and defend Taiwan's sovereignty become statistically insignificant. The coefficient of promoting economic development is the only coefficient that is statistically significant and provides positive effect on the vote for the KMT candidate. In contrast, all but one

Table 5.2 Binary logit of vote choice (KMT = 1; DPP = 0)

	2012		2016	
	Model 1	Model 2	Model 3	Model 4
Cross-Strait Relations (Other=0)	B	B	B	B
	(S.E.)	(S.E.)	(S.E.)	(S.E.)
KMT	.786***	−.042	1.450***	.547
	(.193)	(.351)	(.240)	(.384)
DPP	−2.849***	−1.607**	−1.736**	−2.079*
	(.538)	(.714)	(.609)	(1.093)
Economic Development (Other=0)				
KMT	1.432***	.527	1.497***	.993***
	(.188)	(.350)	(.290)	(.464)
DPP	−1.620***	−.210	−1.544***	−1.295**
	(.326)	(.531)	(.395)	(.588)
Social Welfare (Other=0)				
KMT	.566***	−.394	.636*	−.214
	(.206)	(.376)	(.341)	(.506)
DPP	−1.447***	−.471	−1.025***	.169
	(.190)	(.357)	(.270)	(.458)
Sovereignty (Other=0)				
KMT			.971*	−.339
			(.318)	(.498)
DPP			−1.819***	−1.636***
			(.281)	(.450)
Partisan Favorability (0-10)				
KMT		2.112***		2.435***
		(.397)		(.433)
DPP		−2.016***		−1.201**
		(.336)		(.511)
Candidate Evaluation (0-10)				
KMT candidate		.857***		.883***
		(.098)		(.127)
DPP candidate		−.791***		−.738***
		(.095)		(.124)
Intercept(s)	−.257	.047	−.863***	−.738
	(.145)	(.591)	(.171)	(.684)
N	1390	1324	1137	1067
Cox & Snell R^2	.421	.658	.500	.630
Nagelkerke R^2	.569	.887	.707	.889

Data Source: Chu (2012), Huang (2016)

Notes: (1) ***: $p < 0.01$; **: $p < 0.05$; *: $p < 0.1$; (2) *defending Taiwan's sovereignty* was not included in the 2012 survey

coefficients associated with the DPP's issue competence are statistically significant and bear negative signs. These findings demonstrate that issue politics is more important in the 2016 presidential election, but the associated reputational advantages did not help the KMT candidate. The DPP was able to exploit the perceived competence of many issues while at the same time neutralizing the KMT's issue advantages. The loss of electoral benefits on cross-Strait relations is particularly damaging to the KMT because it is an issue traditionally "owned" by the party. Instead, the DPP turned the table and successfully branded itself as a party that was determined to defend Taiwan's sovereignty while managing the island's relationship with China at the same time. While partisanship and candidate evaluation continue to play an important role in citizens' electoral calculus, the gains of perceived competence by the DPP in part contributed to its electoral success in the 2016 election.

THE AFTERMATH OF THE 2016 ELECTION

As noted above, the majority of Taiwanese citizens want to enjoy the economic benefits of a reasonably close relationship with China, but they also worry about the island's vulnerability to Beijing's control if the relationship becomes too close. Tsai and the DPP effectively responded to this sentiment in the 2016 presidential election on an issue that the KMT had enjoyed a dominant advantage for a long time. However, winning the election on the issue is one thing, while delivering campaign promises is another, particularly when there are competing political forces for conflicting objectives.

Since taking office, Tsai has steered a cautious line between the demands of her core supporters, who have traditionally supported Taiwan's de jure independence, and Beijing's long-standing threats of force against the island's independence, as well as Washington's desire for cross-Strait stability. Thus, Taipei's new government has refused to endorse the 1992 Consensus, which implies that Taiwan and the Chinese mainland are part of one China. Instead, Tsai vowed to maintain the cross-Strait status quo, which is based on the 1992 talks, the outcomes of over two decades of negotiations that followed, the constitutional system of the Republic of China, Taiwan's official name, and the island's democratic principles.[29]

Tsai's call got a cool reception from Beijing leaders. Insisting on the 1992 Consensus as the basis of the cross-Strait relationship, Beijing characterized Tsai's remarks as "an incomplete examination paper."[30] Since

Tsai's inauguration, Beijing has cut official contacts with Taipei's new government and restricted Chinese tourism to Taiwan. By the end of 2016, the number of mainland visitors to Taiwan fell by 27.2 percent year on year, which has had a significant negative effect on Taiwan's tourism industry, leading to a protest organized by 10,000 tourism industry workers.[31] Meanwhile, in breaking the "diplomatic truce," Beijing deprived two of Taipei's few remaining diplomatic allies[32] and effectively blocked Taipei's participation in the World Health Assembly (WHA),[33] further isolating the island country internationally. Taiwanese officials also acknowledged that the recently launched "New Southbound Policy," which attempts to reinvigorate and diversify Taiwan's economy and reduce the island's dependence on the mainland market, has encountered tremendous challenges due to China's powerful presence in Southeast Asian countries.[34] All of these moves by Beijing aim to pressure Tsai to return to the 1992 Consensus or a similar political formula embodying the "one China" principle.

The reality is that Taipei's DPP government is not likely to conform to Beijing's wishes in the foreseeable future. Despite Tsai's low approval rating due to intensifying dissatisfaction with her domestic governance,[35] the majority of the Taiwanese continue to support the maintenance of cross-Strait status quo. In addition, Tsai must heed the demands of her core supporters for independence to avoid an internal backlash.[36] Given Chinese leaders' unyielding position on the "one China" principle, it is reasonable to expect that Beijing's political and economic pressures on Taipei are likely to persist, possibly mixed with implicit and/or explicit military threats as demonstrated by the recent sailing of an aircraft carrier into Taiwan's air defense identification zone.[37]

If the cross-Strait relationship continues to stagnate or even deteriorate, and/or Taiwan's already stagnant economy suffers further as a result of Beijing's political and economic pressure, will the DPP be perceived by voters as a competent political party in managing the cross-Strait relationship? Will the issue ownership in Taiwan's electoral politics revert to pre-2016 status? As noted previously, issue ownership is based on a long record of initiatives, innovations, and accomplishments. Given the long-standing voter perception that the KMT is better able to handle the cross-Strait relationship, the 2016 electoral advantage enjoyed by the DPP may be temporary. Unless the DPP can establish a convincing record, the perceived party competence will be merely a "lease." Because Taiwan's future relationship with China constitutes the key political cleavage on the island, the short-term ownership of the cross-Strait relationship issue may become a liability to the DPP in future elections.

CONCLUSION

This study has aimed to assess the effects of perceived change in issue competence on electoral decisions. Building on the previous research, the findings have shown that issue ownership exists in Taiwan as each principal party is perceived as more competent in handling certain problems of voters' concern. The KMT is generally considered more competent in managing cross-Strait relations, promoting economic development and raising Taiwan's international status. The DPP is perceived as better at advancing democratic reform, enhancing social welfare, and defending Taiwan's sovereignty. That said, the campaign effects of issue ownership vary across the two elections. Indeed, perceived issue competence did not provide much benefits to either political party in the 2012 presidential election, and the electoral outcome was determined largely by partisanship and candidate evaluation. In the 2016 presidential election, partisan differences and the associated candidate evaluation continued to play a major role in voters' electoral calculus. Voters' concerns about Taiwan's increasing economic dependence on China, along with a series of events that tarnished the KMT's image, shifted voters' perceptions of competence on several issue areas, including managing the cross-Strait relationship. These changes in part contributed to the KMT's electoral misfortune in 2016.

These findings again have demonstrated that partisan identification constitutes a dominant factor in Taiwanese citizens' electoral decisions. As noted, Taiwan's future relations with China is the key political cleavage on the island. Because the two main parties take opposite sides on this fundamental cleavage, partisanship embodies the same electoral division. All political issues are examined through partisan lenses. Even though the KMT enjoyed substantial advantages of having maintained peace and stability across the Taiwan Strait, as previous research has demonstrated, such reputational benefits did not help the KMT in the 2012 and the 2016 presidential elections. The DPP, however, was able to employ cross-Strait relations as a key issue to consolidate its core supporters in both elections. When there was a shift in perceived competence in other issue areas, the DPP capitalized on the perceived changes to its electoral advantage. These findings suggest that partisan identification is an important determinant of Taiwan citizens' electoral decisions. However, the role of issue ownership and its accompanied perceived competence cannot be ignored, though the campaign effects of issue ownership may vary from election to election.

Finally, even though the DPP successfully defeated the KMT in the 2016 presidential election, in part due to a shifting perception of party competence, tremendous challenges face Taipei's new government, in no small part due to a stagnant cross-Strait relationship and Beijing's imposed pressures. Unless the Tsai administration can convincingly establish an irrefutable record, the performance reputation on the cross-Strait relationship is likely to be based on a short-term ownership, which may become the party's liability in future elections.

Notes

1. For an analysis of the development Taiwanese citizens' identity, see T.Y. Wang, "Changing Boundaries: The Development of Taiwan Voters' Identity," in *The Taiwan Voter*, eds. Christopher H. Achen and T.Y. Wang. (Ann Arbor: University of Michigan Press, 2017).
2. John Petrocik, "Issue Ownership in Presidential Elections, with a 1980 Case Study," *American Journal of Political Science* 43.3 (1996): 864–87.
3. Shing-yuan Sheng and Hsiao-chuan Liao, "Issues, Political Cleavages, and Party Competition in Taiwan," in *Taiwan Voter*, eds. Christopher H. Achen and T.Y. Wang (Ann Arbor: U of Michigan Press, 2017).
4. The survey data analyzed in this chapter are from "Taiwan's Election and Democratization Study, 2009–2012(III): the Survey of the Presidential and Legislative Elections, 2012 (TEDS 2012)" and "Taiwan's Election and Democratization Study, 2012–2016 (IV): the Survey of the Presidential and Legislative Elections, 2016 (TEDS2016)". The principal investigators are Yun-han Chu and Chi Huang, respectively. Chi Huang is also the coordinator of the multi-year project TEDS. More information is available on the TEDS website (http://www.tedsnet.org). The authors would like to thank the Election Study Center, National Chengchi University in Taiwan, for making the survey data available. All errors are our own.
5. Ian Budge and Dennis Farlie, *Explaining and Predicting Elections* (London: Allen & Unwin, 1983); Ian Budge and Dennis Farlie, "Party Competition-Selective Emphasis or Direct Confrontation? An Alternative View with Data," in *West European Party Systems: Continuity and Change*, eds. H. Daalder and Peter Mair (London: Sage, 1983), 267–305; Petrocik, John. 1989. "The Theory of Issue Ownership: Issues, Agendas, and

Electoral Coalitions in the 1988 Election." Presented at the annual meeting of the American Political Science Association, Atlanta; Petrocik, "Issue Ownership," 864–87.
6. Stephen Ansolabehere and Shanto Iyengar, "Riding the Wave and Claiming Ownership Over Issues: The Joint Effects of Advertising and News Coverage in Campaigns," *The Public Opinion Quarterly* 58.3 (1994): 335–57; Petcock, "Issue Ownership"; John Petrocik, William L. Benoit and Glenn J. Hansen, "Issue Ownership and Presidential Campaigning, 1952–2000," *Political Science Quarterly* 118.4 (2003/2004): 599–626.
7. William H. Riker, *The Strategy of Rhetoric: Campaigning for the American Constitution* (New Haven: Yale University Press, 1996).
8. Karen M. Kaufmann, "Disaggregating and Reexamining Issue Ownership and Voter Choice," *Polity* 36.2 (2004): 283–99.
9. David B. Holian, "He's Stealing My Issues! Clinton's Crime Rhetoric and the Dynamics of Issue Ownership," *Political Behavior* 26.2 (2004): 95–124.
10. David F. Damore, "The Dynamics of Issue Ownership in Presidential Campaigns," *Political Research Quarterly* 57.3 (2004): 391–97; David F. Damore, "Issue Convergence in Presidential Campaigns," *Political Behavior* 27.1 (2005): 71–97; Noah Kaplan, David K. Park, and Travis Ridout, "Dialogue in American Political Campaigns? An Examination of Issue Convergence in Candidate Television Advertising," *American Journal of Political Science* 50.3 (2006): 724–36; Lee Sigelman and Emmett H. Buell, "Avoidance or Engagement? Issue Convergence in US Presidential Campaigns, 1960–2000," *American Journal of Political Science* 48.4 (2004): 650–61.
11. Paolo Bellucci, "Tracing the Cognitive and Affective Roots of Party Competence: Italy and Britain, 2001," *Electoral Studies* 25 (2006): 548–69; Jand Green and Will Jennings, "The Dynamics of Issue Competence and Vote for Parties In and Out of Power: An Analysis of Valence in Britain, 1979–1997," *European Journal of Political Research* 51.4 (2012): 469–503.
12. E. Bélanger and B. Meguid, "Issue Salience, Issue Ownership and Issue-Based Vote Choice: Evidence from Canada," *Electoral Studies* 27.3 (2008): 477–91; Stefaan Walgrave et al., "The Limits of Issue Ownership Dynamics: The Constraining Effect of Party Preference," *Journal of Elections, Public Opinion, and Parties* 24.1 (2014): 1–19.
13. Shana Kushner Gadarian, "Foreign Policy at the Ballot Box: How Citizens Use Foreign Policy to Judge and Choose Candidates," *The Journal of Politics* 72.4 (2010): 1046–62.

14. Hannah Goble and Peter M. Holm, "Breaking Bonds: The Iraq War and the Loss of Republican Dominance in National Security," *Political Research Quarterly* 62.2 (June 2009): 215–29.
15. Petrocik, "Issue Ownership," 864–87.
16. Ching-Ching Chang, "The Effects of Political Advertising: The Role of Issue Ownership," *Chinese Journal of Communication Research* 16 (2009): 93–129; Chiung-chu Lin, "Party Competence and Vote Choice in the 2012 Election in Taiwan," *International Journal of China Studies* 5.1 (2014): 49–70; Sheng and Liao, "Issues."
17. John W. Garver, *Face Off: China, the United States, and Taiwan's Democratization*. Seattle: University of Washington Press, 1997.
18. Damore, "Issue Convergence," 71–97.
19. Executive Yuan, "Employment Promotion Plan of 98–101 (98-101nian chujin jiuye fangan)," The Republic of China, accessed July 6, 2009. http://www.ey.gov.tw/public/Attachment/93102155871.pdf; Ying-jeou Ma, "New Year's Day Celebratory Message," Government Information Office, Republic of China, January 1, 2009, accessed July 6, 2009. http://www.gio.gov.tw/ct.asp?xItem=44972&ctNode=2462.
20. The 1992 Consensus presumably is a verbal agreement between Beijing and Taipei that allows them to interpret what "one China" means in their own ways. See Su Chi and Cheng An-guo, eds., *Yige Zhongguo, gezi biaoshu' gongshi de shishi* (One China, Different Interpretations: An Account of the Consensus) (Taipei: Guojia zhengce yanjiu jijinhui, 2002).
21. J. R., "Politics in Taiwan: Sunflower Sutra," *Economist*, April 8, 2014, accessed January 20, 2015. http://www.economist.com/blogs/banyan/2014/04/politics-taiwan.
22. Sheng and Liao, "Issues."
23. The Da-pu Incident originated from the forceful destruction of a civilian's house by a local county government on the grounds of urban planning and development. The owner committed suicide to protest. The incident was viewed as a matter of social injustice and attracted substantial public attention (see *Taipei Times*, "Miaoli will not fight Dapu ruling, but refuses redress," February 7, 2014, accessed March, 30, 2017. http://www.taipeitimes.com/News/taiwan/archives/2014/02/07/2003582955).
24. Hung Chung-chiu was an enlisted soldier who was abused to death by his commanding officer. The Ministry of Defense resisted the disclosure of information related to the event, which invite public condemnation that led to the resignation of two high ranking officials and Ma's public apology (see BBC, "Taiwan protest over Hung Chung-chiu death," August 3, 2013, accessed March 30, 2017. http://www.bbc.com/news/world-asia-23561244).
25. BBC, "Taiwan Protest."

26. James Soong of the People's First Party (PFP) was the third presidential candidate in both elections. The measurement scheme adopted in this research essentially excludes respondents who supported Soong for two reasons. First, there were few PFP supporters in 2012 and the associated sample size is too small for a meaningful analysis. Second, questions of issue ownership in both surveys only compare the KMT and the DPP, while those on the PFP are not included.
27. The survey question on *defending Taiwan's sovereignty* was not included in the 2012 survey.
28. William Jacoby, "The American Voter," in *The Oxford Handbook of American Elections and Political Behavior*, ed. Jan E. Leighley (New York: Oxford University Press, 2010), 260–77.
29. Ing-wen Tsai, "Inaugural Ceremony of the 14th-term President and Vice President of the Republic of China (Taiwan)," Office of the President, Republic of China (Taiwan), 2016, accessed July 28, 2017. http://english.president.gov.tw/Page/252.
30. Beijing leaders' response to Tsai's inaugural address can be accessed at "http://www.gwytb.gov.cn/wyly/201605/t20160520_11463128.htm (accessed July 28, 2017).
31. Nicola Smith, "China Is Using Tourism to Hit Taiwan Where It Really Hurts," *Times*, November 16, 2016, accessed July 28, 2017. http://time.com/4574290/china-taiwan-tourism-tourists/.
32. The "diplomatic truce" is a tacit understanding between Beijing and Taipei under former President Ma Ying-jeou. Because Ma endorsed the 1992 Consensus, Chinese leaders implicitly agreed to suspend the tug-of-war for diplomatic recognition, an issue on which Beijing has an overwhelming advantage. Since Tsai took office in 2016, Panama and Sao Tome and Principe switched their diplomatic recognition to Beijing, which reduced the number of countries to 20 that formally recognize Taiwan. See Elida Moreno and Philip Wen, "Panama Establishes Ties With China, Ditches Taiwan in Win For Beijing," *Reuters*, June 12, 2017, accessed July 28, 2017. http://www.reuters.com/article/us-panama-china-idUSKBN194054.
33. D.D. Wu, "WHO Déjà Vu: Taiwan Not Invited to World Health Assembly," *The Diplomat*, May 13, 2017, accessed July 28, 2017. http://thediplomat.com/2017/05/who-deja-vu-taiwan-not-invited-to-world-health-assembly/.
34. This observation is based on panel discussions with officials of various ministries in Taiwan, June 19–23, 2017.
35. David G. Brown, "Governing Taiwan Is Not Easy: President Tsai Ing-wen's First Year." May 17, 2017. Accessed July 10, 2017. https://www.brookings.edu/opinions/governing-taiwan-is-not-easy-president-tsai-ing-wens-first-year/ and Michelle Winglee, "On Taiwan, the Honeymoon

Is Over", *The Diplomat,* March 2, 2017. Accessed July 10, 2017. http://thediplomat.com/2017/03/on-taiwan-the-honeymoon-is-over/.
36. This observation is based on a panel discussion with President Tsai, June 20, 2017.
37. Hudson Lockett, "China aircraft carrier enters Taiwan's air defence identification zone," *Financial Times,* July 11, 2017, accessed July 29, 2017. https://www.ft.com/content/fad6ea94-09b8-37fa-b427-5519193c535a.

BIBLIOGRAPHY

Ansolabehere, Stephen, and Shanto Iyengar. 1994. Riding the Wave and Claiming Ownership Over Issues: The Joint Effects of Advertising and News Coverage in Campaigns. *The Public Opinion Quarterly* 58 (3): 335–357.
BBC. 2013. Taiwan Protest Over Hung Chung-chiu Death. August 3. http://www.bbc.com/news/world-asia-23561244. Accessed 30 Mar 2017.
Bélanger, E., and B. Meguid. 2008. Issue Salience, Issue Ownership and Issue-Based Vote Choice: Evidence from Canada. *Electoral Studies* 27 (3): 477–491.
Bellucci, Paolo. 2006. Tracing the Cognitive and Affective Roots of Party Competence: Italy and Britain, 2001. *Electoral Studies* 25: 548–569.
Brown, David G. 2017. *Governing Taiwan Is Not Easy: President Tsai Ing-wen's First Year.* May 17. https://www.brookings.edu/opinions/governing-taiwan-is-not-easy-president-tsai-ing-wens-first-year/. Accessed 10 July 2017.
Budge, Ian, and Dennis Farlie. 1983a. *Explaining and Predicting Elections.* London: Allen & Unwin.
———. 1983b. Party Competition-Selective Emphasis or Direct Confrontation? An Alternative View with Data. In *West European Party Systems: Continuity and Change,* ed. H. Daalder and Peter Mair, 267–305. London: Sage.
Carmines, Edward G., and James A. Stimson. 1989. *Issue Evolution: Race and the Transformation of American Politics.* Princeton: Princeton University Press.
Chang, Ching-ching. 2009. The Effects of Political Advertising: The Role of Issue Ownership. *Chinese Journal of Communication Research* 16: 93–129.
Chu, Yun-han. 2012. *Taiwan's Election and Democratization Study, 2009–2012(III): The Survey of the Presidential and Legislative Elections, 2012* (TEDS 2012).
Damore, David F. 2004. The Dynamics of Issue Ownership in Presidential Campaigns. *Political Research Quarterly* 57 (3): 391–397.
———. 2005. Issue Convergence in Presidential Campaigns. *Political Behavior* 27 (1): 71–97.
Executive Yuan. 2009. Employment Promotion Plan of 98–101 [*98–101nian chu-jin jiuye fangan*]. *The Republic of China.* http://www.ey.gov.tw/public/Attachment/93102155871.pdf. Accessed 6 July 2009.

Gadarian, Shana Kushner. 2010. Foreign Policy at the Ballot Box: How Citizens Use Foreign Policy to Judge and Choose Candidates. *The Journal of Politics* 72 (4): 1046–1062.

Garver, John W. 1997. *Face Off: China, the United States, and Taiwan's Democratization*. Seattle: University of Washington Press.

Goble, Hannah, and Peter M. Holm. June 2009. Breaking Bonds? The Iraq War and the Loss of Republican Dominance in National Security. *Political Research Quarterly* 62 (2): 215–229.

Green, Jand, and Will Jennings. 2012. The Dynamics of Issue Competence and Vote for Parties In and Out of Power: An Analysis of Valence in Britain, 1979–1997. *European Journal of Political Research* 51 (4): 469–503.

Holian, David B. 2004. He's Stealing My Issues! Clinton's Crime Rhetoric and the Dynamics of Issue Ownership. *Political Behavior* 26 (2): 95–124.

Huang, Chi. 2016. *Taiwan's Election and Democratization Study, 2012–2016 (IV): The Survey of the Presidential and Legislative Elections, 2016* (TEDS 2016).

J. R. 2014. Politics in Taiwan: Sunflower Sutra. *Economist*, April 8. http://www.economist.com/blogs/banyan/2014/04/politics-taiwan. Accessed 20 Jan 2015.

Jacoby, William. 2010. The American Voter. In *The Oxford Handbook of American Elections and Political Behavior*, ed. Jan E. Leighley, 260–277. New York: Oxford University Press.

Kaplan, Noah, David K. Park, and Travis Ridout. 2006. Dialogue in American Political Campaigns? An Examination of Issue Convergence in Candidate Television Advertising. *American Journal of Political Science* 50 (3): 724–736.

Kaufmann, Karen M. 2004. Disaggregating and Reexamining Issue Ownership and Voter Choice. *Polity* 36 (2): 283–299.

Lefevere, Jonas, Anke Tresch, and Stefaan Walgrave. 2015. Introduction: Issue Ownership. *West European Politics* 38 (4): 755–760.

Lin, Chiung-chu. 2014. Party Competence and Vote Choice in the 2012 Election in Taiwan. *International Journal of China Studies* 5 (1): 49–70.

Lockett, Hudson. 2017. China Aircraft Carrier Enters Taiwan's Air Defence Identification Zone. *Financial Times*, July 11. https://www.ft.com/content/fad6ea94-09b8-37fa-b427-5519193c535a. Accessed 29 July 2017.

Ma, Ying-jeou. 2009. New Year's Day Celebratory Message. *Government Information Office, Republic of China*, January 1. http://www.gio.gov.tw/ct.asp?xItem=44972&ctNode=2462. Accessed 6 July 2009.

Moreno, Elida, and Philip Wen. 2017. Panama Establishes Ties with China, Ditches Taiwan in Win for Beijing. *Reuters*, June 12. http://www.reuters.com/article/us-panama-china-idUSKBN194054. Accessed 28 July 2017.

Petrocik, John. 1989. *The Theory of Issue Ownership: Issues, Agendas, and Electoral Coalitions in the 1988 Election*. Presented at the annual meeting of the American Political Science Association, Atlanta.

———. 1996. Issue Ownership in Presidential Elections, with a 1980 Case Study. *American Journal of Political Science* 43 (3): 864–887.

Petrocik, John, William L. Benoit and Glenn J. Hansen. (2003/2004). Issue Ownership and Presidential Campaigning, 1952–2000. *Political Science Quarterly* 118 (4), Winter: 599–626.
Riker, William H. 1996. *The Strategy of Rhetoric: Campaigning for the American Constitution*. New Haven: Yale University.
Sheng, Shing-yuan, and Hsiao-chuan Liao. 2017. Issues, Political Cleavages, and Party Competition in Taiwan. In *Taiwan Voter*, ed. Chris Achen and T.Y. Wang. Ann Arbor: University of Michigan Press, forthcoming.
Sigelman, Lee, and Emmett H. Buell. 2004. Avoidance or Engagement? Issue Convergence in U.S. Presidential Campaigns, 1960–2000. *American Journal of Political Science* 48 (4): 650–661.
Simon, Adam F. 2002. *The Winning Message: Candidate Behavior, Campaign Discourse, and Democracy*. New York: Cambridge University Press.
Smith, Nicola. 2016. China Is Using Tourism to Hit Taiwan Where It Really Hurts. *Times*, November 16. http://time.com/4574290/china-taiwan-tourism-tourists/. Accessed 28 July 2017.
Stubager, Rune, and Rune Slothuus. 2013. What Are the Sources of Political Parties' Issue Ownership? Testing Four Explanations at the Individual Level. *Political Behavior* 35: 567–558.
Su Chi, and Cheng An-guo, eds. *Yige Zhongguo, gezi biaoshu' gongshi de shishi* [One China, Different Interpretations: An Account of the Consensus]. Taipei: Guojia zhengce yanjiu jijinhui, 2002.
Taipei Times. 2014. Miaoli Will Not Fight Dapu Ruling, but Refuses Redress. p. 4. February 7, 2014. http://www.taipeitimes.com/News/taiwan/archives/2014/02/07/2003582955. Accessed 30 Mar 2017.
Tsai, Ing-wen. 2016. Inaugural Ceremony of the 14th-term President and Vice President of the Republic of China (Taiwan). *Office of the President, Republic of China (Taiwan)*. http://english.president.gov.tw/Page/252. Accessed 28 July 2017.
Walgrave, Stefaan, Jonas Lefevere, and Anke Tresch. 2014. The Limits of Issue Ownership Dynamics: The Constraining Effect of Party Preference. *Journal of Elections, Public Opinion, and Parties* 24 (1): 1–19.
Wang, T.Y. 2017. Changing Boundaries: The Development of Taiwan Voters' Identity. In *The Taiwan Voter*, ed. Christopher Achen and T.Y. Wang. Ann Arbor: University of Michigan Press.
Winglee, Michelle. 2017. On Taiwan, The Honeymoon Is Over. *The Diplomat*, March 2. http://thediplomat.com/2017/03/on-taiwan-the-honeymoon-is-over/. Accessed 10 July 2017
Wu, DD. 2017. WHO Déjà Vu: Taiwan Not Invited to World Health Assembly. *The Diplomat*, May 13. http://thediplomat.com/2017/05/who-deja-vu-taiwan-not-invited-to-world-health-assembly/. Accessed 28 July 2017.

PART II

The China Factor and Taiwan's Cross-Strait Dilemma

CHAPTER 6

A Comparative Study of the China Factor in Taiwan and Hong Kong Elections

Karl Ho, Stan Hok-wui Wong, Harold D. Clarke, and Kuan-Chen Lee

INTRODUCTION

Globalization and the trend of trade liberalization render a different world in the twenty-first century. Some term it a flat world, while others point out the "Matthew effect," or income inequalities brought to smaller and less industrialized states.[1] One body of research in political economy focuses on the political ramifications of economic integration. Specifically, researchers are interested in the deeper impact of trade openness on political borders and number and size of countries. The core question is whether

K. Ho (✉) • H. D. Clarke
School of Economic, Political and Policy Sciences, The University of Texas at Dallas, Richardson, TX, USA

S. H.-w. Wong
Department of Applied Social Sciences, The Hong Kong Polytechnic University, Hung Hom, Hong Kong

K.-C. Lee
Institute of Political Science, Academia Sinica, Taipei, Taiwan

or not economic integration will lead to better exchange and communications among member states and eventually more political cooperation or integration. Higher efficiency or lower transaction cost due to economy of scale promotes the tendency of forming unions to arrive at better benefits and public goods for member states. Other economists argue that trade openness actually discourages incentives for political integration. Small countries in a world of global markets are better off staying independent and sovereign than bearing higher costs and risks as a member in a bigger union.[2]

At the forefront, the key question is what incentivizes political integration or disintegration, economically speaking. Does economic integration lead to political integration? If more economic cooperation is conducive to political unionization, what are the other factors that motivate further integration, such as full unification? Alesina et al. present formal and empirical evidence that free trade and globalization of markets *actually* eliminate the causes for bigger union or unification.[3] Not only countries will refuse to join borders but also "… small cultural, linguistic and ethnic groups within countries can choose to form smaller and more homogeneous political jurisdictions."[4] In other words, removing global trade barriers can be conducive to separatism. On the other side of the ledger, the European Union (EU) indeed provides the most cited example of political integration due to more open trade, closer economic cooperation, and institutional accommodations.[5] However, new developments in the early 2010s, particularly among the EU's new and peripheral member states, lend weight to skepticism about increasing costs attributed to heterogeneity of citizens and larger jurisdictions. The latest episodes on Brexit and other ensuing or similar movements on dissolution or disintegration in Europe and other regions are clear indicators of this global trend, providing plausible support of Alesina's theory.[6]

In this chapter, we test the theory in the East Asian context, specifically in the cases of Taiwan and Hong Kong, which are regional trade partners of China. In 1949, after retreating from the mainland, the Republic of China moved to Taiwan and remained at odds with the new People's Republic of China (PRC). After half a century of hostilities, the dyad opened trade talks in 2009 between the two quasi-official bodies, Straits Exchange Foundation (SEF) representing Taiwan and the Association for Relations Across the Taiwan Straits (ARATS) representing mainland China, to phase out tariffs in stages for each other. The two sides eventually arrived at a framework agreement primarily preferential to Taiwan's benefits.[7] The bilateral trade pact Economic Cooperation Framework Agreement (ECFA) signed between Taiwan and China in 2010 is considered the preliminary stage for future economic integration.

On a different track was the former British colony Hong Kong. In the 1980s, negotiations between the United Kingdom and the PRC arrived at an agreement returning the city to the latter's sovereignty in 1997 under the "One country, Two systems" arrangement. Under the Sino-British Joint Declaration (1984), Hong Kong retains the British-style system with democratization targeting ultimate full universal suffrage. The popular election promise was initially slated for 2007. Soon after the sovereignty transfer in 1997, the city suffered a severe economic setback due to the Asian Financial Crisis. The economy of the city did not bottom out until 2003. To help boost Hong Kong's economy, the PRC introduced the Closer Economic Partnership Arrangement (CEPA) in 2003, designed to enhance freer trade and introduce more tourist visits.

While the two agreements, the ECFA and CEPA, usher in a new era of economic cooperation with China, many are still doubtful about how the free trade frameworks will play out for smaller states and what political changes they will introduce to Taiwan and Hong Kong. What is the political economy of economic integration between the supersize China and the neighboring states with only a fraction of the former's GDP? To what extent would the economic integration *really* facilitate political cooperation or instead encourage disintegration down the road? Political economists confine the analysis not only to formal economic models but also include a myriad of factors including institutions, international context, and the equally important population heterogeneity. Institutions, for instance, refer to the political systems of trading partners. High volume of trade would not necessarily contribute to integration particularly when partners have dissimilar political systems. Historically, expansion of states through colonialism allowed for less concern over the institutions of the subordinate colonies. These colonized states were not granted rights in participating in colonizers' political processes or institutions, and hence, the colonizers had less worries over bearing too much of heterogeneity cost.[8] Differentials in such costs may be present among sovereign trading partners when policy makers face dissimilar demands for fiscal and redistributive policies.[9] Other institutional variables, such as electoral systems, could also lead to different policy directions and outcome. For example, proportional representation systems generally allow different degrees of

conflicts resulted from agglomerative policies, alleviating inequalities in income and resource distribution.[10] Second, contextual influences from international periods and structure provide impetus or restrictions to integration or disintegration. Interwar periods, for example, saw more examples of unionizations (e.g. Germany in late nineteenth century), while postwar periods witnessed the surge of new, independent nation states.

Last but not least, the factor of population heterogeneity pertains directly to public opinion perceiving the impact and consequences resulting from economic integration and the projected costs that can offset benefits from free trades and mobility due to redistribution of income. Alesina et al. (1997 and 2000) demonstrate that, given the heterogeneity cost, trade openness is positively associated with number of countries. In other words, the high cost of heterogeneity as a result of language and cultural differences among individuals would lead to secessions in the subsequence of freer trade. In this chapter, we specifically probe this micro-level factor and investigate the attitudinal shifts among Taiwan and Hong Kong citizens when economic interactions were instituted through enhanced trade and exchanges. We empirically analyze the relationship between economic cooperation and political integration from the perspective of individual voters. Using survey data from the Taiwan Election and Democratization Study (TEDS) and the Hong Kong Election Study (HKES), we study public opinions of citizens on economic integration with mainland China.

We will first briefly introduce the political economy literature on economic integration and apply suggested models to the cases of Hong Kong and Taiwan. Other studies and analyses focusing on cultural concerns will also be discussed. The subsequent section introduces case studies comparing Taiwan and Hong Kong before the research design, data, and methods, followed by empirical data analysis. In the last section, we discuss the model findings and implications in addition to making proposals for future research.

LITERATURE REVIEW

The Theory: Economic Integration and Political Disintegration

Political economy literature on political integration and disintegration is primarily concerned with analyses of incentives under different scenarios. The formal or rational choice approach focuses on decision making of agents or players under different conditions. Ruta surveys recent studies and provides a good coverage of works pointing to four main factors that determine political integration or disintegration[11]:

1. Economic integration (i.e. increase in trade and factor mobility)
2. International security considerations
3. Existence of international spillovers
4. Institutional setting (mainly decision mechanisms and institutional rules)

Increase in Trade
Each of these factors individually or in combination with others affects the incentives for the political outcome, which is integration or separatism. Among the four, the first factor or increase in trade draws most research interests and also controversies. Alesina and his associates argue that in a world of trade restrictions, open bilateral trade and subsequent political integration will bring in increasing returns and other economic benefits.[12] However, when other bilateral or multilateral free trade agreements are present, these incentives will be reduced. Casella and Feinstein argue that initially economic integration benefits induce political integration, but in time the marginal benefit will diminish and eventually loss of political autonomy will outweigh economic interests.[13]

Other studies concentrate on the long-term effects of redistribution of income under greater factor mobility. When equilibrium policies (i.e. same wages, comparable working conditions, etc.) and perfect mobility exist across borders, obstacles for political integration will be removed.[14] At the crux of this argument is the maintenance and sustainability of free trade and factor mobility in the long run.

International Security
Second, international security considerations regard the link between conflict among nations and incentives for integration. In a relatively stable international environment, when incentives for joining or forming a union decrease, political separatism will ensue. However, in a "bellicose, anarchic world," states will be induced to join union to reduce loss of economic or trade benefits.[15] In time, when stability is resumed or a new world order is achieved and the incentives are reduced or outweighed by other costs, states will again tend to secede, bringing about "its own dose" of new international tensions. Spolaore and Alesina suggest the relationship

between conflict, trade, and integration can go in both directions.[16] While international conflicts discourage trade and, in turn, economic integration, higher trade activities imply greater economic loss in case of war, which actually deter trade partners from entering conflicts. For example, the period following the end of Cold War saw both cases of separatism and integration. Former Soviet Union states sought independence and secession from the Communist bloc, many of whom chose to join the European Union. Economists acknowledge the equilibria for the number and size of states can be reached but more institutional factors need to be considered.[17] These factors include supranational organizations determining the extent of free trade and whether or not democratic institutions and processes are present within the states allowing public involvement in trade and integration decisions, which will be addressed in a later part of this section.

International Spillovers
Similarly, proponents of political integration contend that larger unions can generate international spillovers, providing lower cost public goods, such as environmental rules, infrastructure that benefits citizens beyond national borders, and living in other countries, which are not likely to occur in a fragmented world. The public goods generated are not always better off for citizens of states joining the union.[18] To internalize spillovers, which can be negative or positive, a union could be faced with decisions of strategic policies and redistribution of income across member states that could lead to disintegration. In two formal models, Alesina et al. exhibit the trade-offs between cost and benefits for union member countries with the same and differing policy preferences.[19] The cost of integration can move the equilibrium policy away from the country-specific equilibrium, in particular for the second scenario when countries are positioned on different ends of the policy spectrum. When union policies are introduced as strategic substitutes to allow higher general efficiency, these can be better for outsiders but worse for certain state citizens. One example is the immigration policy that permits visa-free travel for citizens in all member states. The European Union case provides the most recent evidence of how the immigration issue can outweigh the benefits to some part of the population in member states that results in disintegration.[20] The rise of the United Kingdom Independence Party (UKIP) and its role in the Brexit referendum manifests the "disintegration" momentum

that is particularly appealing to voters of older age groups. Their concerns about new immigrants from other ethnic nations motivated their ballot decision in the Brexit vote and in subsequent elections.

Alesina's series of studies consistently emphasizes the inverse effects of globalization and liberalized trade on unionization. Despite apparent enlargement of the union with new joining members, the authors explicitly warn that Europe will "never be a federal state."[21] For other integrationists, a supranational government can generate positive spillovers not possible under political separation, as long as the former can internalize the spillovers entirely and avoid conflicts of preference among different member countries. This explains why and how the EU continues to expand, sustaining an extended period after the Cold War. Yet, recent developments fuel skepticism on the sustainable effects of an expanded union and internalization of positive spillovers. After Brexit, a few other member countries are either considering leaving the union or struggling from internal pressure to hold a similar exit referendum.

Institutional Setting

Last but not least is the institutional setting that involves the decision-making mechanism at the national and supranational levels and the institutional rules governing distribution of power, in particular prerogatives to the union. In general, the more flexible and decentralized the union is, the more likely the political integration. However, high flexibility could lead to harming the functionality of the union government. One key argument Alesina and his group articulate about political separatism is the decision-making mechanism among member states in the union. If the countries are formed through a democratic process and policies are set by majority voting, their voters would prefer remaining sovereign in order to get public goods closer to their preferences, especially for relatively small states at the border of the union. An international union, which is a "social planner maximizing world average utility," is likely to be politically unstable unless secession rules are sufficiently strict.[22] To alleviate the problem, one solution is to use compensation schemes or favorable trade benefits to attract the populations of the joining states. Size of such benefits does matter, but most important is the timing. Voters in the latter countries could foresee the problem including decreasing benefits and other costs, including giving up sovereignty, outweighing the benefit, and casting doubt on votes in the first place.[23] In order to provide stronger incentives, unionization could either offer much higher trade benefits or devise decentralized decision-making mechanisms for agnostic member states. However, both of these measures could result in loss of efficiencies and further disagreements from other member states.

In the case of the Taiwan Strait, the institutional setting problem presents immediate concerns particularly to the potential member states in two aspects. The size difference between China and Taiwan or Hong Kong does matter in expectations of the smaller populations after unionization. Voters are concerned if their policy preferences would be adopted or any equilibrium be reached in their "fair share" of benefits. The second aspect regards the democratic institutions in the new union. Voters cannot trust new institutions that are not equally democratic or representative as in their respective sovereign governments. Another important concern is that different rules and decision mechanisms affect only economic benefits but not "other relevant dimensions of governance including civil liberties and freedom of political participation."[24]

Cultural Differences

Other scholars cite recent developments between China and Taiwan and assess the effects of closer bilateral trade and prospects of political integration through a cultural approach. Chao observes that the economic exchanges between Taiwan and mainland China have grown by leaps and bounds in recent two decades.[25] Citing Samuel Huntington, he suspects if cultural similarities can really be a driving force for further integration. He further argues that despite the economic collaborations and more frequent exchanges, the two sides have fundamental differences in political culture that actually drive the two populations apart. Taiwan citizens harbor a new value system that emphasizes individualism, indigenization, and a Western lifestyle as a result of democratization and development of civil society. On the other side of the Strait, thanks to the economic growth and strengthening of industrial and military capabilities, their counterparts embrace neo-collectivism (in which both collective and newly "transplanted" private ownership are equally important) and nationalism or neo-patriotism, bolstering a new superpower image of China.[26] He concludes that the identity and mindset differences will likely not render the political integration solutions amenable to Taiwan citizens. In another study, Keng cites survey data on Taiwanese identification and contends that economic favors or carrots through preferential trade benefits from the China side can hardly change the "heart" of the Taiwan public in terms of preference for future independence or unification, party support, or Taiwanese identity.[27] Using Beijing's agricultural trade concessions offered to Taiwan as a case, Wong and Wu also empirically show that the trade concessions had no effect on voting behavior in Taiwan. In other words, the public in Taiwan is still apprehensive about political integration despite more favorable economic and trade benefits.[28] Such a skepticism is an aggregation of individual sentiments toward China.

CASE STUDIES: ECONOMIC INTEGRATION WITH CHINA IN TAIWAN AND HONG KONG

Taiwan and Hong Kong are comparable in many respects. Despite the regime disparities (Taiwan being a full democracy, Hong Kong a semi-democracy), both are rooted in Confucian values using the same traditional Chinese language. The two societies have similar historical experience of authoritarian rule but enjoy relatively free markets owing to the capitalist economic structure and strong connections with the West, in particular the United States. Taiwan and Hong Kong share many commonalties in social, cultural, and economic profiles except political developments.

Democratization

Democratization in Taiwan started in late 1980s when the ruling Kuomintang (KMT) government lifted the martial law that had been imposed since 1949. Opposition parties or formerly called *Tangwei* (outside the KMT party) were allowed to register and field candidates to run in elections. Direct and full elections were later introduced to all levels of government, including local councils, mayoral offices, and the Legislative Yuan. In 1996, universal suffrage was extended to the election of the highest political office: the president. Four years later, long-time opposition Democratic Progressive Party (DPP) candidate Chen Shui-bian was elected in the 2000 presidential election and for the first time realized the power transition in a peaceful and democratic manner. Taiwan has since been considered a full-fledged democracy with the two parties alternating control of the presidential office and legislature.

Hong Kong's democracy started to develop also in the 1980s but experienced a much more "tortuous" or convoluted route.[29] After the 1984 Sino-British Joint Declaration pronouncing the decision to return Hong Kong to China in 1997, the British government embarked on a series of political reforms to introduce more democratic, direct elections at different levels of councils in a move parallel to phasing out appointed representatives or councilors. The Chinese government, however, was strongly opposed to the British plan of "expedited" democratization in the city soon to be under its sovereignty. Casting doubt on the motivations of the then Hong Kong British Governor Chris Patten, Beijing insisted a moderate and gradual plan be adopted. As a consequence, the Chinese government appointed a provisional legislature to replace the last Hong Kong legislative council at the 1997 transition and declared its own plan of democratization. After much procrastination in the last two decades, the franchise is extended to only half of the legislature, and the rest is elected indirectly from professional constituencies adapted from the colonial days.

Economic Integration

In the economic dimension, both Taiwan and Hong Kong have a high volume of trade exchanges with China. For the former, major breakthroughs took place in the early 2000s under the DPP President Chen Shui-bian despite his party's pro-independence agenda. Departing from the former KMT cautious policy, the new administration lifted the restrictions on investment in mainland China and implemented a series of reforms allowing development of closer economic ties with the mainland.[30] Within a few years, the investments surged in both volume and dollar amounts by multiple folds. Official data suggested Taiwan projects rose from about US $200 million per year in 1991, to close to US $3 billion in 2002. Actual investments could have ascended to nearly US $100 billion.[31] During the eight years under the Chen administration, China became one of the major investment markets for Taiwan industrialists. In 2008, the KMT returned to power under President Ma Ying-jeou and shortly thereafter inaugurated the "Three Direct Links" policy, setting the stage for further economic cooperation with mainland China.[32] Among the most influential has been the resumption of direct flights across the Strait after decades of indirect transportations mostly via Hong Kong. In 2010, the two sides signed the Economic Cooperation Framework Agreement (ECFA), beginning to remove tariffs to allow freer trade of goods.

Immediate impacts include surging trade and blooming tourism. For the former, during the Ma administration (2008–2015), the figure grew more than double, accounting for 27 percent and 20 percent of Taiwan's entire export and import volume, respectively. Taiwan's annual economic growth during this period was on average about three percent.[33] In terms of tourism, number of mainland visitors to Taiwan increased by tenfold (from 329, 204 in 2008 to over 4 million in 2015) within the eight years under the Ma administration.[34] For every three tourists, one is from mainland China. Considering benefits of economic integration with mainland China, the tourism-related or consumer service industries enjoy the best share. In the first few years, the public was optimistic about opening more exchanges between the two economies and societies, and the sentiment is primarily driven by workers in these industries.

Hong Kong's close economic ties with China were deemed natural due to the vicinity and most importantly the sovereignty transition. The background of such development was, however, quite different from that of Taiwan. After the 1997 turnover, the city suffered a period of economic malaise due to a series of events including the Asian financial crisis (1997–1978), World Trade Center terror attack ("911 terror attack," 2001), and the Severe Acute Respiratory Syndrome (SARS) epidemic (2003). The free trade agreement titled "Closer Economic Partnership Arrangement" (CEPA) was introduced in 2003 as part of a remedy to the ailing Hong Kong economy.[35] The CEPA was designed to provide Hong Kong investors primarily tariff advantages in mainland markets. Since its introduction, Hong Kong's economy has become more and more dependent on China in terms of capital investment to sustain its economic growth.

Like the ECFA in Taiwan, the Hong Kong economy benefits from the CEPA mostly on the mainland tourists. The dramatic surge occurred after 2003, as visitors from across the border accounted for three-quarters of the all tourists in 2016, compared to 41.2 percent in 2002. By number, there were 42.7 million mainland visitors as of 2016, which is six times the city's population.[36] By contrast, the 3.5 million mainland visitors to Taiwan in the same year only account for about one-seventh of the island's population.

To the Hong Kong population, a more complex issue is the mainland immigrants. The so-called "one-way permit" immigration scheme unilaterally issued by China brings in 150 mainlanders to Hong Kong on a daily basis. In other words, about 54,000 permanent Chinese immigrants are added to the already densely populated city every year. These new Chinese immigrants account for around one percent increase of the Hong Kong population annually, which is roughly nine times more than the Taiwanese figure.[37] Most of these immigrants are less skilled workers with generally lower educational backgrounds.[38] They are predominantly employed in low-skilled service industries and in need of public housing. The high volume of tourist visits transformed and homogenized the retail businesses to providing goods primarily catered for mainland visitors such as formula powder, jewelry, and luxury goods. The influx of mainland immigrants also exacerbates the city's housing problem as citizens are already paying for the highest housing cost or most unaffordable apartments in the world (Affordable Housing Index: 19 in 2016[39]).

Within a few years of implementation, CEPA brought quick growth of Chinese investments in Hong Kong and soon recovery to the city's once frail economy.[40] This, however, has come at a high price of introducing China's permeating influence into Hong Kong's institutions and nearly all walks of life.[41] Such development has also been responsible for the public's gradual discord with the central government of China and consequent separatist sentiments among the deprived class, in particular the younger generations.

Sunflower Movement in Taiwan and Umbrella Movement in Hong Kong

In Taiwan, public opinion opposed to the signing of ECFA mounted rapidly in 2013, especially among younger citizens who suspected the trade pact was actually part of a unification scheme conspired by the KMT and China. In 2014, the agreement's second stage Cross-Strait Service Trade Agreement (CSSTA) focusing on services was proposed to the Legislative Yuan for ratification but was met with tremendous opposition from the DPP and protestors from the local activists and college students. Their demonstrations later escalated into occupying the Legislative Yuan building to prevent the Taiwan parliament from passing any bills, including CSSTA. The later-called Sunflower Movement lasted for almost a month. Yet, the repercussions reverberated throughout later elections in Taiwan and similar movements in Hong Kong.

On the heels of the Sunflower Movement, Hong Kong protestors followed suit and started a series of demonstrations also targeting mainland China. This time, they were after a different cause. In protest of Beijing's decision of imposing "draconian" restraints on the upcoming elections, student demonstrators started taking over a government building plaza, followed by a series of protests occupying some of the city's major downtown crossroads and driveways. The Umbrella Movement spread the occupations to multiple locations for over two months, albeit with concessions from neither Beijing nor the Hong Kong government.

Compared to the Sunflower Movement, which prevented the government from closer trade pacts or economic integration with China, the Umbrella Movement fell short of achieving any responsive action from the Hong Kong government or Beijing. The two movements, however, contributed to the rise of new political groups or parties pursuing more "localist" causes or disintegration from China. These parties distinguish themselves from major political parties and promote new agenda demanding self-determination, higher autonomy, or full-fledged national independence. These are the causes that appeal to the "vulnerable" groups composed of younger voters or the most deprived in the age of globalization and economic integration with China. These parties represent the "localism" camp in Hong Kong and the comparable "Third Force" camp in Taiwan.

RESEARCH DESIGN AND DATA

In the model proposed by Alesina et al., freer trade or economic integration leads to separatism. Trading partners will weigh a number of factors when determining whether to join a union or remain sovereign. This calculus is aggregation of individual preferences. Economic integration of Taiwan and Hong Kong with mainland China provides an excellent case for testing the proposition of Alesina et al. Employing the data from the 2016 TEDS survey and the 2016 HKES survey, we can make the models more comparable using data collected from the two legislative elections conducted in the same year. We extract the variables measuring identity of being China in general and benefits of closer trade specifically to test if economic integration leads to sentiments supporting disintegration. We develop the hypotheses as follows:

Hypothesis 1: *More free trade leads to more perceived deprivations.*
Hypothesis 2: *More free trade leads to greater support for disintegration.*
Hypothesis 3: *Younger voters are more supportive of disintegration.*

To put the hypotheses to the empirical test, we operationalize the perception of free trade and support for disintegration using the following questions from the surveys:

1. Political disintegration
   There are no direct or explicit measurements of integration or separatism in both Taiwan and Hong Kong. Instead, we employ the variable of support for pro-independence parties as measurement. In the case of Taiwan, since the Democratic Progressive Party (DPP) is allegedly assuming the position of maintaining the status quo in place of the outgoing Kuomintang (KMT) government, the more outspoken pro-independence party is the new New Power Party (NPP), which positions itself further away from middle-of-the-road status-quo choice, promoting full independence. Its counterpart in Hong Kong is a variety of smaller, new parties under the label of localism. This group of parties takes on positions ranging from self-determination promoting referendum for the city's future to building a fully independent state.
   Namely,
   In Taiwan (2016 TEDS data):
   Support for New Power Party and the "Third Force" camp
   In Hong Kong (2016 HKES data):
   Support for localism camp (e.g. Youngspiration, Demosisto, Hong Kong Indigenous or Civic Passion)
2. Independent variables

   a. "China factor"
      We operationalize the "China factor" by examining the public perception of economic integration with China and evaluations of economy. The variables are created using the following questions:
      In Taiwan (2016 TEDS data):
      After 2008, the cross-Strait economic interactions have intensified. As a result of this, do you think Taiwan's/personal economy has gotten better, worse, or is about the same?
      In Hong Kong (2016 HKES data):
      As a result of increasing economic interactions between mainland and Hong Kong, do you think economy/personal finance has gotten better, worse, or is about the same?

b. Chinese identity versus local Hong Kong/Taiwanese identity
In Taiwan (2016 TEDS data):
In Taiwan, some people think they are Taiwanese. There are also some people who think that they are Chinese. Do you consider yourself as Taiwanese, Chinese, or both?
In Hong Kong (2016 HKES data):
Generally speaking, do you think of yourself as a Hong Konger, Chinese, Hong Kong Chinese, or something else?

In the following section, we analyze the aggregate data in Taiwan and Hong Kong, followed by multivariate models using the voting support for localist party (Hong Kong) or New Power Party (Taiwan) as dependent variables.

ANALYSIS

Freer trade and political separatism go hand in hand, according to Alesina and his co-investigators. For Hong Kong citizens and the Taiwanese, more trade with China and more frequent interactions with mainland Chinese have been part of their lives. After about eight years of "Three Direct Links" and ECFA, whether the economy improves or worsens cannot be easily attributed to the China factor. The 2016 TEDS survey taps into Taiwanese personal perceptions and suggests an ambiguous answer. A slight majority (about 52 percent) thought the economy has been the same, and opinions on either better or worse are not seeing a winner, even though the worse side receives a bit higher support (26 percent versus 23 percent). Respondents in the HKES survey who have longer experience with mainland Chinese (13 years), however, give a different picture: close to 50 percent thought the economy has deteriorated, and only about one out of five felt it is better (see Fig. 6.1). Another 30 percent responded "no difference."

In terms of the identity relative to the concept of "being Chinese," Taiwan and Hong Kong citizens share similar patterns on recognizing a local identity over the last two decades. In the former case, almost 60 percent of Taiwan citizens call themselves "Taiwanese" over the label of "Chinese" or "Both." The ratio was even more pronounced in Hong Kong: almost 70 percent claim themselves to be "Hong Konger" versus others (see Fig. 6.2). The identity of Chinese (or both Chinese and Taiwanese, or both Chinese and "Hong Konger") has been in decline in both societies since the beginning of the 2000s.

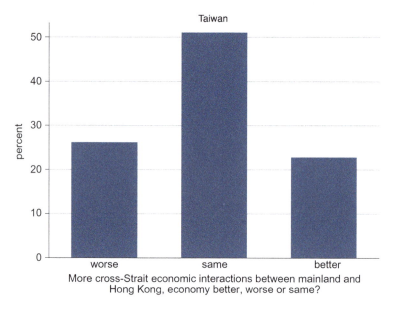
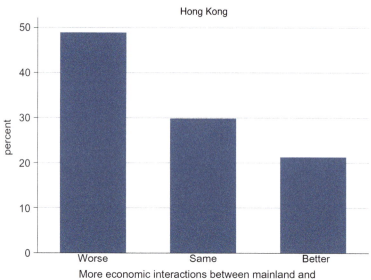

Fig. 6.1 Economic integration: Better, same, or worse for economy? Taiwan and Hong Kong

A COMPARATIVE STUDY OF THE CHINA FACTOR IN TAIWAN... 135

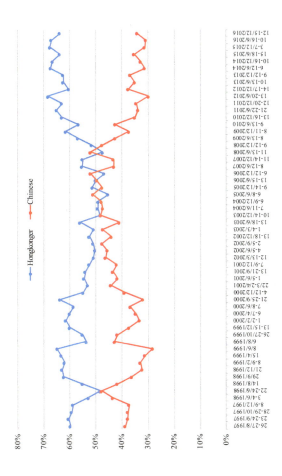

Fig. 6.2 Hong Konger and Chinese identities, 1997–2016 (Source: Public Opinion Programme, The University of Hong Kong (https://www.hkupop.hku.hk/english/popexpress/ethnic/eidentity/poll/datatables.html)

Table 6.1 "Third Force" new voters in 2016 Hong Kong and Taiwan elections

	Localism voter in Hong Kong	Third Force voters in Taiwan	DPP voters in Taiwan
Trade with China better econ. (personal)	−0.115*	0.134	−0.272*
	(0.069)	(0.213)	(0.160)
Support localist parties/NPP	0.828***	1.640***	0.994***
	(0.178)	(0.355)	(0.366)
Localist/DPP parties best in most important issues	0.370**	0.382*	1.115***
	(0.172)	(0.206)	(0.153)
Cantonese/Minnan	0.159**	0.359	0.305*
	(0.079)	(0.227)	(0.160)
Age	−0.0140**	−0.0394***	0.0112**
	(0.006)	(0.007)	(0.004)
Identity (Hong Konger/Taiwanese)	0.362**	0.429*	0.642***
	(0.152)	(0.229)	(0.152)
Support for pan-democrats/DPP	0.457***	0.042	1.868***
	(0.170)	(0.225)	(0.162)
Image of localist candidates/Tsai	0.227***	0.113**	0.430***
	(0.031)	(0.053)	(0.040)
Constant	−4.081***	−2.528***	−4.612***
	(0.315)	(0.648)	(0.493)
Observations	4148	1690	1690
Pseudo R²	0.120	0.114	0.428

Standard errors in parentheses; ***$p < 0.01$, **$p < 0.05$, *$p < 0.1$

To put these variables in perspective, we develop a model of the new parties' supporters in both Taiwan and Hong Kong (see Table 6.1). The dependent variable is the vote for new parties in the camp of so-called "The Third Force or Third Power" in Taiwan and the localism camp in Hong Kong. Interestingly, the binary logit results exhibit two very similar profiles:

- In the Hong Kong case (column 1), these "new voters" are young, strong supporters of localist parties and self-asserting Hong Kongers. They embrace the local dialect as their mother tongue and reject more trade with China (at least under current treaties).

- The Taiwan "new voters" are also younger (column 2), demonstrating strong support of Third Force parties such as NPP and self-identifying as Taiwanese.

We also include the DPP/Tsai voting intention model for comparisons. Compared to others, DPP supporters are the strongest in disapproval of trade with China and highly comparable to the Hong Kong "new voters" in terms of identity, language, and "local" culture. Supporters of the Third Force could likely pool their support for Tsai Ing-wen in lieu of an NPP candidate, for instance.[42] However, compared to the Hong Kong context in which the pan-democrats often face cutthroat competitions from localist opponents, the DPP and Third Force are more often in collaboration with or in complement of each other. That deals volatility to the estimates in the Taiwan Third Force model.

Clearly, age is inversely related to support of liberalization of trade with China, echoing the observations that the two "occupy" movements are action statements for the students and younger citizens in Taiwan and Hong Kong. They perceived economic integration with China as a threat to their localist values and identities. To these young citizens, some could be first-time voters or first-time party supporters. Partisanship cannot explain the vote as much as loyal KMT or DPP supporters voting for their parties. Taiwan's Third Force parties or localist parties in Hong Kong are too new to establish personal connection or provide party benefits or patronage to members, if there are any. This provides further supportive evidence of the China factor in Hypotheses 2 and 3, suggesting young people are casting their votes out of skepticism toward economic integration.

Conclusion and Discussions

Alesina's political economy models predict that trade openness in globalized market entails political disintegration. Smaller and democratic countries face the tradeoff between trade benefits, cultural heterogeneity, and, more importantly, sovereignty and national identity. They could more likely choose separation from the union to keep public goods close to local population's preference even if interests from free trade could outweigh sacrifices of local culture and identities. In this study, we get insights from a comparative study of Hong Kong and Taiwan: both are small economies adjacent to China and subject to globalization influences and high economic growth "gravitational" force from the supersize neighbor. From newly collected public opinion data we learn that Hong Kong and Taiwan are standing in different phrases of economic integration but are pulled in the same direction by the same force. Both are facing the important decision of whether to integrate or not integrate. In the case of Hong Kong, China's integrative effort is deep and ubiquitous.[43] At times, strong interventions such as the controversies in electoral reform to couple universal suffrage elections with Beijing-endorsed nominations have induced strong reactions, particularly among the younger voters.

The Taiwanese citizens are also facing similar dilemmas, including how to build bilateral trade relations with interdependence versus overdependence. It will be costly for Taiwan to stay isolated in the face of rapid economic growth of China. Yet, getting too close may not be politically viable given the high opportunity cost of autonomy and sovereignty. The tension can spread wide if redistribution of income resulting from freer trade barely achieves general satisfaction from benefits of economic growth. Externalities such as more acute income inequalities and structural shift of manufacturing sectors further sabotage the public's faith in government, especially among more vulnerable groups such as students, the unemployed, and workers from sunset industries.

The Brexit experience sheds new light on the externalities equation. Consider union-imposed immigration as a policy outcome, citizens in member states will ignore the benefits from economic integration when they feel a sense of relative deprivation in relation to immigrants. That apprehension was amplified through the campaigns from the UKIP and a few Conservative leaders like Boris Johnson, who won support from the voters who felt "left behind" in the immigration policy choice. They later became determined to voice their say of "leave" in the Brexit referendum.[44] Immigration—in particular the imposition of such policy on member states—is the driver of Euroskeptism.[45] That situation resonates well in the general public perceptions among the younger voters in Hong Kong and Taiwan.

Comparing Taiwan and Hong Kong, political and party systems matter when policy outcome is concerned. In Taiwan, the general public can have viable options to channel policy preferences or oppositions and even unseat the governing party in democratic elections. In contrast, Hong Kong dissidents have little choice except pooling support for radical political propositions. From this study, we learn that the institutional setting is probably among the most important factors to facilitate integration efforts. Member states can more likely reach policy equilibrium with the union when the institutional discrepancies become smaller. Trade liberalization is conducive to political disintegration starting at the micro level. In the context of Taiwan, the democratic system protects public choice from external impositions. In contrast, Hong Kong has little control over integration-oriented policies and, hence, polarizing society, with the younger generation resorting to radical propositions and political actions at one end and the older generation upholding establishment or traditional protest-style opposition parties at the other. Future research in developing a fully structural model is warranted. As more data will be collected, future projects should target systematic study of perception of China at the micro-level and longitudinal studies of impact of immigration and identity evolution.

Notes

1. Thomas L. Friedman, *The world is flat: A brief history of the twenty-first century* (CITY: Macmillan, 2005); Andreas Bergh and Therese Nilsson, "Do liberalization and globalization increase income inequality?" *European Journal of Political Economy* 26, no. 4 (2010): 488–505.
2. Alesina, Alberto, Enrico Spolaore, and Romain Wacziarg. Economic integration and political disintegration. No. w6163. *National Bureau of Economic Research*, 1997; Alberto, Spolaore, and Wacziarg, "Economic Integration," 1276–1296; Michele Ruta, "Economic theories of political (dis)integration," *Journal of Economic Surveys* 19, no. 1 (2005): 1–21.
3. The term "political integration" covers a wide spectrum of "union" forms, including full unification on one end and loose community or regional bloc-based or common institutions on the other. In the case of Taiwan, integration could be in the form ranging from joining the PRC to becoming one country following the Hong Kong model under "one country, two systems" to a loose unionization adopting or adapting the Europe Common Market or European Community model. In this study, we do not limit our definition of political integration to any form but point to a general direction toward closer cooperation or agglomeration through common institutional developments.
4. Alesina, Spolaore, and Wacziarg, "Economic Integration," 1276.
5. Ruta, "Economic theories," 1–21.
6. Harold D. Clarke, Matthew Goodwin, and Paul Whiteley, *Brexit: Why Britain Voted to Leave the European Union* (Cambridge: Cambridge University Press, 2017).

7. According to the trade pact, Taiwan would enjoy a tariff cut as much as $14 billion on 539 exports to China, and corresponding figures for China would be $3 billion and 267 exports. (See the BBC report titled "Historic Taiwan-China trade deal takes effect," http://www.bbc.com/news/world-asia-pacific-11275274. See also Republic of China Mainland Affair Council document titled, "Economic Cooperation Framework Agreement (ECFA) Background," http://www.mac.gov.tw/public/data/051116322071.pdf.)
8. Alesina, Spolaore, and Wacziarg, "Economic Integration," 1291–2.
9. Patrick Bolton and Gerard Roland, "The breakup of nations: a political economy analysis," *The Quarterly Journal of Economics* 112, no. 4 (1997): 1057–1090.
10. Lloyd Gruber, "Globalization."
11. Michele Ruta, "Economic theories," 2.
12. Alesina, Alberto, Enrico Spolaore, and Romain Wacziarg. Economic integration and political disintegration. No. w6163. *National Bureau of Economic Research*, 1997; Alberto, Spolaore, and Wacziarg, "Economic Integration," 1276–1296.
13. Alessandra Casella and Jonathan S. Feinstein, "Public goods in trade: on the formation of markets and jurisdictions," *International Economic Review* (2002): 437–462.
14. Patrick Bolton and Gerard Roland, "Distributional conflicts, factor mobility, and political integration," *The American Economic Review* 86, no. 2 (1996): 99–104.
15. Alberto Alesina and Enrico Spolaore, "War, peace, and the size of countries," *Journal of Public Economics* 89, no. 7 (2005): 1333–1354; Ruta, "Economic theories," 1–21.
16. Enrico Spolaore and Alberto Alesina, *War, peace and the size of countries* (Cambridge: Harvard Institute of Economic Research, Harvard University, 2001).
17. Ruta, "Economic theories," 1–21.
18. Federico Etro, "International policy coordination with economic unions," *Rivista Internazionale di Scienze Sociali* (2002): 187–211.
19. Alberto Alesina and Enrico Spolaore, *The size of nations* (Cambridge: MIT Press, 2003).
20. Clarke, Goodwin, and Whiteley, *Brexit*.
21. Alesina, Spolaore, and Wacziarg, "Economic Integration," 1293.
22. Alesina, Alberto, Enrico Spolaore, and Romain Wacziarg. Economic integration and political disintegration. No. w6163. *National Bureau of Economic Research*, 1997.

23. Ruta, "Economic theories," 13; Alberto Alesina and Enrico Spolaore, "On the Number and Size of Nations," *The Quarterly Journal of Economics* 112, no. 4 (1997): 1027–056.
24. Robert P. Inman and Daniel L. Rubinfeld, "Rethinking federalism," *The Journal of Economic Perspectives* 11, no. 4 (1997): 43–64; Ruta, "Economic theories," 1–21.
25. Chien-min Chao, "Will economic integration between mainland China and Taiwan lead to a congenial political culture?" *Asian Survey* 43, no. 2 (2003): 280–304.
26. Chao, "Will Economic Integration," 302.
27. S. Keng, "Limitations on China's economic statecraft: China's favor-granting policies and their political implications," *Issues and Studies* 48, no. 3 (2009): 1–32; S. Keng, "Understanding integration and 'spillover' across the Taiwan Strait: Towards an analytical framework," *Taiwanese Identity in the Twenty-first Century: Domestic, Regional and Global Perspectives* (2011): 155–175.
28. Stan Hok-wui Wong and Nicole Wu, "Can Beijing Buy Taiwan? An empirical assessment of Beijing's agricultural trade concessions to Taiwan," *Journal of Contemporary China* 25, no. 99 (2016): 353–371.
29. Ming Sing, "Hong Kong's Tortuous Democratisation, op. cit.," *Hsin-chi Kuan, Power Dependence and Democratic Transition: The Case of Hong Kong, The China Quarterly* 128 (1991): 774–793; Stan Hok-wui Wong, "Real estate elite, economic development, and political conflicts in postcolonial Hong Kong," *China Review* 15, no. 1 (2015): 1–38.
30. Wei-chin Lee and Te-Yu Wang, eds., *Sayonara to the Lee Teng-hui era: Politics in Taiwan, 1988–2000* (University Press of America, 2003).
31. Wei-chin Lee, "The Buck Starts Here: Cross-Strait Economic Transactions and Taiwan's Domestic Politics," *American Asian Review* 21, no. 3 (2003): 107.
32. The policy includes opening up direct mail, transportation and trade exchanges between the PRC and ROC Taiwan, according to the Mainland Affairs Council, ROC Taiwan (http://www.mac.gov.tw/en/News_Content.aspx?n=AEC54CE1BB842CD0&sms=7C0CA8982E163402&s=A514E2F510401BC1).
33. According to the Republic of China (Taiwan) National Statistics website, (http://eng.stat.gov.tw/public/data/dgbas03/bs4/ninews_e/10411/enewtotal10411.pdf).
34. According to the Republic of China (Taiwan) Tourism Bureau, Ministry of Transportation and Communication (http://stat.taiwan.net.tw/system/country_years_arrival.html).

35. Yun-wing Sung, "A comparison between the CEPA and the ECFA," *Economic Integration Across the Taiwan Strait: Global Perspectives* (2013): 30.
36. Stan Hok Wui Wong, Kuan-chen Lee, Karl Ho, and Harold D. Clarke, "Regional Socio-economic Integration and Vote Choice of Young People: A Comparative Case Study of Hong Kong and Taiwan," paper presented at the Midwest Political Science Association Annual meeting, Chicago, IL, April 2017.
37. Wong, Lee, Ho, and Clarke, "Regional Socio-economic Integration."
38. Stephen WK Chiu and Tai-lok Lui, "Testing the global city-social polarisation thesis: Hong Kong since the 1990s," *Urban Studies* 41, no. 10 (2004): 1863–1888.
39. According to the 12th Annual Demographia International Housing Affordability Survey (2016), the index is a ratio of average house price and annual income. In the Hong Kong case, an average apartment price is 19 times the citizens' average annual income.
40. Cheng Hsiao, H. Steve Ching, and Shui Ki Wan, "A panel data approach for program evaluation: measuring the benefits of political and economic integration of Hong kong with mainland China," *Journal of Applied Econometrics* 27, no. 5 (2012): 705–740.
41. David A. Rezvani, "Dead autonomy, a thousand cuts or partial independence? The autonomous status of Hong Kong," *Journal of Contemporary Asia* 42, no. 1 (2012): 93–122; Stan Hok-wui Wong, "Real estate elite, economic development, and political conflicts in postcolonial Hong Kong," *China Review* 15, no. 1 (2015): 1–38.
42. For comparison purpose, we did not include the independence/unification variable, but such issue positions can be estimated through the party or leader support variable in the Taiwan case.
43. Rezvani, "Dead autonomy," 93–122.
44. Clarke, Goodwin, and Whiteley. *Brexit.*
45. Clarke, Goodwin, and Whiteley. *Brexit*, 222.

BIBLIOGRAPHY

Alesina, Alberto, and Enrico Spolaore. 1997. On the Number and Size of Nations. *The Quarterly Journal of Economics* 112 (4): 1027–1056.
———. 2003. *The Size of Nations.* Cambridge: MIT Press.
———. 2005. War, Peace, and the Size of Countries. *Journal of Public Economics* 89 (7): 1333–1354.
Alesina, Alberto, Enrico Spolaore, and Romain Wacziarg. 1997. Economic Integration and Political Disintegration. No. w6163. *National Bureau of Economic Research*.

———. 2000. Economic Integration and Political Disintegration. *American Economic Review* 90 (5): 1276–1296.
Bergh, Andreas, and Therese Nilsson. 2010. Do Liberalization and Globalization Increase Income Inequality? *European Journal of Political Economy* 26 (4): 488–505.
Bolton, Patrick, and Gerard Roland. 1996. Distributional Conflicts, Factor Mobility, and Political Integration. *The American Economic Review* 86 (2): 99–104.
———. 1997. The Breakup of Nations: A Political Economy Analysis. *The Quarterly Journal of Economics* 112 (4): 1057–1090.
Chao, Chien-min. 2003. Will Economic Integration Between Mainland China and Taiwan Lead to a Congenial Political Culture? *Asian Survey* 43 (2): 280–304.
Chow, Peter C.Y., ed. 2013. *Economic Integration Across the Taiwan Strait: Global Perspectives*. Cheltenham: Edward Elgar Publishing.
Clarke, Harold D., Matthew Goodwin, and Paul Whiteley. 2017. *Brexit: Why Britain Voted to Leave the European Union*. Cambridge: Cambridge University Press.
Etro, Federico. 2002. International Policy Coordination with Economic Unions. *Rivista Internazionale di Scienze Sociali* 110 (2): 187–211.
Friedman, Thomas L. 2005. *The World Is Flat: A Brief History of the Twenty-first Century*. New York: Macmillan.
Gruber, Lloyd. 2015. Globalization and Domestic Politics: A Call for Theoretical Reorientation. In *Local Politics, Global Impacts: Steps to a Multi-disciplinary Analysis of Scales*, ed. Olivier Charnoz, Virginie Diaz Pedregal, and Alan L. Kolata. Farnham: Ashgate Publishing, Ltd.
Hsiao, Cheng, H. Steve Ching, and Shui Ki Wan. 2012. A Panel Data Approach for Program Evaluation: Measuring the Benefits of Political and Economic Integration of Hong Kong with Mainland China. *Journal of Applied Econometrics* 27 (5): 705–740.
Inman, Robert P., and Daniel L. Rubinfeld. 1997. Rethinking Federalism. *The Journal of Economic Perspectives* 11 (4): 43–64.
Keng, S. 2009. Limitations on China's Economic Statecraft: China's Favor-Granting Policies and Their Political Implications. *Issues and Studies* 48 (3): 1–32.
———. 2011. Understanding Integration and 'Spillover' Across the Taiwan Strait: Towards an Analytical Framework. In *Taiwanese Identity in the Twenty-first Century: Domestic, Regional and Global Perspectives*, 155–175.
Lee, Wei-chin, and Te-Yu Wang, eds. 2003. *Sayonara to the Lee Teng-hui Era: Politics in Taiwan, 1988–2000*. Lanham: University Press of America.
Rezvani, David A. 2012. Dead Autonomy, A Thousand Cuts or Partial Independence? The Autonomous Status of Hong Kong. *Journal of Contemporary Asia* 42 (1): 93–122.

Ruta, Michele. 2005. Economic Theories of Political (Dis) Integration. *Journal of Economic Surveys* 19 (1): 1–21.

Schubert, Gunter, and Jens Damm, eds. 2012. *Taiwanese Identity in the 21st Century: Domestic, Regional and Global Perspectives*. Vol. 5. Abingdon and New York: Routledge.

Sing, Ming. 1991. Hong Kong's Tortuous Democratisation, op. cit. *Hsin-chi Kuan, Power Dependence and Democratic Transition: The Case of Hong Kong, The China Quarterly* 128: 774–793.

Sung, Yun-wing. 2013. A Comparison Between the CEPA and the ECFA. In *Economic Integration Across the Taiwan Strait: Global Perspectives*, ed. P.C.Y. Chow, 30–55. Cheltenham: Edward Elgar.

Wei-chin, Lee. 2003. The Buck Starts Here: Cross-Strait Economic Transactions and Taiwan's Domestic Politics. *American Asian Review* 21 (3): 107.

Wong, Stan Hok-wui. 2012. Authoritarian Co-optation in the Age of Globalisation: Evidence from Hong Kong. *Journal of Contemporary Asia* 42 (2): 182–209.

———. 2015a. *Electoral Politics in Post-1997 Hong Kong*. Singapore: Springer.

———. 2015b. Real Estate Elite Economic Development, and Political Conflicts in Postcolonial Hong Kong. *The China Review* 15 (1): 1–38.

Wong, Stan Hok-wui, and Wu Nicole. 2016. Can Beijing Buy Taiwan? An Empirical Assessment of Beijing's Agricultural Trade Concessions to Taiwan. *Journal of Contemporary China* 25 (99): 353–371.

Wong, Stan Hok-Wui, Ngok Ma, and Wai-man Lam. 2016. Migrants and Democratization: The Political Economy of Chinese Immigrants in Hong Kong. *Contemporary Chinese Political Economy and Strategic Relations* 2 (2): 909.

Wong, Stan Hok Wui, Kuan-chen Lee, Karl Ho and Harold D. Clarke. 2017. *Regional Socio-economic Integration and Vote Choice of Young People: A Comparative Case Study of Hong Kong and Taiwan*. Paper Presented at the 2017 Midwest Political Science Association Annual meeting. Chicago.

CHAPTER 7

Consensus Found and Consensus Lost: Taiwan's 2016 Election, the "1992 Consensus," and Cross-Strait Relations

Wei-chin Lee

Among the electoral campaign slogans and policies appealing for voters' support in the 2016 elections, one issue dominating significant space in media coverage and debates has been the "1992 Consensus." The Nationalist Party (Kuomintang, KMT) has firmly asserted the Consensus as the ultimate foundation for smooth and productive cross-Strait relations. On the contrary, the Democratic Progressive Party (DPP), the largest opposition party prior to the 2016 elections, has constantly challenged the origin and utility of the Consensus. The debate about the 1992 Consensus is a classical display of identity politics that implies an uneasy settling of the collective mindset in charting Taiwan's political future. These divergent identity affiliations in Taiwan, which rely on an emotional sense of belonging and discourse simplification, operate as electoral coalitions working in tandem to obfuscate reality for voters' choices. In the case of

W.-c. Lee (✉)
Department of Politics and International Affairs, Wake Forest University, Winston-Salem, NC, USA

© The Author(s) 2019
W.-c. Lee (ed.), *Taiwan's Political Re-Alignment and Diplomatic Challenges*, Politics and Development of Contemporary China, https://doi.org/10.1007/978-3-319-77125-0_7

the 2016 elections, the tug of war of campaign slogans and narrative propositions between the KMT and the DPP not only provides an interesting examination of major parties' agenda setting and policy direction but also offers a splendid opportunity to see each contender's manipulation of and navigation through the political juggernaut of identity politics and cross-Strait relations. This study begins with a brief genesis of the 1992 Consensus and its distinctive features, followed by an analysis of the campaign agendas and policy stances of both the KMT and the DPP, and ends the discussion with implications for our understanding of Taiwan's identity trend and future cross-Strait relations.

THE GENESIS OF THE "1992 CONSENSUS" FOR CROSS-STRAIT RELATIONS

Taiwan's loss of the UN seat in 1971 to China (People's Republic of China, PRC) was the first major blow to the Republic of China (ROC), diminishing Taiwan's status in the international community. The US switch of recognition from Taiwan to China in 1979 was an additional hit to Taiwan's role as a solid state member in intergovernmental organizations (IGOs), including major economic organizations like the International Monetary Fund (IMF) and the International Bank for Reconstruction and Development (IBRD).[1] China's steady ascent on the world stage meant the shrinking number of Taiwan's IGO affiliations, from 39 in the 1960s to a meager 10 by 1977. Taiwan was concerned that the inability to maintain a visible international profile in the early 1990s might affect its vibrant trade-oriented economic performance.[2]

Several points for consideration took place in the early 1990s. First, as Taiwan's democratization in the late 1980s began to step up its pace and scope, the former ruling establishment and rising opponents had to begin competing for electoral support through populist appeals by advocating disparate nationalistic goals for Taiwan's future status. Taiwan's democratization ended the governmental monopoly on power and ideological systematization and unleashed the force of mass nationalism in a competitive political atmosphere full of prolific ideas and agendas. Aspiring political entrepreneurs hence advocated and politicized Taiwanese indigenous nationalism. At the beginning, they emphasized an ethno-centric notion of primordialism over and against the preceding "China-centered" social constructs in order to broaden their vote shares and electoral approval.[3]

Each contending group tried to carve out a political market niche for targeted constituencies rather than share power for segmental distinction and differentiation in electoral competition. While ethno-nationalism had long existed in Taiwan, the urge to win the majority support of ethnic Taiwanese made politicians adopt identity appeals as a powerful tool for political mobilization between parties, the KMT and the DPP. Each party has since projected its own vision of Taiwan's future relations with China, either unification or independence, to convince voters. The ruling government's identity propositions accordingly have affected Taiwan's cross-Strait policy toward China.

Second, Taiwan fully understood China's accumulating political weight in stifling Taiwan's international space and China's abundant labor force, promising market potential, and rich resources essential for Taiwan's economic growth. Hence, Taiwan eagerly sought a delicate balance between how to resist China's political reunification intent on the one hand and how to reap copious benefits from China via cross-Strait economic interactions on the other hand. Put simply, Taiwan's high degree of economic dependence on China carried political risks of vulnerability and sensitivity. Still, geographic proximity, similar cultural traits, and economic complementarity with China made it impossible to ignore China's existence for Taiwan's economic sustainability. Taiwan has had to find a golden mean without being sucked into the extreme on either side.

Third, although Taiwan has remained close to the US in an informal security cooperation after learning painful lessons of US abandonment in both 1972 and 1979, the lack of an alliance treaty and the implicit nature of the US security guarantee led Taiwan to prepare for future potential setbacks, should China's waxing weight tip the US self-strategic calculation and policy priority unfavorably to Taiwan. Thus, the ever-present fear of US abandonment prompted Taiwan to look deep and hard at the option of engagement with China as a preventive mechanism to mitigate China's military threat.[4] The subtlety rested in how to ensure that the US would not construe Taiwan's engagement with China as a betrayal to the US goodwill commitment nor an act of joining forces against the US regional hegemony. As a result, Taiwan needed to negotiate for an ambiguous but mutually agreeable understanding with China, to which all concerned parties did not object.

Against this backdrop, both Taiwan and China reached an "agree to disagree" understanding through unofficial organizations—Taiwan's Straits Exchange Foundation (SEF) and China's Association for Relations

Across the Taiwan Straits (ARATS) in Hong Kong in October 1992. Taiwan later coined this mutual understanding the "1992 Consensus" (usually referred to in Taiwan as "*yizhong gebiao*"), and China finally adopted it as the fundamental principle to manage cross-Strait interactions as well as Taiwan's participation in international affairs.[5] The 1992 Consensus refers to the idea that there is "one China," but each side reserves the right to interpret the political contents of "one China." In essence, each side does not deny the other's sovereign assertion of "China." The reciprocal moves and responses actually demonstrated a spirit of pragmatism and innovative thinking in reaching a common ground within which a list of principles and actions derived from those principles were practicably reasonable and acceptable to each party.[6] The pledge of the 1992 Consensus was to ensure that each side's inducements to adhere to the Consensus would be higher than their burdens and sacrifices.

There are seveafl features of the 1992 Consensus. First, each side's position virtually reflected its domestic governing power configuration and the identity preferences of political elites and the general public in the 1990s. China's sacred mission of unifying Taiwan with the "mainland motherland" since 1949 had to compromise with its own desperate need for economic reforms, though China remained committed to the military option as a deterrent to Taiwan's declared independence. Likewise, Taiwan's various interpretations of historical, cultural, and political linkages with mainland China and partisan disputes about the "China-oriented" social construct embedded in the KMT's rule clearly showed a public divide in identity preferences in 1991 or 1992.[7] As Taiwan's identity composition and preference evolved and shifted, party leaders would correspondingly adopt an electoral strategy to cultivate and captivate shares of voters as much as possible to ensure winning.

Second, the 1992 Consensus has since aroused a lot of debate concerning its substance and interpretation. The phrase did not exist in the 1992 Hong Kong talk, but it was explicated post facto by Su Chi, Taiwan's former Mainland Affairs Council (MAC) Minister, as a term of reference in April 2000.[8] The DPP President Chen Shui-bian later adopted this term on June 26, 2000, but the following day his MAC minister, Tsai Ing-wen, publicly rescinded Chen's statement. Tsai further clarified what both Taiwan and China had reached: "each side would respectively interpret one China" (*gebiao yizhong*), rather than "one China with different interpretations" (*yizhong gebiao*). The wording rearrangement signifies a different concentration and priority. The DPP staunchly opposed the idea of accepting the "one China" principle and suggested that the order of phrase be correctly reversed to "each side respectively interpret China" (*gebiao yizhong*) in order to show the prominence of the autonomous subject, that is, Taiwan, in making an authoritative determination of the lower ranked object of "China."[9]

Accordingly, the so-called 1992 Consensus has generated various interpretations and concerns over its functionality across the Strait and interparty disputes within Taiwan. The treatment of the 1992 Consensus between China and Taiwan has evolved into Taiwan's reading of "China" as the "Republic of China" in contrast to China's interpretation of "China" being the "People's Republic of China." Within Taiwan's partisan dispute, the KMT has upheld its essentiality in dealing with China; but the DPP has denied the 1992 Consensus and downgraded it as an illustration of the "1992 Spirit" or "1992 Meeting" to facilitate bilateral dialogues, exchanges, and agreements to shelve political disputes across the Strait.

Third, semantics aside, the "agreement to disagree" on the meaning of "China" contained in the 1992 Consensus has not placated Taiwan's pro-independence supporters' anxiety and frustrations. In contrast, China has increasingly embraced the utility of the Consensus and frequently touted the significance of "*yizhong*" (one China) and deliberately ignored the phrase "*gebiao*" (separate interpretation) to assert its sole representation and legitimacy of the whole China. Certainly, the Taiwanese government and general public are aware of China's intentions and action.[10] Taiwan hence consistently has tried to poke China's position as shown in President Lee Teng-hui's 1994 proposal of the "divided-nation" model or the 1999 "two-state theory," an idea designed by the 2016 Presidential candidate Tsai Ing-wen to upend China's one-China principle. However, these revisionist efforts have instantly faced China's dramatic opposition and US alarming concern.[11]

Fourth, be it consensus or spirit, the referred 1992 Consensus appears to have served both sides positively and culminated in a series of bilateral negotiations and agreements since then. Its utility is as much ideational for each side's commitments to its own image of "China" as it is institutional in regulating bilateral interactions. Even so, China has seldom wavered from its one-China principle in stifling Taiwan's international participation. This has surely irked the Taiwanese public regularly. China's controversial 2005 Anti-Secession Law reaffirmed its determination to crush Taiwan's search for autonomy or independence.[12] Since the PRC has been perceived as the sole legitimate government in representing China internationally, China would like to confine Taiwan, the "other" China (ROC), within China's self-defined rigid enclosure of reference framework. In this case, China has failed to nurture a favorable circumstance or present a positive image in winning the hearts and minds of the Taiwanese people in a democratic society.

China's harsh acts have only provided Taiwanese political elites with an impetus to inflame public passion for electoral gains and to endorse a distinctive Taiwanese indigenous identity separate from China. The feeling of "being different" in identity generates an increment of public disinterest and distaste for association with China and the recession of the China-oriented social construct. Concurrently, it helps conscription and construction of a Taiwan-centered mindset in Taiwan. During the Lee Teng-hui era (1988–2000) and followed by Chen Shui-bian's presidency (2000–2008), Taiwan's society and government policies actually dismantled the KMT social constructs through a mostly structured and organized social engineering of the Taiwanese indigenous identity. Chen's well-known three-step process of social construct, that is, "confrontation-compromise-advance," referred to the DPP's political contention and competition with the KMT. This process serves as a perfect example of his regime's repeated efforts at revising institutional names, government procedures, educational policies, and others, during his governance through 2008.[13] While Chen's confrontational tactics might have been disruptive and distasteful, confrontation set the stage for media publicity to "show and tell" as well as ridicule the "alien" KMT regime's "undemocratically imposed" identity and "China-centered" constructs. Thus, confrontation reinforced DPP supporters' commitments and potentially garnered independent voters' sympathy and shuttered their political opposition. Although Chen would make political compromises, the hope was to gain a devoted critical mass of true believers to propagate Taiwan's distinctive status and dismantle the old identification with China for a cascading effect of a full reconfiguration of Taiwan's identity. Any compromise would pave the way for the DPP's advance to the next stage of confrontation to chip away at the KMT's identity base. The whole process has been long, and the speed has been incremental, but the result has spawned doubts, called for self-reflection, and attracted individual sympathy and empathy for the netting and webbing of intersubjective understandings among the public.

In a temporal dimension, the trend of Taiwan's identity politics appears to have evolved toward the "stickiness" of Taiwan-centered identity, as shown in the survey data tracked by the Election Study Center at the National Chengchi University. In June 1992, the year of the 1992 Consensus, solely "Taiwanese" identifiers were 19.5%, in comparison to 25.5% of solely "Chinese identity" respondents and 54.8% of people with "double identity of both Taiwanese and Chinese." When Ma took over from Chen's governance in 2008, "Taiwanese" identity sharply climbed to 48.4%, and the percentage of "double identity" respondents decreased to 43.1%, along with the steep drop of "Chinese" identifiers to 4.5%.

Even after Ma's rapprochement policy toward China, 2008–2016, "Taiwanese" identifiers surged to 59–60%, with "double identity" respondents hovering around 32–33% and "Chinese" identity remaining 3.3–3.5% in 2014 and 2015.[14] Public attitudes toward unification have steadily declined from 20% in 1994 to 9.1% in 2015, if one combines "unification as soon as possible" and "status quo and move toward unification" in survey data. During the same time period, 1994–2015, surveys showed an increase from 11.1% to 21.1% in those preferring "independence as soon as possible" and "status quo and move toward future independence" respectively.

Should one combine all status quo supporters, regardless of their future preference of either unification or independence, the broad category of "status quo" would claim a predominant domain with 83.3% of respondents in 2015, an 11.4% increase from 1994.[15] Similar findings of 87.6% and 89.5% of status quo supporters, respectively, were also registered in Duke University's Taiwan National Security Survey conducted in December 2014 and October 2015.[16]

In sum, identity reconfiguration has been an unending process. Even so, in the deliberation of Taiwan's future, the Taiwanese public has attempted to balance the reality check of China's security threat with their identity calling. Their calculated preference to cross-Strait status quo has become a safe bet, and politicians have been keen to take notice of voters' preferences. With regard to the rise of a Taiwan-centered identity, no major political party in Taiwan would dare to defy the divine gravity of voters' preferences by advocating a campaign platform of unification in a contentious race.

THE KMT: THE RECESSION OF CHINA-CENTERED IDENTITY IN THE 2016 ELECTIONS

In 2008, when Taiwan's President Ma Ying-jeou of the KMT was sworn in, his supporters were exuberant about the end of the turbulent years of the DPP's President Chen Shui-bian's era of governance. In 2012, Ma won a solid mandate for another presidential term in a hotly contested race with the DPP Presidential candidate Tsai Ing-wen, though Ma's vote share shrunk from 58.5% to 51.6%. However, the DPP challenger Tsai has improved the DPP's vote share from 41% in 2008 to 45.6% in 2012, in a voter turnout rate of 74.38%. The discrepancy in the 2012 election between Ma and Tsai was close to 800,000 votes, out of a total of 13.45 million votes cast. Multiple reasons likely contributed to Ma's victory. Pundits and analysts have frequently attributed the loss to the "1992 Consensus"—the Achilles' heel of Tsai's mainland policy.[17]

While the KMT's victory in 2012 reconfirmed the value of the 1992 Consensus, the relatively narrow margin of vote shares also hinted at the diminishing return of the 1992 Consensus as an effective campaign agenda. Although Ma has been accused of being a "China-friendly" leader, his policies have not seen the recession of Taiwanese identity but instead a steady rise of either "Taiwanese" identity (54.3%) or "double identity" (38.5%) in 2012 surveys. Should one add them together, 92.8% of Taiwanese would broadly identify as "Taiwanese." At the same time, 85.4% of the Taiwanese public in 2012 expressed a general desire for maintaining cross-Strait status quo. Going forward, any candidate wishing to grab a larger share of support would have to frame campaign agendas and slogans with this in mind, especially as "Taiwanese" identifiers have passed the 50% mark. Thus, each party's campaigns have since endeavored to project the candidate's sincerity and efforts in doing the right thing, charting a politically correct path of "loving Taiwan" to stir up the voters' inner sense of identity and their enthusiastic Taiwanese spirit.

During Ma's second term, his administration has experienced mounting internal and external economic challenges, mistakes and flip-flops in policy design and execution, problems in coordination and compromise for legislative approval of governmental initiatives, and intra-party fights and elite disunity, not to mention volumes of political accusations, criticisms and ridicules by opposition parties, talk show commentators, and social media bloggers. Meanwhile, the conventional style of politics has mixed with a new style of politics to form a hybrid of the digital age.

Kindness and gentleness in politicking would have difficulty fitting into this sour season of public anger. The increased use of cyber commentaries and sharp critiques has swept aside the traditional retail style of electoral campaigning and policy deliberation through regular media venues, and it has sidestepped traditional vote brokers (*tiao-ka* in Taiwanese) in agenda manipulations. The new role of social media in *dis-intermediation*—a reduction of intermediate layers of communication—has brought political elites closer to their target audience and opened them to the front line of cyber barrages.[18] Communication has transformed from conventional "face-to-face" dialogues into "facebook-to-facebook" cozy chats, unpleasant encounters that are one stroke away, or tweets that arrive 24 hours a day. The availability of anonymity and disguise in virtual identity has made it easy for participants to forego the treasured value of civility in a reasonable and rational deliberation of political issues in a democratic society.

Ma's rivals, partisan opponents, and critics have easily seized the populist momentum to the seething satisfaction of their supporters and audience. Political elites or officials, whoever has declined to growl on cue or failed to perform to public expectation, have had to endure mocking abuses and sharp critiques. The fallout has included low approval ratings, gradual erosion of dignity and legitimacy in governance, and declining public trust for Ma and his government. Ma has surely been neither loved nor feared by opponents, including some of his own party comrades. Failures in governance have been a mantra frequently uttered by commentators.

Public feeling about the ruling elite's governance failure has been compounded by soaring economic inequality, which many have attributed to cross-Strait economic benefits that failed to trickle down from big business enterprises to the ordinary people. Stated differently, Ma's active "China-friendly" policy under the premise of the 1992 Consensus has profited only politically well-connected business corporations and tycoons at the expense of the public. The pace and scope of cross-Strait relations, along with the concern of excessive dependence on the China market, has become the primary culprit for the widening domestic income gap. Ma's accomplishments of cross-Strait flights in 2008, the facilitation of Chinese investments in Taiwan in 2009, and the Economic Cooperation Framework Agreement in 2010, only engendered opponents' vehement charges and criticisms by branding Ma and the KMT for "selling out Taiwan to China," a claim already levied by the DPP in the 2008 presidential election.[19] And critics have championed a reversal or deceleration of Ma's cross-Strait policies. The unabated anti-China sentiments and the shift in public opinion have made Ma's former pledge of "no unification, no independence, and no use of force" lose its luster. The pendulum has swung toward independence. The KMT's expectation, heading into the 2016 election season, to rely on its pro-engagement cross-Strait campaign agenda based on the 1992 Consensus consequently has faced a daunting task in recruiting voters. Against this backdrop, several noted features have also undercut the KMT's efforts in employing its cross-Strait agenda as a salient issue to rejuvenate its slumped 2016 electoral momentum.

First, the selection and replacement of the KMT presidential candidate Hung Hsiu-chu by Eric Chu was a self-inflicted injury to the Party's unity. Hung's haphazard remarks of "*yizhong tongpiao*" (one China with the same interpretation) opened the floodgate for unnecessary confusion and attacks from commentators and contenders. Regardless of journalistic simplicity in reporting or his opponent's deliberate framing, Hung's exclusion of "*gebiao*" (separate interpretations) as a qualification of the 1992 Consensus was construed to be an endorsement of China's long-term practice of omitting Taiwan's insistence on "separate interpretations." Although Hung's party comrades rushed to clarify and defend for damage control, the enduring "1992 Consensus" treasured by the KMT as an electoral agenda began to lose its power of persuasion. It reminded voters of the previous association of the KMT with lingering "Chinese" identity, a link which the KMT has tried to dismiss. It also opened up intra-party disputes between the "indigenous faction" and the "non-indigenous faction" regarding the liability of Hung's candidacy to the legislative election tightly associated with the presidential election. It alienated the younger generation, which has acquired a different collective memory, and younger voters, who have been deeply inspired by the 2014 Sunflower Movement. It drove away some independent voters who strongly identify as Taiwanese but have felt uncomfortable with the DPP rule.[20] Although the KMT candidate Eric Chu attempted to minimize the damage after his replacement, the DPP effortlessly labelled Hung's statement as a general rumination of the KMT's identity profile. This nudged indecisive voters and lukewarm KMT supporters to the center of the political spectrum where Tsai and the DPP (the green camp) have comfortably secured their votes. And despite the unprecedented meeting between Ma and Xi in Singapore in November 2015 that generated media publicity during the election, opponents still sternly portrayed Ma and the KMT as a party without fortitude to boldly reconfirm "one China with different interpretations" in open and official occasions. As follows, opponents portrayed the KMT's 1992 Consensus as an ostrich's head-hiding deceit, rather than an effective principle of strategic ambiguity to facilitate Taiwan's completion of 23 pacts with China during the Ma reign.

Second, political events unfolded in 2014 and 2015 that truly foreshadowed the dilemma the KMT would encounter in the 2016 elections. The debacle of the legislative review and approval process of the Cross-Strait Service Trade Agreement (CSSTA) in 2013–2014 had been a seriously controversial issue among experts and the public concerning its positive and negative impacts on Taiwan. The controversy later erupted into the Sunflower student protest and was followed by the occupation of the Legislative Yuan in March 2014. Some surveys showed that more than half of respondents had no sufficient knowledge about the CSSTA and were concerned with its impact on job opportunities. More than 60% of them nevertheless endorsed the protesters' occupation to force a renegotiation of the CSSTA.[21] This attested to the clear defeat of CSSTA, the challenge of legislative procedures and the KMT legislator's maneuvers, and doubt over Ma's trustworthiness and his government's competence in cross-Strait relations. On the other hand, student protestors and opponents, including the DPP, won support from youngsters and momentum for later contentious acts to block and stall any of the government's cross-Strait policies with China. Thus perceived as "China-friendly" in orientation, the KMT lost its credibility in safeguarding Taiwan's core interests, as illustrated in a circulated slogan of derision: "*Guomindang budao, Taiwan buhui hao*" (Taiwan will not be better, if the KMT still stands). Consequently, 74.5% of the 20–29 age group and 69.9% of the 30–39 age group, higher than the 66.27% of the national voter turnout in the 2016 election, went to the ballot booth in 2016. A majority of the younger generation voted for Tsai, while only a slim 11.4% of them supported the KMT presidential candidates.[22] In brief, an aura of decrepitude shrouds the KMT's political future.

Third, the decision of Lien Chan, the KMT's former chairman, with other pan-Blue politicians (i.e., those elites sharing similar "China-friendly" feelings), to attend China's military parade presided by Xi Jinping on September 3, 2015, in commemoration of China's 70th anniversary of the Sino-Japanese War, reinforced Taiwanese public impression of the KMT's innate affinity to China and exacerbated its already flattened polls. Even under Ma's strenuous request to forego his trip at this critical moment, Lien Chan's disregard of Ma's plea underlined the party's anxiety as well as disunity. While China had its own multiple domestic and international interests for hosting such a huge military spectacle, the parade definitely relayed vibrating waves of sensitivity in Taiwan's identity politics. China's premeditated exclusion and non-recognition of the "ROC's" indelible contributions and immeasurable suffering in the Sino-Japanese War not only gave the pan-Green and DPP's supporters full excuses to mock the KMT's quixotic adherence to the "one China" vision, it also aroused feelings of disgust and humiliation among pan-Blue supporters. After all, the ROC in Taiwan has been so proud of and treasured this particular period of history, wishing for the PRC's reciprocal gesture to validate the KMT's past deeds for the elections.

One noteworthy point in this episode was the incredible level of public support of "ROC" in most of Taiwan's media reports and social media blogging, in defiance of the PRC's military parade. The near-consensus among critics in defense of the national title of ROC might have been an unintended consequence to China. The military parade dispute also rekindled the preceding controversy over the high school textbook revision launched by a group of high school students closely related to the Taiwanese independence movement. The textbook controversy dwelt upon the exact status of the ROC, assessments of sensitive historical events, classification of Japanese colonialism, and even the voluntary or coerced nature of comfortable women in WWII. Basically, the debates intended to delineate the relationship of Taiwan's indigenous and unique development to China as well as Japan. Should the representation of Japanese colonialism and modernization in textbooks be favorable, it would offer a stark contrast to China's backwardness, negligence, or domineering attitudes toward Taiwan. Such a struggle over a sensible assessment of Taiwan's history reflects two former KMT leaders' acts in dealing with China and Taiwan—former KMT chairman Lee Teng-hui's public denunciation of the KMT as an "alien regime" from China and blatant fondness for Japan versus another former KMT Chairman Lien Chan's sentimental affinity with China.

The overall impact has been the diminishing appeal of the KMT's cross-Strait narratives in electoral persuasion, as 65.3% of survey respondents in late October 2015 felt comfortable with Tsai being a future Taiwan president in dealing with China, and only 24.9% of them expressed some degree of concern.[23] And China unsurprisingly lost another perfect opportunity to extend an olive branch to Taiwan, the "ROC," for a symbolic reconciliation and reconnection of both "ROC and PRC" as one big, inclusive China in a united front of defense against Japan in its 70th anniversary of victory. Had it occurred, the bridge-making event would have energized KMT supporters and bolstered the KMT's 1992 Consensus as a positive prelude to the coming Ma-Xi meeting on November 15, 2015. Instead, China's intentional exclusion of Taiwan, the ROC, in the military spectacle as well as ceremonial inference really "hurt Taiwanese people's feeling," as depicted by the usual Chinese government's expression to ward off unfriendly foreign criticisms. Coincidentally, when the Chou Tzu-yu's ROC flag waving incident became an electoral hot button issue, DPP candidate Tsai commented that this incident truly "hurts Taiwanese people's feeling" on the 2016 Election Day.[24]

Fourth, Taiwan seldom had a chance to articulate its national interests in international institutions during the Ma era. A few noted cases of international participation since 2008 have been Taiwan's participation in the World Health Assembly (WHA) and the special guest role in the International Civil Aviation Organization (ICAO). Taiwan's meager wish to join some functional international organizations, such as the International Criminal Police Organization (Interpol), had fallen on China's deaf ears.[25] China's refusal increasingly made younger generations question the usefulness of the "one China" claim and envision that an assertive Taiwan under the DPP might be a better option for their voices to be heard.

In fact, neither China nor the KMT has taken concrete steps to prepare for the impact of Taiwan's demographic changes, that is, the annual passing, addition, and natural increase of eligible voters. Taiwan's eligible voters have increased from 14.3 million in the 1996 presidential election to 18.7 million in 2016, with an approximate increase of 1 million in each past presidential election.[26] The successive alternations of generations in the composition of voters have not meant the successful transmission and adoption of identity knowledge and social constructs without profound modification. Additionally, a series of episodes of cross-Strait confrontations has also increased momentum to challenge the initial Consensus of 1992. Without China's active, public, and reciprocal acquiescence to Taiwan's "one China with different interpretations," the 1992 Consensus is unlikely to remain intact across regime changes. Thus, a major event like the 2016 election becomes a testing ground for the 1992 Consensus.

The DPP: The Upsurge of Taiwanese Identity in the 2016 Elections

Taiwan's social construct is obviously evolving in favor of the DPP due to contextual alternations of demographic composition, recent social climatic changes, and the spirited support of the pan-Green supporters in media visibility and public sentiment. The DPP and Tsai also became more adaptive than the KMT on the front of identity politics to meet voters' expectations. As a front-runner in the 2016 presidential race with a double-digit lead in pre-election polls, Tsai usually remained tight-lipped about details revealing how she would conduct cross-Strait relations, except to announce her principle of "status quo maintenance." Her minimum expression on the cross-Strait agenda prevented her from contenders' frenzied prodding and punching. Nevertheless, her campaign trail revealed part of her strategic framework.

First, Taiwanese voters' identity composition has inched toward the path of independence, though not outright into de jure independence. The majority of Taiwanese voters' wishes have gradually progressed toward the DPP's longstanding platform. Thus, the DPP's safe bet is to stick to the status quo, which does not require extraordinary agitation by the DPP. If necessary, the DPP could simply aggravate China on cross-Strait issues. Any of China's likely forceful countermeasures would only provoke more anger and disgust to convert more believers to the DPP's noble cause. The result would see a further dwindling of China-friendly supporters in Taiwan's future political market. In the DPP's calculation, it is better to stay calm and carry on the current course. Time is on the DPP's side.

Second, Tsai's status quo policy can carve some shares of traditional KMT supporters and calm their previous anxiety and concerns about the appalling governance of former DPP President Chen Shui-bian. During the campaign process, Tsai further revealed that if elected, her cross-Strait policy would be based on the "current constitutional framework of the Republic of China." In addition to pan-Green supporters, her campaign pledge soothed skeptics who feared the DPP's pro-Taiwan independence stand might make her regime a déjà vu of the Chen Shui-bian era. However, later during presidential debates, she advanced a proactive diplomacy vis-à-vis Ma's diplomatic truce with China. Her comments immediately invited KMT's strong critique for a possibility of repeating Chen Shui-bian government's radical approach to cross-Strait relations. Tsai had to retreat back to her defense line afterwards by replying "communication, communication, and communication" to media prodding concerning cross-Strait relations.

No doubt, Tsai's "status quo" policy has been aligned with the majority of Taiwanese people as indicated in various longitudinal surveys for the past two decades. A policy of "status quo" maintenance is self-explanatory, and it easily conveys to most voters that the new DPP regime under Tsai does intend to disturb most current cross-Strait policies and practices. Even though the KMT constantly challenged Tsai for further details regarding how to maintain the current status quo without the "magic wand"—the 1992 Consensus—the DPP simply chanted its status quo mantra in response. Some challengers considered the recitation of maintaining the status quo a cunning move, given DPP's previous track record of anti-China statements on cross-Strait relations. Still, Tsai's status quo policy put her toward the center of the political spectrum, and her verbal promises calmed voters' anxiety and resistance. In the DPP's electoral calculus, as long as the cross-Strait issue becomes inconspicuous, other electoral issues, such as disgust with Ma's incompetence or disappointment with the KMT's intra-party soap opera of power struggles, would captivate media attention and reprioritize voters' issue preferences. Consequently, the DPP won the chance to be a third-time regime change in Taiwan's presidential elections.

Third, should one venture beyond Tsai's cautious campaign statements and electoral profile in commenting on the cross-Strait issue, one could preliminarily conclude that Tsai would try to maintain the status quo as she tried to assure both the US and Japan during her trips abroad. After all, she will chart Taiwan's strategic course tilting toward the US and Japan for powerful balancing wedges against China's security threat and seek the opportunity to join the Trans-Pacific Partnership (TPP) Agreement to lessen Taiwan's economic dependence on China. This has been a perennial issue between the KMT and the DPP concerning the priority of China in Taiwan's overall national security and economic sustainability. While the KMT believes that Taiwan's future relies on peaceful and stable cross-Strait relations as the primary priority due to China's rapid market and global presence, the DPP harbors an opposing logic by arguing for the essentiality of the US, Japan, and other western countries as a check against China's unification threats. In brief, the KMT roadmap would go through a friendly China to connect with the world by defusing China's obstruction; the DPP, on the contrary, would go first through the world, that is, the US and others, prior to detouring back to engagements with China.

It is foreseeable that the Tsai government will follow the DPP path, though this does not imply a complete foreclosure to existing exchanges with China. The electoral mandate naturally gives Tsai and the DPP a chance to carry out their ideas. The future route might be bumpy if Tsai's skillful negotiation is unable to navigate China's layers of obstacles. Moreover, Tsai's dealing with China also depends on the willingness and commitment of the US and Japan to accommodate Taiwan's needs under China's pressures.

Fourth, Tsai's low key, no surprise, cautious "status quo maintenance" message implied no desire to make an abrupt departure from current policies and practices in cross-Strait policies. However, the hidden text of her status quo remarks might imply some necessary deviations from Ma's rapprochement policy. The electoral victory made her feel more confident to express explicitly some concrete principles in managing cross-Strait status quo, mainly "the Republic of China constitutional order, the results of cross-strait negotiations, interactions and exchanges, and democratic principles and the will of the Taiwanese people."[27]

As much as Tsai would acknowledge more or less Ma's past practices and policies, her government may want to reflect the democratic will of the Taiwanese people, particularly pan-Green supporters, exhibited in the 2016 elections as faithfully as possible in policy changes by abiding by the ROC constitutional order and legal stipulations. She would loudly claim her commitment to the wording of status quo. Accompanying this is the intriguing qualification of her status quo pledge in tandem with the shift of public sentiment toward national identity. With China's indisposition to compromise on its self-defined "one China" principle to satisfy Taiwan's public aspiration, the passing of previous "China-centered" generations in voter composition, and the entry of younger eligible voters who tend to be "natural supporters of Taiwan independence" (*tianran du*) in instinct without extensive collective memory of China, one would expect continuous augmentation of Taiwanese identity devotees.

As the status quo continues to evolve, one should not be surprised if one day a critical mass of voters articulates a newly formulated "status quo" of Taiwanese identity through ballots, and the new majority yearns for Taiwan's "independent" status away from China in democratic procedures under the current Republic of China's constitutional stipulation. Clearly, election is the best, peaceful democratic procedure to express the collective will, as the 2016 elections have demonstrated.

Such a future would be fully compliant with President Tsai's prescribed principles in approaching cross-Strait relations, potentially putting both the US and China in a bind. As Tsai explicitly answered in the presidential debate, Taiwanese independence is surely an option available to the public. And her pledge to constitutional rules and democratic will lays out a legitimate institutional way to substantiate the independence calling. An intricate follow-up issue is whether or not the threat of China's persistent military option for unification would be a powerful enough deterrent to the Taiwanese public and elites, convincing them to put the brakes on a Taiwanese declaration of independence. It also depends on whether all concerned parties, i.e., China, the US, and other regional powers, are ready to recalibrate their regional strategic interests for worst-case scenarios, as Taiwan's continuous identity reconstruction rolls toward a brand new Taiwan.

An additional impetus to show the manifest alteration of Taiwan's identity was the Chou Tzu-yu event, days before the 2016 election. It drove the already weakened KMT's electoral support further into a downward spiral in the last days before the election. After waving an ROC national flag in a South Korean televised show in November 2015, Chou faced accusation by another pro-China entertainer for her implied "pro-Taiwan independence" behavior. One day before Taiwan's 2016 general elections, the South Korean entertainment company, JYP, apologized to the Chinese audience for fear of boycotts and profit losses in China by releasing a video of Chou's distressed apology, affirming the one-China principle. China even acquiescently permitted its massive group of Chinese netizens to "*fanqiang*" (climb the wall, bypass China's great cyber firewall of control) to criticize and smash pro-independence opinions. This sparked a cyber clash of Taiwanese nationalism versus Chinese nationalism.[28]

Chou's video vibe instantly stimulated rage that mobilized most Taiwanese youngsters, including 1.34 million newly eligible voters, to rush to vote the next day. While all parties and candidates in the elections as well as the Taiwanese government swiftly condemned such an outrageous event, this incident became an instant reminder of Taiwanese sadness and frustration under China's unreasonable and bullying behavior all these years. It also extracted public sympathy for Chou because of China's harsh treatment of a 16-year-old Taiwanese singer.

As anticipated, public sentiment targeted the Ma government for being responsible for past portrayal of a rosy and unfulfillable promise of "one China with different interpretations," when China had seldom reciprocated sincerely and equally by openly acknowledging Taiwan's legitimate existence. The KMT and other pan-Blue parties suffered from this event, and the DPP and the New Power Party, a party spawned from the Sunflower Movement, naturally reaped electoral benefits in party ballots for legislative seats and also boosted Tsai's presidential bid with a solid 56% winning share, despite the lowest 66.27% voter turnout since Taiwan's first presidential election in 1996.[29]

The incident has caused a political tsunami with multiple implications. The most important consequence of Chou's event is that youngsters swarmed out on Election Day to cast their votes. It is a testimony to younger generations' assertion of their national identity in election. They openly defy China's consistent "bossy and bullying" acts against Taiwan's reasonable request to equality, dignity, and representation in international participation. The younger voters' favorable enthusiasm toward the DPP and other pan-Green parties may continue with the annual addition of eligible voters in sustaining Taiwan's fear and apprehension of China. Their political attitudes will continue to be a crucial variable in charting the course of future cross-Strait relations.

CONCLUSIONS: SLIDING IN AND OUT OF THE "1992 CONSENSUS" BOX

Taiwan's 2016 elections illustrated that the change of identity composition would influence electoral results. As Gillis once remarked, identity is not simply "things we think *about*, but things we think *with*" (original emphasis).[30] When an identity narrative attempts to define and mobilize supporters and believers, it frequently privileges one particular symbolic meaning and magnifies the self-consciousness of the specific community by excluding and scorning those favoring the others. Very much like Duara's study in historicizing China's national identity, Taiwanese elites' initial soft boundaries drawn upon the differentiation of identities based on populist sensationalization has gradually advanced to hardened boundaries in differentiation regarding electoral agenda.[31] After the electoral victory, supporters and parties within the winning coalition will be likely to pressure the fulfillment of identity platforms to assert Taiwanese distinctive constitutive principles of a community in governance. The DPP's main task is to translate the current status quo of Taiwan's identity preferences into concrete policies without endangering Taiwan's security and survival.

Thus, any proclamation of "status quo" refers only to the temporal, spatial, and momentary presence of the situation in allusion. In Taiwan's situation, the formerly proclaimed China-centered imagined community has transformed into an increasingly self-reinforcing, "locked-in," imagined, Taiwan-centered political community, in Benedict Anderson's terms of reference.[32] Ergo, political campaigns and election results provide ample opportunities and battle grounds for multiple contestants to scramble in the game of identity politics by proposing specific institutional agenda and inspiring supporters' enthusiasm in elections.[33]

The 2016 elections testified to several attributes of Taiwan's political development in recent years. First, pundits and analysts unsurprisingly foresaw the KMT's defeat in the 2016 elections as the electoral campaign proceeded. The shock was that the defeat was so catastrophic to the KMT, in losing both the presidency and the legislature, turning Taiwan's political terrain dramatically "green." As the biggest loser, the KMT now faces an immediate crisis in national identity discourses, and its future prospects for re-capturing the political stage remain unpromising.

China is another loser in Taiwan's election and should also bear the burden of blame for its repeatedly missed opportunities to endorse the "separate interpretations" of China as requested by the KMT regime. China neglected the crucial element of reciprocity for the construction of an intersubjective understanding of "Chinese" identity between the "self" ("China" in the PRC) and the "other" ("China" in Taiwan). China's over-confidence in realist calculus and its belief in its own material strength in dealing with Taiwan's cross-Strait asymmetry made China feel that time is on its side, given both Taiwan's unavoidable economic dependence on China and China's powerful military deterrent.

With a similar hope that time is on its side, the DPP is convinced that identity politics in a democratic society will eventually lead to the DPP's promised land—an independent Taiwan. Taiwan's identity politics and the 2016 elections demonstrated a classical match across the Strait between democracy and non-democracy as well as a duel between solid identity conviction and brutish power display. The belief that time is working in their own favor has made both Taiwan, particularly in the case of the DPP, and China reluctant to compromise. The cross-Strait stalemate will continue election after election, unless either side begins to feel that the clock is ticking faster than before.

Second, the 2016 elections are much like a combined repackaging and reframing process, as illustrated by scholars advocating the idea of substantive or symbolic bricolage in institutional change.[34] Although advocating Taiwan's unique identity separate from the "one China" defined by the PRC, the DPP views of Taiwanese independence during the election process have not significantly dismantled or eliminated formerly established symbolic references, rhetorical narratives, or culturally accepted principles essential to the normative and cognitive institutions under the "Republic of China." Regardless of their disgust toward the symbol or substance of ROC, the DPP's identity connotations and historical understandings in this campaign have been partially restrained or compromised under the "status quo maintenance" campaign pledge. This has been demonstrated by its willingness to follow the "Republic of China" constitutional framework, its deliberate display of the ROC flag in Tsai's victory speech, and DPP's political elites' appearances and indistinguishable murmurings of the ROC national anthem at ceremonial events. Apparently, the end justified the choice of electoral means. The electoral result in 2016 perhaps spelt rhetorically the end of the 1992 Consensus, a term that might have exhausted its political functionality. On this point, Tsai and the DPP have bidden farewell to the name of the "1992 Consensus" and sought their own outside-the-box idea for a fresh approach to cross-Strait relations. The DPP has not unveiled any new term or phrase to ensure a peaceful, regular, and steady process of cross-Strait consultation and cooperation. Tsai has, at least, hinted her intent to honor most of Ma's policies in the near future. Naturally, the tempo, scope, and eventual fate of Ma's policies under Tsai's helm might be carefully screened and revised with a plain reference to "status quo maintenance." The pledge of "status quo" is thus a big basic template into which nearly all political interpretations and policies would fit nicely. Also, Tsai does not need to be confined within Ma's pledge of "no unification, no independence, and no use of force," a timely principle contributing to Ma's past electoral victories. However, the first two slogans might restrain Tsai's future freedom of movement in dealing with China.

Consequently, the election results de-legitimized the phrase of the "1992 Consensus" and somewhat rejected China's self-defined "one China" in Taiwan's public discourses and official references. While Taiwan has not been bound by the Consensus nominally and officially, the segment of "different interpretations" of each side's "China" might remain intact to permit either side to blow its own horn. Since Taiwan cannot call for *de jure* outright independence and risk China's possible military threat, the title of ROC serves its purpose of keeping in line with China's "one China" demand. As for the interpretation of the contents of "China," the debate can wait until its substance has been incrementally modified through the Tsai government's skillful policy manipulation for a reconstruction of cultural norm and social constructs, as President Chen Shuibian did before. In line with the idea of "quantity change will naturally lead to quality modification," the consolidation of Taiwan's separate identity from China may pave the way for Taiwan's independence. Based on the DPP's past track record in identity politics, it is almost certain that the DPP will continue to excel in its task of molding the Taiwanese indigenous identity. The general public might not feel the necessity of keeping the 1992 Consensus. Still, pre-election polls steadily show that the principle of "one China with different interpretations" in cross-Strait interactions, without explicit reference to the 1992 Consensus, has public support. Surveys show support from 55.2% and 53.5% of respondents in December 2014 and October 2015, respectively, in comparison to 31.6% and 31.7% in opposition to the phrase.[35]

In other words, Tsai's designation of such a common expression of "status quo" is analogous to the "no brand name" policy initiated by the Japanese well-known apparel company *Muji*'s in cross-Strait interactions. Thus, Tsai and the DPP can avoid the hassle of political disputes triggered by names and connotations as well as the waste of political energy in explicit explanation to voters. It can easily denounce the "illegitimate" and "unfounded" 1992 Consensus, a term long rejected by her party and devoted supporters, and at the same time unobtrusively continue most of the current status quo policies favored by all concerned parties, including the US, Japan, and maybe even China. Thus, Tsai's status quo proclamation is out of the box of the "1992 Consensus," but to some extent parts of its principle remain inside the box.

Third, Taiwan's democratic principles based on popular sovereignty have surely spoken loudly in the 2016 elections. In Tsai's political calculus, as long as the people collectively decide, China would have no choice but to accept Taiwan's democratic terms. Such an expectation for Xi Jinping to concede to Tsai's commanding will be subjected to reality testing in the future. Tsai has nudged Taiwan's public opinion toward the center, close to her party's position. The question is how to harness and consolidate this newly emerged Taiwanese consensus, should the public feel that a non-democratic and nationalistic China chooses not to meet her conditions and cross-Strait relations becomes tense. Above all, China has repeatedly signaled its demand for Tsai to echo China's preferred term of reference. Xi even drew the line to treat the 1992 Consensus as the "divine stabilizer to calm the seas" (*dinghai shenzhen*) to prevent "earth-moving and mountain-shaking" (*didong shanyao*) consequences in cross-Strait relations. Xi also would seek a "final resolution" of cross-Strait difference during his terms of office.[36] Perhaps, Xi would like to wait and see what Tsai can offer. If the 1992 Consensus is impossible, then Tsai may need to come up with concrete substance to ensure China's aspiration of the "one China" principle would be sustained in a pragmatic way.

Tsai certainly could adopt Deng Xiaoping's "black cat and white cat" analogy to convince China that pragmatism in problem-solving is far more important than senseless disputes in naming the consensus. Deng's predominance within the CCP's power hierarchy permitted him to have the luxury to preach his "cat" gospel to convince his skeptics and allies and condemn his opponents. In the cross-Strait power asymmetry, Taiwan's relatively weak position would require more allies, resources, and stamina to persuade a powerful and stronger China to meet Taiwan's terms beyond reasonable and rational dialogues and negotiation.

Fourth, during the 2016 elections, Tsai proclaimed that younger Taiwanese generations have acquired and internalized the idea of Taiwanese independence. And Beijing will have to realize this unpleasant truth in Taiwan's identity composition and will need to deal with this issue in the wake of the DPP's election win. Indeed, more than 89% of Taiwanese respondents endorse the idea of "status quo maintenance," and 80.9% understands Taiwan's insufficient defense capability against China in an October 2015 survey. The intrigue is that only 15.3% of them would be willing to actively resist or join the army to fight against China's military campaign in a worst-case scenario of Taiwan's declaration of independence.[37] It is a paradoxical contrast in the struggle between "the heart versus the head."

Such a dilemma between an idealistic wish and the brutal reality existed even among the young generation in 2015. Despite both the 20–29 age group and the 30–39 age group displaying a higher Taiwanese identity affiliation, those willing to work in China among the 20–29 age group fell from 48% in 2013, 40% in 2014, to 32% in 2015 based on Taiwan's United Daily's long term of track of public opinions. However, those among the

30–39 age group who were interested in a job in China climbed from 24% in 2014 to 35% in September 2015.[38] The boost of Taiwanese identity and anti-China social atmosphere due to the Sunflower Movement seemed to affect the 20–29 age group, but the 30–39 age group might have a stronger desire to explore China's job opportunities because of Taiwan's stifled economic development. This clearly shows Taiwan's public dilemma as well as the DPP's political predicament in searching for a medium between political identity assertion and the economic quest for Taiwan's sustainability.

At this moment, while the US has consistently expressed its desire for the maintenance of the status quo across the Taiwan Strait, China has adopted a wait-and-see approach by not reacting forcefully to the DPP's victory in any concrete measures, except repeated declarations of the 1992 Consensus in governing future cross-Strait relations. Neither China nor the US would stand by should Taiwan drift too far from each country's orbit. So far, the "Republic of China" has endured all clamor and commotion and remained the common denominator in holding all domestic identity contenders together and soothing international anxiety. At the same time, in the first year of Tsai's leadership, cross-Strait relations have remained relatively calm in a stalemate of "cold peace," seeing neither serious provocation nor visible collaboration by both sides.

As Chao Chien-min, former Deputy Minister of the Mainland Affairs Council, aptly put it, "The US does not recognize the Republic of China, but will not allow the Republic of China to give up the Republic of China; Beijing intends to terminate the Republic of China, but will not permit Taiwan to terminate the Republic of China; and Tsai Ing-wen wants to maintain the status quo, the choice remains the status quo under the Republic of China's current constitutional system."[39] Plainly speaking, the identity focal points perceived by all three parties—the US, China, and Taiwan—still converges on the ROC, though the details of the ROC remain unsettled in domestic politics. And the DPP's preferred interpretation of the ROC is the ROC after Taiwan's democratization in the late 1980s, not the ROC favored by the KMT established in China in 1912 or the ROC sustained by the authoritarian KMT after 1949. In conclusion, the "one China" principle will continue to be a controversial issue even after the DPP has won complete governance authority with a confident majority in legislative seats and a majority mandate in presidential votes in the 2016 elections.

Notes

1. Chien-pin Li, "Taiwan's Participation in Inter-Governmental Organizations: An Overview of Its Initiatives." *Asian Survey*, 46, no. 4, 2006, 597–614.
2. Hui-wan Cho, "China, Taiwan Co-representation in IGOs." *Quanqiu zhengzhi pinglun* (English title: *Review of Global Politics*), 26, 2009, 93–130.
3. Jack Snyder and Karen Ballentine, "Nationalism and the Marketplace of Ideas," *International Security*, 21(2), Fall 1996, 5–40. For a discussion of Taiwan's case, see Yun-han Chu, "Taiwan's National Identity Politics and a Prospect of Cross-Strait Relations," *Asian Survey*, 44, no. 4, July/August 2004, 484–512. For a discussion of Chinese national identity, see Prasenjit Duara, "Historicizing National Identity, or Who Imagines What and When," *Becoming National: A Reader*, ed. Geoff Eley and Ronald Grigor Suny (Oxford University Press, 1996), 150–177.
4. For a general introduction of alliance politics, see Glenn H. Snyder, "The Security Dilemma in Alliance Politics," *World Politics*, 36, no. 4, 1984, 461–495; Glenn H. Snyder, *Alliance Politics* (Ithaca, NY: Cornell University Press, 2007).
5. See Su Chi, "Taiwan's Mainland Affairs Council, "Chronology: 1992," www.mac.gov.tw/ct.asp?xItem=67748&ctNode=6605&mp=3.
6. Here the idea of common ground is similar to the zone of indifference. See Chester Irving Barnard, *The Functions of the Executive* (Cambridge, MA: Harvard University Press, 1968), 168–169.
7. Szu-yin Ho and I-chou Liu, "The Taiwanese/Chinese Identity of the Taiwan People in the 1990s," in *Sayonara to the Lee Teng-hui Era, Politics in Taiwan, 1988–2000*, ed. Wei-chin Lee and T.Y. Wang (Lanham, MD: University Press of America, 2003), 171.
8. Shih Hsiu-chuan, "Su Chi Admits the '1992 Consensus" Was Made Up," *Taipei Times*, Feb. 22, 2006, 3.
9. Ying-jeou Ma, "Cross-Strait Relations at Crossroad: Impasse or Breakthrough?" in *Breaking the China-Taiwan Impasse* (Westpoint, CT: Praeger, 2003), 43–44; for China's view, see Xu Shiquan, "The 1992 Consensus," in *Breaking the China-Taiwan Impasse* (Westpoint, CT: Praeger, 2003), 88–94; "1992 Consensus: The Key to Cross-Strait Peace and Prosperity," Mainland Affairs Council, Taiwan, July 2015, www.mac.gov.tw. George W. Tsai, "Cross Taiwan Straits Relations: Policy Adjustment and Prospects," *Cross-Taiwan Straits Relations Since 1979*, ed. Kevin G. Cai (Hackensack, NJ: World Scientific, 2011), 122.

10. See the speech by Li Yafei, China's Vice President of China's Association for Relations across the Taiwan Strait (ARATS), the counterpart of Taiwan's Straits Exchange Foundation (SEF), video.chinatimes.com/video-bydate-cnt.aspx?cid=1&nid=35720. Also, Shiquan Xu, "The 1992 Consensus: A Review and Assessment of Consultations Between the Association for Relations Across the Taiwan Strait and the Straits Exchange Foundation," in *Breaking the China-Taiwan Impasse*, Donald S. Zagoria, ed., with the assistance of Chris Fugarino (Westport, CT: Praeger, 2003), 82–83.
11. Flor Wang, "Taiwan Not to Mention 'Two-State Theory Again: MAC Head," May 2000, fas.org/news/taiwan/2000/e-05-23-00-15.htm; Suisheng Zhao, "Reunification Strategy: Beijing Versus Lee Teng-hui," *Assessing the Lee Teng-hui Legacy in Taiwan's Politics*. ed. Bruce J. Dickson and Chien-min Chao (Armonk, NY: M.E. Sharpe, 2002), 232; Julian J. Kuo, "Cross-Strait Relations: Buying Time without Strategy," *Assessing the Lee Teng-hui Legacy in Taiwan's Politics*. ed. Bruce J. Dickson and Chien-min Chao (Armonk, NY: M.E. Sharpe, 2002), 207.
12. Articles 2, 3, and 8 of the Anti-Secession Law, adopted at the 3rd Session of the 10th National People's Congress, March 13, 2005. english.people.com.cn/200503/14/eng20050314_176746.html. With a proclamation that "both the Mainland and Taiwan belong to one China," the Anti-Secession law also reconfirms its rejection of any interference by outside forces as an apparent reference to Washington's intervention.
13. Wei-chin Lee, "Taiwan's Cultural Reconstruction Movement: Identity Politics and Collective Action since 2000," *Issues and Studies*, 41, no. 1, March 2005, 1–51.
14. Data may vary slightly subject to the date of survey conducted. See Szu-yin Ho and I-chou Liu, "The Taiwanese/Chinese Identity of the Taiwan People in the 1990s," in *Sayonara to the Lee Teng-hui Era, Politics in Taiwan, 1988–2000*, ed. Wei-chin Lee and T.Y. Wang (Lanham, MD: University Press of America, 2003), 171. The Election Study Center, National Chengchi University, "Taiwanese/Chinese Identification Trend Distribution in Taiwan (1992/06~2015/06)," esc.nccu.edu.tw/app/news.php?sn=166#. Duke University's Taiwan National Security Survey result in Oct. 2015 showed 4.5% of respondents considering "Chinese identity" in comparison to 35% of dual identity and 57.4% preferring "Taiwanese identity." See Taiwan National Identity Survey, the Program of Asian Security, Duke University. dl.dropboxusercontent.com/u/43428880/index.html, question C36.
15. The Election Study Center, National Chengchi University, "Taiwan Independence vs. Unification with the Mainland Trend Distribution in Taiwan (1992/06~2015/06)," esc.nccu.edu.tw/course/news.php?sn=167.

16. Various years of "Taiwan National Security Survey" files, 2002–2015, are made available by the Program of Asian Security Studies, Duke University. dl.dropboxusercontent.com/u/43428880/index.html. See Questions C12 and C33 in the 2014 and 2015 survey results.
17. Lii Wen, "'Consensus' View Could Hurt KMT: Survey," *Taipei Times*, May 25, 2015. www.taipeitimes.com/News/taiwan/archives/2015/05/25/2003619121.
18. Donatella Selva and Emiliana De Blasio, "Influence on Elections," *Encyclopedia of Social Media and Politics*, ed. Kerric Harvey (Sage, 2013), 673–677.
19. Shelley Rigger, *Why Taiwan Matters* (Lanham, MD: Rowman and Littlefield, 2011), 159.
20. Ricky Yeh, "The Challenging Road for Taiwan's Newest Presidential Candidate," *The Diplomat*, July 19, 2015. thediplomat.com/2015/07/the-challenging-road-for-taiwans-newest-presidential-candidate.
21. Loa Lok-sin, "MAC Hiding Unfavorable Data: DPP," *Taipei Times*, May 22, 2014, 3; Crystal Hsu, "Trade Pact Siege: Majority Opposes Trade Agreement: Poll," *Taipei Times*, March 27, 2014, 3; "Fumao renzhi luocha da, dujia mindiao baogao" (Wide Gap of the Understanding of CASSA, Exclusive Report of Polls), *Jinzhoukan* (Business Today), No. 901, March 27, 2014. www.businesstoday.com.tw/article-content-92743-106753?page=3.
22. "Taiwan zhiku: nianqingren toupiaolu 74.5%" (Taiwan Thinktank: Youngsters Voting 74.5%), *Liberty Times Net*, Taiwan, January 21, 2016. news.ltn.com.tw/news/politics/breakingnews/1579950. Also see Taiwan Thinktank, Post-2016 election's survey. www.taiwanthinktank.org/chinese/page/2411/2410/3086/0.
23. Taiwan National Security Survey, 2014 and 2015, the Program of Asian Security, Duke University. dl.dropboxusercontent.com/u/43428880/index.html, Question C32.
24. He Meng-kui, "Tsai Ing-wen: Chou Tze-yu shijian, zhongshang Taiwan renmin ganqing" (Tsai Ing-wen: Chou Tze-yu Incident, Severely Hurt the Feeling of Taiwanese People), *Shijie Ribao* (World Journal), US, January 16, 2016. www.worldjournal.com/3669969/.....
25. Bonnie S. Glaser and Jacqueline A. Vitello, *Taiwan's Marginalized Role in international Security*, A Report of the Center for Strategic and International Studies, Washington, D.C., January 2015, Appendix II, 47–52; Bonnie S. Glaser, *Taiwan's Quest for Greater Participation in the International Community*, A Report of the Center for Strategic and International Studies, Washington, D.C., November 2013, 11–15; Wei-chin Lee, *The Mutual Non-denial Principle, China's Interests, and Taiwan's*

Expansion of International Participation (Baltimore, MD: School of Law, University of Maryland, 2014), Maryland Series in Contemporary Asian Studies, March.
26. International Foundation for Electoral Systems, "ElectionGuide: Democracy Assistance and Election News." www.electionguide.org/countries/id/209/.
27. The text of Tsai's speech in Chinese and English after her electoral victory on January 16, 2016, can be found in <iing.tw/posts/533>. The English translation might be slightly different from the Chinese text. For example, Tsai used *xianzheng tizhi* (constitutional framework or order), instead of *xianfa* (constitution). The use of constitutional framework, in her supporters' view, contains all constitutional interpretation, amendments, cases, and others. The use of "constitution" confines on those constitutional articles only.
28. Lawrence Chung, Minnie Chan, Liu Zhen and Ma Jun, "Taiwan Election Blog: Singer Chou Tzu-yu's Apology Steals the Show Early, but Will Tsai In-wen Make History as First Female President," *South China Morning Post*, January 16, 2016. www.scmp.com.
29. Minnie Chan, "Teen Pop Star Chou Tzu-yu's Apology for Waving Taiwan's Flag Swayed Young voters for DPP," *South China Morning* Post, January 17, 2016. Later, some talk show commentators even commented the impact of Chou's incident on some legislators' electoral results overnight and led to the successful election of three legislators from constituencies and two seats allocated from proportional share of party ballots, though there is no openly available documentation for verification of such claims.
30. John R. Gillis, "Introduction: Memory and Identity: The History of a Relationship," in *Commemorations: The Politics of National Identity*, ed. John R. Gillis (Princeton, NJ: Princeton University Press, 1994), 5.
31. Prasenjit Duara, "Historicizing National Identity, or Who Imagines What and When," *Becoming National: A Reader*, ed. Geoff Eley and Ronald Grigor Suny (Oxford University Press, 1996), 168–169.
32. Benedict Anderson, *Imagined Communities*, revised edition (London: Verso, 1999).
33. Paul Pierson, *Politics in Time: History, Institutions, and Social Analysis* (Princeton, NJ: Princeton University Press, 2004).
34. John L. Campbell, *Institutional Change and Globalization* (Princeton, NJ: Princeton University Press, 2004), 69–71.
35. Taiwan National Security Survey, 2014 and 2015, the Program of Asian Security, Duke University. dl.dropboxusercontent.com/u/43428880/index.html, Question C23.

36. "For Voters, Tsai Should Clarify Her Cross-Strait Stance," *The China Post*, January 13, 2016. www.chinapost.com.tw/editorial/taiwan-issues/2016/01/13/455882/For-voters.htm; "A Tsai Is Just a Tsai," *The Economist*, January 9, 2016. www.economist.com/news/asia/21685507-election-independence-leaning-president-would-put-taiwan-back-international.
37. Taiwan National Security Survey, 2015, the Program of Asian Security, Duke University. dl.dropboxusercontent.com/u/43428880/index.html, Questions C22, C28 and C33 in the 2015 Survey. In Question C28, 10.3% of respondents expressed their support whatever the government decides, while 17.5%, higher than 13.5% in 2014, of them would flee or go abroad and 30% of them will follow "the natural development of the situation" (*shunqi ziran*) in 2015. Also, for the complex interaction between emotional attachment and security concerns, see Rou-Lan Chen, "Taiwan's Identity in Formation: In Reaction to a Democratizing Taiwan and a Rising China," *Asian Ethnicity* 14, no. 2, 2013, 229–250.
38. United Daily, "Liangan guangxi tiaocha" (Cross-Strait Relations Survey), Sept. 16, 2015. money.udn.com/money/story/5648/1189933. Guo Zengliang, "Weichi xianzhuang xia, kongqian de jintui liangnan" (Unprecedented back and forth Dilemma under the Status Quo), *Lianhe Bao* (United Daily), Sept. 17, 2015. The survey was conducted by the United Daily.
39. Li Mingxuan, "Zhongguo jiousan dayuebing daodi yange shuikan?" (China's Big Military Parade Was Really a Spectacle for Whom?), *Tianxia zazhi* (Commonwealth Magazine), Sept. 2, 2015, 183.

Bibliography

A Tsai Is Just a Tsai. 2016. *The Economist*, January 9. www.economist.com/news/asia/21685507-election-independence-leaning-president-would-put-taiwan-back-international. Accessed 20 Jan 2016.

Anderson, Benedict. 1999. *Imagined Communities*, rev. ed. London: Verso.

Anti-Secession Law, Adopted at the 3rd Session of the 10th National People's Congress, March 13, 2005. english.people.com.cn/200503/14/eng20050314_176746.html. Accessed 2 Feb 2016.

Barnard, Chester Irving. 1968. *The Functions of the Executive*. Cambridge, MA: Harvard University Press.

Campbell, John L. 2004. *Institutional Change and Globalization*. Princeton: Princeton University Press.

Chan, Minnie. 2016. Teen Pop Star Chou Tzu-yu's Apology for Waving Taiwan's Flag Swayed Young Voters for DPP. *South China Morning Post*, January 17. www.scmp.com. Accessed 20 Jan 2016

Chen, Rou-Lan. 2013. Taiwan's Identity in Formation: In Reaction to a Democratizing Taiwan and a Rising China. *Asian Ethnicity* 14 (2): 229–250.
Cho, Hui-wan. 2009. China, Taiwan Co-representation in IGOs. *Quanqiu zhengzhi pinglun* [English title: *Review of Global Politics*] 26: 93–130.
Chu, Yun-han. 2004. Taiwan's National Identity Politics and a Prospect of Cross-Strait Relations. *Asian Survey* 44 (4): 484–512.
Chung, Lawrence, Minnie Chan, Liu Zhen, and Ma Jun. 2016. Taiwan Election Blog: Singer Chou Tzu-yu's Apology Steals the Show Early, but Will Tsai In-wen Make History as First Female President. *South China Morning Post*, January 16. www.scmp.com. Accessed 20 Jan 2016.
Duara, Prasenjit. 1996. Historicizing National Identity, or Who Imagines What and When. In *Becoming National: A Reader*, ed. Geoff Eley and Ronald Grigor Suny, 151–177. New York: Oxford University Press.
For Voters, Tsai Should Clarify Her Cross-Strait Stance. 2016. *The China Post*, January 13. www.chinapost.com.tw/editorial/taiwan-issues/2016/01/13/455882/For-voters.htm. Accessed 16 Jan 2016.
Fumao renzhi luocha da, dujia mindiao baogao [Wide Gap of the Understanding of CASSA, Exclusive Report of Polls], *Jinzhoukan* [Business Today], No. 901, March 27, 2014. www.businesstoday.com.tw/article-content-92743-106753?page=3. Accessed 20 Feb 2016.
Gillis, John R. 1994. Introduction: Memory and Identity: The History of a Relationship. In *Commemorations: The Politics of National Identity*, ed. John R. Gillis, 3–24. Princeton: Princeton University Press.
Glaser, Bonnie S. 2013. *Taiwan's Quest for Greater Participation in the International Community*, A Report of the Center for Strategic and International Studies, Washington, DC, November 11–15.
Glaser, Bonnie S., and Jacqueline A. Vitello. 2015. *Taiwan's Marginalized Role in International Security*, A Report of the Center for Strategic and International Studies, Washington, DC, January, Appendix II.
He, Meng-kui. 2016. Tsai Ing-wen: Chou Tze-yu shijian, zhongshang Taiwan renmin ganqing [Tsai Ing-wen: Chou Tze-yu Incident, Severely Hurt the Feeling of Taiwanese People]. *Shijie Ribao* [World Journal], US, January 16. www.worldjournal.com/3669969/. Accessed 19 Jan 2016.
Ho, Szu-yin, and I-chou Liu. 2003. The Taiwanese/Chinese Identity of the Taiwan People in the 1990s. In *Sayonara to the Lee Teng-hui Era, Politics in Taiwan, 1988–2000*, ed. Wei-chin Lee and T.Y. Wang, 149–184. Lanham: University Press of America.
Hsu, Crystal. 2014. Trade Pact Siege: Majority Opposes Trade Agreement: Poll. *Taipei Times*, March 27, 3.
International Foundation for Electoral Systems. ElectionGuide: Democracy Assistance and Election News. www.electionguide.org/countries/id/209/. Accessed 1 Mar 2016.

Kuo, Julian J. 2002. Cross-Strait Relations: Buying Time Without Strategy. In *Assessing the Lee Teng-hui Legacy in Taiwan's Politics*, ed. Bruce J. Dickson and Chien-min Chao, 204–217. Armonk: M.E. Sharpe.

———. 2015. Weichi xianzhuang xia, kongqian de jintui liangnan [Unprecedented Back and Forth Dilemma Under the Status Quo]. *Lianhe Bao* [United Daily], September 17.

Lee, Wei-chin. 2005. Taiwan's Cultural Reconstruction Movement: Identity Politics and Collective Action Since 2000. *Issues and Studies* 41 (1): 1–51.

———. 2014. *The Mutual Non-denial Principle, China's Interests, and Taiwan's Expansion of International Participation*, Maryland Series in Contemporary Asian Studies. Baltimore: School of Law, University of Maryland.

Li, Chien-pin. 2006. Taiwan's Participation in Inter-Governmental Organizations: An Overview of Its Initiatives. *Asian Survey* 46 (4): 597–614.

Li, Mingxuan. 2015. Zhongguo jiousan dayuebing daodi yange shuikan? [China's Big Military Parade Was Really a Spectacle for Whom?]. *Tianxia zazhi* [Commonwealth Magazine], September 2, 183.

Li, Yafei. video.chinatimes.com/video-bydate-cnt.aspx?cid=1&nid=35720. Accessed 2 Mar 2016.

Lii, Wen. 2015. 'Consensus' View Could Hurt KMT: Survey. *Taipei Times*, May 25. www.taipeitimes.com/News/taiwan/archives/2015/05/25/2003619121. Accessed 20 Feb 2016.

Loa, Lok-sin. 2014. MAC Hiding Unfavorable Data: DPP. *Taipei Times*, May 22, 3. Also, www.taipeitimes.com/News/taiwan/archives/2014/05/22/2003590950. Accessed 30 Jan 2016.

Ma, Ying-jeou. 2003. Cross-Strait Relations at Crossroad: Impasse or Breakthrough? In *Breaking the China-Taiwan Impasse*, ed. Donald S. Zagoria, with the assistance of Chris Fugarino, 39–66. Westpoint: Praeger.

Mainland Affairs Council. 2015. *1992 Consensus: The Key to Cross-Strait Peace and Prosperity*. Taiwan: Mainland Affairs Council, July. www.mac.gov.tw. Accessed 1 Mar 2016.

Pierson, Paul. 2004. *Politics in Time: History, Institutions, and Social Analysis*. Princeton: Princeton University Press.

Rigger, Shelley. 2011. *Why Taiwan Matters*. Lanham: Rowman and Littlefield.

Selva, Donatella, and Emiliana De Blasio. 2013. Influence on Elections. In *Encyclopedia of Social Media and Politics*, ed. Kerric Harvey, 673–677. Sage: Thousand Oaks, CA.

Shih, Hsiu-chuan. 2006. Su Chi Admits the '1992 Consensus' Was Made Up. *Taipei Times*, February 22, 3. Also, www.taipeitimes.com/News/taiwan/archives/2006/02/22/2003294106. Accessed 2 Jan 2016.

Snyder, Glenn H. 1984. The Security Dilemma in Alliance Politics. *World Politics* 36 (4): 461–495.

———. 2007. *Alliance Politics*. Ithaca: Cornell University Press.

Snyder, Jack, and Karen Ballentine. 1996. Nationalism and the Marketplace of Ideas. *International Security* 21 (2), (Fall): 5–40.
Su, Chi. n.d. Taiwan's Mainland Affairs Council, 'Chronology: 1992'. www.mac.gov.tw/ct.asp?xItem=67748&ctNode=6605&mp=3. Accessed 20 Dec 2015.
Taiwan National Identity Survey, the Program of Asian Security, Duke University. dl.dropboxusercontent.com/u/43428880/index.html. Accessed 1 Mar 2016.
Taiwan National Security Survey, 2014 and 2015, the Program of Asian Security, Duke University. dl.dropboxusercontent.com/u/43428880/index.html. Accessed 20 Feb 2016.
Taiwan Thinktank, Post-2016 Election's Survey. www.taiwanthinktank.org/chinese/page/2411/2410/3086/0. Accessed 27 Jan 2016.
Taiwan zhiku: nianqingren toupiaolu 74.5% [Taiwan Thinktank: Youngsters Voting 74.5%]. 2016. *Liberty Times Net*, Taiwan, January 21. news.ltn.com.tw/news/politics/breakingnews/1579950. Accessed 23 Jan 2016.
The Election Study Center, National Chengchi University. Taiwanese/Chinese Identification Trend Distribution in Taiwan (1992/06~2015/06). esc.nccu.edu.tw/app/news.php?Sn=166#. Accessed 20 Feb 2016.
———. Taiwan Independence vs. Unification with the Mainland Trend Distribution in Taiwan (1992/06~2015/06). esc.nccu.edu.tw/course/news.php?Sn=167. Accessed 20 Feb 2016.
Tsai, George W. 2011. Cross Taiwan Straits Relations: Policy Adjustment and Prospects. In *Cross-Taiwan Straits Relations Since 1979*, ed. Kevin G. Cai, 115–154. Hackensack: World Scientific.
Tsai, Ing-wen. 2016. *Electoral Victory Speech*, January 16. iing.tw/posts/533. Accessed 20 Jan 2016.
United Daily. 2015. Liangan guangxi tiaocha [Cross-Strait Relations Survey], September 16. money.udn.com/money/story/5648/1189933-. Accessed 1 Oct 2015.
Wang, Flor. 2000. *Taiwan Not to Mention 'Two-State Theory Again: MAC Head'*, May. fas.org/news/taiwan/2000/e-05-23-00-15.htm. Now //archive.li/1ZflG. Accessed 10 Oct 2017.
Xu, Shiquan. 2003. The 1992 Consensus: A Review and Assessment of Consultations Between the Association for Relations Across the Taiwan Strait and the Straits Exchange Foundation. In *Breaking the China-Taiwan Impasse*, ed. Donald S. Zagoria, with the assistance of Chris Fugarino, 81–101. Westport: Praeger.
Yeh, Ricky. 2015. The Challenging Road for Taiwan's Newest Presidential Candidate. *The Diplomat*, July 19. thediplomat.com/2015/07/the-challenging-road-for-taiwans-newest-presidential-candidate. Accessed 20 Jan 2016.
Zhao, Suisheng. 2002. Reunification Strategy: Beijing Versus Lee Teng-hui. In *Assessing the Lee Teng-hui Legacy in Taiwan's Politics*, ed. Bruce J. Dickson and Chien-min Chao, 218–240. Armonk: M.E. Sharpe.

CHAPTER 8

The DPP Ascendancy and Cross-Strait Relations

Yu-Shan Wu

Cross-Strait relations are of paramount importance to Taiwan. An abundance of theoretical frameworks have professed to explain cross-Strait relations.[1] Some of these theories concentrate on the interactions between Taiwan and the Chinese mainland.[2] Some stress the importance of domestic political factors on both sides.[3] Some argue that international forces are behind the permutations of cross-Strait relations.[4] Various synthetic theories have also been advanced to claim a higher degree of explanatory power than the "pure" theories.[5] Typically, synthetic models integrate domestic and international factors in an analytical framework. The way the factors are selected and integrated determines how coherent and effective the model is.[6]

If we concentrate on Taiwan's China policy, we find the cycle of general elections (presidential and parliamentary) is of particular importance in shifting the attention of political parties to domestic and international considerations. Typically during the electoral period, political parties take

Y.-S. Wu (✉)
Institute of Political Science, Academia Sinica, Taipei, Taiwan

© The Author(s) 2019
W.-c. Lee (ed.), *Taiwan's Political Re-Alignment and Diplomatic Challenges*, Politics and Development of Contemporary China,
https://doi.org/10.1007/978-3-319-77125-0_8

positions to advance their chances of winning the upcoming elections. During the inter-electoral period, however, the ruling party would take a more practical policy aimed at improving Taiwan's strategic position in the international game (particularly in the Washington-Beijing-Taipei triangle), while the opposition would appeal to its political base in preparation for the next election. In this model, domestic political competition and international strategic games take turns determining the tune of Taiwan's China policy on the basis of the electoral schedule.[7] It proves a useful analytical framework.[8]

The essence of the electoral cycle theory is when faced with political competition (as in elections), political parties and their leaders act to maximize domestic support through their foreign policy stance. They may take either a *median* or *galvanizing* approach. A *median* party believes there is a normal distribution of public opinion on foreign policy issues and moves to capture the "median voter." In this way, there is basically no difference between domestic and foreign policy issues in converging candidates towards the ideological center during the electoral period. A *galvanizing* party senses its weaknesses in the ideological median and decides that a more fundamentalist approach is necessary to galvanize its base and generate electoral momentum. A galvanizing approach is more probable when the distribution of public opinion is bipolar or when people do not hold strong opinions on foreign policy issues and tend to be swayed by jingoistic rhetoric. During the electoral period, political contenders typically cannot afford appearing weak in dealing with foreign powers. This is particularly the case in Taiwan, given its "inherited rivalry" with mainland China.[9] In short, during the electoral period political parties can take either a median or galvanizing approach, depending on the circumstances.

There is another story when it comes to the inter-electoral period. Taiwan's strategic position in the international arena is such that it cannot afford provoking Beijing. There are two equilibria for Taiwan in the Washington-Beijing-Taipei triangle: a semi-partner with the US that always heeds Washington's interest and constrains its own behaviors, or a hedger that sides with the US in geopolitical terms, but extends economic ties with China for a better relationship.[10] Either way, Taiwan has to take a *realistic* approach.[11]

Given the above, Taiwan's political parties may take a median (M) or galvanizing (G) approach towards Beijing during elections, then shift to a realistic (R) approach during the inter-electoral period. However, as the

Blue (pro-unification) and Green (pro-independence) camps occupy different realms on the unification-independence identity spectrum, the Blue and Green parties shift within their ideological realms. This means a Blue party may veer away from Beijing during the electoral period (if it takes a G approach), but its position remains closer to Beijing than a Green party during the inter-electoral period.

With the advent of the second Democratic Progressive Party (DPP) government in 2016, cross-Strait relations took a nosedive. What is the cause of it? How has it evolved? What is the prospect of the bilateral relationship? This chapter starts by identifying the realms of movement of the two major political camps on the unification-independence spectrum, and then uses the electoral cycle theory to answer the three questions.

IDENTITY SPECTRUM AND HISTORICAL TRAJECTORY

Identity conflict lies at the heart of Taiwan politics and cross-Strait relations. We can now lay out the identity spectrum for Taiwan and China. Along the unification-independence scale, three positions are discernable: *one Taiwan, one China*; *two Chinas*; and *one China*. Each larger position area contains multiple positions that fall under the general rubric. One Taiwan one China (or Taiwan independence per se) calls for the establishment of a new nation, the Republic of Taiwan, which is legally separated from China. The Republic of China (ROC) as it exists now, which harks back to its founding on the Chinese mainland in 1912 and still claims the sovereignty of mainland China, will cease to exist. The two-Chinas category allows for the juxtaposition of the ROC and the PRC. Taiwan will not change its official name, but only its content. The ROC under the two-Chinas formula equals Taiwan. The ROC's sovereignty claim on the Chinese mainland is relinquished. Finally, the one-China category contains all the positions that hold the notion of a unified China as both a constitutional norm and a desirable goal. It does not matter whether that one China is the ROC or the PRC. The three areas are designated at the top in Fig. 8.1.

Now we can shift to history to see how different political forces moved their positions on the identity spectrum.[12] The game started with the Kuomintang (KMT) and the Chinese Communist Party (CCP) taking their respective "one China" position, while the DPP clamored for Taiwan independence. During the early period of Lee Teng-hui's reign, the KMT acted to "normalize" cross-Strait relations and to facilitate functional

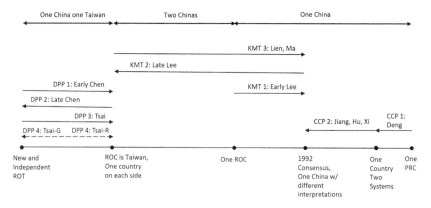

Fig. 8.1 Ideological positions of KMT, DPP, and CCP

interactions that proliferated in the aftermath of the Tiananmen incident in 1989. The ROC maintained its sovereignty claim on the Chinese mainland, but it recognized that its jurisdiction was limited to Taiwan, Penghu, Kinmen, and Matsu in a tacit acknowledgement of the jurisdiction of the PRC. This was the formula of "one ROC, two areas" based on the then new doctrine that separates sovereignty and jurisdiction. Ma Ying-jeou, later the ROC president of 2008–2016, was an active participant in designing the Early Lee formula (KMT 1, see Fig. 8.1).

The KMT's move was reciprocated by Beijing. Under Deng Xiaoping, the CCP's paramount leader, mainland China had designed a "one country, two systems" formula for Hong Kong and Taiwan (CCP 1). After the Tiananmen crackdown and international condemnation, Beijing was eager to seek a breakthrough in cross-Strait relations. The secret envoys from both sides met in Hong Kong and delivered positive messages. The result was an understanding reached in 1992 between Taiwan's Straits Exchange Foundation (SEF) and the mainland's Association for Relations Across the Taiwan Straits (ARATS) for the two sides to orally express the "one China" principle in their respective ways (*yi koutou shengming fangshi gezi biaoda*).[13] From the very beginning, Taiwan's emphasis was on the "respective ways," while the mainland was more interested in the "one China" principle, but there was no denying that the official position of the KMT government was "one China," as clearly stipulated in the "On the Meaning of 'One China'" ("*Yige Zhongguo' de Hanyi*") passed by the National Unification Council in August 1992.[14] A historic compromise was reached between the KMT and the CCP at a time when both sides needed it. In Fig. 8.1, this is CCP 2, a position taken by Jiang Zemin, Deng's successor.

The SEF-ARATS understanding (later named by Su Chi the 1992 Consensus) ushered in the first cross-Strait rapprochement in 1992–1995. The historic meeting between the heads of the SEF (Koo Chen-fu) and the ARATS (Wang Daohan) took place in Singapore in 1993 and facilitated the signing of four agreements to aid cross-Strait interactions. There was an unprecedented exchange of presidential messages in 1995 (Jiang's "Eight Points" and Lee's "Six Items"). The improved atmosphere was foiled after Lee made a landmark visit to the US and delivered a speech at Cornell University, his alma mater. Taiwan's diplomatic breakthrough brought the wrath of China and ignited the missile scare.

After 1995, Beijing began dismissing the 1992 consensus, considering it a pretext that Lee used to achieve Taiwan's diplomatic breakthrough. In 1997 and 1998, Jiang and US President Clinton exchanged state visits in the aftermath of the military standoff between the PLA and the US navy in the Taiwan Strait, plunging Taiwan again into diplomatic isolation. For his part, Lee commissioned an advisory group that came up with the "two-state theory" proposal.[15] Lee then publicly raised his ideas in his famous interview with *Deutsche Welle*. The Late Lee formula (KMT 2 in Fig. 8.1) did not abrogate the ROC, but rather changed its content. In the interview, Lee stated, "the 1991 constitutional amendments have designated cross-Strait relations as a state-to-state relationship or at least a special state-to-state relationship."[16] Lee asserted that the recognition that the ROC's jurisdiction did not reach the Chinese mainland had created an international relation between Taiwan and the mainland. In this way, the ROC was redefined as Taiwan. Thus, under Lee, the KMT shifted to the "two Chinas" position area.

The KMT's tilt towards two Chinas was short-lived. After the defeat of the party in the 2000 presidential election and the excommunication of Lee, the KMT reverted to the old formula. This shift, KMT 3 in Table 1, had to do with the party's attempt to reconnect its political base in preparation for a comeback.[17] The reversion came under the new KMT Chairman Lien Chan. For Beijing, the KMT suddenly became an ally in a united front against the pro-independence DPP government under Chen Shui-bian. For that reason, the CCP welcomed Lien for an ice-breaking visit in April 2005.[18] Lien's position was inherited by Ma, whose mindset was heavily influenced by his own experience in designing the Early Lee formula and reaching a compromise with the mainland on the 1992 Consensus. The Late Lee formula turned out to be a temporary aberration in the KMT's established line.

The DPP started from an ideological position that was diametrically opposite to the KMT's one-China policy. The DPP first adopted the April 17 Resolution in 1988 and stated its intention to pursue Taiwan independence under four conditions.[19] The conditional independence then gave way to the unconditional pursuit of a new nation with a new constitution in Article 1 of the party's platform in 1991, suggesting a radicalization of the DPP. Such repositioning did not serve the party well, as its presidential candidate Peng Ming-min lost in the 1996 race by capturing a meager 21.1 percent of popular vote. Its next presidential candidate Chen Shui-bian learned the lesson and toned down his pro-independence rhetoric significantly to court the middle voters in the 2000 presidential election. The party also adopted a Resolution on the Future of Taiwan in which a grudging recognition of the ROC was granted.[20] The ROC that the DPP reluctantly accepted, of course, was not the country that claims sovereignty over both Taiwan and the mainland, but rather Taiwan per se. This was a move by Early Chen (DPP 1 in Fig. 8.1) through which the DPP literally bridged the divide between Taiwan independence and two Chinas.

Chen was highly cautious at the beginning of his presidency (2000–2002). He restricted his pro-independence rhetoric to the "five no's," a position resembling the DPP's stance in its April 17 Resolution, or "conditional Taiwan independence." Although he did not honor the 1992 Consensus, Chen extolled the "1992 Spirit."[21] He even proposed cross-Strait integration, starting with trade and culture and culminating in political integration. He also took initiative to implement the "three mini links" between the offshore islands of Kinmen and Matsu and the Chinese mainland. Chen's friendly gestures prompted Beijing to reciprocate by affirming the 1992 Consensus and adopting Taiwan's wording in characterizing the "one China" principle as "There is only one China in the world...Both the Mainland and Taiwan belong to that one China."[22] In this "new one-China syllogism" (*yizhong xin sanduanlun*) Taiwan was granted equal status with the mainland under the one-China roof. This was a great improvement on the old one-China syllogism: "There is only one China in the world," "Taiwan is part of China," and "The People's Republic of China is the sole legitimate government of China."[23]

The initial friendly exchanges were terminated abruptly with Nauru shifting diplomatic ties to Beijing at a time when Chen assumed formal party chairmanship of the DPP. Chen fought back with his "Taiwan and China, one country on each side" assertion, radically shifting his position from "two Chinas/conditional Taiwan independence" to "one Taiwan, one China." Later on, Chen would backflip again. Chen's policy shifts had to do with the diametrically opposite forces that he encountered when he ran for reelection. In order to mobilize domestic support when his government's performance was widely deemed poor, Chen concentrated on the DPP's base, the ideologically driven dark Green. He was deliberately provocative when he championed referenda on Taiwan's status and rewriting the constitution. Negative responses from Beijing and Washington came with a vengeance. Even though Chen was forced to tone down his rhetoric a bit after Taipei received mounting pressure from overseas, the tone of his campaign was clearly one of fundamentalism and ethnic mobilization. However, right after he won reelection in March 2004, Chen switched back to international reality, leaving many of his dark Green supporters utterly disappointed. The next serious move towards independence was taken no earlier than January 2006, when Chen abruptly abolished the Council for National Unification, 20 months after he was reelected. The move was followed by the plans to rewrite the constitution and to rejoin the United Nations under the name of Taiwan. This wave of ideological offensive was geared towards the 2008 presidential election. In short, during Chen's reign, he shifted the DPP's ideological position several times to respond to international pressure and domestic political needs. As the two often collided, Chen changed his policy abruptly and frequently. Towards the end of his term, Chen became radicalized again, hence Late Chen (DPP 2) seen in Fig. 8.1.

Compared with Chen's backflips, Ma's mainland policy was amazingly consistent. By embracing the 1992 Consensus, Ma secured the key to cross-Strait rapprochement. For the eight years in office (2008–2016), he tirelessly reiterated that position. Ma made great efforts to counter the DPP's claim that there was no consensus reached in 1992, and he maintained that the adherence to the consensus was the cornerstone of cross-Strait peace and prosperity.[24] The 1992 Consensus was anchored in the amended ROC Constitution and the need to reach a compromise with the mainland for cross-Strait interactions. It resonated well with the core value of Ma's Blue support base and fitted the needs of the middle voters who expected benefits from cross-Strait détente. Beijing ardently embraced it as a most effective curb on Taiwan's tendency towards independence. The US welcomed it for it kept the status quo. There was thus a happy concurrence between the KMT's domestic and cross-Strait/international equilibria. As a result, Ma maintained that position throughout his tenure.

The historic meeting between Ma and Xi Jinping, president of the PRC, on November 7, 2015, in Singapore was set for the two sides to demonstrate their commitment to the 1992 Consensus. In both his opening remarks and behind-the-scenes talk, Ma stressed the 1992 Consensus as the political base for cross-Strait peace and development, the precondition of the 23 agreements signed between Taiwan and mainland China, and the cause of the most stable cross-Strait relationship in 66 years.[25] He knew that the meeting with Xi would be his unprecedented chance of international exposure, and the indispensability of the 1992 Consensus was his foremost message on that occasion. This shows the consistency of Ma's mainland policy and his unswerving ideological position. The contrast with Chen's frequent changes is striking.

The trajectory of interaction between Taiwan and China since the 1990s clearly shows that the cross-Strait relationship is amicable when the identity distance between Taipei and Beijing is short. However, it will plunge into serious confrontation when the identities of the two sides diverge. Much hinges on Taipei's professed stance on Taiwan's identity and its characterization of the cross-Strait relationship. Beijing responds with both carrots and sticks in an effort to steer Taiwan away from *one China, one Taiwan* and towards *one China*. Cross-Strait relations thus experience ups and downs as Taiwan shifts its identity position and China shifts its strategy.

THE FIRST POST-ELECTION YEAR: FROM M TO R

If we take a look at the China policy of the first DPP government under President Chen in 2000–2008, three approaches are identifiable. In the run-up to the 2000 presidential election, Chen took an M approach, mimicking Bill Clinton and Tony Blair. Then an R approach prevailed in 2000–2002, an early inter-electoral period when international strategic thinking dominated. It was replaced by a G approach when elections neared, culminating in the referendum proposals and pledges to rectify the national name and write a new constitution. The G climax ebbed with

Chen's reelection in 2004, and the R thinking made a comeback. However, in 2006 one saw a resurgence of fundamentalist backlash, and the G approach again took the helm. The experience of the first DPP presidency suggests that the party would start with an M approach, then alternate between G and R, with the former dominant in the electoral period and the latter in the inter-electoral period. Each time the G approach surges when the DPP president senses the need to galvanize the party's political base for an imminent uphill fight. It subsides and gives way to the R approach when the president's power is relatively secure and immune from challenge. Is this pattern going to be repeated under the second DPP president Tsai Ing-wen? As a shift from M/R to G is always touched off by political challenge that the president senses, and is almost always related to electoral cycles, we should concentrate on whether such a challenge is likely to emerge in Tsai's tenure.

Tsai began with an M approach that strikingly resembles the one taken by Chen. In 1999, the DPP adopted the Resolution on the Future of Taiwan in which the party grudgingly recognized the legitimacy of the ROC but equated it with Taiwan. This creative reconceptualization of the ROC was to facilitate Chen's presidential campaign by reducing popular anxiety over the DPP's commitment to creating a new and independent nation. If the ROC is Taiwan, then there would be no need to seek independence, for the country is already independent. The reinterpretation appealed to middle voters and contributed to Chen's election. The party thus moved from *one China, one Taiwan* to *two Chinas*.

Such was also Tsai's position in her presidential campaign, an M approach clearly geared towards median voters. For Tsai, her equation of the ROC and Taiwan in 2011 was an early sign of her two-Chinas position.[26] In her second bid for the presidency, Tsai pledged to maintain the status quo, and "push for the peaceful and stable development of cross-Strait relations in accordance with the will of the Taiwanese people and the existing ROC constitutional order."[27] A natural extension of that position is Tsai would uphold the one-China principle inherent in the ROC Constitution, and so should not disagree with the 1992 Consensus. However, Tsai maintains that the 1992 Consensus is but one of the options for the Taiwanese people, suggesting her resistance to that political formula.[28] Her bottom line was that she could accept the ROC as Taiwan, but not anything beyond that. In all, Tsai stepped up her "moderation offensive" (M approach) during the presidential campaign (DPP 3 in Fig. 8.1), which contributed greatly to her winning support from the middle voters and American acquiescence to her candidacy.[29] The fact that Chen and Tsai are both committed to Taiwan independence and are capable of adjustments as the situation requires suggests the possibility of the DPP's position shifts on the identity spectrum, specifically between "One China, One Taiwan" and "Two Chinas."

Tsai's M approach was able to appeal to the majority of Taiwan's voters, hence her resounding victory in the 2016 presidential election. However, from Beijing's point of view, Taiwan shifted from Ma's steadfast commitment to the 1992 Consensus and the one-China principle therein, to Tsai's two-Chinas formula. This was totally unacceptable. The identity gap between the two sides was widened dramatically, leading to a predictable backlash by Beijing. As Xi promised, "if the foundation is undermined, then the ground will move and mountain will be shaken" (*jichu bulao, didong shanyao*).[30] As a result, the number of mainland tourists to Taiwan has been dramatically cut down, semi-official ties between SEF and ARATS was severed, Taiwan was denied attendance at the World Health Assembly (WHA) meeting, Panama was taken away as the most important among Taipei's twentyish diplomatic allies, and the PLA's carrier Liaoning and military aircrafts were sent on missions that circled Taiwan. Even mainland students were discouraged from attending universities on the island.

The Tsai government responded to Beijing's mounting pressure with its New Southbound Policy (NSP) that encourages Taiwan businessmen to shift their investment from China to countries in the South (Southeast Asia, South Asia, Australia, and New Zealand), offers a unilateral visa-free policy to countries in the target area to offset tourist losses from China, promotes educational and academic exchanges between Taiwan and the South, and increases cooperation in the areas of industrial and agricultural development, electronic business, and infrastructure building, among others. The overlap between Taiwan's NSP and China's Maritime Silk Road (MSR) is obvious. Despite much greater resources put into MSR by Beijing, Taiwan has been undeterred in reaching out to the South. It has made some headway in tourism, investment, and student exchanges. From June 2016 to April 2017, travelers from the NSP countries to Taiwan increased by 24.7 percent annually, compared with an overall decrease of 4.4 percent. The number of foreign students from the NSP countries rose by 9.7 percent in the 2016–2017 academic year against a 2.8 percent increase of students from the rest of the world. From June 2016 to May 2017, total trade with the NSP area grew by 11.3 percent, compared with an overall increase by 7.9 percent. Public corporations also increased their investment in the NSP countries to 31 cases that include newly launched projects by China Steel, Taiyen, and Chunghwa Telecom.[31]

The NSP is clearly designed to reduce Taiwan's dependence on the Chinese mainland. It corresponds to the DPP's strategic goal of repositioning Taiwan between the US and China, the rivaling hegemons. It is a realistic shift of position from a hedger to a semi-partner, both of which equilibrium position for Taiwan in the Washington-Beijing-Taipei triangular game. The NSP is thus in line with an R approach, as expected during the early inter-electoral period. One year after Tsai's inauguration, the DPP government's response to the "ground moving and mountain shaking" pressure by Beijing was measured and constrained. Tsai vowed not to "bow to the pressure" over sovereignty issues but did not renege on her moderate stance taken during the presidential election and her inauguration or tinker with Taiwan independence rhetoric.[32] However, pressure was building up.

THE G MOMENT

Three factors are important in determining whether Tsai would shift from R to G as did her predecessor. The first is her approval rating. The second is timing, namely, how close is the presidential election or whether the country has moved from inter-electoral to electoral period. The third is the strength and coherence of her opponents. If the president's popularity is low, the election is near, and the rival camp is strong and coherent, then the need to resort to ethnic/nationalistic mobilization and assertive policy towards Beijing is high (shown in Fig. 8.1 as "DPP4: Tsai-G"). If the president is popular, the election is still far away, and the rival camp is weak and incoherent, then the need for pro-independence rhetoric and actions is low (shown in Fig. 8.1 as "DPP4: Tsai-R"). Assertiveness towards the Chinese mainland is a remedy for the shortfall in popular support during electoral competition. With its well-known negative side effect in cross-Strait and international relations, such a remedy will not be taken lightly. It is the last resort.

Chen's critical shift from the R to G approach occurred when he faced mounting political challenges in mid-2002. The dotcom economic crisis dragged Taiwan's growth to an unprecedented −2.2 percent for 2001, against a backdrop of average growth at 6.93 percent in the preceding decade. Chen's popularity dropped from a high of 77 percent one month after his inauguration to 41 percent when he announced "One Country on Each Side" in August 2002, that is, at the beginning of the latter half of his tenure (see Fig. 8.2). With his popularity plummeting, the groundwork for a strategic shift was laid. He obviously attempted to boost popularity by mobilizing his political base with pro-independence rhetoric, starting with "One Country on East Side" in August 2002.

Like her DPP predecessor, Tsai suffered from plummeting popularity after her inauguration. As shown in Fig. 8.2, Tsai's approval rating took a nosedive from a high of over 47 percent one month after her inauguration to a low of 28 percent in one year's time. Low approval invites challenge from political rivals. Chen's shift from an R to G strategy occurred when his popularity hit 40 percent. In comparison, Tsai suffered from a consistently lower rating than Chen during her first year in office. This suggests she now badly needs a boost in popularity. The groundwork has been laid for a shift to the G strategy.

The second factor is timing. Galvanizing public opinion makes sense only when it is related to elections. G strategy during an inter-electoral period serves no one's interest. However, identifying when exactly a

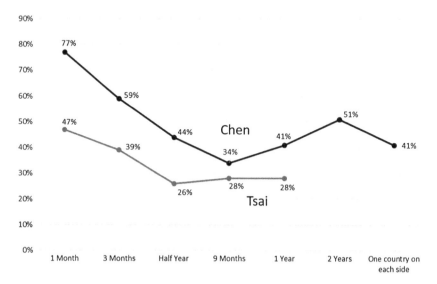

Fig. 8.2 Presidential approval rating: Chen vs Tsai (Source: TVBS opinion polls, http://www.tvbs.com.tw/poll-center, compiled by author)

country crosses the threshold into the electoral period is up to political contenders. Passing half of the inter-electoral period may be a useful rule of thumb. In the case of Chen, his "One Country on East Side" speech was given at the beginning of his third year in office, when he had just passed the middle point of his tenure. Whether that will also be the case for Tsai remains to be seen. The closer it is to the next presidential-cum-parliamentary elections, the greater incentive a DPP president would have to resort to the G approach, for the political benefits the shift in strategy would bestow.

Another electoral cycle factor needs to be heeded. Taiwan's electoral history shows that all power turnovers on the national level have been preceded by the disastrous performance of the ruling party in the preceding local elections. Hence, the KMT lost the largest number of mayoral/magistrate seats to the opposition DPP in 1997, before the first power turnover in 2000. In 2005, the KMT turned the tables and scored great victories in the local elections that foreshadowed its return to power in 2008. The third national power turnover in 2016 was ushered in by the DPP's resounding victories in the local elections of 2014. With such pattern, Taiwan's political parties cannot but give their greatest attention to the 2018 local elections that may well foretell the national results of 2020. If that is the case, and national leaders on both sides must be heavily involved in the 2018 campaign, then the electoral period on the national level will be inadvertently moved forward. A heavy dose of identity stirring may be considered necessary to defend and expand local political turfs in 2018. Put together, the national and local electoral schedules will likely reinforce each other to make 2018 a turning point for a possible shift to the G strategy. If the popularity of the president remains low at that point, so much greater will be the incentive to make a strategy shift.

Finally, the pattern of 2000–2008 brings us to the strength and coherence of the opposition. Even if the president's popularity is low, if there is no plausible challenger on the horizon, then the need to resort to a strategy shift is reduced. Taiwan's presidential election adopts a plurality, not a runoff system, so that whoever grasps the largest number of votes wins. Lack of plausible competitors thus reduces the need to have a popularity boost for the incumbent president. However, competition may arise from multiple sources: the first is the KMT (or Blue camp at large), the second is a within-Green camp challenger, and the third is an intra-DPP rival. In Chen's case, his primary concern was the joining of forces by Lien Chan and James Soong and the alliance of the KMT and the People's First Party (PFP) led by the two men. The intranecine within the Blue camp and the fielding of two Blue candidates made it possible for Chen to grasp presidency with a mere 39.3 percent of popular vote (while Lien and Soong got the remaining 60 percent). Chen realized that if Lien and Soong teamed up before the 2004 presidential bid, it could be a fatal scenario for Chen running for reelection. It was under such overwhelming pressure that Chen resorted to a strategy change in 2002.

Here one finds the reason why the G moment may not come for Tsai after all. The KMT suffered unprecedented electoral defeats in 2014 and 2016, with its top leaders entangled not only in power competition but also in ideological line struggles before and after the elections. President Ma and New Taipei City Mayor Eric Chu stuck to the 1992 Consensus, while the KMT's abortive presidential candidate (from July to October 2015) Hsiu-chu Hung proposed "One China with joint expression" (*yizhong tongbiao*) and sought a peace accord with mainland China. Hung was replaced by Chu as the presidential candidate at an extraordinary party convention precisely because of her advocacy of the new line. The major difference between Hung's proposal and the 1992 Consensus is that the former seeks a common understanding of the status of the ROC and the PRC as two constitutional entities under one China, while the 1992 Consensus leaves the status to the respective interpretation of the two parties. For Hung and her supporters, the "joint expression" is an upgraded version of the "respective interpretation" and can bring about cross-Strait peace and mutual recognition. For those opposed to the idea, Hung was selling out Taiwan's sovereignty by collaborating with mainland China. Hung first won the bid for the KMT's chairmanship in March 2016, after Chu led the party to a predictable electoral fiasco, and then lost the position to Den-yih Wu, former vice president under Ma, in a second chairman election in July 2017. Wu steered the party back to the old line, dropped Hung's commitment to the cross-Strait peace accord, and stopped talking about "joint expression."[33] It is obvious that the dark Blue faction is still restive, while the various branches of the party apparatus remain fragmented.

A further blow to the KMT has been the action taken by the DPP government to take away its properties. Once characterized as KMT, Inc. for the party's immense holdings of various assets, the KMT has been under intense investigation since it lost power by the cabinet-level

Ill-gotten Party Assets Settlement Committee, set up under the Act Governing the Handling of Ill-gotten Properties by Political Parties and Their Affiliate Organizations. The KMT was heavily fined, with its properties seized and offices closed down.[34] Because it could not muster the necessary one third of legislators to file for a constitutional interpretation by the Council of Grand Justices on the constitutionality of the Act, the KMT was rendered helpless in front of the DPP's control of both the administration and legislature.[35] The financial squeeze may not be enough to suffocate the party, but it could surely dampen its momentum, bruise its public image, and delay the emergence of an effective presidential challenger.

Although the KMT has been temporarily paralyzed, challenge to the DPP president may come from an unexpected corner. Taipei Mayor Ko Wen-je is an independent politician, not associated with any political party. He was a political novice when he began campaigning for the mayoral election in 2014. Very rapidly Ko's frank and witty talk, his "slips of the tongue," his use of common men's language, his critique of the political family and big businesses, and his refusal to be tagged in political color made him a darling in the eyes of Taipei's urban voters who detested conventional candidates from establishment parties. Ko's team made good use of new media and big data. His professional background as a surgeon and director at Taipei's National Taiwan University Hospital Intensive Care Unit as well as his exemplary record as an expert on trauma treatment and organ transplant added to his personal charm in a culture that pays great respect to medical doctors. Though not affiliated with any political party, Ko had been an ardent supporter of the DPP and Chen Shui-bian. After Chen was imprisoned for multiple counts of embezzlement, Ko organized a medical team that attested to the need for Chen to be released from prison because of the former president's health conditions. In the 2014 mayoral election, Ko was supported by the DPP which calculated that it could not defeat the KMT's candidate while Ko had a better chance. After Ko took office, his inexperience in public service and his confrontational style cost him some popular support, and yet the much-better-than-expected performance of Taiwan's student athletes in the 2017 Summer Universiade held in Taipei (the third place in medal count) boosted Ko's standing and made him the most popular national political figure. As a result, Ko has great potential to run for president in 2020.[36]

Right after Ko scored political points from Universiade, his realistic approach to mainland China suddenly became an issue. Ko had been sending friendly signals to Beijing since he took office, giving an impression that he is not dogmatic and thus can get things done in cross-Strait, inter-city relations. The "Two City Forum" held alternatively in Taipei and Shanghai has become the only official channel that is still open after 2016. Although Ko did not accept the 1992 Consensus, he nevertheless echoed mainland expressions such as "the two sides are the same family" (*liang'an yijiaqin*) and "share the same destiny" (*mingyun gongtongti*). His diplomatic gesture at the 2017 Two City Forum in Shanghai aroused severe criticism from the Mainland Affairs Council and many DPP politicians.[37] Ko then lamented that he was left to stand alone against China and then deserted.[38] The skirmishes between Ko and the DPP revealed a competitive relationship both over the 2018 mayoral election and the 2020 presidential election. As both elections draw near, tension is bound to rise, for the DPP's need to tap the pro-independence sentiment prevalent among its supporters rises, while Ko is interested in securing a wider support base.

Tsai faces not only the possible threat from Mayor Ko but also from her own competitors in the DPP. In a party that has had an entrenched tradition of factions, Tsai faces great constraints when wielding her power. Not being a member of any established faction, Tsai chose Lin Chuan, an economist-turned-technocrat, as her first prime minister. Lin served 14 months, coinciding with Tsai's R approach to cross-Strait relations. However, because of the government's highly controversial policy on working hours, pensions, same-sex marriage, and so on, Lin's popularity dropped increasingly lower during his tenure. Within the DPP, opposition to Lin stemmed from disgruntlement over the performance of the government and dissatisfaction with its realistic approach to cross-Strait relations.[39] In order to salvage popularity of the government, Tsai was forced, in September 2017, to replace Lin with Ching-te Lai, a rising star county magistrate in Tainan, who had been known for his administrative competence and firm support of Taiwan independence. Furthermore, Lai came from the New Tide Faction, the most organized and disciplined faction in the DPP.[40] Tsai may need Lai to boost the image of the government, but Lai's competence, dark Green credentials, and factional linkage make him a potential challenger to Tsai.[41] The relationship between President Tsai and the new premier would be quite different from the one between Tsai and Lin.

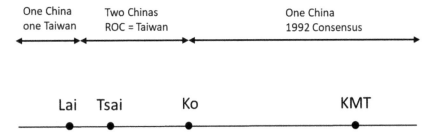

Fig. 8.3 Identity stances and possibility of G moment

The initial tension between Tsai and Lai surfaced when Lai declared during a question-and-answer session at the legislature in September 2017 that he had always been a pro-independence political activist (*zhuzhang taidu de zhengzhi gongzuozhe*), and that "I will never change this stance no matter what office I hold."[42] Such unprecedented remarks from an ROC premier in the parliament sent shockwaves through political circles in Taiwan and mainland China. The timing was extremely inopportune, as the Chinese Communist Party had scheduled to convene its 19th Congress on October 18. Under tremendous pressure to clarify that the government's position had not changed, Lai subsequently announced that Tsai would not announce Taiwan independence, nor would the government hold a referendum on that issue.[43] Both Tsai and Lai also affirmed that cross-Strait policy is the president's prerogative, and that Lai would faithfully execute the president's order.[44] Although Tsai's position (two Chinas and an R approach) has been affirmed, Lai clearly showed his conviction and thus received widespread support from the DPP's base.

Whether there will be a G moment for Tsai depends to a large extent on the political rivalry that she faces. As shown in Fig. 8.3, the KMT candidate (whoever that person may be) is likely to take a One China (1992 Consensus) position; Ko is likely to take a two-Chinas approach (with vague language that stresses commonalities with the mainland); and Lai is likely to take the one China, one Taiwan stance. If Tsai has a considerable lead over her potential rivals, then she need not make a strategic shift from an R to G approach on cross-Strait relations. However, if any of her opponents rises above her in popularity, then there would be tremendous pressure for the president to resort to nationalistic mobilization and claim support from the DPP's base, a la Chen's "One Country on Each Side" in 2002.

CONCLUSION

There are multiple approaches to cross-Strait relations. As far as Taiwan's policy towards mainland China is concerned, the electoral cycle approach is particularly useful. It posits that during the electoral period, political parties take positions on the identity spectrum (separated into three areas: one China; two Chinas; and one China, one Taiwan) to advance their chances of winning the upcoming elections. They have two choices: *median* (M) or *galvanizing* (G) approach. An M approach is taken to capture the median voter under normal circumstances. A G approach is taken when the party is weak at the center of the identity spectrum and thus urgently in need of mobilizing base support. G can also take advantage of the underlying anti-China emotion that finds its outlet in elections. During the inter-electoral period, the ruling party would take a more practical policy aimed at improving Taiwan's strategic position in the international game. There are two equilibria for Taiwan: semi-partner and hedger, both of which suggest a rational, non-provocative policy towards the mainland.

A historical review shows that a DPP president would take an M approach initially, then shift between G and R, with the former dominant in the electoral period and the latter in the inter-electoral period. Each time, the G approach surges when the DPP president senses the need to galvanize its political base for an imminent uphill fight. It subsides and gives way to the R approach when the president's power is relatively secure and immune from challenge. Chen Shui-bian followed this pattern unmistakably. The question is: would Tsai Ing-wen's second DPP government follow the same pattern?

An examination of Tsai's first year in office yields striking similarities with Chen's initial shift from M to R. The "earth moving and mountain shaking" pressure brought on the DPP government after 2016 did not cause Tsai to renege on her moderate stance taken during the presidential election and her inauguration or tinker with Taiwan independence rhetoric. Tsai's response mainly took the form of the New Southbound Policy (NSP), a strategic initiative designed to reduce Taiwan's dependence on mainland China. It was an R response par excellence. However, Chen did not stick to his realistic approach for long. In the second half of his presidential tenure, Chen shifted his strategy and began galvanizing his dark Green base. Would Tsai follow suit?

The factors that cause a DPP president to shift from an R to G approach, that is, the G moment, include the president's approval rating, timing, and the strength and coherence of the opponents. Chen made the strategic shift at the beginning of the second half of his tenure, when his approval plummeted to 40 percent and the prospect of Lien and Soong joining forces against him loomed large. Tsai suffered from a consistently lower rating than Chen during her first year in office; thus, the groundwork has been laid for a shift to the G strategy. As far as timing is concerned, the national and local electoral schedules reinforce each other to make 2018 a turning point for a possible shift to the G strategy. Finally, there is a complicated picture about the strength and coherence of the president's rivals. The KMT has been sufficiently paralyzed with its internal division over party line and the financial squeeze imposed by the DPP government, but challenges to the president may come from unexpected corners: in the pan Green camp and within the DPP, with the former represented by Taipei Mayor Ko and the latter by the newly appointed premier Lai. While Ko is popular among non-committed voters for his flexible cross-Strait policy, Lai has the admiration of the dark Green base for speaking out their aspirations in parliamentary debate. As the president is flanked by the three possible challengers in 2020, her ability to stand above them is crucial. If she is seriously tested by any of her challengers, as Chen was when he faced the presidential election of 2004, the chances for her to shift to galvanizing would increase greatly, and the G moment would come.

There are multiple factors that may impact cross-Strait relations. The Taiwan government's identity position is only one of them. However, it has proven to be the most significant variable as it always triggers strong responses from Beijing. Sino-American relations and regional security also hinge on smooth handling of the issue. And yet, how Taiwan stands on the identity issue is hostage to Taiwan's domestic political competition. Understanding the linkage between domestic politics and Taipei's identity stance is thus of utmost importance. This chapter offers a preliminary exploration of the linkage, both in general terms and in a comparison between the first and second DPP administrations. The pattern that Chen established during his tenure in 2000–2008 serves as an important framework of reference against which we can gauge the possibility of it being repeated under Tsai. Chen's pattern shows an initial M approach, replaced by alternating strategies of R and G. Under similar circumstances, it is possible that such a pattern may repeat itself, with very serious consequences for cross-Strait relations and beyond. The strength and coherence of the president's rivals is a variable that may thwart the repetition. As time progresses and events unfold, we shall understand more about the linkage between domestic politics, identity stance, and cross-strait relations, as well as whether Taiwan would navigate into a storm again.

NOTES

1. Three edited volumes specifically address the theoretical development in cross-Strait studies: Tzong-Ho Bau and Yu-Shan Wu, eds., *Zhengbian Zhong De Liang'an Guanxi Lilun* (*Contending Theories in the Study of Cross-Strait Relations*) (Taipei: Wu-nan, 1999); Tzong-Ho Bau and Yu-Shan Wu, eds., *Chongxin Jianshi Zhengbian Zhong De Liang'an Guanxi Lilun* (*Revisiting Theories on Cross-Strait Relations*) (Taipei: Wu-nan, 2009); Tun-jen Cheng, Chi Huang, and Samuel S.G. Wu, eds., *Inherited Rivalry: Conflict Across the Taiwan Straits* (Boulder, CO: Lynne Rienner, 1995). For a summary of the different approaches, see Yu-Shan Wu, "Theorizing on Relations across the Taiwan Strait: Nine Contending Approaches," *Journal of Contemporary China* 9 (2000): 407–428; Yu-Shan Wu, "Cross-Strait Dialogue and Policies," in *Routledge Handbook of Contemporary Taiwan*, ed. Gunter Schubert (Abingdon, UK: Routledge, 2016). Also see Nancy Bernkopf Tucker, ed., *Dangerous Strait: The U.S.-Taiwan-China Crisis* (New York: Columbia University Press, 2005) for a compendium of different approaches to cross-strait relations without an emphasis on theoretical models.
2. Such as integration theory in Lang Kao, "Cong Zhenghe Lilun Tansuo Liangan Zhenghe De Tiaojian Yu Kunjing" ("Exploring the Conditions and Dilemma of Cross-Strait Integration in the Perspective of Integration Theory"), in *Zhengbian Zhong De Liang'an Guanxi Lilun* (Contending Theories in the Study of Cross-Strait Relations), eds. Tzong-Ho Bau and Yu-Shan Wu (Taipei: Wu-nan, 2004); power asymmetry theory in Yu-Shan Wu, *Kangheng Huo Hucong: Liang'an Guanxi Xinquan* (*Balancing or Bandwagoning: Cross-Strait Relations Revisited*) (Taipei: Cheng-chung, 1997); and Yu-Shan Wu, "Quanli Bu Duicheng Yu Liang'an Guanxi" ("Power Asymmetry and Cross-Strait Relations"), in *Chongxin Jianshi Zhengbian Zhong De Liang'an Guanxi Lilun* (*Revisiting Theories on Cross-Strait Relations*), eds. Tzong-Ho Bau and Yu-Shan Wu (Taipei: Wu-nan, 2009); game theory in Samuel S. G. Wu and Chi-hsin Shih, "Liang'an Tanpan De Shuangceng Saiju Fenxi" ("A Two-Level Game Theoretical Analysis of Cross-Strait Negotiations"), in *Chongxin Jianshi Zhengbian Zhong De Liang'an Guanxi Lilun* (*Revisiting Theories on Cross-Strait Relations*), eds. Tzong-Ho Bau and Yu-Shan Wu (Taipei: Wu-nan, 2009); and Jih-wen Lin and Chih-cheng Lo, "Between Sovereignty and Security:

A Mixed Strategy Analysis of Current Cross-Strait Interactions," *Issues & Studies* 31, no. 3 (1995): 64–91; and divided nation theory in Ya-chung Chang, "Liang'an Guanxi De Guifanxing Yanjiu: Dingwei Yu Zouxiang" ("Normative Analysis of Cross-Strait Relations: Orientation and Trend"), in *Chongxin Jianshi Zhengbian Zhong De Liang'an Guanxi Lilun (Revisiting Theories on Cross-Strait Relations)*, eds. Tzong-Ho Bau and Yu-Shan Wu (Taipei: Wu-nan, 2009).

3. Such as the political competition model in John Fuh-sheng Hsieh, "Chiefs, Staffs, Indians, and Others: How was Taiwan's Mainland China Policy Made?" in *Inherited Rivalry: Conflict Across the Taiwan Straits*, eds. Tun-jen Cheng, Chi Huang, Samuel S.G. Wu (Boulder, CO: Lynne Rienner, 1995); and Yu-Shan Wu, "Does Chen's Election Make Any Difference? Domestic and International Constraints on Taipei, Washington, and Beijing," in *Taiwan's Democratic Politics: Democratization and Cross-strait Relations in the twenty-first Century*, ed. Muthiah Alagappa (Armonk, NY: M.E. Sharpe, 2001); the state-society approach in Tse-Kang Leng, *The Taiwan-China Connection: Democracy and Development across the Taiwan Straits* (Boulder, CO: Westview, 1996); Tse-Kang Leng, "Dalu Jingmao Zhengce De Genyuan: Guojia Yu Shehui De Hudong" ("The Source of Taiwan's Economic Policy toward Mainland China: The Interaction Between the State and Society"), in *Zhengbian Zhong De Liang'an Guanxi Lilun (Contending Theories in the Study of Cross-Strait Relations)*, eds. Tzong-Ho Bau and Yu-Shan Wu (Taipei: Wu-nan, 1999); and Tse-Kang Leng, "Guojia, Quanqiuhua Yu Liang'an Guanxi" ("State, Globalization and Cross-Strait Relations"), in *Chongxin Jianshi Zhengbian Zhong De Lliang'an Guanxi Lilun (Revisiting Theories on Cross-Strait Relations)*, eds. Tzong-Ho Bau and Yu-Shan Wu (Taipei: Wu-nan, 2009); and political psychology theory in Chih-yu Shih, "Zhima! Kaimen Xinli Fenxi Yinling Liangan Zhengce Yanjiu Jinru Xinjingjie" ("Sesame! Open the Door: Psychoanalysis Leads the Study on Cross-Strait Policy to a New Frontier"), in *Zhengbian Zhong De Liang'an Guanxi Lilun (Contending Theories in the Study of Cross-Strait Relations)*, eds. Tzong-Ho Bau and Yu-Shan Wu (Taipei: Wu-nan, 1999); T.Y. Wang and I-Chou Liu, "Contending Identities in Taiwan: Implications for Cross-Strait Relations," *Asian Survey* 44 (2004): 568–590; and Yu-Shan Wu, "Taiwanese Nationalism and Its Implications: Testing the Worst-Case Scenario," *Asian Survey* 44 (2004): 614–625.

4. Such as systems theory in Chu-cheng Ming, "Guoji Tixi Lilun Yu Liangan Guanxi" ("International Systems Theory and Cross-Strait Relations"), in *Zhengbian Zhong De Liang'an Guanxi Lilun (Contending Theories in the Study of Cross-Strait Relations)*, eds. Tzong-Ho Bau and Yu-Shan Wu (Taipei: Wu-nan, 1999); and Chu-cheng Ming, "Guoji Tixi Cengci Lilun Yu Liang'an Guanxi: Jianshi Yu Huigu" ("International System-level

Theory and Cross-Strait Relations: A Review in Retrospect"), in *Chongxin Jianshi Zhengbian Zhong De Liang'an Guanxi Lilun (Revisiting Theories on Cross-Strait Relations)*, eds. Tzong-Ho Bau and Yu-Shan Wu (Taipei: Wu-nan, 2009); the strategic triangle model in Tzong-Ho Bau, "Zhanlue Sanjiao Getilun Jianshi Yu Zongtilun Jiangou Ji Qi Dui Xianshi Zhuyi De Chongji" ("Review of the Micro Theory of Strategic Triangles and Construction of the Macro Theory: Impact on Realism"), in *Chongxin Jianshi Zhengbian Zhong De Liang'an Guanxi Lilun (Revisiting Theories on Cross-Strait Relations)*, eds. Tzong-Ho Bau and Yu-Shan Wu (Taipei: Wu-nan, 2009); and Yu-Shan Wu, "From Romantic Triangle to Marriage? Washington-Beijing-Taipei Relations in Historical Comparison," *Issues & Studies* 4, no. 1 (2005): 113–159; and constructivist exposition in Yi Yuan, "Anquan Dianzhi Yu Mei 'Zhong' Guanxi: Yige Renzhishequnlun De Fenxi Jiagou" ("The Security Regime and U.S.-PRC Relations: An Analytical Framework of Perception Community") in *Zhengbian Zhong De Liang'an Guanxi Lilun (Contending Theories in the Study of Cross-Strait Relations)*, eds. Tzong-Ho Bau and Yu-Shan Wu (Taipei: Wu-nan, 1999); and Yi Yuan, "Guifan Jiangou Zhuyi Yu Liang'an Guanxi: Lilun Yu Shijian" ("Normative Constructivism and Cross-Strait Relations: Theory and Practice"), in *Chongxin Jianshi Zhengbian Zhong De Liang'an Guanxi Lilun (Revisiting Theories on Cross-Strait Relations)*, eds. Tzong-Ho Bau and Yu-Shan Wu (Taipei: Wu-nan, 2009).

5. Such as the one that combines power asymmetry theory and the political competition model in Yu-Shan Wu, "Taiwan De Dalu Zhengce: Jiegou Yu Lixing" ("Taiwan's Mainland Policy: Structure and Reason"), in *Zhengbian Zhong De Liang'an Guanxi Lilun (Contending Theories in the Study of Cross-Strait Relations)*, eds. Tzong-Ho Bau and Yu-Shan Wu (Taipei: Wu-nan, 1999); and the one that put together integration theory and divided nation theory in Yung Wei, "From 'Multi-System Nations' to 'Linkage Communities': A New Conceptual Scheme for the Integration of Divided Nations," *Issues & Studies* 33, no. 10 (1997): 1–19; and Yung Wei, "Recognition of Divided States: Implication and Application of Concepts of 'Multi-System Nations,' 'Political Entities,' and 'Intra-National Commonwealth," *The International Lawyer* 34 (2000): 997–1011.

6. There has been a long tradition in international relations and foreign policy theories that address the integration of international and domestic factors. The most famous model is two-level game. See, for example, Christopher H. Achen, "Two-Level Games and Unitary Rational Actors," in *Zhengzhi Fenxi De Cengci (Level-of-Analysis Effects in Political Research)*, eds. Yungming Hsu and Huang Chi (Taipei: Weber, 2000); Peter Evans, Harold K. Jacobson, and Robert Putman, eds., *Double-Edged Diplomacy:*

International Bargaining and Domestic Politics (Berkeley, CA: University of California Press, 1993); Keisuke Iida, "When and How Do Domestic Constraints Matter? Two-Level Games with Uncertainty," *Journal of Conflict Resolution* 37 (1993): 403–426; Jongryn Mo, "The Logic of Two-Level Games with Endogenous Domestic Coalitions," *Journal of Conflict Resolution* 38 (1994): 402–422; Jongryn Mo, "Domestic Institutions and International Bargaining: The Agent Veto in Two-Level Games," *American Political Science Review* 89 (1995): 914–924; Robert D. Putnam, "Diplomatic and Domestic Politics: The Logic of Two-Level Games," *International Organization* 42 (1998): 427–460. For an application of the two-level game perspective to cross-Strait relations, see Jih-wen Lin, "Two-Level Games Between Rival Regimes: Domestic Politics and the Remaking of Cross-Strait Relations," *Issues & Studies* 36, no. 6 (2000): 1–26.

7. For elections and Taiwan's mainland policy, see Yu-Shan Wu, "Taiwan's Domestic Politics and Cross-Strait Relations," *The China Journal* 53 (2005): 35–60; and Richard Bush, *Untying the Knot: Making Peace in the Taiwan Strait* (Washington, D.C.: Brookings Institution Press, 2005), 142–198.

8. See Yu-Shan Wu, "The Evolution of the KMT's Stance on the One China Principle," in *Taiwanese Identity in the Twenty-first Century*, eds. Gunter Schubert and Jens Damm (New York: Routledge, 2011).

9. See Cheng, Huang and Wu, eds., *Inherited Rivalry: Conflict Across the Taiwan Straits (Boulder, Colo.: Lynne Rienner, 1995 CITY: PUBLISHER, YEAR)*.

10. For a discussion of Taiwan's strategic choice as a lesser power caught in the rivalry between the US and the PRC, see Yu-Shan Wu, "Pivot, Hedger, or Partner: Strategies of Lesser Powers Caught between Hegemons," in *Taiwan and China: Fitful Embrace*, ed. Lowell Dittmer (Berkeley: University of California Press, 2017).

11. Yu-Shan Wu, "Under the Shadow of a Rising China: Convergence towards Hedging and The Peculiar Case of Taiwan," in *Globalization and Security Relations across the Taiwan Strait: In the Shadow of Power*, eds. Ming-chin Monique Chu and Scott L. Kastner (Oxon, UK: Routledge, 2014).

12. The following analysis draws on Yu-Shan Wu, "Heading towards Troubled Waters? The Impact of Taiwan's 2016 Elections on Cross-Strait Relations," *American Journal of Chinese Studies* 23, no. 1 (2016): 59–75.

13. Chi Su and An-kuo Cheng, eds., *"Yige Zhongguo, Gezi Biaoshu" Gongshi de Shishi* ("One China, with Respective Interpretations"—A Historical Account of the Consensus of 1992) (Taipei: National Policy Foundation, 2002), p. i.

14. It is stated in the document that "The two sides of the Strait have different opinions as to the meaning of 'one China.' It should mean the Republic of China (ROC), founded in 1912 and with *de jure* sovereignty over all of

China. The ROC, however, currently has jurisdiction only over Taiwan, Penghu, Kinmen and Matsu…Since 1949, China has been temporarily divided, and each side of the Taiwan Strait is administered by a separate political entity. This is an objective reality." See National Unification Council, "'*Yige Zhongguo' de Hanyi*" ("On the Meaning of 'One China'"), http://www.mac.gov.tw/ct.asp?xItem=68275&CtNode=5836&mp=4, accessed January 1, 2016.

15. In August 1998, the advisory group on strengthening the ROC's sovereignty (*qianghua Zhonghuaminguo zhuquan diwei xiaozu*) was formed, and their report was finished in May 1999. In July Lee announced the group's "two-state theory" in the famous interview with *Deutsche Welle*. He was trying to torpedo the visit to Taiwan by Wang Daohan, the mainland's chief negotiator. It is worth noting that Tsai Ing-wen, who later joined the DPP government under Chen Shui-bian and won the 2016 presidential election, was a member of the advisory group that proposed the "two-state theory." This foretells her later position.

16. Mainland Affairs Council, *Lee zongtong teshu guoyuguo guanxi—Zhonghua minguo zhengce shuoming wenjian* (Special State to State Relationship by President Lee Teng-hui: An Explanatory Note on the ROC's Policy), (Taipei: Mainland Affairs Council, 1999).

17. Yu-Shan Wu, "The Evolution of the KMT's Stance on the One-China Principle: National Identity in Flux," in *Taiwanese Identity in the twenty-first Century: Domestic, Regional and Global Perspectives*, eds. Gunter Schubert, Jens Damm (London: Routledge, 2011).

18. During Lien's trip to China, he made a fervent speech at Peking University that appealed to the audience with liberalism and Chinese nationalism. Lien also openly denounced Taiwan independence in his speech. He was given a standing ovation. Lien's trip was the first time that a KMT chairman had visited the mainland since the end of the Chinese civil war. Common commitment to Chinese nationalism and opposition to Taiwan independence bridged the gap between the KMT and the CCP, an unthinkable pair of strange bedfellows.

19. The four conditions are: if the KMT enters into negotiation with the CCP, if the KMT betrays the interest of the Taiwanese people, if the CCP rules Taiwan, and if the KMT does not practice bonne fide constitutional democracy.

20. The Resolution states, "Taiwan, although bearing the name of the Republic of China according to the current constitution, is not subject to the PRC's sovereignty, and vice versa." This was the first time when the DPP granted legitimacy to the ROC, under the condition that the ROC was simply the current name of Taiwan.

21. Chen even mentioned his willingness to accept the consensus reached by the SEF and the ARATS, namely "one China with respective interpretations," as long as the other side was willing to do the same. That position was denied by his own minister of mainland affairs, Tsai Ing-wen, one day later. For Chen's remarks, see "Zongtong jiejian meiguo yazhou jijinhui huizhang Fuller boshi" (The President received Dr. William Fuller, President of The Asia Foundation), *News Release*, June 27, 2000, Office of the President, http://www.president.gov.tw/Default.aspx?tabid=131&itemid=7712, accessed February 10, 2016.
22. The same wording can be found in "On the Meaning of 'One China'" passed by the ROC's National Unification Council in 1992. For the concessions by Beijing and the adoption of Taiwan's wording in redefining "one China," see Chi-hung Wei, "China-Taiwan Relations and the 1992 Consensus, 2000–2008," *International Relations of the Asia-Pacific* 16, no. 1 (January 2006): 67–95.
23. Hsi-tang Pan, "'Yizhong' xin sanduanlun shifou neng fuzhu xingdong 'neiwai wubie'?" ("Can the new 'one-China' syllogism be put into practice 'without differentiating between cross-Strait and international relations?"), *NPF Backgrounder*, March 7, 2002, http://old.npf.org.tw/PUBLICATION/NS/091/NS-C-091-087.htm, accessed January 10, 2016.
24. *President Ma Delivers Address at Symposium on "1992 Consensus"* (Taipei: Mainland Affairs Council, 2013).
25. "Ma-Xi hui dengchang: Ma Ying-jeou Xi Jinping kaishang fayan quanwen" (Ma-Xi meeting on stage: full text of the opening remarks by Ma Ying-jeou and Xi Jinping), *chinatimes.com*, November 7, 2015YEAR?, http://www.chinatimes.com/realtimenews/20151107003702-260401.
26. Tsai mentioned, "The KMT leans towards greater China and performs poorly, but the DPP can tolerate the KMT, and tolerate the ROC, because they are both included in Taiwan" ("baorong zai Taiwan limian"), *Apple Daily*, October 9, 2011, http://www.appledaily.com.tw/appledaily/article /headline/20111009/33725978/, accessed February 10, 2016.
27. "Tsai Ing-wen 2016: Taiwan Faces the Future," June 3, 2015, CSIS, http://csis.org/event/tsai-ing-wen-2016, accessed February 20.
28. "Tsai bashes Ma's advocacy of '1992 Consensus'," November 10, 2015, *The China Post*, http://www.chinapost.com.tw/taiwan/national/nationalnews/2015/11/10/450530/Tsai-bashes.htm, accessed February 10.
29. The US reception of Tsai in 2015 was qualitatively different from four years before. When she came to the US as the DPP's presidential candidate in 2011, her stance on cross-Strait relations was considered ambiguous. Four years later, Tsai became more moderate and reassuring in her approach to cross-Strait affairs. See Douglas H. Paal, "Maintaining Peace Across

Taiwan Strait Can Benefit All," *China Daily*, January 21, 2016, http://carnegieendowment.org/2016/01/22/maintaining-peace-across-taiwan-straits-can-benefit-all/it2u, accessed February 20, 2016.

30. Xi made this stern warning when he attended a meeting of the Chinese People's Political Consultative Conference (CPPCC) on March 4, 2015. See "Xi chongshen jiuer gongshi: jichu bulao, didong shanyao" (Xi reaffirmed the 1992 Consensus: if the foundation is undermined, then the ground will move and mountain will be shaken), worldjournal.com, March 5, 2015, http://www.worldjournal.com/2610831/article-習近平重申九二共識:基礎不牢地動山搖/.
31. Concerning Taiwan's New Southbound Policy, see the official website at http://www.moea.gov.tw/MNS/otn/news/News.aspx?kind=1&menu_id=2629&news_id=71631.
32. See, for example, Tsai's Double Tenth (national day) address on October 10, 2016. "Taiwan 'will not bow' to Beijing on sovereignty issue, says President," DW, http://www.dw.com/en/taiwan-will-not-bow-to-beijing-on-sovereignty-issue-says-president/a-36003201.
33. See the KMT's platform adopted after Wu's inauguration in August 2017 at: http://www.kmt.org.tw/p/blog-page_3.html.
34. Sean Lin, Article author? "KMT assets to be seized for unpaid fine," *Taipei Times*, August 27, 2017YEAR?, http://www.taipeitimes.com/News/front/archives/2017/08/27/2003677254.
35. Stacy Hsu,Author? "KMT seeks Grand Justices ruling on ill-gotten assets," *Taipei Times*, July 27, 2016YEAR?, http://www.taipeitimes.com/News/front/archives/2016/07/27/2003651870.
36. Ben Bland Author?, "Maverick mayor shakes up Taiwan politics," *Financial Times*, September 29, 2017, https://www.ft.com/content/031106c0-a4f1-11e7-9e4f-7f5e6a7c98a2.
37. Tsai Ya-hua, Su Fang-he Author?, "Ko's 'Two Sides are the Same Family' shook collaboration with DPP" (Ko 'liang'an yijiaqin chongji yu luying hezuo), *Liberty Times*, July 5, 2017, http://news.ltn.com.tw/news/politics/paper/1116243.
38. Lee I-chia Author?, "MAC defends itself over Ko's complaint," *Taipei Times*, September 14, 2017, http://www.taipeitimes.com/News/taiwan/archives/2017/09/14/2003678404; Lee I-chia Author?, "City government did its job: Ko," *Taipei Times*, September 27, 2017 Year?, http://www.taipeitimes.com/News/taiwan/archives/2017/09/27/2003679233.
39. In the Lin cabinet, all the ministers in charge of national security, such as defense, foreign affairs, and mainland affairs, including Lin himself, are "mainlander" professional bureaucrats, a sign of Tsai's pro-stability cross-Strait policy.

40. Factions in the DPP were officially dissolved in 2006, but many of them continue to operate, particularly the New Tide Faction.
41. According to a poll commissioned by Taiwan Trust Brain, Lai is more popular than Tsai among DPP supporters if he were to run for president in 2020, and he has a better chance than Tsai to defeat the KMT rival. See Author? NO AUTHOR, "Press conference for the release of a survey on 'Government Crisis in Poll Numbers: An Analysis on the 2020 Presidential Election'" (Cong zuixin mindiao kan zhizheng weiji: 2020 zongtong xuanqing guancha pingxi), Taiwan Brain Trust, http://www.braintrust.tw/article_detail/2150.
42. Sean Lin Author?, "Lai reaffirms support for independence," *Liberty Times*, September 27, 2017, http://www.taipeitimes.com/News/front/archives/2017/09/27/2003679217.
43. Lin Ching-yin, Chiu Tsai-wei, Hsu Chia-yu Author?, "Lai: Tsai government would not announce Taiwan independence, nor would it hold an independence referendum" (*Laikui: Tsai zhengfu buhui xuanbu taidu buhui taidu gongtou*), UDN News Network, October 4, 2017, https://udn.com/news/story/11515/2738316.
44. Lin Ching-yin Author?, "Did the president know beforehand? Lai: She knows my personal beliefs" (*Zongtong shiqian zhiqing? Lai: Ta zhidao wo geren zhuzhang*), UDN News Network, September 29, 2017, https://udn.com/news/story/11515/2729216.

Bibliography

Achen, C.H. 2000. Two-Level Games and Unitary Rational Actors. In *Zhengzhi Fenxide Cengci* [Level-of-Analysis Effects in Political Research], ed. Yung-ming Hsu and Huang Chi, 35–47. Taipei: Weber,.
Bau, T.H. 2009. Zhanlue Sanjiao Getilun Jianshi yu Zongtilun Jiangou ji qi dui Xianshizhuyide Chongji [Review of the Micro Theory of Strategic Triangles and Construction of the Macro Theory: Impact on Realism]. In *Chongxin Jianshi Zhengbianzhonge Liangan Guanxi Lilun* [Revisiting Theories on Cross-Strait Relations], ed. Tzong-Ho Bau and Yu-Shan Wu, 345–360. Taipei: Wu-nan.
Bau, T.H., and Y.S. Wu, eds. 1999. *Zhengbianzhongde Liangan Guanxi* [Contending Theories in the Study of Cross-Strait Relations]. Taipei: Wu-nan.
———. 2009. *Chongxin Jianshi Zhengbianzhonge Liangan Guanxi Lilun* [Revisiting Theories on Cross-Strait Relations]. Taipei: Wu-nan.
Bush, R. 2005. *Untying the Knot: Making Peace in the Taiwan Strait*. Washington, DC: Brookings Institution Press.
Chang, Y.C. 2009. Liangan Guanxide Guifanxing Yanjiu: Dingwei yu Zouxiang [Normative Analysis of Cross-Strait Relations: Orientation and Trend].

In *Chongxin Jianshi Zhengbianzhongde Liangan Guanxi Lilun* [Revisiting Theories on Cross-Strait Relations], ed. Tzong-Ho Bau and Yu-Shan Wu, 87–114. Taipei: Wu-nan.

Cheng, T.J., C. Huang, and Samuel S.G. Wu, eds. 1995. *Inherited Rivalry: Conflict Across the Taiwan Straits*. Boulder: Lynne Rienner.

Evans, P., H.K. Jacobson, and R. Putman, eds. 1993. *Double-Edged Diplomacy: International Bargaining and Domestic Politics*. Berkeley: University of California Press.

Hsieh, J.F.S. 1995. Chiefs, Staffs, Indians, and Others: How Was Taiwan's Mainland China Policy Made? In *Inherited Rivalry: Conflict Across the Taiwan Straits*, ed. Tun-jen Cheng, Chi Huang, and Samuel S.G. Wu, 137–152. Boulder: Lynne Rienner.

Iida, K. 1993. When and How Do Domestic Constraints Matter? Two-Level Games with Uncertainty. *Journal of Conflict Resolution* 37 (3): 403–426.

Kao, L. 2004. Cong Zhenghe Lilun Tan Liangan Zhenghede Tiaozhan yu Kunjing [Exploring the Conditions and Dilemma of Cross-Strait Integration in the Perspective of Integration Theory]. In *Zhengbianzhongde LianganGuanxi* [Contending Theories in the Study of Cross-Strait Relations], ed. Tzong-Ho Bau and Yu-Shan Wu, 41–75. Taipei: Wu-nan.

Leng, T.K. 1996. *The Taiwan-China Connection: Democracy and Development Across the Taiwan Straits*. Boulder: Westview.

———. 1999. Dalu Jingmao Zhenghede Genyuan: Guojia yu Shehuide Hudong [The Source of Taiwan's Economic Policy Toward Mainland China: The Interaction Between the State and Society]. In *Zhengbianzhongde Liangan Guanxi Lilun* [Contending Theories in the Study of Cross-Strait Relations], ed. Tzong-Ho Bau and Yu-Shan Wu, 211–263. Taipei: Wu-nan.

———. 2009. Guojia, Quanqiuhua yu Liangan Guanxi [State, Globalization and Cross-Strait Relations]. In *Chongxin Jianshi Zhengbianzhongde Liangan Guanxi Lilun* [Revisiting Theories on Cross-Strait Relations], ed. Tzong-Ho Bau and Yu-Shan Wu, 143–166. Taipei: Wu-nan.

Lin, J.W. 2000. Two-Level Games Between Rival Regimes: Domestic Politics and the Remaking of Cross-Strait Relations. *Issues & Studies* 36 (6): 1–26.

Lin, J.W., and C.C. Lo. 1995. Between Sovereignty and Security: A Mixed Strategy Analysis of Current Cross-Strait Interactions. *Issues & Studies* 31 (9): 64–91.

Mainland Affairs Council. 1999. *Lee Zongtong Teshu Guoyuguo Guanxi—Zhonghua Minguo Zhengce Shuoming Wenjian* [Special State to State Relationship by President Lee Teng-hui: An Explanatory Note on the ROC's Policy]. Taipei: Mainland Affairs Council.

Ming, C.C. 1999. Guoji Tixi Lilun yu Liangan Guanxi [International Systems Theory and Cross-Strait Relations]. In *Zhengbianzhongde Liangan Guanxi Lilun* [Contending Theories in the Study of Cross-Strait Relations], ed. Tzong-Ho Bau and Yu-Shan Wu, 365–388. Taipei: Wu-nan.

———. 2009. Guoji Tixi Cengci Lilun yu Liangan Guanxi: Jianshi yu Huigu [International System-level Theory and Cross-Strait Relations: A Review in Retrospect]. In *Chongxin Jianshi Zhengbianzhongde Liangan Guanxi Lilun* [Revisiting Theories on Cross-Strait Relations], ed. Tzong-Ho Bau and Yu-Shan Wu, 313–336. Taipei: Wu-nan.
Mo, J. 1994. The Logic of Two-Level Games with Endogenous Domestic Coalitions. *Journal of Conflict Resolution* 38 (3): 402–422.
———. 1995. Domestic Institutions and International Bargaining: The Agent Veto in Two-Level Games. *American Political Science Review* 89 (4): 914–924.
Putnam, R.D. 1988. Diplomatic and Domestic Politics: The Logic of Two-Level Games. *International Organization* 42 (3): 427–460.
Shih, C.Y. 1999. Zhima! Kaimen: Xinli Fenxi Yinling Liangan Zhengce Yanjiu Jinru Xin Jingjie [Sesame! Open the Door: Psychoanalysis Leads the Study on Cross-Strait Policy to a New Frontier]. In *Zhengbianzhongde Liangan Guanxi Lilun* [Contending Theories in the Study of Cross-Strait Relations], ed. Tzong-Ho Bau and Yu-Shan Wu, 265–336. Taipei: Common Wealth Culture, 20ei: Wu-nan.
Su, Chi, and A.K. Cheng, eds. 2002. *"Yige Zhongguo, Gezi Biaoshu" Gongshi de Shishi* ["One China, with Respective Interpretations"—A Historical Account of the Consensus of 1992]. Taipei: National Policy Foundation.
Tucker, N.B., ed. 2005. *Dangerous Strait: The U.S.-Taiwan-China Crisis*. New York: Columbia University Press.
Wang, T.Y., and I.C. Liu. 2004. Contending Identities in Taiwan: Implications for Cross-Strait Relations. *Asian Survey* 44 (4): 568–590.
Wei, Y. 1997. From 'Multi-System Nations' to 'Linkage Communities': A New Conceptual Scheme for the Integration of Divided Nations. *Issues & Studies* 33 (10): 1–19.
———. 2000. Recognition of Divided States: Implication and Application of Concepts of 'Multi-System Nations,' 'Political Entities,' and 'Intra-National Commonwealth'. *The International The Lawyer* 34: 997–1011.
Wei, C.H. 2006. China-Taiwan Relations and the 1992 Consensus, 2000–2008. *International Relations of the Asia-Pacific* 16 (1): 67–95.
Wu, Y.S. 1999. Taiwande Dalu Zhengce: Jiegou yu Lixing [Taiwan's Mainland Policy: Structure and Reason]. In *Zhengbianzhongde Liangan Guanxi Lilun* [Contending Theories in the Study of Cross-Strait Relations], ed. Tzong-Ho Bau and Yu-Shan Wu, 153–210. Taipei: Wu-nan.
———. 2000. Theorizing on Relations Across the Taiwan Strait: Nine Contending Approaches. *Journal of Contemporary China* 9 (25): 407–428.
———. 2001. Does Chen's Election Make Any Difference? Domestic and International Constraints on Taipei, Washington, and Beijing. In *Taiwan's Presidential Politics: Democratization and Cross-Strait Relations in the 21st Century*, ed. Muthiah Alagappa, 167–179. Armonk: M.E. Sharpe.

———. 2004. Taiwanese Nationalism and Its Implications: Testing the Worst-Case Scenario. *Asian Survey* 44 (4): 614–625.

———. 2005a. From Romantic Triangle to Marriage? Washington-Beijing-Taipei Relations in Historical Comparison. *Issues & Studies* 4 (1): 113–159.

———. 2005b. Taiwan's Domestic Politics and Cross-Strait Relations. *The China Journal* 53: 35–60.

———. 2009. Quanli Buduichen yu Liangan Guanxi [Power Asymmetry and Cross-Strait Relations]. In *Chongxin Jianshi Zhengbianzhongde Liangan Guanxi Lilun* [Revisiting Theories on Cross-Strait Relations], ed. Tzong-Ho Bau and Yu-Shan Wu, 31–60. Taipei: Wu-nan.

———. 2011. The Evolution of the KMT's Stance on the One China Principle. In *Taiwanese Identity in the Twenty-first Century*, ed. Gunter Schubert and Jens Damm, 51–71. New York: Routledge.

———. 2014. Under the Shadow of a Rising China: Convergence Towards Hedging and The Peculiar Case of Taiwan. In *Globalization and Security Relations Across the Taiwan Strait: In the Shadow of Power*, ed. Ming-chin Monique Chu and Scott L. Kastner, 25–36. Abingdon: Routledge.

———. 2016a. Cross-Strait Dialogue and Policies. In *Routledge Handbook of Contemporary Taiwan*, ed. Gunter Schubert, 393–409. Abingdon: Routledge.

———. 2016b. Heading Towards Troubled Waters? The Impact of Taiwan's 2016 Elections on Cross-Strait Relations. *American Journal of Chinese Studies* 23 (1): 59–75.

———. 2017. Pivot, Hedger, or Partner: Strategies of Lesser Powers Caught Between Hegemons. In *Taiwan and China: Fitful Embrace*, ed. Lowell Dittmer, 197–220. Berkeley: University of California Press.

Wu, Samuel S.G., and C.H. Shih. 2009. Liangan Tanpande Shuangceng Saiju Fenxi [A Two-Level Game Theoretical Analysis of Cross-Strait Negotiations]. In *Chongxin Jianshi Zhengbianzhongde Liangan Guanxi Lilun* [Revisiting Theories on Cross-Strait Relations], ed. Tzong-Ho Bau and Yu-Shan Wu, PAGE. Taipei: Wu-nan.

Yuan, Y. 1999. Anquan Dianze yu Mei-Zhong Guanxi: Yige Renzhi Shequande Fenxi Jiegou [The Security Regime and U.S.-PRC Relations: An Analytical Framework of Perception Community]. In *Zhengbianzhongde Liangan Guanxi Lilun* [Contending Theories in the Study of Cross-Strait Relations], ed. Tzong-Ho Bau and Yu-Shan Wu, 389–432. Taipei: Wu-nan.

———. 2009. Guifanjiangouzhui yu Liangan Guanxi: Lilun yu Shijian [Normative Constructivism and Cross-Strait Relations: Theory and Practice]. In *Chongxin Jianshi Zhengbianzhongde Liangan Guanxi Lilun* [Revisiting Theories on Cross-Strait Relations], ed. Tzong-Ho Bau and Yu-Shan Wu, PAGE. Taipei: Wu-nan.

PART III

Taiwan's International Way-out

CHAPTER 9

American Policy Toward Taiwan-China Relations in the Twenty-First Century

Robert Sutter

INTRODUCTION

Both the Bill Clinton and George W. Bush administrations took actions in support of Taiwan that went beyond past practice of most US governments since President Richard Nixon in giving primacy to positive relations with China, making compromises over Taiwan, and avoiding actions toward Taiwan that would seriously upset the US-China relationship. The two US presidents came to regret their past initiatives, which began and exacerbated major tensions in cross-Strait relations, starting with President Clinton, under enormous pressure from the US Congress and American media favoring Taiwan, who reversed existing policy in granting a visa for Taiwan President Lee Teng-hui to visit the United States in 1995.

By Robert Sutter, Professor of Practice of International Affairs, George Washington University. The author is grateful for the constructive comments received when this chapter was presented on a panel at a conference entitled "Taiwan in the Realm of East Asia," Wake Forest University, October 22, 2016.

R. Sutter (✉)
George Washington University, Washington, DC, USA

There ensued 13 years of turmoil and repeated crises in the Taiwan Strait and in US relations with China and Taiwan, turmoil which did not subside until a new Taiwan president, Ma Ying-jeou, was elected in 2008 and dramatically reversed Taiwan's contentious approach to China. He sought to reassure, accommodate, and engage much more closely with Beijing. The outgoing George W. Bush administration and the incoming Barack Obama administration strongly endorsed Ma's approach, which reduced the importance of the so-called Taiwan issue as the US government pursued pragmatic engagement with China on an increasingly wide range of international and bilateral issues, where rising China played a more important role impacting American interests.

The 13 years of tense cross-Strait and US-Taiwan-China relations reinforced a strong tendency in the US government to manage issues with Taiwan in ways that avoided major friction in what was viewed as a much more important relationship with China. The strength of that tendency was seen during the escalation in recent years of US-Chinese frictions over a range of security, economic, and political issues, which from the American side were seen as caused by the newly assertive actions of Chinese party leader and President Xi Jinping (2012–). The Obama government showed a pattern of very deliberative and transparent foreign policy making that in the case of China saw gradual escalation of rhetorical criticism and eventually some serious actions to deal with disputes with China. The pattern showed that specific differences and disputes with China were dealt with separately; they were not linked to other issues in US-China relations or to the overall state of the relationship, which continued to be portrayed by President Obama and his lieutenants in a positive and optimistic way, with priority given to areas of increased constructive engagement and a creditworthy foreign policy legacy for President Obama. Under these circumstances, Taiwan policy was not allowed to change in ways that could seriously aggravate Beijing.

The recent direction of US policy is now challenged by new circumstances. For one thing, Ma Ying-jeou's approach to China was strongly questioned by Taiwan voters who rejected his party and in January of 2016 elected in a landslide vote a new president and legislature, now led by officials prepared to be firmer in protecting Taiwan's sovereignty in the face of Chinese pressure. Tension in cross-Strait relations has continued to rise; the Obama government predictably doubled down on its efforts to foster cross-Strait communication to avoid serious instability. Meanwhile, the US election campaign of 2016 featured acrimony with China and some support for Taiwan. The victor, Donald Trump, said little about Taiwan during the campaign.

Once elected, Mr. Trump shifted policy. In December 2016, he broke ranks with past practice in accepting a phone call from Taiwan's president and publicly questioning past deference to Beijing over Taiwan. Facing pressure from Beijing and seeking Chinese support in dealing with North Korea, he reverted to discreet handling of Taiwan issues of previous US governments, affirming in April that he would not accept another phone call from the Taiwan president. In June, the president led administration officials expressing disappointment with China's help on North Korea; a concurrent hardening of US policy on issues sensitive to China included prominent statements of firm support for Taiwan and provision of US$1.4 billion in arms for the island.[1]

To support the findings noted in this summary, the following sections of this chapter first provide the relevant background of US policy toward Taiwan-China relations since the mid-1990s. Then it explains why the rising tensions in cross-Strait relations and in US-China relations, as well as a gradual hardening of the Obama administration's approach to China have not spilled over to change US policy toward Taiwan. Finally, it moves into a discussion of how and in what ways the US 2015–2016 presidential election debates involving China and Taiwan have impacted US policy toward Taiwan at the end of the Obama era and foreshadow the new US presidency.

THE CONTEXT OF RECENT US POLICY TOWARD TAIWAN-CHINA RELATIONS

Tumultuous events characterized US-China-Taiwan relations at the turn of the twentieth century. Following Taiwan President Lee Teng-hui's success in lobbying the US government to allow him to visit the United States in 1995, Beijing reacted with strident rhetoric against alleged plots of Lee to foster Taiwan independence from China, and it employed impressive military shows of force in the Taiwan Strait up to the Taiwan presidential election of March 1996. The Clinton administration eventually felt compelled to send two aircraft carrier battle groups to the Taiwan area in an effort to deter Chinese attack. Taiwan thereby became the focus of an ongoing massive buildup of Chinese military forces, now more than ever before aiming to deter and if necessary defeat intruding American forces. US military planners felt compelled to respond in kind, resulting in respective arms buildups targeting one another that continue to the present.[2]

Seeking to ease tensions and avoid military confrontation, the Clinton administration shifted to a policy of close positive engagement with China and viewed Lee's government as a troublemaker. It followed the pattern of several previous US governments since President Richard Nixon in seeking to give top priority to improving relations with China and in the process to assure that the so-called Taiwan issue would not seriously upset that effort.

The Taiwan electorate's choice of Chen Shui-bian as president in 2000 represented the first time a person held this powerful post who was not a member of the Kuomintang (KMT) party, which stresses that Taiwan is part of China. Chen's party, the Democratic Progressive Party (DPP), had struggled for many years against the KMT, employing a platform that stressed independence and/or self-determination for Taiwan—an anathema for Beijing.

At first Chen was moderate on cross-Strait issues. The incoming George W. Bush administration was very favorably inclined to Taiwan and more reserved than the Clinton administration in seeking positive ties with China. However, Chen came to be seen by the Bush government as manipulating US support in seeking greater separation of Taiwan from China despite repeated warnings from Beijing. The Bush administration's wars in Afghanistan and Iraq as well as major problems with North Korea's development of nuclear weapons saw the US government revert to the approach of its predecessor in seeking to strengthen positive engagement with Beijing and manage the Taiwan issue in ways that would avoid serious disruption of US relations with China. That task proved to be very difficult as Chen repeatedly provoked Beijing with legislative, constitutional, and other initiatives that fundamentally challenged Beijing's view of one China with Taiwan as part of China.

A major turning point came with the 2008 election of Ma Ying-jeou of the Kuomintang (KMT) Party and his policy of stressing reassurance and accommodation of China in the interests of cross-Strait peace and closer interchange and development. From an historic perspective, President Ma's policies toward China represented a fundamental reversal of the highly competitive and often militarily tense and confrontational policies of previous Taiwan governments since Chiang Kai-shek retreated to

Taiwan after losing the Chinese Civil War on the mainland in the late 1940s. The Taiwan electorate turned against the approaches to cross-Strait issues challenging Beijing that were favored by Lee Teng-hui and Chen Shui-bian. Its opposition to the turmoil in cross-Strait relations was a major reason for Ma's landslide victory and the KMT's dominance in the legislative elections in 2008. And Ma's reelection, along with the legislature staying under KMT control in voting in 2012, was widely seen as an endorsement of his moderate cross-Strait policies aimed at accommodating Beijing. Seeking to foster peace and stability in the Taiwan Strait, as they gave primacy to developing constructive relations with China, the US governments of Republican President George W. Bush and Democratic President Barack Obama strongly endorsed the dramatic change in direction in the Taiwan government's approach to China.

As explained in detail below, the Obama government managed to sustain an approach of avoiding change in American policy toward Taiwan that would have substantially upset Beijing. It did so even though this US government resorted to increasingly tougher measures to deal with what it came to see as major challenges to important American interests by the more assertive use of coercive means and other negative practices affecting American interests by the government of Party Leader and President Xi Jinping. And it did so even though the Taiwan electorate shifted to opposing Ma Ying-jeou's accommodation of China. Indeed, Taiwan voters in January 2016 strongly favored the Democratic Progressive Party (DPP), electing Tsai Ing-wen in a landslide victory in the presidential race and dominating the legislative races for candidates and supporters with much greater determination to defend the interests of Taiwan as a sovereign government separate from Beijing.

President Tsai and the Democratic Progressive Party (DPP) government seek to preserve the peace, economic benefits, and positive interchange of the cross-Strait status quo. Reflecting the wishes of the vast majority of Taiwan people, they seek no confrontation with China. However, they refuse to endorse the concept of "one China" seen in the so-called 1992 consensus—an agreement used by Beijing and the Ma government to meet China's requirement for acknowledgment that Taiwan is part of China as a foundation for cross-Strait peace and the more than 20 economic and other agreements reached between the two sides over the past eight years. Insistence on endorsing the 1992 consensus comes amid Chinese warnings of serious consequences for cross-Strait peace and development without it. Beijing's resolve accompanies continued massive

Chinese military buildup across the Strait to intimidate Taiwan, tight control of Taiwan's limited international diplomatic space as an independent government, and use of economic and social interchange to deepen Taiwan's connection to the Chinese mainland. The negative and positive incentives are all part of a clearly focused Chinese goal of eventually unifying Taiwan with the People's Republic of China (PRC), an outcome strongly opposed by the DPP and most voters in Taiwan. Meanwhile, Beijing's insistence underlines its deeply rooted distrust of President-elect Tsai and the DPP leadership, viewed by Chinese officials as seeking ways to block moves toward unification and promote moves toward Taiwan de jure independence.

In sum, the future of peace and stability in the Taiwan Strait is more in doubt following the Taiwan election. For China, the election of Tsai Ing-wen and the DPP government is a clear setback in efforts to move Taiwan toward reunification. Chinese officials from President Xi Jinping on down have warned in sometimes ominous language of consequences of the Tsai government not endorsing the "one China" concept of the 1992 consensus. Thus, the key gap between the two sides now is over a statement of principle. Smoother relations may follow a possible compromise on this issue, but opposing interests and resolve on both sides promise a much rockier road in China-Taiwan relations than existed under President Ma.

AMERICA'S RECENT CHINA POLICY DEBATE AND THE TAIWAN ISSUE

Will the results of the Taiwan elections and greater uncertainty about cross-Strait peace and stability lead to a change in US policy and practice toward Taiwan? Despite a significant American debate over its China policy and a hardening of the Obama administration policy toward China, US government policy toward Taiwan did not change during the Obama administration. American advocates for closer ties with Taiwan at odds with China may find the Tsai Ing-wen government more open to their initiatives than the Ma Ying-jeou government, which stressed accommodation of China. But whatever support they receive in the US government now depends heavily on the Donald Trump administration and depends probably on how seriously US-China relations may deteriorate during its tenure.

The American debate over China policy has grown over the past few years. Harry Harding said in the *Washington Quarterly* that the debate is the "most intense" China policy debate since the Tiananmen Crisis of 1989, if not before.[3] As explained in more detail in the following sections, the debate had some impact during the 2015–2016 presidential campaign, notably in the pronouncements of Senate Foreign Relations Committee Member Marco Rubio who ran for the Republican nomination. The debate on China is part of a larger foreign policy narrative of Republican and other critics of the Obama government regarding perceived weakness in foreign affairs, which also focuses on more urgent threats posed by Islamic extremists and Russia.

The China debate highlights differences in US-China relations that also came to receive more prominent attention in the highly deliberative foreign policy of the Obama administration. The importance of US-China differences has evolved over time. They were generally held in check as the two powers normalized and improved relations in the 1970s and 1980s with a common framework of working constructively together to offset the perceived menacing power of the then-expanding Soviet Union. That framework shattered with the Tiananmen Crisis of 1989, the end of the Cold War, and the end of the Soviet Union. Subsequent efforts to establish a new framework of cooperation failed. They included a try at creating a "strategic partnership" during the Clinton administration, an effort to have common understanding as "responsible stakeholders" during the Bush administration, and the now-failing effort to create a "new type of great power relationship" during the Obama-Xi Jinping years.[4]

In the first decade of the twenty-first century, both sides managed to establish pragmatic understandings that saw the wisdom of emphasizing positive engagement and managing differences for three basic reasons. Both governments benefited from positive engagement; close interdependence meant that pressuring the other would hurt both parties; and both leaders were preoccupied with many other problems and sought to avoid serious problems with the other. Incoming President Xi Jinping gave those pragmatic understandings lower priority as he coercively advanced Chinese control of claimed maritime territories at the expense of neighbors backed by the United States. He also initiated a variety of multilateral financial institutions, economic agreements, and related initiatives that undermined existing US-backed bodies and accords, and he ignored US complaints and persisted in cyber espionage for economic benefit against American companies and in-state intervention in economic matters undermining American companies. Additionally, President Xi Jinping repressed human rights in ways grossly offensive to American values and accelerated China's large and wide-ranging military buildup targeting American forces in the Asia-Pacific region.[5]

President Obama for many years rarely criticized China, but Xi's practices prompted a remarkable rhetorical and to some degree substantive hardening of US government policy. The president's wide-ranging and often sharp criticism notably did not include Taiwan. Rather, the president and his administration continued to adhere to an approach inherited from the George W. Bush administration that Taiwan issues should be handled in ways that avoid serious negative consequences for American policy toward China. For example, the president's signature rebalance policy in the Asia-Pacific region was repeatedly and sometimes harshly criticized by China. The Obama government nonetheless went ahead with a wide range of initiatives with Japan, the Philippines, Vietnam, and other areas around Taiwan though initial administration statements about the policy failed to even mention Taiwan. In response to various queries, the administration began stating routinely that Taiwan was included in the rebalance policy, though it avoided discussing any details of what the United States and Taiwan were doing, presumably to avoid offending the PRC in ways seen adverse to administration interests.

The record of the Obama administration's dealing with differences with China over in its last two years showed carefully measured management of disputes, not allowing them to spill over and impact other more positive elements in the relationship, resulting in an overall positive image of continued progress in US-China relations.[6] This pattern underlined an approach that did not reverse the administration's cautious moderation in dealing with Taiwan-China relations.

As noted, President Obama rarely criticized China during his first six years in office. However, after 2014 he became outspoken about Chinese behavior. President Xi ignored the complaints, which were dismissed by lower-level officials. As he did in his March 31, 2016, meeting with President Obama, Xi emphasized a purported "new model of major country relations" with the US critics increasingly seeing Xi playing a double game at America's expense.

Since a strained US-China summit in Washington in September 2015, Obama had less to say about China. Rather, he and his administration took stronger actions. For example:

- The United States applied much stronger pressure than seen in the past to compel China to rein in rampant cyber theft of American property;
- The United States applied much stronger pressure than seen in the past to compel China to agree to international sanctions against North Korea;
- China's continued militarization of disputed South China Sea islands followed President Xi's seemingly duplicitous promise made during the September 2015 summit not to do so. In tandem came much more active US military deployments in the disputed South China Sea, along with blunt warnings by US military leaders regarding China's ambitions;
- More prominent cooperation developed with allies Japan, the Philippines, and Australia along with India and concerned Southeast Asian powers; the cooperation strengthened regional states and complicated Chinese bullying;
- US action in March 2016 halted access to American information technology that impacted China's leading state-directed electronics firm ZTE. The company reportedly had earlier agreed under US pressure to halt unauthorized transfers to Iran of US-sourced technology and then clandestinely resumed them;
- The United States rebuked negative Chinese human rights practices in an unprecedented statement to the UN Human Rights Council in March 2016 that was endorsed by Japan, Australia, and nine European countries.

However, the impact of these actions was less than it appeared at first. The public pressure regarding cyber theft and Chinese support for sanctions against North Korea subsided once bilateral talks on cyber theft began, and China went along with tougher UN sanctions against North Korea. Cutting off ZTE was reversed after a few days of secret consultations. Much later, during the early Trump administration, came the news that the United States had negotiated a punishment with ZTE which required payment of a fine of over US$1 billion.[7] The rebuke in the Human Rights Council turned out to be a one-time public occurrence. Meanwhile, the so-called Taiwan issue in Sino-American relations became more sensitive following the landslide election in January of Democratic Progressive Party (DPP) candidate Tsai Ing-wen and a powerful majority of DPP legislators. Avoiding actions that might "rock-the-boat," the Obama government, as noted, eschewed controversy and emphasized constructive cross-Strait dialogue.

In sum, the Obama government's greater resolve against China's challenges came to focus on the South China Sea disputes and related American maneuvering with Japan, Australia, India, and some Southeast Asian nations to respond to China's destabilizing and coercive measures. Defense Secretary Ashton Carter and Pacific Commander Admiral Harry Harris repeatedly spoke of China's "aggressive" actions and what Harris called Chinese "hegemony in East Asia." They and others pointed to US military plans "to check" China's advances through deployments, regional collaboration, and assistance to Chinese neighbors. American officials also expected and were pleased by the Chinese defeat in a ruling on July 12, 2016, by the Arbitral Tribunal associated with the Permanent Court of Arbitration in The Hague, undermining the broad and vague Chinese claims used to justify expansion in the South China Sea.

Looking out in late 2016, the case for continued opportunistic and incremental Chinese expansion in the South China Sea seemed strong, despite opposition from the United States. The benefits of Xi's challenges appeared to outweigh the costs. Notably, President Xi appeared in China as a powerful international leader, while President Obama appeared weak. China's probing expansion and intimidation efforts in the East China Sea ran up against firm and effective Japanese efforts supported strongly by the United States; and they were complicated for Beijing by China's inability to deal effectively with provocations from North Korea. The opportunities for expansion in the South China Sea were greater, given the weaknesses of governments there. And the case at The Hague may have given incentive to Chinese expansion, enabled by a new Philippines government more anxious to negotiate with China than its predecessor.

While as shown above the Obama government's efforts to counter China in the South China Sea were more substantial, resolute, and significant than in the cases of its other recent disagreements with China, they remained carefully measured to avoid serious disruption in the broader and multifaceted US-China relationship. They were not allowed to spill over to impact other elements of the relationship or to impact the development of greater Sino-American cooperation on other issues. The Obama government signaled that measured resolve would continue. It favored transparency and predictability in Sino-American relations. Unpredictability was generally not favored, notably by US officials responsible for managing

US-China relations, in part because of all the work involved in managing uncertainty. Unfortunately, smooth policy management seen fostered by the predictability and transparency of Obama policy allowed the opportunistic expansionism of China to continue without danger of serious adverse consequences for Chinese interests. In a word, the Obama government showed little danger of taking strong actions that would dissuade continued probing for advantage by Beijing. Beijing's continued probing could lead to a face-off with US forces in the South China Sea, but China had some confidence in past Obama government practice that the US president would take only small incremental steps in transparent ways, allowing China to pull back if necessary in one area while it prepared probes elsewhere. Obama's restraint seemed reinforced by the President's intent to leave office with a legacy of smoothly running Sino-American relations.[8]

Thus, it is not surprising that the carefully calibrated hardening of the Obama government's stance on various aspects of China policy was not accompanied by any change or hardening in its policy toward China over Taiwan. US officials highlighted progress in relations with Taiwan less likely to prompt frictions with China. They avoided taking sides against Tsai Ing-wen as they did in using a prominent news leak to voice concerns with her cross-Strait policy during Tsai's run for the presidency in the elections in January 2012.[9] As noted, the delicate cross-Strait situation following the January 2016 election caused the US government to double down on efforts to encourage both Beijing and Taipei to avoid provocations, seek constructive communications, and reach compromise formulas or understandings that would avoid a break in cross-Strait interchange detrimental to peace and stability.

Posed against the administration's treatment of Taiwan in ways that avoided friction with China were Americans in three schools of thought seeking to advance relations with Taiwan in ways that risked antagonizing Beijing. The victory to the DPP government, notably less deferential to Beijing than the Ma Ying-jeou government, raised the possibility that the Taiwan government might be more open and supportive of their initiatives.

Some Americans strongly urged US policy to deal with Taiwan for its own sake, rather than in a contingent way dependent on US interests with China. They opposed the US government intervention in Taiwan's domestic politics in voicing concern about Tsai Ing-wen's cross-Strait policies in 2011. They favored more forthright American government support for Taiwan's entry into the Trans-Pacific Partnership (TPP) multilateral economic agreement, more frequent US cabinet-level visits to Taiwan, and the sale of more advanced US military equipment to Taiwan; and they aver that recently strident American leadership complaints about Chinese bullying and intimidation of neighbors using military and other coercive means needed also to highlight and condemn China's two decades of massive bullying, coercion, and intimidation toward Taiwan.

A second group of Americans focus on using Taiwan's strategic location in opposition to what they saw as Chinese efforts to undermine the American strategic position around China's rim and achieve overall dominance in the region contrary to longstanding American interests. In their view, to counter such perceived efforts required a clear American strategy working with China's neighbors involving maritime control, and interdiction if necessary. Because of its location at the center of the so-called first island chain, Taiwan looms large in plans to counter Chinese expansion along its rim. The plans involve gaining the Taiwan government's cooperation in setting and monitoring sensors and other means of surveillance, preparing mobile units with anti-ship missiles to deploy to various locations in the first island chain, and preparing the use of mines and other means to deny access to Chinese ships and submarines.

A third group of Americans focused on the Xi Jinping government's recent coercive expansionism at American expense along China's rim and the other practices grossly at odds with US interests to argue that America should take actions showing greater support for Taiwan as part of a cost imposition strategy to counter Xi Jinping's anti-American practices. In their view, the kinds of steps forward in US relations with Taiwan advocated by the previous two groups should be considered and used as the United States endeavored to show Beijing that its various challenges to US interests would not be cost free and actually would be counterproductive for Chinese concerns on the all-important Taiwan issue.[10]

Given the deeply rooted American government practice to deal with Taiwan with an eye toward avoiding friction with China, a change in US government practice seemed unlikely without substantial change in the circumstances influencing that policy. The election of the DPP government, which was less deferential to Beijing than the KMT government, did not change Obama government's Taiwan policy. Meanwhile, despite its recent hardening, the Obama government remained on the moderate side of the American China policy debate. Most of the Republican candidates and Democratic candidate Hillary Clinton promised stronger resolve against foreign challenges such as those posed by Xi Jinping's China.

In sum, the likelihood of change in US Taiwan policy more supportive of Taiwan and less sensitive to Beijing seemed contingent on which candidate was elected. The likelihood also seems to depend on the status and salience of US differences with China amid seemingly more urgent policy matters deserving the attention of the incoming US government.

2015–2016 ELECTION DEBATES IMPACT US POLICY TOWARD CHINA-TAIWAN RELATIONS

The foreign policy debate in Washington in this period featured perceived American weaknesses throughout the world, including Asia. Republican leaders in Congress and supporting think tanks and interest groups joined media and other commentators in depicting major shortcomings in the Barack Obama government's policies in Europe, the Middle East, and Asia. One target was the so-called Obama Doctrine laid out in the President's speech to graduating West Point cadets in 2014 that showed greater administration wariness regarding security engagements abroad. The president's cautious approach seemed in line with prevailing American public opinion, even though the Republican-led critics in Congress and various media stressed the president's approach reflected weakness.[11]

The Obama government approach to Asia was defined by its "pivot" or rebalance to Asia policy announced in 2011. The United States accompanied military pullbacks from Iraq and Afghanistan with greater attention to a broad range of countries in Asia, from India in the west to Japan in the northeast and the Pacific Island states in the southeast. US diplomatic activism increased; existing substantial military deployments were maintained and strengthened in some areas; trade and investment remained open and were poised to increase, notably on the basis of the Trans-Pacific Partnership (TPP) free trade arrangement.[12]

The new US activism was widely welcomed by the governments in the region, with the notable exception of China. Under a new leadership of Communist Party Chief and President Xi Jinping (2012–), China used economic enticements on the one hand and coercive and intimidating means short of direct military force on the other hand in order to compel neighbors to accept Chinese claims to disputed territories and to side with China against American foreign policy initiatives. American critics of the Obama rebalance claimed that the US government was not resolute enough in defending the US role as regional security guarantor and not active enough in promoting greater American trade, investment, and diplomatic engagement in competition with China's state-directed efforts. For example, the Republican-leaning Heritage Foundation summed up critics' concerns by offering far-reaching political-security recommendations for Asia that added to the Foundation's longstanding support for greater free trade and investment there. The recommendations included more robust military spending to allow for a long-term goal of 350 naval ships (there are now about 280 ships in the Navy), increased support for allies and partners, expanded involvement with the Association of Southeast Asian Nations (ASEAN) and other regional groups, and greater firmness in dealing with Chinese challenges to regional and American interests.[13]

Relevant 2015–2016 Election Debates on Overall Policy Toward Asia

Most candidates talked about eroded or challenged US international power and influence, and the need to re-affirm America's role in the world. Candidates Hillary Clinton, Ted Cruz, John Kasich, Marco Rubio, and Donald Trump in varying ways favored strengthening US power and leadership. Bernie Sanders favored less muscular approaches than the other candidates, emphasizing negotiations over military means and pressure. Most affirmed strengthened relations with allies without much emphasis on greater reciprocity on the part of the allies.[14]

On specific issues involving US leadership that are discussed in more detail below, John Kasich joined free trade advocates in Congress, like House Speaker Paul Ryan, to support the TPP. Clinton, Cruz, Sanders, and Trump voiced varying opposition to the trade pact. Donald Trump was alone in insisting that allies do more to reciprocate American costs in maintaining their security and overall regional stability or face American withdrawal. And he accepted the possibility that allies without US support like Japan and South Korea might be compelled to develop nuclear weapons to protect themselves. All the candidates emphasized applying pressure to get the North Korean leader to denuclearize, but Mr. Trump was alone in also calling for direct talks with North Korea's leader, Kim Jung Un.

China remained the main country of concern regarding challenging US leadership in Asia. Relevant election discourse focused on how China was an unfair partner and how the United States needed to counter negative features of China's rise. China generally was not seen as an adversary; rather, it was depicted as neither an enemy nor a friend. Candidates

Clinton, Cruz, and Rubio argued for greater firmness against China; Sanders urged negotiations as did Trump, who also favored military buildup and trade sanctions if needed.

Hillary Clinton's priorities included holding China accountable.[15] She spoke highly of Obama's policies, played up her part in the rebalance, and called for continuity of the rebalance policies.[16] Ted Cruz said that Presidents Obama and Clinton had weakened America and jeopardized its global interests.[17] Bernie Sanders believed in resolving international conflicts in a peaceful manner. Sanders said, "…we must move away from policies that favor unilateral military action… and that make the United States the de facto policeman of the world." Sanders, like Trump, blamed current economic problems in the US on "disastrous trade policies" involving China and other countries.[18] Donald Trump said "… we have to rebuild our military and our economy." He held that international trade agreements were not beneficial; he preferred bilateral trade deals and opposed the TPP. Trump also fixed on currency manipulation, citing China and Japan. He usually did not find fault with China and others for taking advantage of perceived maladroit US trade policies. He promised swift and dramatic retaliation against Chinese and other unfair economic practices.[19]

Implications

Broad American concern with China remained active but secondary in the campaign debates. It was overshadowed by strong debate on international trade and the proposed Trans-Pacific Partnership (TPP) accord, as well as debate on candidate Donald Trump's controversial proposals on allied burden sharing, nuclear weapons proliferation, and North Korea.

Mr. Trump's strong opposition to the TPP and other US trade efforts was at odds with the free trade policies favored by Republican congressional leaders, but the Trump position had a strong appeal among both Republican and Democratic voters. He and Sanders reinforced each other's arguments; Clinton, Cruz, and others reversed or modified their positions to accord with the changed politics surrounding the TPP.

Candidate Trump's unique emphasis on getting Japan, South Korea, and other allies to compensate America for its role as regional security guarantor prompted serious negative reactions that promised significant complications for US alliance relations if Trump were elected president and attempted to follow through on his demands. His calls for Japan and

South Korea to compensate the United States for American security support were at odds with proposals by Speaker Ryan, Senator John McCain, and other Republican congressional leaders as well as many Republican-leaning think tanks and media. Some of these Republicans publicly opposed such policies.

Trump's acceptance of Japan or South Korea developing nuclear weapons for self-defense following a US pullback was a major departure from longstanding policies of Republican and Democratic US governments that was widely seen to add to the danger of war in northeastern Asia.

Trump's abrupt announcement that he would seek direct talks with North Korea's leader undermined existing US, South Korean, and Japanese policy and deviated sharply from the tough US posture on this issue favored by the Obama government and by Republican congressional leaders and Republican-leaning think tanks and media.

In summary, these three sets of controversial proposals by Mr. Trump garnered little support in the United States and prompted opposition, including from prominent congressional Republicans.

There was consensus among American and Asian observers consulted for an East-West Center report[20] that the election discussion politicized American foreign policy and weakened the American leadership position in Asia. The style of the campaign featured repeated personal attacks, gross language, and salacious accusations which degraded America's image and provided fodder for Chinese and others stressing the weaknesses of US democracy.

On policy issues, the success of the Sanders and Trump campaign attacks on the TTP surprised American and Asian commentators, notably by underlining seemingly weak popular American support for this important component of US policy in the region. The fact that the Republican Party—widely seen in the region as strongly committed to US defense ties with Asia—selected Mr. Trump, despite his controversial views on military disengagement from Asia and Europe and acceptance of proliferation of nuclear weapons, raised serious doubts about America's future regional role. Among Asian countries depending on military support from the United States, Japanese non-government commentators seemed the most concerned. On the other side of the spectrum of Asian views were Chinese commentators who saw opportunities for Chinese gains in competition with the United States for leadership in Asia as a result of the election's negative impact on the credibility of American commitments to Asian allies and friends.

For the most part, the Asian observers juxtaposed the above developments with evidence that strong engagement with Asia in the US rebalance policy would likely continue. The result was a muddled picture of US leadership sustainability. In particular, even if Hillary Clinton, an avowed supporter of the rebalance policy (with the exception of the TPP) had been elected president, the election debates over Asia meant trouble ahead for US leaders. The debates notably added to disturbing developments at home (e.g., terrorist attacks and racially motivated killings) and abroad (e.g., a weakened European Union and major crises involving the Middle East and Russia), seen likely to preoccupy the new American president and complicate steady American engagement with the region.

CHINA POLICY

That often sharp criticism of China remained at the center of the 2015–2016 election debates over Asia is consistent with an overall hardening of American policy toward the Chinese government and a wide range of its policies. Specialists detected a broad sense of American disappointment at the apparent failure in longstanding US efforts to constructively interact with China's leaders in expectation that those leaders would conform more to international norms in line with American interests. Instead, they found an ever more powerful Chinese state under the often bold leadership of President Xi Jinping seeking unfair advantage at America's expense and posing ever larger challenges to important US interests.[21]

China's egregious behavior reached a point in 2014 where President Obama became outspoken in repeatedly criticizing Chinese actions on the important issues. President Obama particularly singled out China in an effort to garner US congressional support for the TPP. At the same time, President Obama and President Xi continued to pursue greater cooperation in areas where interests overlapped; they appeared determined not to allow their disputes to undermine efforts to move the overall relationship in a positive direction.[22]

Relevant 2015–2016 Election Debates on China Policy

Though most presidential candidates voiced harsh criticism of Chinese policies and behavior, the mix of strong differences and positive engagement seen in the Obama administration's policy toward China was reflected in the candidates' similarly mixed policy recommendations. The contenders' views also were in line with American public opinion that, on balance, was disapproving of the Chinese government but ranked China lower than in the recent past as an economic threat and viewed China's military as less threatening to US interests than terrorism, nuclear weapons development in North Korea and Iran, various conflicts in the Middle East, climate change, refugee flows, and infectious diseases.[23]

Hillary Clinton's discourse on China showed a general theme of injustice. China was seen as manipulative as it maneuvers for selfish gains at the expense of US international interests and American workers. Clinton underlined her past record and continued resolve to rectify various wrongs, abuses, unfair practices, and China's threatening of allies. Key themes in her campaign included:

- Holding China accountable. "As secretary of state, Clinton reasserted America's role as a Pacific power and called out China's aggressive actions in the region. If elected, she promised to work with friends and allies to promote strong rules of the road and institutions in Asia, and encourage China to be a responsible stakeholder, including on cyberspace, human rights, trade, territorial disputes, and climate change, and hold it accountable if it does not."[24]
- China's rise. "How we handle that, how we respond to it will determine our future and the world's future. I want to see a peaceful rise for China,... but we also have to be fully vigilant. China's military is growing very quickly, they're establishing military installations that again threaten countries we have treaties with.... They're also trying to hack into everything that doesn't move in America. Stealing commercial secrets...from defense contractors, stealing huge amounts of government information, all looking for an advantage."[25]
- Chinese abuses. "I've gone toe – to – toe with China's top leaders on some of the toughest issues we face, from cyber-attacks to human rights to climate change to trade and more. I know how they operate and they know if I'm your president they are going to have to toe the line because we are going to once and for all get fair treatment, or they're not going to get access to our markets. When you know how somebody operates and you know they're always trying to game the system and you know that they really don't care about the rules of the road, you have to get tough, and you have to be ready to really draw the line. And I think we are at that point."[26]

Clinton's Democratic opponent Bernie Sanders focused primarily on trade and how China's development has come at the cost of American workers. He opposed international trade treaties in general and with China in particular, because he said it led to job losses in the United States and the weakening of labor unions. "I voted against [permanent normal trade relations] with China. That was the right vote, and if elected president I will radically transform trade policies." "I want to see the people in China live in a democratic society with a higher standard of living. I want to see that, but I don't think that has to take place at the expense of the American worker." Sanders also advocated working with China to curb fossil fuel consumption and address global climate change.[27]

Ted Cruz said the best way to approach China is to emphasize US military and economic might. He cited former President Ronald Reagan's "peace through strength" approach toward the Soviet Union during the Cold War as a model for contemporary US-China relations. At the first Republican primary debate, Cruz declared that China had committed acts of "cyberwar" against the United States, and later he recommended "counter attacks" to emphasize that there "will be a price to be paid." On human rights, Cruz joined other senators in petitioning for a plaza outside the Chinese embassy in Washington to be named after Liu Xiaobo, a human rights activist and 2010 Nobel Laureate who was then imprisoned in China.[28]

John Kasich was moderate about China. Kasich listed four major issues with China: North Korea, the South China Seas, cyber attacks, and currency manipulation. He advised, "We don't seek confrontation with China. But then why would we? Just as we have worked with China since President Nixon's historic initiative of 45 years ago, together we should forge innovative solutions and institutions that respect and accommodate the national security interests of every Pacific nation."[29]

Marco Rubio's well-developed approach to China was much tougher than what he saw as the "disaster" of Clinton's tenure as Secretary of State and the failed engagement policy of President Obama. He favored major increases in defense spending and strengthened relations with allies and partners in the Asia-Pacific, strong retaliation against Chinese economic misconduct and use of the Trans-Pacific Partnership and other free trade agreements to strengthen strategic ties with regional partners, and use of US leadership statements, visa bans, asset freezes, and other means against Chinese officials involved with human rights abuses and internal repression in China.[30]

According to Donald Trump, the main problem the United States has with China was that the United States has lost China's respect and is not using its power to influence them. The source of US power over China, according to Trump, is economic strength. Trump proposed tariffs of 45 percent on Chinese imports to counter unfair Chinese economic practices. Overall, Trump was not hostile to or confrontational with China. "We desire to live peacefully and in friendship with Russia and China. We have serious differences with these two nations, and must regard them with open eyes, but we are not bound to be adversaries. We should seek common ground based on shared interests." Trump saw the blame for the massive US trade deficit and negative impact on American manufacturing and job losses resting with maladroit American policies. Trump favored a strong military with "maximum firepower," but tended to avoid discussing China as a national security threat. He averred that issues with China can be dealt with through negotiations using American strengths as leverage.[31]

Implications

US policies dealing with China were seen as not working in several important areas. However, China was not seen as an enemy by the candidates or American public opinion. Most of the candidates, including leaders Hillary Clinton and Donald Trump, favored tougher policies, with Trump focused on seeking leverage in negotiations centered on economic issues, while Clinton's broader scope of concern included salient national security and human rights problems. The overall upshot of all the discussion of China in the campaign was moderate controversy over proposed remedies, with the possible exception of sometimes strident warnings against Donald Trump's threat to impose 45 percent tariffs on Chinese imports to the United States.

Observers in Beijing saw negatives with both Hillary Clinton and Donald Trump. Like many Americans, they were frustrated with the downward trend in US-China relations and judged that trend would worsen at least to some degree if Clinton were elected. Some in Beijing nonetheless voiced confidence that mutual interests and highly integrated US-China government relationships would guard against relations going seriously off track. Chinese derision of Donald Trump earlier in the campaign shifted to seeking advantage given the candidate's disruption of US alliances along China's rim and emphasis on seeking common ground with China through negotiations. Overall, a common view was that China could "shape" President Trump to behave in line with its interests as Mr. Trump was seen as less ideological and more pragmatic than Ms. Clinton.

Commentators in Japan urged tougher US policy toward China and South Koreans—like many in Southeast Asia—stressed avoiding increased US-China tensions. In Taiwan, the new government of President Tsai Ing-wen of the Democratic Progressive Party (DPP) sought to avoid confrontation with China over China's demand that the government accept the so-called 1992 consensus. Taiwan supporters of the DPP judged that some increase in US-China tensions on other issues might lead to more US support for the Tsai government. Taiwan supporters of the now opposition Kuomintang Party judged that US-China tensions would "squeeze" Taiwan between China and the US, providing no good options. Some observers in Taiwan cautioned that Donald Trump's proposed negotiations with China could lead Beijing, as in the past, to demand US concessions on Taiwan as "a price to be paid" for better US relations with China.

Disputes with China over the South China Sea

Heading the list of disagreements in the troubled Sino-American relationship entering the US 2016 election year was the disagreement over Chinese expansion using coercive means generally short of direct military force to advance its control at the expense of other claimants to wide swaths of disputed territory in the South China Sea.

As discussed above, President Obama's response to this and other Chinese challenges was measured. President Obama became more publicly vocal against Chinese expansionism in the South China Sea in 2014 and 2015, and over time he followed his vocal complaints with actions. In this period, China's continued massive dredging and construction of military and other installations on newly created South China Sea islands. In tandem came much more active US military deployments in the disputed South China Sea, along with blunt warnings by US military leaders of China's ambitions. Meanwhile, more prominent US cooperation with allies Japan, the Philippines, and Australia along with India and concerned Southeast Asian powers strengthened regional states and complicated Chinese expansion.

Rising tensions over the South China Sea saw US armed combat aircraft repeatedly patrol with Philippine forces over Scarborough Shoal beginning in April 2016. This large Chinese-claimed maritime feature near the main islands of the Philippines was long used by Philippine fishermen and patrolled by Philippine security forces until stronger Chinese Coast Guard forces expelled the fishermen, took control, and occupied it in 2012. Other episodes of tension over the past year included Chinese armed fighter jets harassing US surveillance planes by flying dangerously close to those planes, and US naval forces disregarding Chinese military warnings and shadowing Chinese warships and aircraft in carrying out so-called freedom on navigation exercises near land features occupied by China in the disputed South China Sea. A highpoint of China-US disagreement came when the arbitral tribunal affiliated with the Permanent Court of Arbitration ruled in July against China's vague claims to much of the South China Sea in a case brought by the Philippines and strongly backed by the United States, Japan, and Australia. Beijing had prepared for a possible adverse ruling with a large-scale propaganda campaign to discredit the tribunal and the Philippines case; it repeatedly warned against US and other "outside" infringements on China's claimed territorial sovereignty. A newly installed Philippines government reacted moderately to the judgment as did the United States and other concerned powers, avoiding an immediate crisis in relations with China.

Some American specialists and media commentary questioned the wisdom of the tough American stance on South China Sea issues, but the Republican-led Congress held hearings, passed legislation, and issued letters and statements arguing for more forthright American opposition to China's expansionist behavior that came at the expense of the US treaty ally, the Philippines, and Vietnam, a partner of rising importance for the United States.[32]

Relevant 2015–2016 Election Debates on South China Sea Disputes

The candidates did not add much to the ongoing discussion on the South China Sea disputes. The debate over what the United States should do remained active, but the presidential candidates had at best a secondary influence on the debate. Thus, for example, the Clinton and Trump campaigns responded to the arbitral tribunal ruling in July with brief statements of support.[33]

Earlier, Hillary Clinton supported the Philippines saying, "We've got challenges in the South China Sea because of what China is doing in building up these military installations. [...]" She added, "I have been very strongly in support with the Philippines in this dispute and I am proud of the Philippines for taking their dispute to the international court ... I thought that was a very wise decision, because there should not be a seizure of any territory until there's some kind of resolution that is legal."[34]

John Kasich recommended the US increase its presence in the South China Sea and other nearby waters to signal to China that its actions will not be tolerated. His campaign said, "In order to stand by our allies who feel threatened by China's aggressive actions in the South China Sea, the US must work with regional allies to significantly increase our military presence in region and ensure freedom of navigation for the $5.3 trillion in annual trade that passes through the Western Pacific. We must help Japan defend its territorial waters with advanced seabed acoustic sensors, anti-ship missiles and other defensive equipment. We must also forward deploy our Pacific combat commander to Guam and station additional Air Force and Marines Corps units in the Western Pacific where they can conduct regular joint regional amphibious landing exercises."[35]

Bernie Sanders mentioned the need to keep peace in the South China Sea in this way: "With China, the United States has to continue to work with our allies and partners in the region to maintain peace and prosperity. That means ensuring freedom of navigation in the South China Sea, which is critical to global commerce. It also means preventing tensions having to do with overlapping maritime claims from spiraling out of control between China, which claims much of the South China Sea, and other countries with overlapping claims of their own."[36]

Donald Trump mentioned China in the South China Sea as a threat but without much evidence or explanation. He said, "building a military island in the middle of the South China Sea, a military island. ... They built it in about one year, this massive military port. They're building up their military to a point that is very scary. You have a problem with ISIS. You have a bigger problem with China."[37]

Implications

The South China Sea dispute could have easily risen in importance for the presidential candidates in the event of such setbacks as a shooting incident or face-off of armed forces in the contested territory. In late 2016, it appeared that the ongoing debate would continue along recent lines without resolution or serious worsening, passing from the Obama to the Trump administration.

Observers in Beijing generally supported China's truculent response to the arbitral tribunal ruling. They advised the United States to react to the ruling in a low key way in order to avoid further worsening in US-China relations over the South China Sea disputes.

Interlocutors in Tokyo and Seoul had little to add to prevailing patterns: Japan continued supporting a tougher US stance on differences with China, and South Korea continued seeing such tensions working against its interests to avoid having to choose between Washington and Beijing. To varying degrees, observers in Southeast Asia shared the South Korean perspective. Australia was forthright in publicly backing the American reaction to the tribunal's judgment.

Observers in Taipei said that the Taiwan government had been working closely with the US government in preparing to respond in measured terms to the tribunal's ruling. Taiwan sought to maintain good terms with Washington while avoiding major retreat from its traditional expansive South China Sea claims, which mirror Beijing's. To retreat from its traditional expansive South China Sea claims could have caused problems with Beijing at this delicate time in Taiwan-China relations by signaling that Taiwan was moving away from its support of territorial claims associated with one China. However, the ruling had a negative impact on elite and public opinion in Taiwan. In particular, the ruling used a phrase very offensive to people in Taiwan in referring to the Taiwan government. And to the reported surprise of Taipei and Washington, the tribunal made a ruling regarding Taiping Island, the largest natural land feature in the Spratly Islands of the South China Sea, which is controlled by Taipei. The ruling said that Taiping Island did not qualify as an island under the terms of the UN Law of the Sea. Thus, it was not eligible for the large Exclusive Economic Zone (EEZ) given to islands as opposed to "rocks" permanently above sea level or above sea level at low tide. This development came as a significant setback to Taiwan's claims of fishing and other territorial rights in the South China Sea and prompted strong negative reaction in Taiwan that had to be accommodated by the government, according to observers in Taipei. The result was a strong statement from the Taiwan government criticizing the US-backed ruling and affirming Taiwan's territorial claims.

US Policy Toward Taiwan

As discussed earlier, the Xi Jinping government's territorial expansion, cyber theft, unfair economic practices, and internal repression drew strong rebukes from President Obama and hardened the administration's overall policy toward China. The president's wide-ranging and often sharp criticism notably refrained from including China's policy toward Taiwan. Rather, the president and his administration continued to adhere to an approach inherited from the George W. Bush administration that Taiwan issues should be handled in ways that avoid serious negative consequences for American policy toward China. Thus, the hardening of the Obama government's stance on various aspects of China policy was not accompanied by a hardening in its policy toward China over Taiwan.

US officials highlighted progress in relations with Taiwan involving cooperation on global issues, increased official interchanges at levels somewhat higher than in the recent past, assisting Taiwan membership in international bodies, and other matters that were deemed less likely to prompt frictions with China. They avoided taking sides against then-presidential candidate and now-President Tsai Ing-wen of the Democratic Progressive Party (DPP), who refused to endorse a view of "one China" demanded by Beijing. They encouraged both Beijing and Taipei to avoid provocations, seek constructive communications, and reach compromise formulas or understandings that would avoid a break in cross-Strait interchange detrimental to peace and stability. American critics of the administration's policy toward Taiwan included Republican leaders in Congress, Republican-leaning think tanks, media, and interest groups, along with many Democrats and progressive think tanks, media, and interest groups advocating change in existing US Taiwan policy less deferential to China.[38]

Relevant 2015–2016 Election Debates Regarding Taiwan

Taiwan received limited attention during the 2015–2016 election debates. A few Republican candidates and the Republican Party Platform used the arguments of the three schools of thought described above in calling for change in policy toward Taiwan. Before, during, and after his stint as a presidential candidate, Senator Marco Rubio has been active in congressional measures to support Taiwan along the lines of the first group of critics noted above who urge treating Taiwan on its own terms and without so much deference to Beijing. He frequently highlighted those initiatives during his campaign. Rubio notably backed a US military buildup to insure Taiwan's protection in the face of China's military power. He advised that US policy should be guided by historic American reassurances of support for Taiwan and not by reputed need to avoid exacerbating tensions with China over the issue.[39]

Senator Cruz released a statement on the results of Taiwan's January 2016 presidential elections lauding Taiwan on ideological grounds as a beacon for Democracy inspiring those in China and Hong Kong seeking freedom against the oppressive Communist government.[40]

Senator McCain and other senators visited Asia in May–June 2016 to reassure US allies and partners of continued strong American regional engagement despite Donald Trump's call for allies depending on US military protection to do more to offset the US costs or face American withdrawal. McCain and six of the visiting senators stopped in Taiwan to affirm support for recently installed President Tsai Ing-wen. The visit marked the first by the Chair of the Senate Armed Services Committee in 26 years and the largest group of US senators to visit Taiwan in 10 years.[41]

Though Mr. Trump said little about Taiwan, one of his policy advisors on Asian issues, Professor Peter Navarro, published in July an extensive assessment of the importance of stronger US support for Taiwan, using the arguments of the three schools of thought noted above.[42]

Implications

The US election debates on Taiwan deviated little from the arguments seen in Congress and the media prior to and during the American campaign. How Hillary Clinton's promised hardening of policy on disputes with China would impact her approach to Taiwan remained undefined. Her senior staff member Jake Sullivan said in July that Hillary Clinton would not change Taiwan policy.[43] Candidate Donald Trump devoted little attention to the issue.

In July 2016, observers in Taipei were concerned that Taiwan would suffer if Donald Trump were to follow through with pledges to negotiate major agreements with China, as the Taiwan issue would likely be raised by the Chinese side in those negotiations. There also was worry in Taipei that candidate Trump's approach to US ally Japan would seriously weaken the US ability to support Taiwan in the face of China's military intimidation. Observers in Taiwan appreciated the resolve shown by McCain and his colleagues to continue support for US allies and partners in Asia regardless of the results of the American presidential election. They were encouraged by interactions with Trump campaign Asia expert Peter Navarro during a recent visit to Taiwan as well as strong support for Taiwan registered in the Republican Party platform. The July 12 arbitral tribunal led observers in Taiwan to complain that its interests in the South China Sea have less priority than other concerns in current US policy. There was broad worry among Taiwan observers on how they could advance Taiwan's importance in US administration's policy deliberations. In particular, the Taiwan government was preparing actively for future entry into the TPP and hoped the agreement would be approved by Congress, allowing Taiwan to be supported for entry by the United States in the next round of membership for the body.

Taiwan issues did not figure prominently in comments by interlocutors in China or elsewhere in Asia. High-level interlocutors in Beijing judged that Hillary Clinton's tougher approach would not involve major moves on Taiwan.

Outlook

In December 2016, then-President-elect Trump sharply broke with past practice by accepting a congratulatory phone call from Taiwan President Tsai Ing-wen, publicly questioning US government support for the policy of "one China" including Taiwan, and reacting promptly to Chinese criticisms with blunt public complaints about unfair Chinese economic policies and military expansion in the disputed South China Sea. The phone call was facilitated by representatives in the President-elect's entourage and the Republican Party leadership who favored an American policy toward Taiwan less deferential to Beijing.[44]

The moves upset Chinese forecasts of smoother sailing with Donald Trump than with Hillary Clinton. In a few gestures, the President-elect showed President Xi and his lieutenants that the new US leader was capable of a wide range of actions that would surprise Chinese counterparts with serious negative consequences. During the long US election campaign, Mr. Trump made clear that he values unpredictability and does not place the high value President Obama did on policy transparency, carefully measured responses, and avoiding dramatic actions. He is much less constrained than the previous US administration by a perceived need to sustain and advance US-China relations. Like President Xi and unlike President Obama, President Trump does not eschew tension and presumably seeks advantage in tensions between the two countries. And like his Chinese counterpart and unlike President Obama, he is prepared to seek leverage through linking his policy preference in one area of the relationship with policies in other areas of the relationship.

What all of the above meant for the full range of US relations with China and especially policy toward Taiwan remained very uncertain as Mr. Trump took office. As time passed the US president in February saw the wisdom in meeting Xi Jinping's requirement for consultations by saying in a phone conversation with Xi that he supported the traditional one China policy of the United States. A summit with Xi at President Trump's resort Mar-a-Lago in Florida in April came amid intensified US pressure on China to do more to stop North Korea's development of nuclear weapons. The strong US focus on China and North Korea caused the president and the administration for a few weeks to avoid actions that would have alienated Beijing such as freedom of navigation naval demonstrations along China's coast and arms sales to Taiwan. It was against this background that President Trump told the media in April 2017 that he would not accept another phone call from Taiwan's president until he had discussed the matter with President Xi.[45]

Showing a remarkable inclination to change American policy in ways that complicated Chinese efforts to seek the advantageous stability it desired in relations with the United States, President Trump in June expressed disappointment with China's efforts to curb North Korea's nuclear weapons. What followed were US freedom of navigation exercises in much faster sequence than in the recent past in the disputed South China Sea, an announced major US arms sales package for Taiwan, strong public statements from Secretary of Defense James Mattis and Secretary of State Rex Tillerson in support of American military and other commitments to Taiwan, and substantial US sanctions against a Chinese bank and Chinese individuals seen by the United States as aiding North Korea to circumvent international sanctions against its nuclear weapons program. Administration officials privately indicated that more measures were to come demonstrating American resolve against Chinese actions seen opposed to US security, economic, and other interests.[46]

Whether or not there is some sort of decisive outcome from such twists and turns on sensitive issues in US-China relations remains very uncertain. One path forward could involve constant shifting, depending a various circumstances. The Trump administration seems at bottom wary of Xi

Jinping's China, and if Xi and his officials had thought that Trump would be easy to deal with, one suspects that such views are now a thing of the past. Signs to watch for include an articulated strategy of the Trump government in foreign affairs and the Asia-Pacific region in particular that China could respond to negatively or positively with a sense of clarity. Present circumstances—notably a volatile US president with a still very poorly staffed administration—see that strategy as far off.

Regarding Taiwan, it is possible but unlikely that President Trump will succeed in persuading President Xi to accept some improvement in US-Taiwan relations and other changes in China policy favorable to the United States rather than risk major disruption and confrontation in Sino-American relations at this sensitive time of leadership transition in China. On the other end, President Xi may, out of a sense of power and confidence or a sense of vulnerability, resort to massive demonstrations of Chinese economic and military power to compel the Trump government to reverse its Taiwan initiatives and accommodate China's demands. In between are many possibilities, including negotiations and deal making favored by Mr. Trump and many in China where compromises will be reached allowing for smoother progress in the relationship. Taiwan presumably would benefit from the first outcome; it would be at the center of any US-China military face-off seen in the second outcome; and as noted above, observers in Taiwan remain concerned that Taiwan will be "the price to pay" in any US-China grand bargain governing future Sino-American relations.

NOTES

1. For relevant overviews, see Steven M. Goldstein, *China and Taiwan* (Polity 2015); Richard Bush, *Untying the Knot* (Brookings 2005); Richard Bush, *Unchartered Strait* (Brookings 2013); US Congress, House Foreign Affairs Committee, "Subcommittee Hearing: The Future of U.S.-Taiwan Relations," Feb 11, 2016 (Statements of R. Schriver, B. Glaser and S. Rigger), https://foreignaffairs.house.gov/hearing/subcommittee-hearing-the-future-of-u-s-taiwan-relations/; recent developments are reviewed triannually in David Brown "China-Taiwan Relations," *Comparative Connections* http://cc.csis.org/, and in articles by Alan Romberg in *Chinese Leadership Monitor* http://www.hoover.org/publications/china-leadership-monitor.

2. In addition to the sources in note 44, see Bonnie Glaser, *Prospects for Cross-Strait Relations as Tsai Ing-wen assumes the Presidency in Taiwan* (CSIS April 2016); Shelley Rigger, *Why Taiwan Matters*, updated ed. (Rowman and Littlefield 2014); Russell Hsiao, "U.S.-Taiwan Relations: Hobson's Choice and the False Dilemma," *Strategic Asia 2014–2015* (National Bureau of Asian Research 2014): 256–287; Brantly Womack and Yufan Hao, *Rethinking the Triangle: Washington-Beijing-Taipei* (World Scientific 2016); Yun-han Chu et al., *Taiwan's Democracy Challenged: The Chen Shui-bian Years* (Lynne Rienner 2016); Robert Sutter, *U.S.-Chinese Relations* (Rowman & Littlefield 2013): 229–248.
3. Harry Harding, "Has U.S. China Policy Failed?" *The Washington Quarterly* 38, no. 3 (2015): 95–122.
4. This review is taken from Robert Sutter, "Taiwan's Elections, China's Response and America's Policy," *The Diplomat Magazine*, February 1, 2016, http://thediplomat.com/2016/02/taiwans-elections-chinas-response-and-americas-policy/; See also Robert Sutter, *U.S.-Chinese Relations* (2013).
5. David Michael Lampton, "A Tipping Point in U.S.-China Relations is Upon Us," *US-China Perception Monitor*, May 11, 2015; Robert Blackwill and Ashley Tellis, *Council Special Report : Revising U.S. Grand Strategy toward China* (Washington, DC: Council on Foreign Relations, April 2015); Orville Schell and Susan Shirk, Chairs, *US Policy toward China: Recommendations for a new administration* (New York: Asia Society, 2017).
6. Robert Sutter, "Obama's Cautious and Calibrated Approach to an Assertive China," *YaleGlobal* (2016), http://yaleglobal.yale.edu/content/obamas-cautious-and-calibrated-approach-assertive-china; Jeffrey Bader, *A Framework for U.S. Policy Toward China* (Brookings March 2016); Deputy Secretary Blinken Testimony on U.S.-China Relations: Strategic Challenges and Opportunities, Senate Foreign Relations Committee, April 27, 2016.
7. "ZTE to pay massive U.S. fine over Iran, North Korea," *EURONEWS*, March 7, 2017 http://www.euronews.com/2017/03/07/china-s-zte-to-pay-massive-us-fine-over-iran-north-korea-sanctions-busting.
8. Author consultations with U.S. administration officials, Washington, DC, August, 2016 and January, 2017.
9. Anna Fifield, Robin Kwong and Katherin Hille, "US Concerned about Taiwan Candidate," *Financial Times* September 15, 2011 https://www.ft.com/content/f926fd14-df93-11e0-845a-00144feabdc0?mhq5j=e1.
10. These differing approaches are seen in these and among others: Richard C. Bush III, "Cross-Strait relations: Not a one-way street," *Brookings Institution*, April 22, 2016, http://www.brookings.edu/blogs/order-from-chaos/posts/2016/04/22-cross-strtait-relations-bush; Mark Stokes

and Sabrina Tsai, "The United States and Future Policy Options in the Taiwan Strait," *Project 2049*, February 1, 2016, http://www.project2049.net/documents/Future_US%20Policy%20Options%20in%20the%20Taiwan%20Strait_Project%202049.pdf; T.X. Hammes, "Strategy for an Unthinkable Conflict," *The Diplomat*, July 27, 2012, http://thediplomat.com/2012/07/military-strategy-for-an-unthinkable-conflict/; John Bolton, "China-Taiwan tensions are rising," *John Bolton PAC*, April 25, 2016, http://www.boltonpac.com/2016/04/bolton-china-taiwan-tensions-rising-obama-responds-critical/; William Lowther, "US presidential candidate pledges to defend Taiwan," *The Taipei Times*, January 9, 2016, http://www.taipeitimes.com/News/taiwan/archives/2016/01/09/2003636798.
11. See among others, Leon Hadar, "Obama's West Point Realism, *The American Conservative*, May 30, 2014, http://www.theamericanconservative.com/articles/obamas-west-point-realism/.
12. Mark E. Manyin et al., *Pivot to the Pacific? The Obama Administration's "Rebalancing" toward Asia*, Report 42448 (Washington, DC: Library of Congress, Congressional Research Service, March 28, 2012); Robert Sutter, Michael Brown, and Timothy Adamson, *Balancing Acts: The U.S. Rebalance and Asia Pacific Stability* (Washington, DC: George Washington University, Elliott School of International Affairs, 2013); Timothy Adamson, Michael Brown, and Robert Sutter, *Rebooting the U.S. Rebalance to Asia* (Washington, DC: George Washington University, Elliott School of International Affairs, 2014); Hugo Meijer, ed., *Origins and Evolution of the U.S. Rebalance toward Asia: Diplomatic, Military and Economic Dimensions* (London: Palgrave Macmillan, 2015); Kurt Campbell, *The Pivot: The Future of American Statecraft in Asia* (New York: Twelve: The Hachette Group, 2016.
13. Walter Lohman, *Top Five Political-Security Priorities for the Asia-Pacific in 2016* (Washington, DC: Heritage Foundation, February 5, 2016).
14. This section is adapted from Robert Sutter and Satu Limaye *Washington Asia Policy Debates: Impact of 2015–2016 Presidential Campaign and Asian Reactions*, East-West Center (Washington September 2016). The principal findings and US policy implications of this report are based on the author's assessment of campaign statements and other materials made available in the East-West Center Washington 2016 Presidential Candidates on Asia, http://www.asiamattersforamerica.org/asia/2016-presidential-candidates-on-asia; other news and commentary as well as interviews and discussions with senior Republican and Democratic Asian specialists conducted in Washington, DC, during June 2016 and with Asian specialists, commentators, and officials in Beijing, Seoul, Taipei, Tokyo, and Washington, DC, during July 2016.

15. "Issues: National Security: With policies that keep us strong and safe, America can lead the world in the 21st century," *Hillary for America* https://www.hillaryclinton.com/issues/national-security, accessed June 10, 2016.
16. "Hillary Clinton Addresses The Iran Nuclear Deal," presentation at The Brookings Institution (Washington, DC, September 9, 2015),. http://www.brookings.edu/events/2015/09/09-clinton-iran-nuclear-deal, accessed July, 5 2016.
17. "Defend Our Nation," *Cruz for President*, https://www.tedcruz.org/issues/defend-our-nation, accessed June 20, 2016.
18. "Issues: War and Peace," *Bernie 2016*, https://berniesanders.com/issues/war-and-peace/, accessed June 10, 2016; "Bernie Sanders: On Trade," Council on Foreign Relations, *Campaign 2016: The Candidates & The World*, http://www.cfr.org/campaign2016/bernie-sanders/on-trade,accessed June 10, 2016.
19. "'America First' Foreign Policy Speech," Washington, DC, April 27, 2016 http://time.com/4309786/read-donald-trumps-america-first-foreign-policy-speech, accessed July 5, 2016.
20. Sutter and Limaye *Washington Asia Policy Debates: Impact of 2015–2016 Presidential Campaign and Asian Reactions.*
21. Harding, "Has U.S. China Policy Failed?" (2015).
22. Sutter, "Obama's Cautious and Calibrated Approach to an Assertive China," (2016).
23. Jeffery M. Jones, "Americans See China's Economic Power as Diminished Threat," *Gallup*, February 26, 2015, http://www.gallup.com/poll/181733/americans-china-economic-power-diminished-threat.aspx; Saad, "Americans See China as Top Economy Now, but U.S. in Future." Lydia Saad, "Americans See China as Top Economy Now, but U.S. in Future." *Gallup.* February 22, 2016. http://www.gallup.com/poll/189347/americans-china-top-economy-future.aspx.
24. Hillary Clinton, "Issues: National Security: With policies that keep us strong and safe, America can lead the world in the 21st century," *Hillary for America.*
25. Hillary Clinton, "Campaign Rally in New Hampshire," campaign speech in New Hampshire (June 5, 2015), http://www.bbc.com/news/world-us-canada-33399711.
26. Hillary Clinton, "Remarks to AFL-CIO," AFL-CIO Convention in Philadelphia, PA, (April 6, 2016).
27. Bernie Sanders, interview by Ezra Klein, *Vox*, July 28, 2015, http://www.vox.com/2015/7/28/9014491/bernie-sanders-vox-conversation.

28. Council on Foreign Relations, "Ted Cruz: On China," *Campaign 2016: The Candidates & The World*, http://www.cfr.org/campaign2016/ted-cruz/on-china.
29. John Kasich, "A Conversation With John Kasich," (Council of Foreign Relations, Washington, DC, December 9, 2015) http://www.cfr.org/united-states/conversation-john-kasich/p37304; John Kasich, "Republican Presidential Debate in Miami, Florida," Televised Broadcast, *CNN*, March 10, 2016, http://www.cnn.com/2016/03/10/politics/republican-debate-transcript-full-text/index.html.
30. Marco Rubio, "How My Presidency Would Deal With China," *The Wall Street Journal*, August 27, 2015, http://www.wsj.com/articles/how-my-presidency-would-deal-with-china-1440717685.
31. Maggie Haberman, "Donald Trump Says He Favors Big Tariffs on Chinese Exports," *New York Times*, January 7, 2016, http://www.nytimes.com/politics/first-draft/2016/01/07/donald-trump-says-he-favors-big-tariffs-on-chinese-exports/; *Donald* Trump, "'America First' Foreign Policy Speech," Washington, DC, April 27, 2016.
32. Ronald O'Rourke, "Maritime Territorial and Exclusive Economic Zone (EEZ) Disputes Involving China: Issues for Congress," *Congressional Research Service*, May 31, 2016, https://www.fas.org/sgp/crs/row/R42784.pdf.
33. "Parties Should Accept South China Sea Decision: Donald Trump's Adviser," *India Express*, July 13, 2016.
34. Hillary Clinton, "Democratic Presidential Debate in Des Moines, Iowa," Televised Broadcast, CBS, November 15, 2015; Hillary Clinton, interview by *ABS-CBN, ABS-CBN News North America*, February 24, 2016, http://news.abs-cbn.com/global-filipino/02/23/16/clinton-backs-ph-moves-in-sea-dispute-with-china.
35. John Kasich, "A Comprehensive Outline For American Security In A Chaotic World," *Kasich for America*.
36. Bernie Sanders, interview with *Brooklyn Daily Eagle, Brooklyn Daily Eagle*, April 19, 2016, http://www.brooklyneagle.com/articles/2016/4/19/exclusive-qa-hillary-clinton-and-bernie-sanders-brooklyn-national-issues.
37. Donald Trump, "Presidential Campaign Announcement," (New York, New York, June 16, 2015) http://blogs.wsj.com/washwire/2015/06/16/donald-trump-transcript-our-country-needs-a-truly-great-leader/.
38. Robert Sutter, "The Taiwan elections: Don't expect a US policy change," *The Interpreter*, January 20, 2016,
    http://www.lowyinterpreter.org/post/2016/01/20/The-Taiwan-elections-Dont-expect-a-US-policy-change.aspx.
39. William Lowther, "US presidential candidate pledges to defend Taiwan," *The Taipei Times*, January 9, 2016, http://www.taipeitimes.com/News/taiwan/archives/2016/01/09/2003636798.

40. Ten Cruz, "Sen. Cruz: Taiwan Is Exemplar of Liberty and Best Hope for Peace in East Asia," *Senate Office of Ted Cruz*, January 16, 2016, https://www.cruz.senate.gov/?p=press_release&id=2576.
41. William Lowther, "Tsai has 'very successful' US meetings," *The Taipei Times*, June 4, 2015, http://www.taipeitimes.com/News/front/archives/2015/06/04/2003619870.
42. Peter Navarro, "America Can't Dump Taiwan," *The National Interest*, July 19, 2016 http://nationalinterest.org/feature/america-cant-dump-taiwan-17040, accessed July 29, 2016.
43. William Lowther, "Clinton would not change US' Taiwan policy: aide," *Taipei Times*, July 27, 2016, 3.
44. Bonnie Glaser and Alexandra Viers, "U.S.-China Relations," *Comparative Connections*, 18, no. 3, January 2017:21–22.
45. David Brown and Kevin Scott, "China-Taiwan Relations, "*Comparative Connections* Vol. 19, No. 1 (May 2017): pp. 62–63.
46. Shi Jiangtao, "US doubts over one-China linchpin to stalk Sino-US security talks," *South China Morning Post* June 16, 2017 p. 1; Mark Landler, "Trump takes more aggressive stance with U.S. friend and foes in Asia," *New York Times* June 30, 2017, https://www.nytimes.com/2017/06/30/world/asia/trump-south-korea-china.html.

Bibliography

Bader, Jeffrey. 2012. *Obama and China's Rise*. Washington, DC: Brookings Institution.
Bush, Richard. 2005. *Untying the Knot: Making Peace in the Taiwan Strait*. Washington, DC: Brookings Institution.
———. 2012. *Unchartered Strait: The Future of China-Taiwan Relations*. Washington, DC: Brookings Institution.
Center for a New American Security. 2015. *More Willing and Able: Charting China's International Security Activism*. Washington, DC: Center for a New American Security.
Chi, Su. 2008. *Taiwan's Relations with Mainland China: A Tail Wagging Two Dogs*. New York: Routledge.
Christensen, Thomas. 2015. *The China Challenge: Shaping the Choices of a Rising Power*. New York: W.W. Norton.
Copper, John. 2016. *Taiwan's 2016 Presidential/Vice Presidential and Legislative Elections*. Baltimore: Maryland Series in Contemporary Asian Studies.
Fravel, M. Taylor. 2011. China's Strategy in the South China Sea. *Contemporary Southeast Asia* 33 (3): 292–319.
Friedberg, Aaron. 2011. *A Contest for Supremacy: China, America, and the Struggle for Mastery in Asia*. New York: W.W. Norton.

———. 2014. *Beyond Air-Sea Battle: The Debate over US Military Strategy in Asia*, Adelphi Paper 444. London: International Institute for Strategic Studies.
Glaser, Charles. 2011. Will China's Rise Lead to War. *Foreign Affairs* 90 (2): 80–91.
Glaser, Bonnie. 2016. *Prospects for Cross-Strait Relations as Tsai Ing-wen assumes the Presidency in Taiwan*. Washington, DC: CSIS.
Goldstein, Lyle. 2015a. *Meeting China Halfway*. Washington, DC: Georgetown University Press.
Goldstein, Steven. 2015b. *China and Taiwan*. New York: Polity.
Goldstein, Steven, and Julian Chang, eds. 2008. *Presidential Politics in Taiwan: The Administration of Chen Shui-bian*. Norwalk: Eastbridge.
Hachigian, Nina. 2014. *Debating China*. New York: Oxford University Press.
International Crisis Group. 2005. *China-Taiwan: Uneasy Détente*, Asia Briefing 42. Brussels: International Crisis Group.
Johnson, Christopher. 2014. *Decoding China's Emerging "Great Power" Strategy in Asia*. Washington, DC: Center for Strategic and International Studies.
Lampton, David Michael. 2014. *Following the Leader: Ruling China from Deng Xiaoping to Xi Jinping*. Berkeley: University of California Press.
Lee, David Tawei. 2000. *The Making of the Taiwan Relations Act*. New York: Oxford University Press.
Lieberthal, Kenneth, and Wang Jisi. 2012. *Addressing U.S.-China Strategic Distrust*. Washington, DC: Brookings Institution.
Medeiros, Evan. 2005–2006. Strategic Hedging and the Future of Asia-Pacific Stability. *Washington Quarterly* 29 (1): 145–167.
Murray, William S. 2008 Summer. Revisiting Taiwan's Defense Strategy. *Naval War College Review* 61: 13–38.
O'Rourke, Ronald. 2015. *China's Naval Modernization*, Report RL33153. Washington, DC: Library of Congress, Congressional Research Service.
Pillsbury, Michael. 2015. *The Hundred Year Marathon*. New York: Henry Holt and Company.
Rigger, Shelley. 2006. *Taiwan's Rising Rationalism: Generations, Politics, and "Taiwanese Nationalism"*. Washington, DC: East-West Center.
———. 2014. *Why Taiwan Matters*. Lanham: Rowman and Littlefield.
Ross, Robert S. 2006. Taiwan's Fading Independence Movement. *Foreign Affairs* 85 (2): 141–148.
Roy, Denny. 2003. *Taiwan: A Political History*. Ithaca: Cornell University Press.
Su Ge. 1998. *Meiguo: Dui hua Zhengce yu Taiwan wenti* [America: China Policy and the Taiwan Issue]. Beijing: Shijie Zhishi Chubanshe.
Sutter, Robert, and Satu Limaye. 2016. *America's 2016 Election Debate on Asia Policy and Asian Reactions*. Washington, DC: East-West Center.
Swaine, Michael. 2011. *America's Challenge: Engaging a Rising China in the Twenty-First Century*. Washington, DC: Carnegie Endowment for International Peace.

Tellis, Ashley. 2014. *Balancing Without Containment*. Washington, DC: Carnegie Endowment for International Peace Report, January 22, 2014.
Tucker, Nancy Bernkopf. 2009. *Strait Talk: United States-Taiwan Relations and the Crisis with China*. Cambridge, MA: Harvard University Press.
Wachman, Alan. 2007. *Why Taiwan: Geostrategic Rationales for China's Territorial Integrity*. Stanford: Stanford University Press.
Yan Xuetong. 2010. The Instability of *China-US* Relations. *The Chinese Journal of International Politics* 3 (3): 1–30.

CHAPTER 10

Rethinking US Security Commitment to Taiwan

Yuan-kang Wang

The Taiwan Strait is widely regarded as the most dangerous flash point in US-China relations, leading a top US expert on Asia to warn that "a Taiwan clash is the only conflict in which the US could confront a nuclear power with a huge military establishment."[1] Historically, power transitions have often resulted in war.[2] With China's expanding military capabilities and growing political ambitions, the likelihood of a US-China conflict appears to be rising. Should the United States end its security commitment to Taiwan to avoid war with an increasingly powerful China?

International relations scholars propose accommodation as a strategy of peaceful power transition, arguing that if the dominant states gradually accommodate the interests of rising powers, share systemic leadership, and accept separate spheres of influence, a peaceful transformation of the system is possible.[3] In the case of the US-China power transition, accommodationists advocate ending the US security commitment to Taiwan as a war-avoidance strategy.[4] For them, Taiwan is a strategic liability and an

---

Y.-k. Wang (✉)
Department of Political Science, Western Michigan University,
Kalamazoo, MI, USA

© The Author(s) 2019
W.-c. Lee (ed.), *Taiwan's Political Re-Alignment and Diplomatic Challenges*, Politics and Development of Contemporary China,
https://doi.org/10.1007/978-3-319-77125-0_10

unnecessary provocation to China. To accommodate China, the United States should terminate its quasi-alliance with Taiwan, repeal the Taiwan Relations Act, or at least reduce arms sales. Once the thorny issue of Taiwan is removed, so the argument goes, both countries can engage in cooperative activities and build mutual trust.

This article evaluates the "abandon Taiwan" literature and argues that accommodating China on Taiwan will increase—not decrease—the probability of conflict in East Asia. Rather than moderating China's foreign policy ambitions, accommodation would expand them, making the region more prone to conflict. Moreover, accommodation would destroy the delicate balance between deterrence and reassurance in the Taiwan Strait. By deassuring Taiwan of US protection, accommodation would push Taiwan into taking risky political initiatives that might provoke China and create new security dynamics that could increase tensions and destabilize the region.

I identify five major errors in the "abandon Taiwan" argument. First, accommodationists misidentify Taiwan as the main cause of US-China security competition and strategic mistrust. What is causing tensions in US-China relations is structural, not issue-specific. Second, accommodationists wrongly assume that Chinese foreign policy is driven by limited aims. The foreign policy goals of a state are inherently difficult to ascertain with confidence. Third, accommodating China on Taiwan will damage US credibility for honoring its security commitments to other allies and partners. A decision to abandon Taiwan could trigger unintended consequences that undermine US security interests and substantially increase the costs of restoring the status quo. Fourth, forsaking Taiwan contradicts the US interest in upholding the values of human rights, freedom, and democracy. The US security commitment to Taiwan is compatible with both American strategic interests and democratic values. Finally, accommodating China on Taiwan would jeopardize the US policy of dual deterrence in the Taiwan Strait. By deassuring Taiwan, accommodation would destroy the delicate balance between deterrence and reassurance, thus destabilizing the region.

The chapter proceeds as follows. The first section distills the main arguments of abandoning Taiwan and traces the theoretical foundation of accommodation to defensive realism. I question the explanatory power of defensive realism and adopt offensive realism as my theoretical baseline. Next, I analyze the five errors of accommodationist proposals: underestimation of structural pressures; mistaken assumption of China's limited aims; damage to US alliance credibility; downplaying of Taiwan's democratic and strategic values; and destruction of the delicate balance between deterrence and reassurance. Finally, I argue for a strengthening of US-Taiwan security and economic ties as part of the US grand strategy toward Asia.

Accommodating China

The US security commitment to Taiwan is enshrined in the Taiwan Relations Act (TRA) of 1979, which replaced the bilateral mutual defense treaty that was terminated after Washington recognized the People's Republic of China and derecognized the Republic of China (Taiwan). In the TRA, the United States retains its security commitment to Taiwan in two important ways. First, the United States considers any threat to Taiwan as "a threat to the peace and security of the Western Pacific area and of grave concern to the United States." In response to such danger, the United States promises to take "appropriate action" to restore peace. This became known as the policy of strategic ambiguity. Second, the United States will "provide Taiwan with arms of a defensive character." These arms sales help Taiwan strengthen self-defense capabilities, enable Taiwan to negotiate with China from a position of strength, and give the United States sufficient lead time to respond to a Taiwan crisis.

Over the decades, the US security commitment has kept the peace in the Taiwan Strait, allowing cross-Strait social and economic exchanges to flourish. China's rapid rise, however, puts stress on the international system and foreshadows a dangerous power transition with the United States. The structural stress is such that both the rising power's dissatisfaction with the current system and the existing hegemon's fear of being overtaken significantly increase the likelihood of war. Graham Allison coins the term "Thucydides Trap" to capture the danger of power transition.[5] The high probability of war apparently prompted Chinese President Xi Jinping to publicly deny the existence of the Thucydides Trap during his visit to the United States in 2015: "There is no such thing as the so-called Thucydides trap in the world. But should major countries time and again make the mistakes of strategic miscalculation, they might create such traps for themselves."[6] Avoiding a potential US-China war has become one of the most important issues for policymakers as well as academic communities.

Accommodation emerges as a war-avoidance strategy during power transition. T.V. Paul defines accommodation as "mutual adaptation and acceptance by established and rising powers, and the elimination or substantial reduction of hostility between them."[7] The term "accommodation" is a variant of the disgraced strategy of appeasement. Given the emotional baggage of appeasement, most analysts choose to use the term "accommodation" instead. Culling through various definitions, Norrin M. Ripsman and Jack S. Levy summarize that appeasement is "conventionally defined as the satisfaction of grievances through unilateral concessions, with the aim of avoiding war."[8] Charles Glaser defines accommodation synonymously with appeasement: "unilateral territorial concessions to an adversary designed to reduce the probability of war."[9] Like appeasement, the strategy of accommodation attempts to reduce the probability of war by making unilateral concessions to a dissatisfied adversary in hopes of turning it into a status quo power.

Proponents of accommodating China on Taiwan offer three arguments. First, Taiwan is the most dangerous issue in US-China relations and the main source of potential conflict. Removing it would pave the way for better bilateral relations. In the words of Chas Freeman: "The Taiwan issue is the only one with the potential to ignite a war between China and the United States.... The kind of long-term relationship of friendship and cooperation China and America want with each other is incompatible with our emotionally fraught differences over the Taiwan issue. These differences propel mutual hostility and the sort of ruinous military rivalry between the two countries that has already begun."[10] Similarly, Charles Glaser writes, "the United States should consider backing away from its commitment to Taiwan. This would remove the most obvious and contentious flash point between the United States and China and smooth the way for better relations between them in the decades to come."[11] Forsaking Taiwan, so the thinking goes, defuses the most explosive issue in US-China relations and prevents a future conflict.

Second, accommodationists argue that abandoning Taiwan could moderate the security dilemma between the United States and China. Military competition is already intensifying. China is expanding anti-access area denial (A2/AD) capabilities (which the Chinese military refers to as "counter-intervention," *fan jieru*) to thwart US intervention in the Taiwan Strait, while the United States is developing its AirSea Battle concept to counter China. Charles Glaser writes, "A decision by the United States to end its commitment to Taiwan could moderate this security dilemma...."[12] Similarly, Bruce Gilley argues that ending the US security commitment would "allow Taiwan to break this cycle by taking itself out of the game and moderating the security dilemma that haunts the Washington-Beijing relationship."[13] In this view, abandoning Taiwan enables trust-building and facilitates cooperation between the United States and China.

Third, accommodationists claim that China has limited aims in its foreign policy. "From the United States' perspective," writes Charles Glaser, "there is broad agreement on Taiwan—China's goal of unification makes China a limited-aims expansionist state."[14] Chas W. Freeman, Jr., avers that "China does not...have a history of global power projection, seek to export an ideology, or propose to expand beyond its traditional frontiers."[15] In this view, China's security objective is defense of the homeland, not expansionism. China does not seek regional hegemony, nor does it wish to push the United States out of Asia. If China has no desire beyond Taiwan, abandoning Taiwan would not risk creating a more dangerous China. Once this key source of bilateral tension is removed, both Beijing and Washington could then proceed to build a more cooperative relationship. Bruce Gilley goes even further: "Beijing has no interest in occupying or ruling Taiwan; it simply wants a sphere of influence that increases its global clout and in which Taiwan is a neutral state, not a client state."[16] Since China is motivated by the limited aims of defending the mainland, Gilley proposes that Washington should stop antagonizing China and end its security commitment to Taiwan, letting the island become a Finlandized neutral state.

Taken together, accommodationists believe that by making unilateral concessions on Taiwan, the United States would remove the principal source of conflict and disagreement with China, thereby satisfying China's grievances, reducing bilateral tensions, and potentially avoiding war.

Although most accommodationists do not explicitly ground their argument in international relations theory, their proposal parallels defensive realism.[17] Defensive realism takes an optimistic view about the effects of anarchy, arguing that the structure of the international system is generally benign and does not always lead to competitive policies. In the offense-defense balance, military technology and geography often favor the defense. Security is thus plentiful.[18] The best means for states to be secure is to maintain the status quo. States should not attempt to maximize relative power because it would trigger counterbalancing. Defensive realists argue that states can convey reliable information about their motives through costly signaling and policy choices. Both China and the United

States are secure because they enjoy "defensive advantage" created by nuclear weapons and geographical separation. As Glaser argues, "China's rise need not be nearly as competitive and dangerous…because the structural forces driving major powers into conflict will be relatively weak."[19] The dangers come from secondary disputes such as Taiwan. A US accommodation on Taiwan would indicate US benign motives toward China. If China reciprocates, such as on the South China Sea or other issues, it would convey information about the limited extent of China's foreign policy aims. China could thus rise peacefully, a view that is in stark contrast to offensive realism.[20]

As a theory, defensive realism is an intellectual cousin of idealism. It describes how the world should work instead of how the world actually works. As Glaser makes clear, defensive realism "analyzes the strategies a state *should* choose" (emphasis original) to achieve their goals and as such, "it is a prescriptive, normative theory."[21] The problem with normative theory such as defensive realism is that it does not have much explanatory power, as John Mearsheimer points out.[22] The historical record is often at odds with defensive realism, with great powers having behaved in ways that contradict the theory. Defensive realism often attempts to explain away these anomalies by incorporating non-structural variables such as domestic politics or misperception into their theory.[23] Like idealism, the policy prescriptions of defensive realism may appear desirable, but they are politically infeasible.[24] Their proposals provide little guidance to realistic policy making.

In this article, I draw on offensive realism to highlight the dangers of accommodating China on Taiwan.[25] Unlike defensive realism, offensive realism argues that the structure of the international system drives states to compete for power. To be secure, major states will maximize relative power until they have dominated the system. Great powers seek to establish hegemony in their region, while preventing rival powers from dominating another region. The offense-defense balance emphasized by defensive realism offers little guidance to international politics because it is inherently difficult both to distinguish defense from offense and to operationalize the concept.[26] States cannot reliably convey their motives or intentions to others. The intentions of states are difficult to know, and even if known, present intentions can still change in the future.[27] Because states face uncertainty about the intentions of others under anarchy, the security dilemma cannot be moderated. As Mearsheimer points out, "little can be done to ameliorate the security dilemma as long as states operate in anarchy."[28] Adopting offensive realism as the theoretical baseline reveals the flaws of accommodationist arguments favored by defensive realists.

Structural Causes of US-China Rivalry

Accommodationists misidentify Taiwan as the principal cause of US-China problems. Rather, the root cause of US-China tensions lies in the anarchic structure of the international system, not Taiwan. Structural pressures permit war to happen, and Taiwan is only one of the many issues (such as the Korean peninsula and territorial disputes in the East and South China Seas) that could ignite a war between the United States and China. It is anarchy, the absence of a central authority above states, that makes China and the United States fear the power of each other. It is anarchy that makes them suspicious of each other's intentions. It is also anarchy that makes mutual assurances of goodwill fall flat in each other's capital. Taiwan operates independently of this structure; abandoning it will not remove the structural cause of US-China tensions. In anarchy, great powers base their strategic decisions on the capabilities of others, not intentions. In an anarchic world in which each state can hurt one another, great powers will compete for power to become substantially stronger than the others. The ideal situation is to become the hegemon in one's own region.[29] The United States accomplished this feat in the Western Hemisphere through a series of determined pursuits of power in the nineteenth century. Washington also enforced the Monroe Doctrine to exclude outside powers from meddling in its backyard.

The same strategic logic applies to China. As power brings security, the pursuit of power has been the top priority of Chinese statecraft. The Chinese people know very well about the "century of humiliation" when Qing China suffered disgraceful defeat at the hands of technologically superior European powers in the nineteenth century. The lesson is well learned: weakness invites aggression; strength begets security. Henceforth, a recurrent theme in modern Chinese politics is how to build a strong country that is secure from foreign encroachment. Today, the Communist Party's sloganeering of the China Dream and the "great rejuvenation of the Chinese nation" reflects this long-held aspiration. The ideal outcome is a maximization of its power advantage over neighbors, as exemplified by the "era of strength and prosperity" (*shengshi*) during the Han, Tang,

Ming, and Qing dynasties. Those were the days when China was the regional hegemon and enjoyed plentiful security. Hence, China's strategic aims are far broader than acquiring Taiwan. If China's present military and economic power continues to grow, it will continue on the path to becoming the most powerful state in Asia.

China's rise, however, is incompatible with US dominance. As a regional hegemon, the United States believes that its security interests will be best served by not allowing another power to dominate Asia (or Europe). "The interest of the United States of America," declared President John F. Kennedy in 1963, "is best served by preserving and protecting a world of diversity in which no one power or no one combination of powers can threaten the security of the United States."[30] Simply put, the United States does not want a peer competitor. Henry Kissinger emphasizes that "it is in the American national interest to resist the effort of *any* power to dominate Asia" (emphasis original).[31] Joseph S. Nye, former US Assistant Secretary of Defense for International Security Affairs, argues that maintaining regional stability and "deterring the rise of hegemonic forces" constitutes the rationale for stationing American troops in East Asia.[32] There is consensus among US policymakers and commentators that it is in the national interest to prevent any power from dominating Asia and Europe. Washington should maintain a regional balance of power to preserve US preeminence in international affairs.

Apparently, the two structural factors—China's rising power and US dominance—are not compatible. Both countries are locked in a security dilemma in which one's moves to increase its own security will invariably decrease the security of the other. The security dilemma is a product of states' uncertainty about each other's intentions under anarchy. It is a constant, not a variable. Therefore, accommodating China on Taiwan will not fundamentally transform the problem of uncertainty about intentions, nor will it moderate the security dilemma.

The structural contradiction in US-China relations foretells a competitive dynamic in the years ahead. China's suspicions about US motives and intentions are structurally driven, just as US suspicions of China are driven by the same structural conditions. Uncertainty about intentions is a built-in characteristic of an anarchic system, generating the security dilemma and strategic distrust. US policy toward Taiwan is tangential to the distrust between Beijing and Washington. Because Taiwan is not a direct cause of US-China security competition, abandoning Taiwan to China will not ameliorate the security dilemma. The structural tension remains. Aside from Taiwan, other issues could also ignite a conflict, such as flare-ups in the Korean peninsula, the South China Sea, or the East China Sea. It is worth noting that the only war between China and the United States was the Korean War of 1950–1953. It was not fought over Taiwan.

Does China Have Limited Aims?

The claim of a limited-aims China is not backed up by logic and evidence. To begin with, whether a state has limited aims is private information that outsiders cannot discern with confidence. States also have incentives to conceal or misrepresent their true aims to mislead others and to gain advantages. More importantly, present aims can change in the future as a state's power increases. A state that professes status quo aims today may shift to an expansionist stance in the future when it has developed the capabilities to alter the status quo, such as existing territorial arrangements and alignment patterns among states. Thus, claiming that China is motivated by limited aims is logically unpersuasive and empirically unknowable.

In addition, there is no conclusive evidence to support a limited-aims China. There is no agreement, let alone consensus, among analysts when it comes to China's foreign policy goals. Some view China as a conservative, defensive power intent on protecting its territory, while others see China as an aggressive, expansionist state seeking to dominate Asia.[33] To complicate matters further, there are no widely accepted guidelines for determining a state's foreign policy goals. After a conflict has occurred, scholars often find themselves debating whether the initiator was motivated by security or by greed. For instance, one hundred years after the outbreak of World War I, there is still no consensus among scholars about whether Germany was driven by the limited aims of insecurity or by a greedy desire for hegemony. As Sebastian Rosato persuasively argues, "if scholars armed with definitions and the documentary record cannot agree about what states wanted long after the fact, it is unlikely that great powers can do so in real time."[34]

Since we face uncertainty about China's foreign policy goals, abandoning Taiwan to China is highly risky and dangerous. It would not convince Beijing that Washington harbors only benign intentions toward China and seeks cooperative relations. Instead, Beijing is likely to see such a concession as a sign of growing US weakness and as a vindication of China's successful pursuit of power. US concession on Taiwan would also fuel

Chinese nationalism.[35] It is dangerous to assume that, once Washington abandons Taiwan, Beijing would restrain its foreign policy ambitions or become a status quo power. On the contrary, by acquiring a forward base in the First Island Chain, China's capabilities to project power would be substantially enhanced should Taiwan fall into Beijing's orbit. Rather than limiting its aims, Beijing would likely push for more concessions on other issues. As John Mearsheimer points out, "appeasement is likely to make a dangerous rival more, not less, dangerous."[36] The structurally driven imperatives for China to maximize relative power in Asia will not stop at the waters of Taiwan.

We have evidence that accommodation encourages more aggressive behavior by China. In the early years of the Obama administration, the United States attempted to accommodate China by refraining from criticizing China's human rights records, postponing arms sales to Taiwan, demonstrating willingness to respect China's "core interests," and delaying meeting with the Dalai Lama. Instead of moderating its foreign policy aims, China took these unilateral concessions as "signs of American weakness, and proof that China could get away with more assertiveness."[37]

The outbreak of World War II in Europe exemplifies the danger of accommodation as well as the inherent difficulty of discerning an adversary's foreign policy goals. Before the war, many European leaders and analysts considered Nazi Germany a limited-aims state driven by its security needs. They found excuses for Hitler's demands and proposed a policy of appeasement. Winston Churchill's warning about Hitler, which turned out to be correct, was considered alarmist. During the Munich Crisis, Sir Neville Henderson, the British ambassador in Berlin, found excuses in Hitler's action and rationalized it in this way: "One must also try to understand the German point of view. If we were in Germany's place what would we, in the midst of all this war psychosis, be doing: exactly what I think the Germans are today doing."[38] In hindsight, policymakers misread Germany's foreign policy goals and chose the disastrous policy of appeasement.

US Credibility

A third error in the "abandon Taiwan" argument is its damaging effect on US credibility for defending allies and partners. For extended deterrence to work, the credibility of the state for defending an ally is critical. The deterrent state must make the adversary believe that its commitment to defend the ally is credible. A state's credibility is linked across issues that share similar dimensions such as geography, history, and strategic value. The state's action on one issue sends a signal to the adversary about the extent of its interests on that issue. Because of issue linkage, the adversary may use the information to update its assessment of the extent of the state's interests on another similar issue. The state's concession on one issue could cause the adversary to raise doubt about the state's resolve in protecting another similar interest. Ending a security commitment to an ally would likely lead the adversary to question the credibility of the state's commitment to another ally. Moreover, for allies, the same logic applies to their assessment of the credibility of the state's security commitment to them. The state's concession on another similar issue could lead its allies to doubt the state's credibility for meeting its commitments to them. This in turn could cause the ally to reevaluate its strategic alignment, seek an alternative partner, or embark on a military buildup.[39]

The US security commitment to Taiwan is linked to the credibility of the United States for defending allies and partners in Asia. A decision to abandon Taiwan would damage US credibility throughout the region. First, China would likely view the concession as a weakening of US resolve for protecting other interests in Asia. If China concludes that US accommodation on Taiwan is a result of China's rising military capabilities, the same shift in the military balance would likely lead China to reduce its assessment of US resolve for defending other interests in Asia. This might encourage China to adopt a more hardline approach toward the Senkaku/Diaoyu Islands dispute with Japan, believing that China's rising power had weakened US resolve to defend Japan. Seeing the United States as a "paper tiger," China might also become more aggressive in pursuing its territorial interests in the South China Sea. Thus, abandoning Taiwan would have a weakening effect on the credibility of similar US commitments in Asia. As Nancy Tucker and Bonnie Glaser argue, "China would respond to appeasement as have virtually all governments: It would conclude that a weaker United States lacking vision and ambition could be pressured and manipulated."[40]

Second, abandoning Taiwan would reduce allies' confidence in the credibility of US security commitment to them. Given the similarity in geographical location, Japan would likely see the accommodation of China on Taiwan as a weakening of US resolve in contesting Beijing's claims to disputed oil fields and islands in the East China Seas. The change in regional balance of power in China's favor combined with a perceived weakening of US credibility could lead Tokyo to relax its constitutional constraint on the armed forces. A remilitarized Japan would amplify security concerns across the region. South Korea, facing the diminished credibility of the US alliance, might calibrate that its security is better served by realigning with China, as ancient Korea did in the Chinese tribute system. Likewise, Southeast Asian states would see US accommodation on Taiwan as a weakening of credibility in contesting Chinese territorial claims in the South China Seas. At a time when Asian states need the United States to counterbalance Chinese power, a US decision to abandon Taiwan would be particularly alarming, sending shock waves across the region. As Shelley Rigger argues, "If Washington appears to be backing away from its commitment to the alliances and institutions in which it has invested so much, other governments will take that as a sign that they may not be able to rely on US-backed security arrangements to ensure their future security, forcing them to become more competitive and individualistic."[41]

The history of the Korean War demonstrates the logic of issue linkage for the credibility of extended deterrence. Despite North Korean leader Kim Il Sung's repeated requests for Soviet assistance in attacking South Korea, Stalin rejected him for fear of a possible US intervention. When US Secretary of State Dean Acheson made an important speech in January 1950 outlining US defense perimeter in Asia, the line of defense extended from the Aleutians through Japan and Okinawa to the Philippines—both Korea and Taiwan were conspicuously left out. This omission led to the Communist assessment that the United States would not intervene in the Korean peninsula, which caused US deterrence failure. As one North Korean official recounted, after the Acheson speech Kim Il Sung "was convinced that the US would not enter the Korean War."[42] North Korea's invasion of South Korea on June 25, 1950, caught the United States by surprise. At stake was US credibility. "A North Korean victory," writes historian Chen Jian, "would damage the credibility of American policy in East Asia."[43] The outbreak of the Korean War compelled the United States to send troops to shore up its credibility in Asia. As Thomas Christensen points out, "Truman dispatched American forces in order to punish aggression and save American reputation for resolve against communist expansion."[44] In the end, the United States paid a high price to shore up its credibility.

Thus, if Washington ends its commitment to Taiwan and China uses military force against the island, it would be extremely difficult for the United States to stand on the sidelines without damaging US credibility across Asia. Circumstances would likely compel the United States to intervene and to save its reputation from further deteriorating—but at a much higher cost.

Democratic and Strategic Values

The fourth error in the "abandoning Taiwan" argument is its damage to the US policy of promoting democracy and freedom around the world.[45] US policymakers have spoken of Taiwan as a "beacon of democracy."[46] Abandoning a democracy to an authoritarian government would undercut Washington's stated interests in supporting democracy and freedom around the world. Both Taiwan and the United States share common democratic values. Forsaking Taiwan would jeopardize these values. Charles Glaser agrees: "The United States has a significant interest in promoting and protecting freedom and democracy around the globe. Cutting the US commitment to Taiwan would put these values at risk."[47] But he argues that these values could be sacrificed for national security interests: "Nevertheless, states usually should, and usually do, give priority to their key national security interests. The United States should not be an exception: it should pursue these political and ideological interests only if the risks to its national security are relatively small in comparison."[48] In his view, supporting a democratic Taiwan is incompatible with US national security interests, and therefore, the United States should accommodate China on Taiwan.

What Glaser and others fail to recognize is that protecting Taiwan serves *both* US national security interests and democratic values. Taiwan's geostrategic location is of particular value to US national security interests. Taiwan's democracy reinforces its strategic values to the United States. As noted earlier, the US security objective in Asia is to maintain a balance of power and to prevent any country from dominating the region. Taiwan is strategically situated between the East China Sea and the South China Sea, two areas of rising importance. Taiwan controls the sea lines of communication (SLOCs) extending from Japan to Southeast Asia and serves as a check on China's maritime expansions into the East and the South China Seas. As China rises, Taiwan's strategic value to the United States will rise as well. Taiwan has substantial economic and military resources to contribute to America's Asia strategy. The imperatives of the balance of power will prompt Washington to give more—not less—thought to Taiwan's geopolitical importance. As John Mearsheimer points out, for their own strategic interests, "[US policy makers] will be inclined to back Taiwan no matter what."[49]

Taiwan's geography serves as a strategic constraint on the PLA's maritime expansion in the East and South China Seas. PLA leaders have stressed the necessity of breaking out of the First Island Chain that runs from Japan, Taiwan, and the Philippines, through the Indonesian archipelago. In PLA writings, Taiwan is described as "Gibraltar of the East" and a "springboard" to the Pacific: "if the Taiwan problem is resolved, the door to the Pacific Ocean will be opened for mainland China, thus breaking the first island chain."[50] Taiwan is crucial to the PLA's attainment of command of the sea from the Yellow, East China, and South China seas, which are critical to protecting China's commercial interests and energy security. The PLA's authoritative *Science of Military Strategy* goes so far as to link Taiwan to the rejuvenation of the Chinese nation: "If Taiwan should be alienated from the mainland ... China will forever be locked to the west side of the first chain of islands in the West Pacific.... [If so], the essential strategic space for China's rejuvenation will be lost."[51]

Far from being a strategic liability, as advocates of abandoning Taiwan believe, Taiwan is a strategic asset for the United States and its allies. During the Cold War, Gen. Douglas MacArthur famously referred to Taiwan as an "unsinkable aircraft carrier." Today, China's strategic planners see Taiwan as an integral part of its future naval power, as a way to break out of the encirclement of the First Island Chain. In the PLA's strategic planning, Taiwan is part of the First Island Chain that the Chinese navy must have access to. Beijing's acquisition of Taiwan would enhance China's naval capabilities and give the PLA Navy greater strategic depth. It would adversely affect Japan's maritime security, making it more difficult for the United States to defend its ally. Taiwan's close location to the Philippine Sea and the Luzon Strait would also provide the PLA Navy easy access to the South China Sea, an area fraught with territorial disputes.

Deterrence and Reassurance

Last but not least, abandoning Taiwan would destroy the delicate balance between deterrence and reassurance, a balance that is critical to regional stability. Current US policy toward Taiwan aims to achieve dual deterrence. Aside from deterring China from attacking Taiwan, Washington also seeks to deter Taiwan from taking political initiatives that could destabilize the situation.[52] Deterrence alone, however, is not sufficient to maintain the peace. Effective deterrence requires both coercive threats and credible reassurances. In addition to issuing the threats, the deterring state also needs to reassure the target state that if it does not alter the status quo, its core interests would not be deprived. Otherwise, the target will have no incentives to heed the threats. As Thomas Schelling points out, "any coercive threat requires corresponding assurances."[53] Thomas Christensen notes that successful deterrence requires "a mix of credible threats and credible reassurances" about the conditions under which those threats would be carried out.[54] The same logic applies to dual deterrence. In such a situation, the deterring state needs to deter not one but two states from destabilizing the status quo. On the one hand, the deterring state communicates coercive threats to both target states about not changing the status quo. On the other hand, it needs to reassure the target states that their interests will not be sacrificed if they do not take steps to change the status quo. Without reassurance that their interests would not be jeopardized, the target states would have no incentives to abide by the deterrent threats.

The 1995–1996 Taiwan Strait Crisis demonstrates the imperatives of maintaining a delicate balance between deterrence and reassurance. When Washington decided to issue a visa to Taiwan President Lee Teng-hui to visit his alma mater, Cornell University, in 1995, it deassured Beijing about the US commitment to the one-China policy. Beijing responded to "creeping Taiwan independence" by launching missiles off Taiwan's ports, prompting Washington to dispatch two aircraft carriers to the region. In the aftermath of the crisis, President Bill Clinton attempted to calm Beijing's fear while visiting Shanghai in 1998 by publicly announcing the "Three Noes" (no support of Taiwan independence; no support of "two Chinas" or "one China, one Taiwan"; and no support of Taiwan's membership in any international organization that requires statehood). But he overcorrected. As Andrew Nathan points out, this "intentional tilt toward

Beijing" was counterproductive. It led President Lee to harden Taiwan's position by declaring that cross-Strait relations were akin to "special state-to-state relationship." Tensions quickly escalated, with Beijing freezing all contacts with Taiwan. Nathan concludes, "The United States' policy of reassuring Beijing has also deassured Taiwan, thus worsening rather than easing tensions."[55]

Thus, accommodating China on Taiwan would have the similar effect of deassuring Taiwan and raising tensions. It would destroy the delicate balance between deterrence and reassurance. Accommodation would force Taiwan into taking risky political initiatives that could further destabilize the Taiwan Strait, as it did after President Clinton's "three noes" announcement in 1998. The current US policy of strategic ambiguity has kept the peace in the region, and there is no sound strategic rationale to change a successful policy.

Recalibrating US-Taiwan Relations

Both Taipei and Washington share a common interest in deterring China from using force in the Taiwan Strait. As China continues to rise in power, we can expect US-China security competition to intensify. If Washington wishes to maintain its preeminent position in Asia, it is in US strategic interest to include Taiwan in its overall Asia strategy, along with Japan, South Korea, and other allies. Given Taiwan's strategic value, the changing international structure will likely push Washington and Taipei into closer defense cooperation. The security interests of both countries are compatible. It makes good strategic sense for the United States to help strengthen Taiwan's defense capabilities to deter a Chinese attack. Strong US-Taiwan security ties ameliorate the power asymmetry across the Taiwan Strait and increase the costs of China's military coercion.

Accommodationists argue that US arms sales to Taiwan are an unnecessary provocation to China. Ending arms sales, however, would be risky and dangerous. A weakly defended Taiwan could tempt the Chinese leadership to use the implied threat of force to coerce the island into negotiations for unification. Once this process is started, it would be politically difficult for the United States to stay on the sidelines and watch a democracy being incorporated into an authoritarian state under duress. For their part, the Chinese leaders would find it difficult to back down without losing domestic legitimacy. A spiral of escalation would generate perilous security dynamics and threaten regional peace. Conversely, a well-defended Taiwan would reduce this source of dangerous miscalculation, which, counterintuitively, is also in China's interest.[56]

Thus, contrary to accommodationist argument, US arms sales to Taiwan strengthen regional stability. A basic requirement for effective deterrence in the Taiwan Strait is that Taiwan should at least have the capabilities to withstand an initial Chinese attack until the United States has sufficient time to respond. The arms sales not only fulfill a legal obligation under the Taiwan Relations Act but also serve US strategic interests. The $1.4 billion arms sales approved by the Trump administration in June 2017 are consistent with the US policy to support Taiwan to maintain a sufficient self-defense. A robust defense makes Taiwan less vulnerable to China's military coercion and helps preserve regional peace.

China is opposed to US arms sales for the simple reason that a militarily weak Taiwan would be more compliant to Beijing's demands. China has continued its military buildup across the Taiwan Strait to shift the military balance of power further in its favor, despite evident improvements in cross-Strait relations during Taiwan's Ma Ying-Jeou administration (2008–2016). China has made significant advances in military hardware, demonstrated its anti-satellite capabilities, continued development and deployment of short- and medium-range conventional ballistic missiles, and upgraded its A2/AD capabilities. In the Taiwan Strait, the Chinese military aims to raise the risks and costs of US intervention to deter Washington from coming to Taiwan's rescue.

For its part, Taiwan needs to make an earnest effort to beef up its defense. Its defense spending has remained at a low two percent of GDP for years, below its stated target of three percent. Calls for strengthening the military and increasing arms purchases often fall into acrimonious partisan accusations of benefiting the US military-industrial complex. But Taiwan's subpar commitment to its own defense gives rise to US suspicion of free riding. To counter Beijing's military coercion, Taiwan needs to strengthen its defense to raise the costs for China before US intervention arrives.[57] Upon her election in 2016, President Tsai Ing-wen has made plans to raise Taiwan's defense budget to three percent of GDP, but whether that target can be achieved remains to be seen.

In addition to military self-defense, Taiwan's economic dependence on China raises another security concern.[58] China is Taiwan's largest trading partner and the top destination of Taiwan's outward foreign direct investment (FDI). Cross-Strait trade flows skyrocketed from $2 billion in 1994 to $128 billion in 2011. Taiwan's trade dependence on China is even more striking if we consider the share of cross-Strait trade in Taiwan's total foreign trade. Taiwan's trade with China as a percentage of total foreign trade surged from only 2.3 percent in 1998 to 21.3 percent in 2012.[59] An overwhelming majority of Taiwan's outward FDI went to China, reaching as high as 83.8 percent in 2010. Cumulatively, China accounts for 62.62 percent of Taiwan's total outward investment from 1991 to 2012.[60] As Richard Bush writes, "Taiwan is becoming more dependent on China economically while China is becoming less dependent on Taiwan."[61]

To lessen its economic dependence on China, Taiwan needs to diversify its foreign trade and investment. Taiwan's efforts to diversify its economy have been hampered by China's growing international clout over other countries, with its economy being increasingly marginalized in Asia's movement toward greater economic integration. The abandonment of the Trans-Pacific Partnership (TPP) by the Trump administration in 2017 has complicated Taiwan's efforts to participate in regional economic integration. Nonetheless, a bilateral US-Taiwan free trade agreement, such as the one between the United States and South Korea, could provide Taiwan with the much-needed economic boost and sustain long-term global competitiveness. A US-Taiwan FTA could have a "demonstration effect" by encouraging other countries to follow suit.[62] A prosperous Taiwan will be in better position to resist China's economic coercion.

CONCLUSION

Accommodating China on Taiwan is risky and dangerous. It would lead to false optimism about US-China relations and increase the probability of conflict. The fundamental cause of US-China strategic distrust lies in the anarchic structure of the international system, not Taiwan. Even without the Taiwan issue, the international structure would still push China and the United States into intense security competition, generating strategic distrust and mutual suspicion. Abandoning Taiwan would not make for a more cooperative relationship between the United States and China, nor would it prevent future conflict. The US security commitment to Taiwan is consistent with American democratic values and strategic interests. Failing to come to Taiwan's defense would jeopardize US credibility in protecting its Asian allies and create new security dynamics that could further destabilize the region. Appeasing China by giving up Taiwan would increase, not reduce, China's foreign policy ambitions. It is risky to assume that China's foreign policy is guided by limited aims and will remain unchanged as its power grows. Rising states tend to expand,[63] and we have no good reason to expect China to behave otherwise.

The emerging international structure foretells a deepening of US-Taiwan security cooperation in the foreseeable future. Taiwan may take comfort that US accommodating China on Taiwan is mainly an academic discussion and does not reflect a change in US policy, but Taiwan must take measures consistent with the dictates of international structure. To reduce its vulnerability to China's military coercion, Taiwan needs to strengthen itself, diversify its foreign trade and investment, and maintain strong ties with the United States. The ultimate objective of US grand strategy toward Asia is to maintain a regional balance of power. In that regard, Taiwan is an asset, not a liability.

Notes

1. Nancy Bernkopf Tucker, *Strait Talk: United States-Taiwan Relations and the Crisis with China* (Cambridge, MA.: Harvard University Press, 2009), 1. There is general agreement on Taiwan's war-triggering potential. For instance, Chas Freeman observes: "The Taiwan issue is the only one with the potential to ignite a war between China and the United States." Chas W. Freeman, Jr., "Beijing, Washington, and the Shifting Balance of Prestige: Remarks to the China Maritime Studies Institute (May 10, 2011)," http://www.mepc.org/articles-commentary/speeches/beijing-washington-and-shifting-balance-prestige. Alan Romberg contends that "the Taiwan question is the only issue in the world today that could realistically lead to war between two major powers." Alan D. Romberg, *Rein in at the Brink of the Precipice: American Policy toward Taiwan and U.S.-PRC Relations* (Washington, D.C.: Henry L. Stimson Center, 2003), 14.
2. Robert Gilpin, *War and Change in World Politics* (New York: Cambridge University Press, 1981); A.F.K. Organski and Jacek Kugler, *The War Ledger* (Chicago: Chicago University Press, 1982).
3. T. V. Paul, ed., *Accommodating Rising Powers: Past, Present, and Future* (Cambridge: Cambridge University Press, 2016).
4. Bill Owens, "America Must Start Treating China as a Friend," *Financial Times*, November 17, 2009; Bruce Gilley, "Not So Dire Straits: How the Finlandization of Taiwan Benefits U.S. Security," *Foreign Affairs* 89, no. 1 (January/February 2010): 44–60; Freeman, "Beijing, Washington, and

the Shifting Balance of Prestige: Remarks to the China Maritime Studies Institute (May 10, 2011)"; Charles L. Glaser, "Will China's Rise Lead to War? Why Realism Does Not Mean Pessimism," *Foreign Affairs* 90, no. 2 (March/April 2011): 80–91; Charles L. Glaser, "A U.S.-China Grand Bargain? The Hard Choice between Military Competition and Accommodation," *International Security* 39, no. 4 (Spring 2015): 49–90.
5. Graham T. Allison, "The Thucydides Trap: Are the US and China Headed for War?" *The Atlantic*, September 24, 2015, http://www.theatlantic.com/international/archive/2015/09/united-states-china-war-thucydides-trap/406756/.
6. "Full text of Xi Jinping's speech on China-US relations in Seattle," *Xinhua*, September 22, 2015, http://news.xinhuanet.com/english/2015-09/24/c_134653326.htm.
7. Paul, *Accommodating Rising Powers*, 4. Paul, however, does not distinguish between "accommodation" and "appeasement." He lists "When is accommodation not appeasement?" as one of the research questions, but does not offer a clear distinction between accommodation and appeasement. Ibid., 29.
8. Norrin M. Ripsman and Jack S. Levy, "Wishful Thinking or Buying Time? The Logic of British Appeasement in the 1930s," *International Security* 33, no. 2 (Fall 2008): 148–181 at 149. See also Daniel Treisman, "Rational Appeasement," *International Organization* 58, no. 2 (Spring 2004): 345–373.
9. Glaser, "A U.S.-China Grand Bargain? The Hard Choice between Military Competition and Accommodation," 56, n. 16.
10. Freeman, "Beijing, Washington, and the Shifting Balance of Prestige: Remarks to the China Maritime Studies Institute (May 10, 2011)."
11. Glaser, "Will China's Rise Lead to War? Why Realism Does Not Mean Pessimism," 87.
12. Glaser, "A U.S.-China Grand Bargain? The Hard Choice between Military Competition and Accommodation," 72.
13. Gilley, "Not So Dire Straits: How the Finlandization of Taiwan Benefits U.S. Security," 56.
14. Glaser, "A U.S.-China Grand Bargain? The Hard Choice between Military Competition and Accommodation," 64.
15. Freeman, "Beijing, Washington, and the Shifting Balance of Prestige: Remarks to the China Maritime Studies Institute (May 10, 2011)."
16. Gilley, "Not So Dire Straits: How the Finlandization of Taiwan Benefits U.S. Security," 51.
17. Glaser explicitly draws on defense realism. Glaser, "A U.S.-China Grand Bargain? The Hard Choice between Military Competition and Accommodation." For his exposition of defensive realism, see Charles

L. Glaser, *Rational Theory of International Politics: The Logic of Competition and Cooperation* (Princeton, N.J.: Princeton University Press, 2010); Charles Glaser, "Realists as Optimists: Cooperation as Self-Help," *International Security* 19, no. 3 (Winter 1994/95): 50–90; Charles L. Glaser, "The Security Dilemma Revisited," *World Politics* 50, no. 1 (October 1997): 171–201.
18. For defensive realism, security can be scare when offense has the advantage.
19. Glaser, "Will China's Rise Lead to War? Why Realism Does Not Mean Pessimism," 81.
20. For an offensive realist view, see John J. Mearsheimer, "Can China Rise Peacefully?" *The National Interest*, October 25, 2014, http://nationalinterest.org/commentary/can-china-rise-peacefully-10204.
21. Glaser, *Rational Theory of International Politics*, 2, 23.
22. John J. Mearsheimer, "Realists as Idealists," *Security Studies* 20, no. 3 (2011): 424–430.
23. See, for example, Jack L. Snyder, *Myths of Empire: Domestic Politics and International Ambition* (Ithaca, N.Y.: Cornell University Press, 1991); Stephen Van Evera, *Causes of War: Power and the Roots of Conflict* (Ithaca, N.Y.: Cornell University Press, 1999).
24. This may be the key reason why Glaser insists on a separation between the desirability of his grand bargain proposal and its political feasibility: "Analytically, the desirability and political feasibility of U.S. security policy can often be productively separated." See Glaser, "A U.S.-China Grand Bargain? The Hard Choice between Military Competition and Accommodation," 55. It is worth noting that the two rejoinders to his article faults him on the political infeasibility of his proposal. Leif-Eric Easley, Patricia Kim, and Charles L. Glaser, "Correspondence: Grand Bargain or Bad Idea? U.S. Relations with China and Taiwan," *International Security* 40, no. 4 (Spring 2016): 178–191.
25. The definitive work is John J. Mearsheimer, *The Tragedy of Great Power Politics* (New York: W. W. Norton, 2001).
26. Kier A. Lieber, "Grasping the Technological Peace: The Offense-Defense Balance and International Security," *International Security* 25, no. 1 (Summer 2000): 71–104.
27. Sebastian Rosato, "The Inscrutable Intentions of Great Powers," *International Security* 39, no. 3 (Winter 2014/15): 48–88.
28. Mearsheimer, *The Tragedy of Great Power Politics*, 36.
29. Ibid.
30. Quoted in John Lewis Gaddis, *Strategies of Containment : A Critical Appraisal of Postwar American National Security Policy* (New York: Oxford University Press, 1982), 201.

31. Henry Kissinger, *Does America Need a Foreign Policy? Toward a Diplomacy for the 21st Century* (New York: Simon & Schuster, 2001), 135.
32. Joseph S. Nye, "The Case for Deep Engagement," *Foreign Affairs* 74, no. 4 (July/August 1995): 90–102 at 91.
33. For a contrasting view, see Michael D. Swaine, *America's Challenge: Engaging a Rising China in the Twenty-First Century* (Washington, DC: Carnegie Endowment for International Peace, 2011); Aaron L. Friedberg, *A Contest for Supremacy: China, America, and the Struggle for Mastery in Asia*, 1st Ed. (New York: W. W. Norton & Co., 2011).
34. Rosato, "The Inscrutable Intentions of Great Powers," 59.
35. Nancy Bernkopf Tucker and Bonnie Glaser, "Should the United States Abandon Taiwan?," *The Washington Quarterly* 24, no. 4 (Fall 2011): 23–37 at 25; Shelley Rigger, "Why Giving up Taiwan Will Not Help Us with China," *AEI Asian Outlook*, no. 3 (November 2011): 1–9. Rigger writes: "If the United States withdraws its support, we should expect nationalists and hardliners in the PRC to press the Chinese Communist Party leadership to solve the Taiwan problem sooner rather than later."
36. Mearsheimer, *The Tragedy of Great Power Politics*, 164.
37. Edward Friedman, "China's Ambitions, America's Interests, Taiwan's Destiny, and Asia's Future," *Asian Survey* 53, no. 2 (2013): 225–244 at 244.
38. Quoted in Richard K. Betts, "Realism Is an Attitude, Not a Doctrine," *The National Interest*, September/October 2015, http://nationalinterest.org/print/feature/realism-attitude-not-doctrine-13659.
39. For a summary of the literature on credibility, see Glaser, "A U.S.-China Grand Bargain? The Hard Choice between Military Competition and Accommodation," 58–60.
40. Tucker and Glaser, "Should the United States Abandon Taiwan?," 33.
41. Rigger, "Why Giving up Taiwan Will Not Help Us with China."
42. Sergei. N. Goncharov, John W. Lewis, and Litai Xue, *Uncertain Partners: Stalin, Mao, and the Korean War* (Stanford, CA: Stanford University Press, 1993), 142.
43. Jian Chen, *China's Road to the Korean War: The Making of the Sino-American Confrontation* (New York: Columbia University Press, 1994), 126.
44. Thomas J. Christensen, *Useful Adversaries: Grand Strategy, Domestic Mobilization, and Sino-American Conflict, 1947–1958* (Princeton, NJ: Princeton University Press, 1996), 151.
45. Tucker and Glaser, "Should the United States Abandon Taiwan?."; Rigger, "Why Giving up Taiwan Will Not Help Us with China."
46. The White House, "Statement by President George W. Bush on Taiwan's Election," March 25, 2008, http://www.ait.org.tw/en/officialtext-ot0802.html.

47. Glaser, "A U.S.-China Grand Bargain? The Hard Choice between Military Competition and Accommodation," 72.
48. Ibid., 73.
49. John J. Mearsheimer, "Taiwan's Dire Straits," *The National Interest*, no. 130 (March/April 2014): 29–39 at 35. Mearsheimer is often mistakenly categorized in the "abandon Taiwan" camp. His view is actually more nuanced. He holds that before China reaches power parity with the United States, Washington will go out of its way to support Taiwan, not abandon it. It is only when China becomes as powerful as the United States (which may not happen) that Washington, no longer capable of protecting Taiwan, would be reluctantly forced to give it up. Note that the title of Mearsheimer's article ("Taiwan's Dire Straits") in the printed journal *The National Interest* is different from the one on its website ("Say Goodbye to Taiwan"), which was chosen by the website editor, not by Mearsheimer.
50. Quoted in Toshi Yoshihara and James R. Holmes, *Red Star over the Pacific: China's Rise and the Challenge to U.S. Maritime Strategy* (Annapolis, Md.: Naval Institute Press, 2010), 52–53.
51. Quoted in ibid., 21.
52. Richard C. Bush, *Untying the Knot: Making Peace in the Taiwan Strait* (Washington, D.C.: Brookings Institution Press, 2005), 259–265.
53. Thomas C. Schelling, *Arms and Influence* (New Haven, CT: Yale University Press, 1966), 74.
54. Thomas J. Christensen, "The Contemporary Security Dilemma: Deterring a Taiwan Conflict," *The Washington Quarterly* 25, no. 4 (Autumn 2002): 7–21 at 10.
55. Andrew J. Nathan, "What's Wrong with American Taiwan Policy," *The Washington Quarterly* 23, no. 2 (Spring 2000): 93–106 at 97, 102.
56. Steve Tsang, "The U.S. Military and American Commitment to Taiwan's Security," *Asian Survey* 52, no. 4 (2012): 777–797.
57. Vincent Wei-cheng Wang, "The U.S. Asia Rebalancing and the Taiwan Strait Rapprochement," *Orbis* 59, no. 3 (Summer 2015): 361–379.
58. On the security externalities of trade, see Joanne Gowa, *Allies, Adversaries, and International Trade* (Princeton, NJ: Princeton University Press, 1994); Scott L. Kastner, *Political Conflict and Economic Interdependence across the Taiwan Strait and Beyond* (Stanford, Calif.: Stanford University Press, 2009).
59. Mainland Affairs Council, *Liangan jingji tongji yuebao* (Cross-strait economic statistics monthly), no. 238 (2012).
60. Investment Commission, Ministry of Economic Affairs, Republic of China (Taiwan), http://www.moeaic.gov.tw/system_external/ctlr?PRO=Public ationLoad&id=135
   http://www.moeaic.gov.tw/system_external/ctlr?PRO=PublicationLo ad&lang=1&id=134.

61. Richard C. Bush, *Uncharted Strait: The Future of China-Taiwan Relations* (Washington, DC: Brookings Institution Press, 2013), 141.
62. Wang, "The U.S. Asia Rebalancing and the Taiwan Strait Rapprochement," 378.
63. Fareed Zakaria, *From Wealth to Power: The Unusual Origins of America's World Role* (Princeton, NJ: Princeton University Press, 1998); Mearsheimer, *The Tragedy of Great Power Politics*.

Bibliography

Allison, Graham T. 2015. The Thucydides Trap: Are the US and China Headed for War? *The Atlantic*, September 24. http://www.theatlantic.com/international/archive/2015/09/united-states-china-war-thucydides-trap/406756/.

Betts, Richard K. 2015. Realism Is an Attitude, Not a Doctrine. *The National Interest*, September/October. http://nationalinterest.org/print/feature/realism-attitude-not-doctrine-13659.

Bush, Richard C. 2005. *Untying the Knot: Making Peace in the Taiwan Strait*. Washington, DC: Brookings Institution Press.

———. 2013. *Uncharted Strait: The Future of China-Taiwan Relations*. Washington, DC: Brookings Institution Press.

Chen, Jian. 1994. *China's Road to the Korean War: The Making of the Sino-American Confrontation*. New York: Columbia University Press.

Christensen, Thomas J. 1996. *Useful Adversaries: Grand Strategy, Domestic Mobilization, and Sino-American Conflict, 1947–1958*. Princeton: Princeton University Press.

———. 2002. The Contemporary Security Dilemma: Deterring a Taiwan Conflict. *The Washington Quarterly* 25 (4, Autumn): 7–21.

Easley, Leif-Eric, Patricia Kim, and Charles L. Glaser. 2016 Spring. Correspondence: Grand Bargain or Bad Idea? U.S. Relations with China and Taiwan. *International Security* 40 (4): 178–191.

Freeman, Chas W. Jr. 2011. Beijing, Washington, and the Shifting Balance of Prestige: Remarks to the China Maritime Studies Institute, May 10. http://www.mepc.org/articles-commentary/speeches/beijing-washington-and-shifting-balance-prestige.

Friedberg, Aaron L. 2011. *A Contest for Supremacy: China, America, and the Struggle for Mastery in Asia*. 1st ed. New York: W. W. Norton & Co.

Friedman, Edward. 2013. China's Ambitions, America's Interests, Taiwan's Destiny, and Asia's Future. *Asian Survey* 53 (2): 225–244.

Gaddis, John Lewis. 1982. *Strategies of Containment: A Critical Appraisal of Postwar American National Security Policy*. New York: Oxford University Press.

Gilley, Bruce. 2010. Not So Dire Straits: How the Finlandization of Taiwan Benefits U.S. Security. *Foreign Affairs* 89 (1): 44–60.

Gilpin, Robert. 1981. *War and Change in World Politics*. New York: Cambridge University Press.

Glaser, Charles L. 1994/95. Realists as Optimists: Cooperation as Self-Help. *International Security* 19 (3, Winter): 50–90.

———. 1997. The Security Dilemma Revisited. *World Politics* 50 (1): 171–201.

———. 2010. *Rational Theory of International Politics: The Logic of Competition and Cooperation*. Princeton: Princeton University Press.

———. 2011. Will China's Rise Lead to War? Why Realism Does Not Mean Pessimism. *Foreign Affairs* 90 (2): 80–91.

———. 2015. A U.S.-China Grand Bargain? The Hard Choice Between Military Competition and Accommodation. *International Security* 39 (4, Spring): 49–90.

Goncharov, Sergei N., John W. Lewis, and Litai Xue. 1993. *Uncertain Partners: Stalin, Mao, and the Korean War*. Stanford: Stanford University Press.

Gowa, Joanne. 1994. *Allies, Adversaries, and International Trade*. Princeton: Princeton University Press.

Kastner, Scott L. 2009. *Political Conflict and Economic Interdependence Across the Taiwan Strait and Beyond*. Stanford: Stanford University Press.

Kissinger, Henry. 2001. *Does America Need a Foreign Policy? Toward a Diplomacy for the 21st Century*. New York: Simon & Schuster.

Lieber, Kier A. 2000. Grasping the Technological Peace: The Offense-Defense Balance and International Security. *International Security* 25 (1, Summer): 71–104.

Mearsheimer, John J. 2001. *The Tragedy of Great Power Politics*. New York: W. W. Norton.

———. 2011. Realists as Idealists. *Security Studies* 20 (3): 424–430.

———. 2014a. Can China Rise Peacefully? *The National Interest*, October 25. http://nationalinterest.org/commentary/can-china-rise-peacefully-10204.

———. 2014b. Taiwan's Dire Straits. *The National Interest* 130 (March/April): 29–39.

Nathan, Andrew J. 2000. What's Wrong with American Taiwan Policy. *The Washington Quarterly* 23 (2, Spring): 93–106.

Nye, Joseph S. 1995. The Case for Deep Engagement. *Foreign Affairs* 74 (4): 90–102 at 91.

Organski, A.F.K., and Jacek Kugler. 1982. *The War Ledger*. Chicago: Chicago University Press.

Owens, Bill. 2009. America Must Start Treating China as a Friend. *Financial Times*, November 17.

Paul, T.V., ed. 2016. *Accommodating Rising Powers: Past, Present, and Future*. Cambridge: Cambridge University Press.

Rigger, Shelley. 2011. Why Giving Up Taiwan Will Not Help Us with China. *AEI Asian Outlook* 3 (November): 1–9.

Ripsman, Norrin M., and Jack S. Levy. 2008 Fall. Wishful Thinking or Buying Time? The Logic of British Appeasement in the 1930s. *International Security* 33 (2): 148–181.

Romberg, Alan D. 2003. *Rein in at the Brink of the Precipice: American Policy Toward Taiwan and U.S.-PRC Relations.* Washington, DC: Henry L. Stimson Center.

Rosato, Sebastian. 2014/2015. The Inscrutable Intentions of Great Powers. *International Security* 39 (3, Winter): 48–88.

Schelling, Thomas C. 1966. *Arms and Influence.* New Haven: Yale University Press.

Snyder, Jack L. 1991. *Myths of Empire: Domestic Politics and International Ambition.* Ithaca: Cornell University Press.

Swaine, Michael D. 2011. *America's Challenge: Engaging a Rising China in the Twenty-First Century.* Washington, DC: Carnegie Endowment for International Peace.

Treisman, Daniel. 2004 Spring. Rational Appeasement. *International Organization* 58 (2): 345–373.

Tucker, Nancy Bernkopf. 2009. *Strait Talk: United States-Taiwan Relations and the Crisis with China.* Cambridge, MA: Harvard University Press.

Tucker, Nancy Bernkopf, and Bonnie Glaser. 2011 Fall. Should the United States Abandon Taiwan? *The Washington Quarterly* 24 (4): 23–37.

Van Evera, Stephen. 1999. *Causes of War: Power and the Roots of Conflict.* Ithaca: Cornell University Press.

Wang, Vincent Wei-cheng. 2015. The U.S. Asia Rebalancing and the Taiwan Strait Rapprochement. *Orbis* 59 (3, Summer): 361–379.

Yoshihara, Toshi, and James R. Holmes. 2010. *Red Star Over the Pacific: China's Rise and the Challenge to U.S. Maritime Strategy.* Annapolis: Naval Institute Press.

Zakaria, Fareed. 1998. *From Wealth to Power: The Unusual Origins of America's World Role.* Princeton: Princeton University Press.

CHAPTER 11

Beyond Diplomacy: The Political Economy of Taiwan's Relations with Southeast Asia

Samuel C. Y. Ku

INTRODUCTION

In October 1971, the ROC withdrew from the United Nations and the Republic of China (ROC) on Taiwan has been diplomatically isolated from the international community ever since. However, due to sustained political and economic developments it has never been fully excluded. Taiwan's relationship with Southeast Asia presents a good example of this.

Although Taiwan does not maintain any full diplomatic partnerships in Southeast Asia, it has maintained very stable relationships with major countries in the region. Economically, Taiwan has for years been a major trading partner throughout the region, with Southeast Asian migrant workers making up more than 95% of Taiwan's foreign labor force.[1]

This however, does not trivialize the importance of diplomacy for Taiwan in an increasingly globalized world and the subsequent challenges it faces with continued political isolation. This situation often prevents it

S. C. Y. Ku (✉)
Department of International Affairs, Wenzao Ursuline University of Languages, Kaohsiung, Taiwan

© The Author(s) 2019
W.-c. Lee (ed.), *Taiwan's Political Re-Alignment and Diplomatic Challenges*, Politics and Development of Contemporary China, https://doi.org/10.1007/978-3-319-77125-0_11

271

from participating in crucial international activities. Also, since the turn of the century, Taiwan has faced regional economic marginalization, such as when it was not allowed to join organizations such as ASEAN Plus One, ASEAN Plus Three and ASEAN Plus Six. It continues to struggle to participate in agreements such as the Regional Comprehensive Economic Partnership (RCEP) and the Trans-Pacific Partnership (TPP).

This chapter aims to demonstrate how Taiwan has gone beyond diplomacy by driving a thriving political economy and developing multiple partnerships throughout Southeast Asia, which has subsequently allowed it to survive and thrive internationally. However, it can also be argued that given China's recent rise in political and economic might, the ROC government cannot avoid the influence this Asian giant has over the international community. Taiwan's continued diplomatic isolation and ongoing economic marginalization are two grave challenges that the Taiwanese government and its people will have to face in years to come.

Taiwan's Economic Relations with Southeast Asia

Taiwan's economic relations with Southeast Asia are the foundation of Taiwan's overall connection with other countries in the region. Prior to the mid-1980s, Taiwan experienced a strained relationship with most of the Southeast Asian countries. In 1975, the ROC on Taiwan lost its last diplomatic partner in the region and maintained few economic ties with Southeast Asia. However, during the mid-1980s, things began to change and throughout the 1990s, Taiwan's trade and investment greatly increased, demonstrating the development of sound economic relations with several countries in the region. It also laid out a solid foundation to create opportunities to improve its political relationships. As a result, in the 1990s, diplomatically isolated Taiwan began engaging more with major Southeast Asian countries, bringing about the "Golden Age of Relationships."

Since the turn of the century, Taiwan has signed a number of economic agreements and memorandums, cementing economic ties throughout Southeast Asia. In September 2011, Taiwan and Vietnam signed the Customs Administrative Cooperation Agreement and in October 2014, Taiwan and the Philippines signed a memorandum of understanding on the promotion of trade and investment, which empowered and strengthened economic relations in the following four areas:

(1) Increasing Taiwan's economic relations with Southeast Asian countries.
(2) Developing greater channels for economic assistance and cooperation.
(3) Providing a platform for regional economic interactions.
(4) Providing additional opportunities to create relationships that could facilitate greater participation in regional economic blocs.

Increasing Taiwan's Economic Relations with Southeast Asia

Foreign investment and the volume of foreign trade are two important indicators of a country's international economic strength and diplomatic relationships. The more foreign trade and investment a country engages in with another country, the closer the economic ties between the two countries. On the contrary, when two countries engage in a limited foreign trade and investment, it implies a low level of economic exchange exists.

Taiwan's economic development was limited during the first three decades after World War II and therefore the island did not have much trade and investment in Southeast Asia. However, Taiwan's currency appreciated against the American dollar during the early 1980s and its economy grew tremendously. This allowed for economic relations with Southeast Asian countries to begin to strengthen.[2]

In 1975, Taiwan's total trade volume with the ten ASEAN countries was less than US$1 billion. However, in 1987, this figure increased to US$5 billion, in 1990 it was US$11.02 billion, in 1995, US$25.54 billion and in 2000, US$38.71 billion.[3] Since 2000, Taiwan has continued to augment its trade with Southeast Asia. In 2005, the total volume of Taiwan's trade in the region expanded from US$48.53 billion to US$70.84 billion in 2010 and US$93.64 billion in 2014, despite a drop in 2016 to US$78.4 billion. In 1990, Taiwan's entire trade in Southeast Asia expanded by 9%. In 2000, it continued to increase to 13.4% and in 2014 it increased to 15.9%, at which point it leveled out throughout 2015 and 2016.[4] Another significant fact is that since 2010, the Southeast Asian region has become Taiwan's second largest trading partner, second only to China.

Since the turn of the century, the ROC government has been consistently strengthening its economic relations with other Asian countries, many of which are located in Southeast Asia. At the opening ceremony of the 2014 Asian MICE Forum in September 2014, W. S. Chiang (Taiwan's Deputy Director of the Bureau of International Trade) pointed out that Asia was gradually becoming the main exhibition platform of global enterprises and manufacturing industries and that Taiwan would continue to make efforts in developing its economic presence throughout this part of the world.[5]

When President Tsai Ing-wen was sworn in on 20 May 2016, she further promoted Taiwan's New Southbound Policy. This "people-centered" initiative was designed to strengthen Taiwan's multi-faceted relations with countries throughout Southeast Asia. While the new policy emphasizes cultural, social and educational exchanges, it has also been designed to increase economic relations through trade and investment.[6] For instance, Economic Ministry and a few nation corporate groups jointly organized the Committee on Asia-Pacific Industrial Cooperation (APIC) in early March 2017, which aims to promote business and trade between Taiwan and its southern neighbors, including Vietnam, Malaysia, Thailand, Indonesia, the Philippines and India.[7]

It is obvious the development of this new policy is due to Taiwan's economic foundation that had been previously developed in Southeast Asia. Certainly, if it had not been for these previous cordial connections, President Tsai's New Southbound Policy would perhaps not have been possible.

Taiwan's investment in Southeast Asia also exhibits a strengthening in economic relations throughout the region. Prior to the mid-1980s, Taiwan did not have much foreign investment in Southeast Asia. However, since the early 1990s, its foreign investment in Southeast Asia has been steadily increasing.[8] Taiwan's investment in Southeast Asia peaked at US$5.1 billion in 1994. However, since 1998, with the outburst of the Asian financial crisis, it has steadily been in decline. During the 1990s and golden age of foreign investment in Southeast Asia, Taiwan was economically vibrant and one of the leading foreign investors in the region. For two decades Vietnam ranked Taiwan as either its largest or second largest source of foreign investment.

Since the turn of the century, Taiwan's investment in Southeast Asia has had its ups and downs. Taiwan's investment in Southeast Asia peaked in 2008, with a total investment of US$10.07 billion. After the 2008 global economic tsunami, Taiwan's investment in Southeast Asia declined for three years. However, it has been up and down ever since, with the investment expansion of US$5.93 billion in 2012, then in decline again in 2014 with investments of US$1.16 billion, a slight increase to US$2.62 billion in 2015 and US$3.45 billion in 2016.[9]

These figures demonstrate Taiwan's continuing economic interest in Southeast Asia, providing for more trade and other economic developments, along with increased employment opportunities for the Southeast Asian people. In 2015, during the first year of President Tsai's administration, Taiwan's investments in Southeast Asia slightly increased and continued increasing throughout 2016. With the implementation of the New Southbound Policy, the ROC government has promoted a series of initiatives, in order to get further involved with infrastructure development in Southeast Asia and to encourage Taiwanese businessmen to invest there. These include the development of power plants, the petrochemical industry and industries related to environmental preservation.[10] With these government-funded initiatives, Taiwan will be able to offer greater investment to its southern neighbors.

Establishing Channels for Economic Assistance and Cooperation

Although at first, it was not to such a large extent, in the early 1970s, Taiwan began to engage in economic development and cooperation projects with various countries throughout Southeast Asia. One of these more prominent projects was Taiwan's agricultural assistance to Thailand. In 1973, the ROC government still maintained official diplomatic relations with the Thai Kingdom. This project was to assist in agricultural development along the borders of northern Thailand and Burma. This initiative was quite successful in transforming opium farming into an agricultural industry that focused on tea and fruit. It continued into the 1990s and has not only transformed northern Thailand from an opium based agricultural industry, to one of fruit, but has also helped the communities of ROC military and their families, whom in 1949 had retreated into northwestern Thailand and Burma.[11] Due to the ROC's assistance to Thailand, these displaced ROC families were mostly granted citizenship and allowed to stay permanently in Thailand. During the 1970s and 1980s, along the borders of Thailand and Burma, these families' poor living conditions were also greatly improved and slums were upgraded into modern villages.[12]

Despite the 1975 termination of diplomatic ties between Taiwan and Thailand, throughout the 1980s, the ROC government continued to assist in northern Thailand, by dispatching agricultural and technical missions. Since the early 1990s, private businessmen from Taiwan increased investment and development in northern Thailand. Through agriculture, transportation, infrastructure and northern hillside community development, Taiwan has greatly contributed to Thailand's development.

In 1976, an agreement on agriculture was signed between the Islamic state of Indonesia and Taiwan and a subsequent agricultural and technical mission from Taiwan to Indonesia was developed and still continues there today. Throughout the 1970s and 1980s, the ROC Agricultural and Technical Mission had offices in Surabaya and Yogyakarta, where they assisted local farmers in advancing their agricultural skills. In 1996, the government sponsored agency, International Cooperation and Development Fund (ICDF) was established and continues to manage Taiwan's agricultural and technical assistance to Southeast Asian countries. In 1998, the ICDF reorganized and merged the two offices into the Misi Teknik Taiwan Di Indonesia (Taiwan Technical Mission in Indonesia), which would be based in Bogor. In 2007, the ICDF signed an agreement at a central government level, with Indonesia's Ministry of Agriculture upgrading agricultural cooperation with Taiwan. Taiwanese experts and technicians assisted local farmers in Bali and Bandung.[13]

Taiwan also granted a low interest loan to the Philippines, in order to establish the Subic Bay Gateway Park, which is an industrial zone for foreign investment. In November 1996, Taiwan established a development center, mobilized investment and set up a number of Taiwanese enterprises there. In the mid-1990s, Taiwan granted Vietnam a substantial loan in order to construct Highway #5 which connects Hanoi and Ha-long Bay.

Taiwan continues to assist Southeast Asian countries in terms of loans, resources and humanitarian assistance. In December 2004, Taiwan's government issued tsunami relief to Aceh, Indonesia. In November 2013, when the Philippines were hit badly by Typhoon Haiyan, Taiwan mobilized US$200,000 and 150 tons of relief supplies, which were dispatched by eighteen ROC Air force C-130 cargo planes.[14] Historically, it was the first time the ROC military aircraft and naval vessels had landed on the Philippines, in order to provide humanitarian assistance.

One report highlights that Taiwan's humanitarian assistance and disaster relief (HA/DR) to the Philippines after Typhoon Haiyan was a great example of its capability to mobilize partnerships between governments, military and NGOs. During his administration, President Ma Ying-jeou allocated an annual budget of US$6–8 million to Taiwan's HA/DR, which has contributed to its international achievements, survival and visibility. However, due to the United Nations-centered aid system, Taiwan did not receive much recognition.[15] Within the same report, there are also concerns that in the future, Taiwan may face challenges over its HA/DR policy, due to President Tsai Ing-wen's unwillingness to endorse the 1992 Consensus, which is resulting in deteriorating relations across the Taiwan Straits.[16] China and possibly the United Nations could block Taiwan's HA/DR initiatives in strategic countries. Only time will tell if these fears will be well-founded.

Since May 2016, one of the key elements of President Tsai's New Southbound Policy is to establish a comprehensive mechanism of foreign assistance and to readjust its budgetary allocation of foreign assistance resources. In 2016, Taiwan increased its amount of Overseas Development Assistance with a number of projects in Myanmar, Thailand and Indonesia, and, the island plans to spend US$49.7 million in 2018, according to Minister without Portfolio John Deng, to support local banks to loan up to US$3.5 billion to allied and New Southbound Policy countries for development projects.[17] Taiwan's Ministry of Economics even initiated the Industry Innovation and Development Project on 4 September 2016, which ended on 2 November 2016. This special training class recruits students from Vietnam, Laos, Indonesia and Thailand.[18] In addition, the ROC government announced, in early August 2017, that Taiwan will train 200 medical professionals from Southeast Asia every year and establish 16 agricultural demonstration parks in South and Southeast Asia in the coming years.[19] It is believed that throughout President Tsai's administrations more of these types of assistance and development projects will continue throughout the Southeast Asian region, where the ROC on Taiwan does not have any diplomatic partner.

Connecting Taiwan with Regional Economies

Since the early 1990s, in addition to increasing trade, investment and assistance to Southeast Asia, Taiwan has initiated a series of policies that have also developed economic relations with countries throughout the Asia-Pacific region. In the late 1990s, the Kuomintang (KMT) government proposed an Asia-Pacific Regional Operations Center (APROC), in an attempt to establish Taiwan as a pivotal economy in the region. The proposal, however, was never fully developed due to a change in political power. In May 2000, the first Democratic Progressive Party (DPP) President, Chen Shui-bian was sworn in. His administration proposed the "Green Silicon Island" initiative to become Taiwan's economic focus. Unfortunately, this plan also never got fully developed due to another switch in political leadership, when, in May 2008, KMT President Ma Ying-jeou came to power.

President Ma also tried to implement the APROC proposal earlier on in his first term, but in 2012, he switched to the Free Economic Pilot Zones (FEPZ) initiative and developed Taiwan into an economically free zone, in order to upgrade economic relations with other Asia-Pacific countries. The main directives of the FEPZ included deregulation, an open market, internationalization, institutional reform and an international alignment. This would align Taiwan with other economies and allow for the free movement of people, goods and money. It would provide tax incentives and convenient land acquisition, promote cross-border industrial cooperation and allow for a freer environment to attract international businesses and investment.

FEPZ's first phase included six of Taiwan's harbors, which were designed to make Taiwan a platform for connecting sea lane transportation from Northeast Asia to Southeast Asia. The second phase was to be carried out during President Ma's second term from 2012 to 2016 and required certain laws to be passed in order to continue. Unfortunately, there was a series of disputes between the then ruling KMT and the opposing DPP and the FEPZ did not reach its full potential.

With the implementation of President Tsai's New Southbound Policy, Taiwan is willing to share resources with Southeast Asian countries, specifically in the realms of medicine, culture, tourism, technology and agriculture.[20] According to this policy, Taiwan plans to establish a Taiwan Agricultural Development Company in order to promote Taiwan's agricultural technology with its southern neighbors. The company will supervise various agricultural demonstration parks in South and Southeast Asia, as indicated earlier. Because Taiwan's economic and industrial development is comparable to most Southeast Asian countries, it provides Taiwan an opportunity to share its resources with its neighbors to the South. While it is too early to assess whether the New Southbound Policy will allow Taiwan to build sustainable relationships with Southeast Asia, the Tsai administration continues to make great efforts in the region.

Attempts at Joining Regional Economic Blocs

Since the early 1990s, free trade, economic regionalization and the development of a number of regional economic blocs have become the trend in Southeast Asia. ASEAN has been playing a pivotal role in the development of regional economics and has initiated free trade agreements with neighboring powerful economies, such as China, India and Australia. Ten ASEAN members have successfully accomplished a number of free trade agreements, including 10+1, 10+3 and 10+6. Neighboring countries have also been able to develop greater economic cooperation and regional integration.

The Regional Comprehensive Economic Partnership (RCEP) and the Trans-Pacific Partnership (TPP) are newly developed economic blocs that have created some grave international attention. The RCEP was introduced in November 2011, at the 19th ASEAN Summit and would include ten member countries from the previous 10+6.[21] In November 2012, at the 21st ASEAN Summit, it was formally endorsed by leaders of 16 member countries. The RCEP was developed to boost economic growth through open trade and investment, enhance economic cooperation and deepen economic integration in the region. By the end of December 2014, all 16 member states engaged six times in negotiations over issues regarding trade, goods and services, investment, intellectual property, dispute settlement and technical cooperation and so on. It is expected that the RCEP agreement later concluded at the end of 2017.

TPP originated from the Pacific Three Closer Economic Partnership (P3 CEP) that was initiated by Chile, Singapore and New Zealand. In 2005, it was renamed the Trans-Pacific Strategic Economic Partnership Agreement (TPSEPA, or P4), which also included Brunei. In January 2008, the United States showed interest in entering into talks with the P4 countries. In January 2009, after President Barack Obama took office, he reaffirmed America's commitment to TPP. When the US began to dominate, more countries in the Asia-Pacific region (mostly American allies) followed suit. By the end of 2014, participating countries had held 19 formal rounds of TPP negotiations regarding cooperation, capacity building, cross-border services, e-commerce, financial services, government procurement, intellectual property, investment, the elimination of tariffs and other trade barriers and so on. When President Donald Trump was sworn in January 2017, he fulfilled his campaign promise to withdraw the United States from the TPP, subsequently making the future of the TPP uncertain.

Taiwan is part of the Asia-Pacific, but due to its political isolation and China's sustained political barriers, opportunity for formal involvement in regional economic blocs has become tremendously challenging.[22] This continues to threaten Taiwan's economic development. Since the mid-1980s, Taiwan has strived to join regional blocs, including the most significant organization in the region, ASEAN, which would essentially offer four methods of participation. Options include becoming a full member, with the second of becoming an observer, the third as a candidate member and the fourth as a dialogue member. Although Taiwan has made great efforts over the last three decades, it has failed to establish any connection with ASEAN.[23]

In September 2013, the ROC government officially announced its interest in joining RCEP and the TPP. At a conference on 17 February 2014, President Ma Ying-jeou stated that it was an "unshakeable goal" for Taiwan to enter these organizations and Taiwan's bid to join should be carried forth simultaneously and with the greatest possible momentum.[24] President Ma also indicated that about 34.4% of Taiwan's trade in 2013 was already being carried out with 12 of the nations that were currently in negotiations with the TPP. Trade between Taiwan and 16 member states of the RCEP accounted for 56.6%.[25] At the Boao Forum on 29 March, 2015, then Vice-President Vincent Siew and his delegation met with PRC President Xi Jinping and expressed Taiwan's willingness to join the Asian Infrastructure Investment Bank (AIIB).[26] Two days later, on 31 March, 2015, the ROC government sent an official application to join the China-financed AIIB. However, China was unwilling to allow Taiwan to become one of its founding members.[27]

Despite its bumpy road in joining regional economic blocs, Taiwan has successfully negotiated quasi free trade agreements with China, Singapore and New Zealand. In August 2010, the Cross-Straits Economic Cooperation Framework Agreement (ECFA) went into effect. On 1 December 2013, the Economic Cooperation (ANZTEC) was established between New Zealand and Taiwan's Separate Customs Territory, Penghu, Kinmen and Matsu. The Economic Partnership (ASTEP), between Singapore and Taiwan's Separate Customs Territory, Penghu, Kinmen and Matsu, became effective on 19 March 2014. In March 2013, in order to develop its Trade and Investment Framework Agreement, Taiwan also resumed negotiations with the United States.

In 2010, according to Professor Chen-Yuan Tung's study, approximately 23–27% of private enterprises would have increased investments in Taiwan, if it were permitted membership into East Asia's emerging economic organizations.[28] When President Tsai Ing-wen took office, Tung served as her first Executive Yuan Spokesman (May–September 2016) and an advisor to the National Security Council (September 2016–July 2017). In August 2017, Tung was appointed as the Representative to Taipei Economic and Cultural Office in Thailand. He has been a key figure in implementing President Tsai's New Southbound Policy. According to the Policy, Taiwan will continue its attempt to join regional economic blocs, revise and strengthen existing economic agreements, develop new agreements and widen Taiwan's economic partnerships with countries in Southern and Southeast Asia.[29] Actually, linkage with regional countries is a major policy under the guidance of Ministry of Economics, whose main task is to strengthen Taiwan's bilateral and multilateral connections with countries in Southeast Asia, particularly through the channels of non-governmental organizations.[30]

TAIWAN'S POLITICAL RELATIONS WITH SOUTHEAST ASIAN COUNTRIES

Devoid of any official diplomatic relations in the region, the ROC on Taiwan continues to maintain a relatively stable relationship with countries in Southeast Asia. This is exemplified by the following four indicators:

(1) Taiwan's offices in Southeast Asia
(2) Agreements signed between Taiwan and various Southeast Asian countries
(3) Exchanges and visits to Taiwan by high-level officials and delegations from Southeast Asian countries
(4) Visitor visa waivers for Taiwanese people visiting Southeast Asian countries

Taiwan's Offices in Southeast Asia

It was in the mid-1970s, when the ROC lost its last diplomatic Southeast Asian ally.[31] Since then, Taiwan has been forced to set up unofficial offices in major Southeast Asian countries. Originally, they bore ambiguous names and maintained very basic, unofficial political relationships. Major Southeast Asian countries also set up non-governmental offices in Taiwan, but could only offer minimal services.[32] In Indonesia, for example, Taiwan's office was called the Chinese Chamber of Commerce and the Indonesian office in Taiwan was called the Indonesian Chamber of Commerce. Taiwan's office in the Philippines was called the Pacific Economic and Cultural Center in Manila and the Philippine's office in Taiwan was called the Asia Exchange Center. These vague names confused not only governmental officials from both sides but also ordinary citizens of both countries, when they wanted to apply for visas to visit one another.

Since the late 1980s, due to Taiwan's great economic contributions to the region, Taiwan's offices began changing its names throughout Southeast Asia, to include Taipei, in order to emphasize the ROC's capital. In October 1989, Taiwan's Office in Indonesia changed its name to the Taipei Economic and Cultural Office (TECO) in Indonesia and in December 1989, the Taipei Economic and Cultural Office (TECO) in the Philippines. In May 1992, Thailand's office was changed to the Taipei Economic and Cultural Office and in November 1992, in Vietnam, the name was changed to the Taipei Economic and Cultural Office and so on.[33] Most Southeast Asian countries allowed Taiwan to upgrade its status, granted more privileges and more formal diplomatic relations. The Trade offices began to function similarly to a regular Embassy. Taiwan's officials that were dispatched to Southeast Asia were also granted diplomatic privileges and immunities like those of diplomats from countries with formal diplomatic relations and followed the stipulations stated in the Vienna Convention on Diplomatic Relations (1961).

Diplomats, whose countries have official diplomatic relations with another country, enjoy at least 15 diplomatic privileges, including tax exemption, immunity from criminal persecution, civil lawsuits and preferential, expediential processing at airports and so on. Diplomats from the United States and Canada, for example, enjoy the highest level of reciprocal diplomatic privilege. However, countries without formal diplomatic relationships receive fewer diplomatic privileges, such as during the Cold War, when some diplomats from the Soviet Union were not allowed to leave the Washington, D.C., area without permission from the US State Department.

Prior to 1990, most countries in Southeast Asia granted Taiwanese diplomats a very limited number of diplomatic functions and minimum diplomatic privileges. However, after the office names changed, Taiwan's officials stationed in Southeast Asia began to enjoy more diplomatic privileges and since the turn of the century, in major Southeast Asian countries, Taiwan's diplomats have been granted diplomatic privileges and immunities to a level that is equivalent of international governmental organizations (the United Nations, for example).[34]

Agreements Between Taiwan and Several Southeast Asian Countries

Signing official agreements and other documents is an important indicator of how diplomatically close two countries are. The closer the relations between the two countries, the more agreements they pursue. The United Kingdom and the United States are examples of this. However, it is difficult to sign official agreements and documents if they do not maintain a friendly relationship, such as in North Korea and South Korea. During the 1980s, due to its political isolation and minimal diplomatic relationships, Taiwan had only a few agreements throughout Southeast Asia. However, in the 1990s, Taiwan's signing of official documents and memorandums with major Southeast Asian countries rapidly increased, which resulted in increased economic relations.

Throughout the golden age of the 1990s, in order to facilitate greater investment in major countries in Southeast Asia, Taiwan developed a greater number of agreements and memorandums. One major example of this was the number of agreements Taiwan and the Philippines engaged in, including the Promotion and Protection Investment, Aviation, Fishing and Agricultural Co-operation, the Customs Co-operation, the Science and Technology Co-operation and so on.

Since the turn of the century, Taiwan has continued to sign many more agreements, most of which have been with regard to economic cooperation with major countries in Southeast Asia. Although Taiwan continues to be isolated, in 2010, Taiwan and Singapore began talks on a bilateral economic agreement. On 7 November, 2013, the Agreement between Singapore and the Separate Customs Territory of Taiwan, Penghu, Kinmen and Matsu on Economic Partnership (ASTEP) was signed between Singapore and Taiwan.[35] The ASTEP is likely to promote trade between the two countries and provides leeway for Taiwan to connect its economy with other countries in Southeast Asia. This could certainly be seen as participating in emerging economic regionalization.

In early December 2012, Taiwan and Indonesia also signed an MOU to assist with the development of North Maluku Province's Morotai Island in Indonesia. Rich in fisheries, aquaculture, forestry and ecotourism, the MOU was designed to provide incentives for Taiwanese investment, while the Indonesian government was responsible for the construction of the necessary infrastructure.[36] Although Morotai Island is extremely undeveloped and remote, the MOU exemplifies the potential for diplomatically isolated Taiwan to sign agreements with significant countries in Southeast Asia.[37] During the last couple of years, Taiwan has also signed various agreements with other countries in Southeast Asia, which exemplify well-constructed substantial relations between Taiwan and its Southeast Asian neighbors.[38]

Cross-Strait relations between China and Taiwan have recently gone into serious decline, since President Tsai refuses to accept the 1992 consensus. This has caused the Chinese government to cease communications and has provoked them to block Taiwan's initiatives in various international realms. This is in sharp contrast to President Ma Ying-jeou's 2008–2016 administration. It currently remains unclear what potential Taiwan will have in reaching further agreements with its Southeast Asian neighbors.

Exchanges of Visits Among High-Level Officials

Another indicator of Taiwan's political relations with its Southeast Asian neighbors is the frequency of high-level official exchanges and visits, which are similar to other nation-states that maintain official diplomatic relations. Countries in Western Europe are an example this. However, countries with unstable or hostile relations do not engage in such exchanges. Israel and its neighboring countries are an example of this.

Since the ROC on Taiwan lost its last Southeast Asian diplomatic partner in 1975, it has been diplomatically isolated and barred from participating international organizations in the region. Since the late 1980s, thanks to its economic achievements, there has been some improvement. In the early 1990s, Taiwan began hosting high-level Southeast Asian officials. In February 1994, Former President Lee Teng-hui paid unofficial visits to the Philippines, Indonesia and Thailand. During that time, Taiwan's cabinet ministers also went on pseudo-diplomatic exchanges in the region.[39] During the 1990s, Taiwan's golden age of strong relations with its neighbors to the south, President Lee visited several Southeast Asian countries under the guise of "vacation diplomacy." This gave rise to opportunities for him to engage in historical talks with three regional leaders.

During President Chen Shui-bian's administration from 2000 to 2008, Taiwan, however, experienced a series of diplomatic challenges, since President Chen was more confrontational in his relationship with the PRC. Beijing reacted by demanding Southeast Asian governments to adhere to the one-China policy, which claims that there is only one China and Taiwan is part of China. This resulted in far fewer exchanges of high-level officials between Taiwan and its Southeast Asian neighbors.

In May 2008, when President Ma Ying-jeou took power, he initiated a policy of diplomatic truce with the PRC. During his administration from 2008 to 2016, Taiwan engaged in greater, more peaceful diplomatic interactions with the international community.[40] This can be exemplified in the increase of exchanges between Taiwan and Southeast Asia's high-level officials. Taiwan's improved relationship with Singapore could be exemplified as one of the most notable examples of this. On 25 March 2015, after former Singaporean Prime Minister Lee Kuan Yew passed away, President Ma made a private visit to Singapore to pay tribute to its founding father. This was carried out under a special circumstances agreement. President Ma visited Singapore again in early November 2015, for a historic meeting with his counterpart President Xi Jinping. This was the first time since 1949 that a meeting had occurred between the Chinese Nationalist government of Taiwan and the Chinese Communist government of Beijing.[41] Although President Ma and President Xi did not come to any formal agreements, their meeting in Singapore implied Taiwan's would be maintaining long-term substantial relations with Singapore.

Throughout President Ma's administration, Taiwan's high-level officials frequently visited other countries in Southeast Asia; however, most of these remained unpublicized. One example of this was in 2015, when Mr. Y. L. Lin, the then Foreign Minister of the ROC made a private visit to Indonesia. Other such exchanges also occurred during the Ma administration; however, they were mostly unpublicized. These exchanges exemplified great cordial relations between Taiwan and its neighboring countries.[42]

Southeast Asia Visa Waivers for Taiwanese People

Since the ROC passport was not formally recognized, the Taiwanese people previously experienced great challenges when applying for visas to travel abroad. In December 1979, when the ROC and the United States terminated their diplomatic ties, entry visas became a requirement for Taiwanese citizens visiting the United States and until 1997 these were only issued through the US Council General's Office in Hong Kong. When the American Institute in Taiwan was established, they became authorized to issue entry visas to ROC citizens. In 2015, due to President Ma's visa waiver policy, the United States began issuing the Taiwanese people electronic visas. Although ROC passport holders still face some challenges when going overseas, President Ma's administration was able to negotiate visa waivers for multiple countries around the world. This can be considered one of his greatest diplomatic achievements. It was particularly extraordinary, given the fact that Taiwan had only 22 diplomatic partners during his presidency.[43]

Due to Taiwan's successful political economy and the prevalence of the internet, most foreign offices in Taiwan are now authorized to issue entry visas to Taiwanese citizens regardless of whether or not they maintain official diplomatic recognition with the ROC. Six major Southeast Asian countries have offices in Taipei and are now authorized to issue entry visas to Taiwanese citizens.[44]

The "visa free policy" encompasses three types of issuance, the first being the completely visa free policy, with no requirement to obtain an entry visa in advance. Singapore is one example of this. The second type of issuance allows Taiwanese visitors to obtain a landing visa upon arrival. Again, it does not require any advance application, such as in Thailand and Indonesia. The final issuance method allows Taiwanese visitors the opportunity to obtain entry visas through an electronic visa application system, prior to the visit. As of August 2016, the Taiwanese people can utilize one of these three issuing methods in 164 countries.[45]

Most Southeast Asian countries now grant Taiwanese visitors either full visa waivers such as the case in Singapore and Malaysia or entry visas issued upon arrival, such as in Thailand, Indonesia, Cambodia, Laos, Brunei and East Timor (Timor-Leste). Singapore was the first country in Southeast Asia to sign on to the visa free policy and in 2011 Malaysia became the last. Due to these privileges, the Taiwanese now enjoy easier access to travel, trade and investment. It also gives rise to greater opportunity for more social and cultural interactions around the region and exemplifies that Taiwan has clearly developed trustworthy, integral relationships throughout Southeast Asia.

CHALLENGES FOR TAIWAN'S RELATIONS WITH SOUTHEAST ASIA

Political Isolation and an Uncertain Future

As indicated earlier in this chapter, Taiwan has successfully established stable substantial relationships with major Southeast Asian countries and has consistently participated in political interactions with them. However, a substantial relationship does not equate formal diplomatic ties. Despite the awkward situation that Taiwan has endured for more than 30 years, it has flourished internationally. However, there does not seem to be much opportunity for Taiwan to overcome such isolation in the near future, which will be a major challenge that Taiwan will have to face.

Despite China's political and economic dominance, one of the key factors of Taiwan's survival in the international community has been due to substantial American support. However, with China's political economy on the rise and its strategic relationship strengthening with the United States, Taiwan will now be at greater risk. President Donald Trump has recently been illustrating increased goodwill towards China, which juxtaposes his electoral platform prior to January 2017, when he took office.[46] China's influence on international politics is consistently increasing, which is augmented with a possible American alliance. It now becomes obvious that Taiwan will suffer increased isolation and is questionable regarding how well the island will be able to thrive internationally.

Another consequence of President Tsai's unwillingness to endorse the "1992 Consensus" has been the suspension of dialogue between Taiwan and China and an increase in blocking Taiwan's international participation. In late September 2016, Taiwan was barred from attending the International Civil Aviation Organization (ICAO) assembly. Both President Tsai Ing-wen and Foreign Minister David Lee expressed grave dissatisfaction regarding this matter.[47] During President Ma's administration, Taiwan had been invited to attend the ICAO.

More recently in May 2017, China refused Taiwan's attendance to the World Health Association's (WHA) annual meeting, though Taiwan had been invited to attend under President Ma's administration. In early May 2017, Director of China's Taiwan Affairs Office Mr. Zhang Zhijun told reporters that unless Taiwan accepted the 1992 consensus, they would be in no way permitted to attend international meetings and participation in the international community would need to be condoned by China. It is evident that cross-Strait relations are currently strained.[48] Nevertheless, Taiwan continues to make its case to the world and raise support from major countries; however, it has been to no avail.[49]

Another mater of significance is that since May 2016, the ROC has lost two of its diplomatic allies. Sao Tome Principe cut relations on 20 December 2016 and 13 June 2017 marked the significant loss of the Republic of Panama. Panama was the ROC's longest standing diplomatic partner. The previous Manchu empire established relations with Panama in 1910. Panama then continued diplomatic relations with the ROC after the establishment of the Republic of China in January 1912. Panama was also Taiwan's most powerful diplomatic partner. Taiwan's international status rested on diplomatic recognition. The loss of Panama may prompt Taiwanese allies in Central America to follow suit. Eleven of the ROC's remaining 20 diplomatic allies are located in Latin America, and countries such as Dominican, El Salvador and Honduras are beginning to show signs of bowing to China's rising political economic clout.

Since October 1971, when the PRC took the ROC's United Nations seat, Taiwan has struggled diplomatically. However, at that time China was in a much weaker position and Taiwan received greater support from the United States. Yet, since May 2016, China has taken an increasingly tough stance towards Taiwan, and despite President Tsai's promotion of the New Southbound Policy, she will most likely face greater diplomatic isolation during her administration in light of China's powerful presence and influence in global affairs.

Economic Marginalization and Future Development

During the Cold War era, Taiwan was branded as one of Asia's four Dragon Economies. This was mainly due to how it had opened itself to the world's market earlier on. This chapter has outlined how Taiwan's economic relations with Southeast Asia have been on the rise since the early 1980s. The early 1990s marked the end of the Cold War and Southeast Asian countries began opening their market economies up to the world. More recently, these countries have been actively engaging in the development of economic regionalization. With trade deals such as ASEAN Plus One, Three and Six, countries in the region have established a steadfast economic community and have been making great economic strides. Taiwan, unfortunately, remains excluded. Previously, Taiwan's economic relations with Southeast Asia were developed on bilateral terms; however, more recently more multilateral interactions have come into play and are now the cornerstone of regional economic integration. Although Taiwan continues efforts to join these regional economic groupings, political difficulties continue to keep it marginalized and prevent it from joining. It will indeed be a great challenge for Taiwan to deal with greater economic marginalization in the years ahead.

In mid-June 2002, Taiwan's dynamic and vibrant democracy was referred to at an Asia Society annual dinner, in a speech by former US Secretary of State, Colin Powell. He said, "The Taiwan problem is one of a success story."[50] Taiwan's economic achievements have made it world famous and this continues to be the cornerstone of its political democratization and modernization.

However, Taiwan has experienced great economic decline since 2000 when it was at a 6.42% growth at that time, it then declined to 5.62% in 2006, 2.23% in 2013 and 1.5% in 2016. Since 2011, its economic growth has been less than 5%. However, since 2013, most Southeast Asian countries have illustrated growth rates of over 5%. One more concern regarding Taiwan's economic development is the decline in shared government capital and public enterprises, which had previously been a cornerstone of its GDP. In 2000, shared public/private enterprises comprised of 5.44% of GDP revenue, yet in 2004 it went into sharp decline to 4.13%, in 2008 and 2.86% in 2014. There was however a slight increase to 2.9% in 2016.[51] These figures have revealed a declining trend in public investment, which has subsequently hindered its economic development.

Taiwan continues to be isolated from regional trade agreements and economic integration with countries in the region. Taiwan's continued economic marginalization could potentially impact the people's livelihoods. Maintaining its economic growth is certainly a grave challenge that Taiwan will have to face in the coming years.

CONCLUSION

Taiwan's economic developments have contributed greatly to its integral relationships with Southeast Asian countries and an increasing political economy in the region. It, however, remains uncertain what sort of impact its continued diplomatic and economic isolation will have on these future developments.

China is currently creating diplomatic challenges for Taiwan, which is also subsequently making it more marginalized. Unfortunately, its democratization seems to have also contributed to its isolation in the realm of international politics. However, China does receive criticism for its authoritarian governance, whereas Taiwan is receiving some positive recognition for their democracy. Taiwan does not intend to compete with China's rising political economy; however, it is clearly ahead in its democratization.

During the 1950s to the 1980s, Asian values contrasted universal values advocated by Western scholars. However, today these Asian values are used as the foundation of political authoritarianism. China is considered to be the strongest modern leader to advocate these traditional Asian cultural ideas and values.

Many Asian countries began the democratization process in the mid-1980s. In February 1986, The Philippines overthrew their former dictator Ferdinand Marcos. This was the first Asian country to undergo a democratization process. In July 1987, martial law was lifted in Taiwan making it the second country in the region to begin its journey towards democratization. In February 1988, President Roh Tae-woo was democratically elected in South Korea. In 1997, Thailand successfully revised its 1932 constitution. However, Thailand's road to democracy remains bumpy. After President Suharto was overthrown in May 1998, Indonesia also began implementing a democracy and according to *Freedom House* (2006), it was ranked as the world's most politically free Muslim state.

Asia's political developments over the past two or three decades have demonstrated that political democratization has become a universal value. Various countries, including Islamic Indonesia, Catholic Philippines, Confucian Taiwan and Buddhist Korea have all successfully adopted democratic systems. Despite its isolation, Taiwan's democratic transformation makes it a role model in the region. China and its leaders will also have to consider these factors in the years to come.

Notes

1. By the end of 2016, there were 624,768 foreign migrant workers in Taiwan, mostly from Vietnam, Indonesia, Thailand and the Philippines.
2. Before 1985, US$1 was the equivalent of 40 Taiwan dollars but throughout 1986–1988, Taiwan's currency appreciated to 25–26 Taiwan dollars to US$1.
3. The Republic of China's Bureau of Foreign Trade, Ministry of Economics.
4. Figures in this paragraph are from http://cus93.trade.gov.tw/FSCI/, accessed on 15 May 2017.
5. https://www.trade.gov.tw/App_Ashx/File.ashx?FilePath=../Files/PageFile/b8efa1ee-91b2-4c6c-8624-4aed8e9b8370.pdf.
6. For more about the New Southward Policy, see Chen Hui-ping, "Foreign Affairs: Tsai to chase 'New Southward Policy'" *Taipei Times*, 21 March, 2016. http://www.taipeitimes.com/News/taiwan/archives/2016/03/21/2003642086; "Taiwan's New Southward Policy must go beyond chasing," *Straits Times*, 20 May, 2016. http://www.straitstimes.com/asia/east-asia/taiwans-new-southward-policy-must-go-beyond-chasing-the-china-post.
7. For details, see Christine Chou, "Call the APIC team: Industry, government launch 'New Southbound Policy' task force," *The China Post*, March 7, 2017. http://www.chinapost.com.tw/taiwan/business/2017/03/09/493168/call-the.htm.
8. Regarding Taiwan's early investment in China and Southeast Asia, see Xiang Ming Chen, "Taiwan Investments in China and Southeast Asia: "Go West, but Also Go South"," *Asian Survey*, Vol. 36, No. 5, May 1996, pp. 447–467; Rong Yung King, "Taiwan and ASEAN: Another Approach to Economic Cooperation," *Issues and Studies*, Vol. 34, No. 11/12, November/December 1998, pp. 181–201.
9. Figures in this paragraph are from https://www.dois.moea.gov.tw/Home/relation3, accessed 15 May 2017.
10. For the details of the New Southbound Policy, please visit: http://www.newsouthboundpolicy.tw/PageDetail.aspx?id=cbf0a167-7c9e-4840-ba5b-2d47b5badb00&pageType=SouthPolicy.
11. In 1949, after the Chinese Communists took over mainland China, roughly 100,000 ROC military and their families retreated from Yunnan province into northern Burma. The Burmese government sued the Nationalist army through the United Nations. In the early 1960s, a UN resolution forced most of them out of Burma and into Thailand. These displaced ROC military were also not welcomed by the Thai government. However, in the early 1970s, the ROC assisted Thailand in putting down a Thai communist insurgency in its northern region. King Bhumibol Adulyadej and the Thai government publicly acknowledged and appreciated

their contribution and as a result granted the Chinese Nationalist soldiers Thai citizenship.
12. *The New York Times* recently reported on one of these villages in northwestern Thailand. See Amy Qin, "In Remote Thai Villages, Legacy of China's Lost Army Endures", *The New York Times*, 14 January, 2015. http://www.nytimes.com/2015/01/15/world/asia/in-remote-thailand-the-lost-soldiers-of-the-kuomintang.html?_r=0.
13. See http://www.icdf.org.tw/ct.asp?xItem=4283&ctNode=29793&mp=1.
14. http://www.mofa.gov.tw/en/News_Content.aspx?n=C7C822667A8F469F&sms=11233CCF2D9FD7A7&s=545375B51DA41425, accessed 2 October, 2016.
15. Alain Guilloux, *Taiwan's humanitarian aid/disaster relief: wither or proper?*, Taiwan-US Quarterly Analysis, Brookings, August 2016. https://www.brookings.edu/opinions/taiwans-humanitarian-aiddisaster-relief-wither-or-prosper/, accessed 4 October 2016.
16. Ibid.
17. For the 2016 information, see Ministry of Foreign Affairs, 2016 Annual Report of the International Cooperation and Development Affairs (Taipei: Ministry of Foreign Affairs of the Republic of China) (http://www.mofa.gov.tw/Upload/RelFile/17/262/a2fe53f1-8839-4a82-819b-d0dd45e2d73d.pdf). For the 2018 figures, see http://focustaiwan.tw/news/aeco/201711040011.aspx.
18. Ibid, p. 26.
19. http://ocacnews.net/overseascommunity/article/article_story.jsp?main=255&sub=106&third=0&id=223444, accessed 6 August 2017.
20. Ministry of Economics: http://www.newsouthboundpolicy.tw/PageDetail.aspx?id=cbf0a167-7c9e-4840-ba5b-2d47b5badb00&pageType=SouthPolicy.
21. The members of the RCEP include the ten ASEAN countries, China, Japan, South Korea, India, Australia and New Zealand.
22. Due to the "One-China policy", China continues to block Taiwan from joining these economic organizations. See, Christopher M. Dent, "Taiwan and the New Regional Political Economy of East Asia," *The China Quarterly*, Vol. 182, June 2005, pp. 385–386.
23. With regard to Taiwan's economic relations with ASEAN, see Hong Zhao, "Taiwan-ASEAN Economic Relations in the Context of East Asian Regional Integration," *International Journal of China Studies*, Vol. 2, No. 1, April 2011, pp. 39–54.
24. http://www.mofa.gov.tw/EnMobile/News_Content.aspx?s=812442E092DF7B2B.
25. Ibid.

26. "Siew delivers message to Xi as Boao Forum opens," *Taipei Times*, 29 March, 2015: http://www.taipeitimes.com/News/front/archives/2015/03/29/2003614643.
27. Taiwan's bid for the AIIB was a last minute submission, just before the deadline for applications closed. See Lawrence Chung, "Taiwan in last-minute bid to join AIIB as founding member," *South China Morning Post*, 31 March, 2015. http://www.scmp.com/news/china/article/1751994/taiwan-last-minute-bid-join-aiib-founding-member.
28. Chen-Yuan Tung, "The East Asian Economic Integration Regime and Taiwan", *Asian Perspective*, Vol. 34, No. 2, April/June 2010, pp. 83–112.
29. http://www.newsouthboundpolicy.tw/PageDetail.aspx?id=cbf0a167-7c9e-4840-ba5b-2d47b5badb00&pageType=SouthPolicy.
30. Ibid.
31. The ROC terminated diplomatic ties with then the Republic of Vietnam (South Vietnam) in April 1975 when the Democratic Republic of Vietnam (North Vietnam), led by Ho Chi Minh, was taken over by the Vietnamese Communists.
32. Issuing visas for visitors was one of the few functions that could be carried out.
33. Taiwan now has two offices in Indonesia, located in Jakarta and Surabaya, and two offices in Vietnam, located in Hanoi and Ho Chi Minh City.
34. Interviews conducted with high-level Taiwanese officials in Southeast Asian countries, July 2016.
35. ASTEP commenced on 19 April 2014
36. Shih Hsiu-Chuan, "Taiwan, Indonesia ink MOU to develop Indonesian island," *Taipei Times*, December 6, 2012.
37. Interview with a Taiwanese businessman in Jakarta, August 2015.
38. Based on the author's two decades of field studies in Southeast Asia, it can be concluded that Taiwan does not face significant problems in initiating and signing agreements with desired countries in Southeast Asia.
39. The Foreign Minister and Defense Minister did not, however, participate in these exchanges.
40. The ROC President serves up to two four-year terms. President Ma was successfully reelected, serving two full years; President Chen Shui-bian also served for eight years.
41. For more information, see Charles Hutzler and Jake Maxwell Watts, "China's Xi Jinping and Taiwan's Ma Ying-jeou Meet in Singapore," *The Wall Street Journal*, November 8, 2015. http://www.wsj.com/articles/china-s-xi-jinping-and-taiwan-s-ma-ying-jeou-meet-in-singapore-1446880724.
42. Mr. Lin served as Foreign Minister from September 2012 to May 2016 and was Taiwan's Representative to Indonesia from 2003 to 2007.

43. Throughout the Ma administration, there were 22 diplomatic partners, but as of July 2017, there are now only 20. In November 2013, Gambia withdrew its diplomatic recognition and then established diplomatic relations with China in March 2016. Since May 2016, President Tsai's administration has lost another two, Sao Tome Principe on 20 December, 2016 and the Republic of Panama on 13 June, 2017.
44. These six countries include Singapore, Malaysia, Indonesia, Thailand, Vietnam and the Philippines.
45. http://fl00clt.blogspot.tw/p/visa.html.
46. One US reporter points out, "Mr. Trump's antagonism towards China is a gamble without an upside." (Edward Luce, "Donald Trump's collision course with China", *Financial Times*, 18 December 2016. (https://www.ft.com/content/5d9df7d4-c3c3-11e6-81c2-f57d90f6741a, accessed 19 May 2017).
47. Alison Hsiao, "Ministry regrets lack of ICAO invitation", *Taipei Times*, 24 September 2016. http://www.taipeitimes.com/News/front/archives/2016/09/24/2003655812.
48. "No 1992 consensus, no basis for Taiwan to attend WHA: China," *Focus Taiwan*, May 8, 2017. http://focustaiwan.tw/news/acs/201705080010.aspx.
49. Chris Horton, "Blocked by China, Taiwan Presses to Join U.N. Agency's Meeting," *The New York Times*, May 8, 2017. https://www.nytimes.com/2017/05/08/world/asia/taiwan-world-health-china-.html?_r=0.
50. "Taiwan problem is one of "success story": Powell," *The China Post*, 12 June, 2002. Available at: http://www.chinapost.com.tw/news/2002/06/12/27410/Taiwan-problem.htm.
51. Figures in this paragraph are from http://dmz9.moea.gov.tw/GMWeb/common/CommonQuery.aspx, accessed 15 May, 2017.

BIBLIOGRAPHY

Chen, Xiang Ming. 1996. Taiwan Investments in China and Southeast Asia: 'Go West, but Also Go South'. *Asian Survey* 36 (5, May): 447–467.

Chung, Lawrence. 2015. Taiwan in Last-Minute Bid to Join AIIB as Founding Member. *South China Morning Post*, March 31. http://www.scmp.com/news/china/article/1751994/taiwan-last-minute-bid-join-aiib-founding-member.

Dent, Christopher M. 2005. Taiwan and the New Regional Political Economy of East Asia. *The China Quarterly* 182 (June): 385–386.

Guilloux, Alain. 2016. *Taiwan's Humanitarian Aid/Disaster Relief: Wither or Proper?* Taiwan-US Quarterly Analysis. Brookings, August. https://www.brookings.edu/opinions/taiwans-humanitarian-aiddisaster-relief-wither-or-prosper/. Accessed 4 Oct 2016.

Hsiao, Alison. 2016. Ministry Regrets Lack of ICAO Invitation. *Taipei Times*, September 24. http://www.taipeitimes.com/News/front/archives/2016/09/24/2003655812.
Hsiu-Chuan, Shih. 2012. Taiwan, Indonesia Ink MOU to Develop Indonesian Island. *Taipei Times*, December 6.
Hui-ping, Chen. 2016. Foreign Affairs: Tsai to Chase 'New Southward Policy.' *Taipei Times*, March 21. http://www.taipeitimes.com/News/taiwan/archives/2016/03/21/2003642086.
Hutzler, Charles, and Jake Maxwell Watts. 2015. China's Xi Jinping and Taiwan's Ma Ying-jeou Meet in Singapore. *The Wall Street Journal*, November 8. http://www.wsj.com/articles/china-s-xi-jinping-and-taiwan-s-ma-ying-jeou-meet-in-singapore-1446880724.
King, Yung Rong. 1998. Taiwan and ASEAN: Another Approach to Economic Cooperation. *Issues and Studies* 34 (11/12, November/December): 181–201.
Ku, Samuel C.Y. 2005. The Changing Political Economy of Taiwan's and China's Relations with Southeast Asia. In *China and Southeast Asia: Global Changes and Regional Challenges*, ed. Ho Khai Leong and Samuel C.Y. Ku, 259–280. Singapore: Institute of Southeast Asian Studies and Taiwan: Center for Southeast Asian Studies, National Sun Yat-sen University.
Qin, Amy. 2015. In Remote Thai Villages, Legacy of China's Lost Army Endures. *New York Times*, January 14. http://www.nytimes.com/2015/01/15/world/asia/in-remote-thailand-the-lost-soldiers-of-the-kuomintang.html?_r=0.
Tung, Chen-Yuan. 2010. The East Asian Economic Integration Regime and Taiwan. *Asian Perspective* 34 (2, April/June): 83–112.
Zhao, Hong. 2002. Taiwan Problem Is One of 'Success Story': Powell. *The China Post*, June 12. http://www.chinapost.com.tw/news/2002/06/12/27410/Taiwan-problem.htm.
———. 2011. Taiwan-ASEAN Economic Relations in the Context of East Asian Regional Integration. *International Journal of China Studies* 2 (1, April): 39–54.
———. 2015. Siew Delivers Message to Xi as Boao Forum Opens. *Taipei Times*, March 29. http://www.taipeitimes.com/News/front/archives/2015/03/29/2003614643.
———. 2016. Taiwan's New Southward Policy Must Go Beyond Chasing. *Straits Times*, May 20. http://www.straitstimes.com/asia/east-asia/taiwans-new-southward-policy-must-go-beyond-chasing-the-china-post.

CHAPTER 12

The Japan-Taiwan Relationship Under the Tsai Ing-wen Administration

Madoka Fukuda

INTRODUCTION

This chapter mainly focuses on the process of institutionalization and maturity in the relationship between Japan and Taiwan under the Ma Ying-jeou administration and analyzes the factors that have enabled this relationship. Then, it analyzes whether or not these factors have continued after the inauguration of Tsai Ing-wen in 2016, and shows the forecast for Japan-Taiwan relations under the Tsai administration.

Since Taiwan's historic regime change in 2000, which is often described as the completion of Taiwanese democratization, the Japan-Taiwan relationship has become steadily closer while still facing one structural constraint in the form of the Sino-Japanese political agreement that has existed since 1972. Former Taiwanese Presidents Chen Shui-bian (2000–2008) and Ma Ying-jeou (2008–2016) both publicized their own policies toward

This chapter expands upon research presented in Fukuda (2014). And this work was supported by JSPS KAKENHI Grant Numbers 15K17006 and 16H02005.

M. Fukuda (✉)
Department of Global Politics, Faculty of Law, Hosei University, Tokyo, Japan

© The Author(s) 2019
W.-c. Lee (ed.), *Taiwan's Political Re-Alignment and Diplomatic Challenges*, Politics and Development of Contemporary China, https://doi.org/10.1007/978-3-319-77125-0_12

Japan, with each one asserting that his government had brought Taiwan into the best phase ever of its relationship with Japan. In fact, the substantial partnership between Japan and Taiwan has continued to grow since 2000, especially in the areas of economy, culture, and interpersonal interaction.

It is important to note, despite the remaining lack of official diplomatic ties, the extent to which substantial relations between Taiwan and Japan have developed. On the one hand, while being largely limited to economic and cultural interactions in the private sector, the Japan-Taiwan connection has been characterized as having de facto "normal" relations, much like other nations that have official diplomatic ties with each other. On the other hand, however, the relationship has still been restrained in some areas by the lack of formal diplomacy. To answer these questions, this chapter will examine the following two points. The first point is what factors have enabled the Japan-Taiwan relationship to progress as far as it has already done. The second point is whether or not those factors have sufficient force to push the Japan-Taiwan partnership beyond the limits posed by the lack of a diplomatic relationship.

This chapter will not only summarize current developments in Japan-Taiwan relations based on newspapers, memoirs, and interviews from both sides but will also characterize factors that promote a mature relationship between Japan and Taiwan—two neighboring societies sharing the fruits of democracy.

JAPAN-TAIWAN RELATIONS AFTER TAIWANESE DEMOCRATIZATION

Factors Inhibiting the Political Relations

Since 1972, successive Japanese administrations have basically taken the same position on the issue of Taiwan, that is, to maintain unofficial relations with Taiwan and hope for stability in the Taiwan Strait, respecting the Japan-China Joint Communiqué of 1972. This so-called 1972 regime has defined the unofficial relationship between Japan and Taiwan, which has been mainly limited to the economic and cultural fields.[1] Under that regime, the channels between the members of the Nikkakon from the Liberal Democratic Party (LDP) of Japan and the Kuomintang (KMT) politicians in Taiwan had mainly taken the form of unofficial political dialogue to promote economic and cultural exchanges until the 1980s.[2]

Taiwan's democratization since the 1990s has added a new dimension to the Japan-Taiwan relationship. This democratization has led to a relaxation of controls on public opinion in Taiwan, allowing positive memories of the Japanese colonial era to be expressed along with increased public appreciation and affinity for Japanese culture. Lee Tung-hui, who served as Taiwanese president from 1988 to 2000, often made reference to his own Japanese connections when calling on Japan to further develop its tie with Taiwan without submitting to China's threats. At that time, Lee's words appealed to many Japanese, and they began to reconsider their country's relationship with Taiwan.[3]

Furthermore, many in Japan have begun to consider China a potential threat, as it holds a different ideology from the Western democratized countries including Japan. The Tiananmen Square incident in 1989 surprised many Japanese by showing how strongly the authoritarian regime in China opposed democratization, and the event caused them to have a higher regard for Taiwanese democratization on the other side of the Taiwan Strait. The Taiwan Strait missile crisis in 1995 and 1996 shocked many Japanese people as the People's Liberation Army (PLA) took a menacing attitude toward Taiwan's first presidential election, which was one of the fruits of Taiwanese democratization.[4]

In this context, President Lee's policy toward Japan was an important piece of his "pragmatic diplomacy," which identified his country not as "China" but as "Taiwan" in the international community to fit the reality of Taiwan's status. Lee's diplomatic strategy confused China, because it brought about great changes in its struggle with the Taiwanese regime, which had contended for recognition as the legitimate "China." At that time, the People's Republic of China (PRC)'s only way to counter Lee's initiative was to call on the Japanese government to follow the "One China" principle that was agreed upon in the Japan-China Joint Communiqué of 1972.[5]

As a result, Japan has found itself in a dilemma between Taiwan's appeals for the further promotion of relations and the PRC's adamant protests against any such measures. On the one hand, Japan has welcomed Taiwanese democratization and strengthened its ties with Taiwan, as will be explored in detail later. On the other hand, Japan has been inhibited from promoting its connection with Taiwan, out of respect for the 1972 political agreement with the PRC regarding the Taiwan issue. Since 1972, Japan and the PRC have repeatedly reconfirmed their commitment to the "four basic documents," which are the 1972 Joint Communiqué, the

1978 Peace Treaty, the 1998 Joint Declaration, and the 2008 Joint Statement. Each document has clarified their position respecting their agreement on the Taiwan issue in 1972.[6]

Factors Promoting the Maturity of the Substantial Relationship

Since Taiwanese democratization, Japan-Taiwan relations have continued to lead to enhance substantial and multilateral ties, notwithstanding the "One China" principle that the PRC government has used to protest its improvement. On the relevant question as to why the relationship between Japan and Taiwan has progressed, many studies have indicated that Japan-Taiwan cooperation has resulted from Sino-Japanese rivalry as well as cross-Strait rivalry. The progress of Japan-Taiwan relations under the Ma Ying-jeou administration, however, cannot be explained by this argument. Therefore, this section will explain what factors beyond the balance-of-power theory have led to improvements in recent Japan-Taiwan relations.

Changing Regional Power Balance and the Stability of the Taiwan Strait

Since the Taiwan Strait Crisis in 1996, Japanese government has regarded the stability of the Strait as an increasingly important issue and has clearly stated its concern. When the crisis occurred, the Japanese government was negotiating with the United States for the redefinition of their security treaty. Therefore, the Japan-US commitment to the peace and stability of the Taiwan Strait was the focus of public attention when both the Japan-US Security Communiqué was published in 1996 and the Japan-US guidelines, including the concept of the "situations in areas surrounding Japan," was agreed upon in 1997. Though the Japanese government did not define "the situations in areas surrounding Japan" in geographical terms and did not clarify the connection between the Japan-US treaty and the stability of the Strait, some influential persons in Japan clearly stated that it would include the Taiwan Strait.[7]

Since the establishment of the Chen Shui-bian government and its tense relations with the PRC government in 2000, the Japanese government has repeatedly expressed concern over both Taiwan and mainland China regarding the current status of the Taiwan Strait and has called for self-restraint. For example, when President Chen proposed "a nationwide consultative referendum" at the same time as the election in 2004, the chief of the Exchange Association Taipei Office Katsuhisa Uchida urged the NSC Secretary-General Chiou I-jen to take a cautious position on the stability of the Taiwan Strait.[8] In addition, when Chen decided to suspend the operation of the guidelines and the committee for national unification in 2006, a Japanese Ministry of Foreign Affairs (MOFA) spokesperson commented that they could not support any attempt to change the status quo of the Taiwan Strait by either side and conveyed their position to the Taiwanese representative office in Japan.[9]

At the same time, the Japanese government clarified the position to restrain the PLA's use of force against Taiwan. In February 2005, soon after the reelection of President Chen, the Japan-US security consultative committee published the Joint Statement and specified that Japan and the United States would "encourage the peaceful resolution of issues concerning the Taiwan Strait through dialogue" as one of their common strategic objectives.[10] In addition, when the PRC's anti-secession law was established in 2005, the MOFA of Japan expressed that Japan worried about the law from the viewpoint of the peace and stability of the Taiwan Strait, and Japan would oppose any non-peaceful resolution of this issue.[11] These actions of the Japanese government on the one hand showed its clear respect for the Japan-China Joint communiqué in 1972 on the Taiwan issue and strengthened its commitment toward the peace and stability of the Strait on the other hand.

Japan's disapproval about Taiwanese search for independence from the mainland China sometimes surely aroused opposition from Taiwanese people. Still, Taiwan has generally welcomed the strengthening of the Japan-US alliance and its commitment to the Taiwan Strait. In this context, various voices have promoted a bilateral dialogue between Japan and Taiwan focused on mutual security. In addition, facing China's expansion in the East China Sea and the South China Sea in recent years, both sides have realized the importance of cooperation on the maritime issue.

Economic Exchanges and Regional Integration
Second, Japan and Taiwan are geographically close, and they have a complementary relationship in the areas of industry and trade. Even after the rupture of the diplomatic relationship between Japan and Taiwan in 1972, many Japanese private enterprises maintained their economic ties with Taiwan, and trade between Japan and Taiwan expanded remarkably through the 1980s and 1990s. The value of exports from Japan to Taiwan

was two times as much as the value of imports during the 1980s, and this trade imbalance expanded further in the 1990s. Taiwanese dissatisfaction about this trade imbalance with Japan grew during that time, but more recently it has disappeared as Taiwan has found Japan to be an important supplier of raw materials and capital goods for Taiwanese industries. Additionally, Taiwanese companies can obtain Japanese information technology through importing IT product parts. Taiwan's trade deficit with Japan has been offset by surpluses with other countries that have imported finished products from Taiwan.[12]

The economic ties between Japan and Taiwan have complemented the development of the Chinese economy and its regional impact. Both Japan and Taiwan have become more interdependent economically with China, especially since 2000. This economic interdependence with China and the improvement of Japan-Taiwan economic relations are not necessarily in conflict. For example, when Taiwanese enterprises export their finished goods to China, their parts and technology imported from Japan add value to those products. Many Japanese enterprises enter the Chinese market through collaborations with Taiwanese counterparts, who have considerable experience in doing business with Chinese enterprises.[13] Consequently, Japan is now Taiwan's second-largest import and fourth-largest export partner, and Taiwan is the seventh-largest import and fourth-largest export partner for Japan.[14]

Additionally, the recent development of regional economic cooperation initiatives has encouraged the Japan-Taiwan economic cooperation. Since the Asian Financial Crisis in 1997, the Association of South East Asian Nations (ASEAN) +3 (Japan, China, and South Korea) has increased its importance as a framework for developing practical cooperation in East Asia. Especially since 2000, a rising China has strengthened its influence on the progress of regional cooperation in the area.[15] Conversely, Taiwan became a member of the Asia Pacific Economic Cooperation (APEC) in 1991, and the World Trade Organization in 2002, along with China, under the name of "Chinese Taipei." Taiwan, however, has not been invited to participate in other organizations of regional cooperation such as the ASEAN Regional Forum and the Association of South-East Asian Nations (ASEAN)+3, which have a principle of noninterference in the domestic affairs of other countries and consider China's claim that the Taiwan issue is a domestic affair for China.[16]

Japan has tried to solidify practical agreements with Taiwan and further stabilize their relationship as a way to substantially include Taiwan in the process of regional economic cooperation in East Asia. As discussed in the next section, under Ma's tenure, Japan and Taiwan have been solidifying their economic and cultural ties by signing numerous unofficial and practical agreements, upon which they have also tried to build a de facto Free Trade Agreement (FTA).

Cultural Exchange and Common Values
Third, along with economic development and democratization, the civil societies in Japan and Taiwan have come to reflect a sense of common values and solidarity with each other. Although Japan's GDP is still more than two times as large as that of Taiwan, the latter has exceeded 10,000 dollars per person and has been at a level commensurate with that of developed countries since the 1990s. In addition, the Human Development Index of the United Nations Development Program (UNDP) shows that only Japan (0.903 points, ranked 17th in the world in 2016), South Korea (0.901 points, ranked 18th), Hong Kong (0.917 points, ranked 12th), and Taiwan (0.882 points in 2014, according to calculations by the Legislative Yuan, equivalent to 21st of the UNDP's ranking in the same year) have been ranked as "very high" among Asian countries in terms of human development.[17] These social welfare indicators show that both the Japanese and Taiwanese have enjoyed high living standards in recent times.

On the base of shared social affluence, cultural exchanges between Japan and Taiwan have been heavily promoted, especially in the area of popular culture for the younger generation. While Taiwanese society was under martial law until 1987, there were strict limitations on placing Japanese cultural contents in circulation. Since Taiwanese democratization took off, broadcasts of Japanese movies, cartoons, and television dramas have opened up greater public appreciation for and affinity with Japanese culture. Taiwanese young people have specifically become more interested in Japanese popular culture, and the phrase Ha-Ri-Zu (Japan mania) has come into fashion.

Though there are some signs of Ha-Ri-Zu among young people in mainland China too, young people in Taiwan and Hong Kong remarkably love Japanese popular culture when compared with the people of other

Asian nations. According to a survey conducted by Hakuhodo in 2010 and 2012, people in Taiwan and Hong Kong tend to like not only Japanese cartoons and comic books but also Japanese fashions and television dramas more than Korean ones, while other Asian countries prefer Korean fashions and television dramas over Japanese ones.[18]

As a result of the factors mentioned above, people-to-people interactions between Japan and Taiwan have also strengthened over the past few years. Under martial law, public education and propaganda by the KMT regime often included anti-Japanese materials such as reminders of the Sino-Japanese War. Taiwan's democratization has led to a relaxation of controls on public opinion, allowing the expression of various perceptions about Japan, including the positive memories of the Japanese colonial era along with increased public appreciation for Japanese popular culture. President Lee's "practical diplomacy" toward Japan took advantage of the positive aspects of Japan-Taiwan historical ties and succeeded in arousing strong affinity with the Taiwanese people in Japan. Shared social affluence and cultural exchanges among the members of the younger generation have caused mutual feelings of closeness between Japanese and Taiwanese people to swell. Recent opinion polls indicate that about 80 percent of Taiwanese and 66 percent of Japanese respondents feel close or relatively close to each other today.[19]

JAPAN-TAIWAN RELATIONS UNDER THE MA YING-JEOU ADMINISTRATION (2008–2016)

Ma's "Anti-Japan" Image and His Attempt to Remove It

When President Ma took office, some Japanese policymakers were concerned that his administration might neglect Japan because of his cooperative policy toward China. Unlike Chen Shui-bian and the DPP, Ma Ying-jeou and the KMT agreed to the 1992 Consensus on the subject of the "One China" principle, which was a precondition of recovering the relations with mainland China.[20] Some Japanese were concerned that this might be a drastic change of Taiwan's position in regional politics. In addition, President Ma himself had a background as a mainlander born in Hong Kong and had engaged in a study about the maritime issue around the Senkaku islands as a scholar of international law. Referring to the above points, the Democratic Progressive Party (DPP)'s candidate Frank Hsieh raised the issue of Taiwan's policy toward Japan in the 2008 presidential campaign, and he cast doubt on whether or not Ma Ying-jeou could keep a good relationship with Japan.[21]

After the election, Ma Ying-jeou made efforts to counter his image of favoring China over Japan and further proposed that his government could improve economic and cultural ties with Japan because of the decreased tensions in the Taiwan Strait. In the area of foreign policy, he promised "viable diplomacy" that aimed at improving relations across the Taiwan Strait while seeking to improve Taiwan's relations with other countries.[22] In that context, Ma welcomed the Japan-US alliance in the region, encouraged cooperation between Japan-Taiwan companies to break into the mainland China market, and worked to establish the Japan-Taiwan FTA in the near future.[23] Ma repeated those ideas and policies in his visits to Japan in June 2006 and November 2007. As a result of Ma's efforts, respecting his election for presidency in 2008, the Japanese government published the Foreign Minister's talk on the Taiwanese elections for the first time and expected to keep Japan-Taiwan ties despite a thaw in cross-Strait relations.[24]

Soon after Ma came to office, however, the Lianhe Hao incident occurred in the waters around the Senkaku Islands in June 2008, which deteriorated the Japan-Taiwan relationship. The incident started with the sinking of a Taiwanese private boat named Lianhe Hao, which had collided with a Japanese coast guard patrol ship in territorial waters around the Senkaku Islands. Some Taiwanese people protested the reaction of the Japanese coast guard, and Taiwanese patrol vessels briefly entered territorial waters around the Senkaku Islands despite repeated advance warnings from Japan. Though the situation was settled when that Japanese coast guard apologized to the captain of the boat again, the Ma administration's tough stance during the incident and its firm position on the issue of Senkaku Islands surprised many in Japan.[25]

The Lianhe Hao incident had a great effect on President Ma's subsequent policy toward Japan as he realized the importance of the relationship with Japan in the context of both domestic and international politics. Although Ma had already decided to break up the "special group of policies toward Japan," which the Chen administration established in the Ministry of Foreign Affairs (MOFA) of Taiwan, before the incident, he had to set up another group to restore the relationship with Japan in the MOFA after the incident.[26] He also established a new "special group of policies toward Japan" in the Office of the President to strengthen its ties with Japan.[27] A few months after the incident, legislators from the KMT visited Japan to provide assurance that President Ma was not an "anti-Japan" statesman and that he hoped for progress in dialogues about the fisheries agreement and the FTA with Japan.[28]

In the end, President Ma presented a new concept, namely, a Japan-Taiwan "special partnership," to counter his image as an "anti-Japan" statesman and stress his intention to strengthen ties with Japan.[29] He indicated that the Taiwanese government would do three things: first, seek progress in substantial relations with Japan, mainly in the economic and cultural areas; second, assure the Japanese government that the cross-Strait détente would not contradict Japan-Taiwan cooperation; and third, pursue dialogue about the fisheries agreement with Japan, separating it from the territorial claim about the Senkaku Islands.[30] The Ma administration declared that the year 2009 would be a year to promote this "special partnership" and strengthen ties with Japan in five areas: economics and trade, culture, the younger generation, tourism, and dialogue.[31]

Strengthen Japan-Taiwan Economic and Cultural Ties

After 2009, Japan and Taiwan solidified their economic and cultural ties under the condition that the pressure from Beijing was reduced. First, in 2009, they reached some agreements that would promote people-to-people exchanges and tourism, including the Japan-Taiwan Working Holiday and the establishment of a branch of the Representative Office of Taiwan in Sapporo. In 2010, they agreed to establish new direct flights between Haneda Airport in Tokyo and Songshan Airport in Taipei. When the East Japan earthquake and tsunami disaster occurred in 2011, the contributions from Taiwan totaled 20 billion yen, greater than the amount from any other country except the United States, and the Japanese people were deeply impressed by the "kizuna (bond)" with the Taiwanese people.[32] Japan and Taiwan finally announced the Kizuna Initiative to reaffirm and advance their people-to-people exchanges still further.[33]

Since 2010, when the Ma administration concluded the Economic Cooperation Framework Agreement with mainland China, the administration has begun to raise sensitive issues that could conflict with the PRC's position regarding Japan-Taiwan relations, including the Japan-Taiwan FTA. For example, in February 2010, Ma talked with the new Japanese representative, Tadashi Imai, and asked him to open dialogue about the Japan-Taiwan FTA.[34] Although Japan and Taiwan have never started official negotiations about the FTA, they have accumulated numerous practical agreements, based upon which they have tried to build a de facto FTA. In particular, the Taiwanese have assumed that the Japan-Taiwan Investment Agreement, concluded in September 2011, was a very important step toward the future completion of the Japan-Taiwan FTA.[35] Although the Investment Agreement liberalized mutual investments between Japan and Taiwan more than the Japan-China investment agreement had done, the PRC government has not officially protested against it.

The Japan-Taiwan Open Skies Agreement, which concluded in November 2011, was the second open skies agreement for the Japanese government, following a similar one with the United States. It was somewhat surprising that the PRC did not officially protest this agreement or conduct any reprisals, because the PRC had previously expressed concerns about the issue of air service between Japan and Taiwan. Presumably, China viewed these agreements as within the scope of unofficial economic ties and felt that it would not be beneficial to offend Taiwanese feelings by objecting to its efforts to strengthen ties with Japan before the Taiwanese election in 2012.

Japan-Taiwan Fisheries Agreement

The Japan-Taiwan fisheries agreement, which was concluded in April 2013 after 17 years of negotiation, was a highlight of the Japan-Taiwan partnership under the Ma Ying-jeou administration. The main reason that the agreement was concluded at that time was the sense of crisis felt by both Japan and Taiwan about heightening tensions over the Senkaku Islands and surrounding waters. During the 17 years of Japan-Taiwan fisheries talks, the Taiwanese negotiators presented their Japanese counterparts with claims to a fishing zone even larger than that sought by Japan, and they asserted the Republic of China (ROC)'s sovereignty over the Senkaku Islands and fishing operations within the surrounding seas. Further adding to the tension was the lack of official diplomatic relations between Japan and Taiwan since 1972, as well as China's successful blocking of political talks between Japan and Taiwan in keeping with the "One China" principle.

Following the Lianhe Hao incident in 2008, the Ma administration objected to the Japanese government's purchase of three of the Senkaku Islands in the summer of 2012 and asserted their own territorial claims. In cooperating with these claims, the PRC declared the Senkaku Islands to be "territory belonging to the Chinese people" and called on Taiwan to stand with it against Japan on the Senkaku Islands issue.[36] A united front with Taiwan was important for the PRC both in asserting territorial claims to the Senkaku Islands and in maintaining the idea of "One China."

The Ma administration, however, gradually clarified its position that Taiwan would not cooperate with mainland China on the issue of the East China Sea.[37] The Taiwanese administration has been advocating the "East China Sea Peace Initiative" since August 2012, calling on Japan and mainland China to shelve sovereignty issues, peacefully resolve their disputes, and engage in joint development of resources. Taiwan has regarded the resumption of negotiations with Japan on fisheries as the first step in that approach.[38] Then, in February 2013, the Ma administration released a statement confirming that it would not be coordinating with mainland-China on the Senkaku Islands issue because Taiwan's ideas for resolving the dispute differ from those of the PRC and because its intervention would adversely impact the Japan-Taiwan fisheries talks.[39]

Responding to Taiwan's call for negotiation, the Japanese government agreed to restart the fisheries talks and sent an exceptional statement by the foreign minister on relations with Taiwan. [40] Presumably, Japan's wish to avoid being entangled in simultaneous disputes with Taiwan as well as the PRC prompted the resumption of talks and compromises on fishing zones. In the "Agreement on the Establishment of a New Order in the Fishing Industry between the Interchange Association, Japan and the Association of East Asian Relations" in 2013, the Japanese government, on the one hand, allowed Taiwanese fishing boats to operate in almost all areas that they claimed south of latitude 27 degrees north. On the other hand, both governments agreed not to mention the territorial rights of the Senkaku Islands, and such rights would not be applied to the territorial and connecting waters that Japan claimed around the islands.[41]

As the above account shows, the Japan-Taiwan fishing talks were wrapped up via political decisions made by both sides, who both hoped to reduce tensions among Japan, China, and Taiwan. The official title of the Japan-Taiwan fisheries agreement evidenced the fact that this agreement was concluded within a framework of the unofficial Japan-Taiwan relationship since 1972. The content of the Japan-Taiwan fisheries agreement also in no way contradicts the Japan-China fisheries agreement that went into force in 2000.

The Sensitive Issues Between Japan and Taiwan

The Japan-Taiwan relationship under the Ma Ying-jeou administration reached its climax when the Japan-Taiwan fisheries agreement concluded in 2013. It has rapidly cooled in the last two years, although the Abe administration, which would be friendly toward Taiwan, has stabilized its base in Japanese domestic politics. Prime Minister Abe is well known as a politician who has a close relationship with Taiwanese leaders. He has visited Taiwan twice and promoted friendship with Lee Tung-hui, Ma Ying-jeou, Tsai Ing-wen, and other politicians after the resignation of his first cabinet. Then, in his second cabinet since December 2012, Abe put his preference toward Taiwanese friends into practice; for example, he invited a Taiwanese representative to the ceremony in memory of 311 earthquakes in different former governments of the Democratic Party of Japan (DPJ). And, it was reported that the prime minister himself made the final decision to conclude the Japan-Taiwan fisheries agreement on the conditions mentioned above.

Ma Ying-jeou, however, failed to build a good relationship with Abe after the Japan-Taiwan fisheries agreement. Especially, in the last two years of the Ma administration, President Ma searched for the possibility of the Cross-Strait Summit meeting and made light of its policy toward Japan. In this environment, the Abe administration was indifferent to Ma's claim about the historical and territorial issue. For his part, Ma's excessive emphasis of the ROC's identities would not fit with Abe's views on history and international politics.

At first, the reinforcement of the ban on foods from the five prefectures around Fukushima seemed to be the beginning of the mutual distrust between Ma and Abe. Since soon after the Fukushima Daiichi nuclear disaster in 2011, the Taiwanese government has prohibited food imports from Fukushima, Ibaraki, Tochigi, Gunma, and Chiba. In addition to this prohibition, the Taiwanese government decided to require all import foods from Japan to attach certificates of origin at a prefecture level, and to require some "high risk items" to attach certificates of radiological examinations. Those decisions were announced suddenly in May 2015, when the Taiwanese officials had not finished negotiating about substantial operations with the Japanese yet. The process above incurred the distrust of the Japanese government, which had requested that the Taiwanese government to relax restrictions on food imports since 2011.[42]

Then in 2015, commemorating the 70th anniversary of the end of WWII, Ma repeatedly proclaimed the ROC-oriented understanding of historical issues, for which the Abe administration was criticized especially by the PRC and the Republic of Korea (ROK). On November 7, 2015, Ma succeeded in holding the Cross-Strait Summit meeting with Xi Jinping in Singapore, and in a closed meeting he agreed with Xi's proposal to collaborate in studies about "anti-Japanese war."[43] Then, at the end of 2015, when Japan and the ROK agreed about the issue of comfort women, Ma claimed that Japan should also discuss this issue with Taiwan. Referring to Ma's claim, Japanese Chief Cabinet Secretary stated that the Japanese government had already compensated comfort women in Taiwan through the Asian Women's Fund and would not consider further dialogue about this issue with Taiwan.[44]

Finally, in the beginning of 2016, when a regime change in Taiwan became inevitable, Ma put his ideas about the territorial and maritime issue into action. In January 2016, he landed at Taiping Island, of which Taiwan had effective control in the South China Sea, and released the roadmap toward the South China Sea Peace Initiative on the island.[45] Then in April, Ma visited Pengjia Islet for the first time since his visit in September 2012, and he unveiled a monument to peace in the East China Sea and border defense of the ROC.[46] At the end of the month, when the Japanese coast guard detained a Taiwanese fishing boat and its crew in adjacent waters around Okinotori Islands, Ma began to claim that Taiwan could not accept Japanese Exclusive Economic Zone (EEZ) around Okinotori because it was not an island but a reef, then ordered the Taiwanese coast guard to patrol these waters.[47]

In the last two years of the Ma administration, political relations between Japan and Taiwan cooled and left each with unpleasant feelings over the above problems. The Abe administration got the impression that Taiwan suddenly raised these issues without enough negotiations, and Japan's insufficient responses to Taiwan made the Ma administration stiffen its attitude. As a result of the mutual distrust between Abe and Ma, on the day of the Taiwanese presidential election in 2016, the Chair of the Exchange Association, who visited Taipei to congratulate Tsai Ing-wen, did not meet Ma Ying-jeou. It was a rare case that the Chairman of the Exchange Association did not visit an active president in Taipei.[48]

JAPAN-TAIWAN RELATIONS AFTER TSAI ING-WEN'S INAUGURATION

Expectation from Each Side

In reaction to the mutual distrust with Ma, the Abe administration gave Tsai Ing-wen a cordial reception on her visit to Japan and welcomed her election, expecting her to keep close relations with Japan. When she visited Japan as the DPP's presidential candidate last October, though she and Abe did not publicize their meeting, it was no secret that they were in the same hotel at the same time.[49] At the time of Tsai's election in January, the Japanese government soon published an official message by the foreign minister and emphasized a partnership between Japan and Taiwan, the warmest message in the history of Taiwanese presidential elections.[50] In addition, Prime Minister Abe himself also congratulated Tsai's election in the House of Representatives.[51]

President Tsai also regards the relations with Japan as much more important than with the United States. The new administration appointed Frank Hsieh as the representative in Japan and Chiou I-jen as the chair of the Association of East Asian Relations, which the Japanese considered to be positive examples of how Tsai attached a lot of importance to Japan-Taiwan relations. In addition, Tsai referred to the necessity to revise the Ma administration's stances on both the maritime issue and the ban on Japanese food before her inauguration. Tsai, however, could not change these policies drastically, because of local protests in Taiwan and the PRC's watchful eyes behind the KMT's criticism.

On the issue of Okinotori, Tsai tried to withdraw Ma's claim and worked toward maritime dialogue with Japan. On May 23, 2016, the administration, apparently reversing the previous administration's position, stated that the government had no "specific position" on whether the Okinotori reefs constitute an island and hoped to set up a bilateral mechanism on maritime affairs with Japan.[52] The first Japan-Taiwan Maritime Affairs Cooperation Dialogue was held in Tokyo on October 31, 2016, to discuss fisheries cooperation, search and rescue cooperation, and marine scientific research. Those at the meeting agreed to regularize the dialogue once a year. About the issue of Okinotori, however, the Taiwanese officials announced that it claimed to protect fishermen's interests in the surrounding waters, but the Japanese officials did not mention this issue at all.[53]

Regarding the issue of the South China Sea, Tsai's position was little different from Ma's, which was only to claim possession of the Dongsha and Taiping Islands and their "related waters," and not to frequently state the so-called eleven dots line. On the day before the decision of the Permanent Court of Arbitration (PCA) was announced, the presidential office of Taiwan confirmed its basic positions: (1) assertions and actions under international law and the UN Convention on the Sea of Law, (2) Taiwan's participation in multilateral dispute settlement mechanism, and (3) freedom of passage in territorial seas and airspace.[54] When the decision was announced on July 12, however, the presidential office announced that it was "unacceptable" because it stated Taiwan as "Taiwan Authority of China" and considered all islands of the Spratly Islands to be "rocks."[55] As a result, countries that welcomed the decision from the point of "the rules based international order," like the United States and Japan, reaffirmed their difference in position from Taiwan on that issue.

Soon after the Japan-Taiwan maritime dialogue, the Tsai administration announced a lift on the ban for food imported from four Japanese prefectures except Fukushima on the condition that a safety certification be attached on each food. The administration, then, decided to hold public hearings about this issue in each district in Taiwan, responding to demand from opposition parties in the Legislative Yuan. As a result, protests from opposition parties and consumer organizations rushed into the public hearings and forced the administration to hear many more public opinions. Under the circumstances, the news that foods from those prefectures were sold in some markets and restaurants in Taiwan encouraged Taiwanese voices that objected to relax restrictions on food imports.[56] Tsai finally announced that the relaxation would be postponed indefinitely, which disappointed the Japanese.

Promoting and Inhibiting Factors in the Near Future

Though the Japan-Taiwan relationship temporary cooled because of the food ban issue, the relationship recently has looked like it is warming. In January 2017, the Interchange Association changed its name to the Japan-Taiwan Exchange Association, and in May its counterpart in Taipei also changed its name to the Association of Taiwan-Japan Relations. Those changes, which include officially adding the names "Japan" and "Taiwan," constitute a significant breakthrough in their relationship since 1972.

Moreover, in March a Japanese Senior Vice-Minister, who has been a government official at the highest level since 1972, visited Taiwan to attend a Japanese tourism fair.

However, it is unclear that Japan and Taiwan can continue to achieve significant breakthroughs in their relationship under the Tsai administration. Against the backdrop of both associations' name changes and the Japanese Vice-Minister's visit to Taiwan, the PRC's Foreign Ministry spokesperson expressed dissatisfaction with Japan's decisions. As a background to the PRC's protest and is different to the era of President Ma, the Tsai administration has not reached a consensus about the 1992 Consensus with the PRC government yet, and the PRC has intensified pressure on Taiwan in international politics since Tsai's inauguration in May 2016.

The above situation has raised the possibility that developments in the Japan-Taiwan relationship will be obstructed by the PRC's opposition. In recent years, under the condition that the North Korea crisis has entered a critical phase, Japan has regarded the relationship with the PRC as more important than before. As such, it will be difficult for the Japanese government to make a breakthrough in its relationship with Taiwan, which would arouse strong protest from the PRC government. Thus, the peace and stability of cross-Strait relations is vitally important for the further progress of the Japan-Taiwan relationship, and the Japanese government will expect both Taiwan and mainland China to recover dialogue between them.

Though the PRC's pressure to the Japan-Taiwan political relationship has been strengthened since Tsai's inauguration, substantial exchanges between Japan and Taiwan have expanded in recent years. For example, an increase of Japanese tourists has partly provided supplement to a decrease in tourism from mainland China since 2016. In terms of next steps in the Japan-Taiwan bilateral relationship, there is the question of how Japan can integrate Taiwan into bilateral and regional Economic Partnership Agreements. About this subject, both the governments of Japan and Taiwan should make efforts to foster domestic discussions and arrange the necessary conditions, while ensuring a desirable international situation.

As a result of close economic and cultural exchange and people-to-people interaction between Japan and Taiwan today, both governments are now facing some problems that require them to understand various voices from each society. For example, on the maritime issue, the historical issue, and the issue of the food ban, both governments should understand various voices on each side and maintain dialogue between both.

Conclusion

This chapter began by introducing the developments in the Japan-Taiwan relationship after Taiwanese democratization, focusing on the factors that are improving the relationship and restricting it. It then examined how those factors worked in the relationship during the eight years of the Ma Ying-jeou administration and the first year of the Tsai Ing-wen administration.

With regard to the improvement of the Japan-Taiwan relationship during these eras in Taiwan, the following four points have been revealed. First, although both the DPP and the KMT in Taiwan criticized each other regarding their policies toward Japan, the Japan-Taiwan relations during this time have remained fairly consistent rather than changing with the different Taiwanese administrations. This chapter characterizes this consistency as the result of the institutionalization of channels between the two governments, the enhancement of practical agreements, and the progress of relationships between the two societies.

Second, the institutionalization and progress of the relationship between Japan and Taiwan have been consistent with the political agreements contained in the Japan-China Joint Communiqué in 1972 and their results. Japan and Taiwan have institutionalized and promoted their mutual relationship by taking full advantage of the ambiguity of those political agreements.

Third, it is undeniable that the possibility of cooperation between Japan and Taiwan has occasionally depended on the reaction of the PRC government. This has been confirmed by the fact that some forms of cooperation that Chen Shui-bian failed to achieve have become possible in the Ma Ying-jeou era because the PRC's policy toward Taiwan has changed. Conversely, in the current situation in which the two societies share many common interests, international structural constraints are losing the influence upon the Japan-Taiwan relationship that they once had.

Fourth, the importance of having no official diplomatic relationship has been declining in the context of greater social interaction between Japan and Taiwan as the modern world has become increasingly borderless. In recent years, the dialogues and agreements of significance to the people of Japan and Taiwan have not been in matters of power politics and security, but in the areas of the economy, culture, and people-to-people exchange. With regard to these issues, the role of the two governments consists largely of approving existing relationships between both societies.

If cross-Strait relations come to a standstill under the Tsai administration, it is possible that Japan's ties to Taiwan will once again incur protests from China. As recent developments show, Japan and Taiwan now enjoy ever closer economic and sociocultural ties, and the two sides share the common values of freedom and democracy. In fact, Japan and Taiwan have been enhancing these ties while simultaneously respecting the Japan-China Joint Communiqué of 1972. Japan, therefore, should continue on its current course of further solidifying practical agreements with Taiwan and should encourage the cross-Strait dialogue.

NOTES

1. The following three documents were primarily responsible for providing this so-called 1972 regime: "The Sino-Japanese Joint Communiqué (September 29, 1972)"; "The Record of the Press conference by Foreign Minister Masayoshi Ohira and the Minister's Secretariat Susumu Nikaido about the Sino-Japanese Normalization (September 29, 1972)"; and "The Declaration about Breaking off Diplomatic Relations with Japan by the ROC's Ministry of Foreign Affairs (September 29, 1972)." All are available from the Japan and World Database (Project Leader: Akihiko Tanaka), http://worldjpn.grips.ac.jp.
2. About the Nikkakon, see Wu Mingshang, "Tai-ri Guohui Waijiao de Xingcheng yu Fazhan," in "Qiernian Tizhi" Xia Tairi Guanxi de Huigu yu Zhanwang, eds. He Sishen and Cai Zengjia (Taipei: Yanjing Jijinhui, 2009), 71.
3. For example, the following books were typical writings that spread Lee's words: Ryotaro Shiba, *Taiwan Kiko*, (Tokyo: Asahishimbunbunko, 1997) and Yoshinori Kobayashi, *Taiwan Ron*, (Tokyo: Shogakukan, 2000).
4. With regard to Japan-Taiwan relations in the 1980s, see Yasuhiro Matsuda, "Nittai Kankei no Anteika to Henka e no Taidou" in *Nittai Kankei Shi*, eds. Shin Kawashima, Urara Shimizu, Yasuhiro Matsuda, and Yang Yongming (Tokyo: Tokyo University Press, 2009), 129–151.
5. With regard to how Taiwanese democratization influenced Japan-Taiwan relations in the 1990s, see Yasuhiro Matsuda, "Taiwan no Minshuka to Aratana Nittai Kankei no Mosaku" in *Nittai Kankei Shi*, eds. Shin Kawashima, Urara Shimizu, Yasuhiro Matsuda, and Yang Yongming (Tokyo: Tokyo University Press, 2009), 153–171.
6. The texts of the "four basic documents" are available at the website of the MOFA of Japan, "Japan-China Relations (Archives)," http://www.mofa.go.jp/region/asia-paci/china/archives.html.

7. For example, the Chief Cabinet Secretary Kajiyama Seiroku stated that it was no wonder that the conflict between Taiwan and China was included in "the situations in areas surrounding Japan" on a TV show in August 1997, (Author unknown), "Chutai Funsouji Nihon ga Beigun Shien," *Asahi Shimbun*, Aug. 18, 1997.
8. Katsuhisa Uchida, *Daijyoubu ka Nittai Kankei* (Tokyo: Sankei Shimbunsha, 2006), 186–194.
9. "The Spokesperson's Talks of the MOFA of Japan on Feb. 28, 2006," MOFA of Japan, http://www.mofa.go.jp/mofaj/press/danwa/18/dga_0228.html.
10. "About the Japan-US Security Consultative Committee (2+2) on Feb. 19, 2005," MOFA of Japan, http://www.mofa.go.jp/mofaj/area/usa/hosho/2plus2.html.
11. "The spokesperson's talks of the MOFA of Japan on Mar. 14, 2005," MOFA of Japan, http://www.mofa.go.jp/mofaj/press/danwa/17/dga_0314.html.
12. "The relationship between Japan and Taiwan," Japan External Trade Organization (JETRO), http://www.jetro.go.jp/world/asia/tw/.
13. Shingo Ito, "Taiwan Keizai ga Kakaeru Kadai to Nittai Keizai Kanke no Yukue", *Toa* 557 (November, 2013): 15–17.
14. The Interchange Association, *Taiwan no Keizai Data Book 2016*, (Tokyo: The Interchange Association, 2016): 66–67.
15. Mitoji Yabunaka, "Ajiataiheiyo ni Okeru Chiiki Togo Koso de Omoukoto", *Kokusai Mondai* 622 (June, 2013): 1–2.
16. Sachiko Hirakawa, "Ajia Chiikitougou to Chutai Mondai", *Kokusai Seiji* 158 (December, 2009): 158–160, and Takayuki Takeuchi, *Taiwan Honkon to Higashiajia Chiikisyugi*, (Chiba: IDE-JETRO, 2011), 36–37.
17. "Human Development Report," United Nations Development Programme, http://hdr.undp.org/sites/default/files/2016_human_development_report.pdf, and Shu-yuan Lin and Maubo Chang, "Taiwan ranks 21st in world human development index," *CNA Focus Taiwan*, Sep. 18, 2014. (http://focustaiwan.tw/news/asoc/201409180039.aspx). In addition, many countries in East Asia, including the PRC, have been ranked at the medium level in human development.
18. Hakuhodo Global HABIT, "Comparative statistics about people's preferences for contents of Japan, Korea, and Western countries in 10 cities in Asia," Hakuhodo, July 5, 2011, http://www.hakuhodo.co.jp/uploads/2011/07/20110705.pdf, and Hakuhodo Global HABIT, "Comparative statistics about people's preferences for contents of Japan, Korea and Western countries in 10 cities in Asia," *Hakuhodo*, May 22, 2013, http://www.hakuhodo.co.jp/archives/newsrelease/10642.

19. Japan-Taiwan Exchange Association, "Dai 5 kai Taiwan ni okeru Tainichi Yoron Chosa (2015)." https://www.koyu.or.jp/taipei/ez3_contents.nsf/Top/7B4C76E0FC259BAF49257FF400394934?OpenDocument, and the Taipei Economic and Cultural Representative Office in Japan, "Nihonjin no Taiwan ni Taisuru Yoron Chosa," http://www.roc-taiwan.org/jp_ja/post/42473.html.
20. Madoka Fukuda, "Shindankai wo mukaeru Chutai Kankei," *Toa* 488 (February 2008): 30–39.
21. Kazuo Asano, *Taiwan no Rekishi to Nittai Kankei* (Tokyo: Waseda University Press, 2010), 201–203.
22. Yen Anlin, "Lun MaYingjiu Waijiao Linian yu Zhuzhang, Tedian ji Qi Yingxiang" *Taiwan Yenjiu Qikan*, No. 2 (2009): 15.
23. The National Policy Foundation, "Ma-Hsiao Waijiao Zhengce," http://www.npf.org.tw/printfriendly/4114.
24. "The Foreign Minister's comments on Mar. 22, 2008," MOFA of Japan, http://www.mofa.go.jp/mofaj/press/danwa/20/dkm_0322.html.
25. For example, see Toshinao Ishii, "Ba Eikyu seiken no tainichi seisaku", *Yomiuri Shimbun*, June 25, 2008.
26. Wang Kuang-Tze and Lee Chih-Te, "Duiri Gongzuo Jiang Chengri Zhuanze Xiaozu", *Lianhe Bao*, July 6, 2008.
27. Chen Lo-wei and Hsiao Hsu-tsen, "Qianghua Tairi Fu She Kuabuhui Xiaozu", *Zhongguo Shibao*, July 24, 2008.
28. Chou Yongjie, "Jiang Bingkun Min Lutan Fangri", *Zhongyang Tongxun*, August 24, 2008.
29. "Ma Zongtong Zhuchi Zhonghua Minguo Jianguo 97nian Guoqing Dianli Zhici Quanwen (October 10, 2008)," Mainland Affairs Council, ROC (Taiwan), https://www.mac.gov.tw/News_Content.aspx?n=8940E5C0456177C3&sms=2A725F666F2160C6&s=662E1A9DF8898172.
30. (Author unknown) "The Taiwan–Japan Special Partnership (October 2008)," *Mondai to Kenkyu*, 37 (October 2008): 171–76.
31. Huang Juei-hung, "Ma Zongtong; Jinnian Shi Tai-Ri Tebie Huoban Guanxi Cujin Nian", *Zhongyang Tongxun*, January 7, 2009.
32. "Donations from Taiwan," The Interchange Association, http://www.koryu.or.jp/ez3_contents.nsf/0/6be18444c925cc364925785c00299f24?OpenDocument.
33. "The Japan-Taiwan 'Kizuna' Initiative," The Interchange Association, http://www.koryu.or.jp/ez3_contents.nsf/15aef977a6d6761f49256de4002084ae/f1252464ed5760474925787d000a8b87/$FILE/07-01.pdf.
34. Li Jia-fei, "Ma Zongtong Duiri Xinxiwang", *Zhongyang Tongxun*, February 4, 2010.

35. "Ba Eikyu Soutou, Nihon no Shinnin Cyutai Daihyo to Kaiken", *CNA Taiwan Today*, May 17, 2012. http://jp.taiwantoday.tw/news.php?unit=149&post=69623.
36. For example, see Kazuhide Minamoto and Satoshi Saeki, "'Senkaku Kougi' Chutai ni Rentaikan," *Yomiuri Shimbun*, Sep. 15, 2010.
37. "Zongtongfu Guanyu Diaoyutai zhi Shengming (Oct. 5, 2010)," available from the Japan and World Database, http://worldjpn.grips.ac.jp, and "Ma Zongtong Jieshou Riben 'Dumai xinwen' ji 'Riben Jingji xinwen' Lianhe Xinfang (Jul. 22, 2011)," The Mainland Affairs Council, ROC (Taiwan), https://www.mac.gov.tw/News_Content.aspx?n=8940E5C0456177C3&sms=2A725F666F2160C6&s=13F919E0D70A5C1C.
38. "Ma Zongtong Chuxi 'Zhongri Heyue Liushi Zhounian Jinian Huodong (Aug. 15, 2012)," The Mainland Affairs Council, ROC (Taiwan), https://www.mac.gov.tw/News_Content.aspx?n=21595FA41A9EE70A&sms=DFBE7BE3EE0DB6AE&s=2275E2B118E6B06D.
39. "Zai Diaoyutai Lieyu Zhengduan, Woguo buyu Zhongguo Dalu Hezuo zhi Lichang," MOFA of ROC (Taiwan), http://www.mofa.gov.tw/News_Content.aspx?n=C641B6979A7897C0&sms=F9719E988D8675CC&s=56A84BD617A31604.
40. "The foreign minister Genba's message to Taiwanese friends," the Interchange Association, http://www.koryu.or.jp/taipei/ez3_contents.nsf/Top/8595D637B3D1966C49257A8E000E39D9.
41. "Agreement on the Establishment of a New Order in the Fishing Industry between the Interchange Association, Japan and the Association of East Asian Relations," the Interchange Association, http://www.koryu.or.jp/ez3_contents.nsf/0/2CD490BD755BBCC649257B4900248AAD?OpenDocument.
42. Yasuto Tanaka, "Taiwan, Jyugonichi kara Nihon Shokuhin no Yunyuu Kisei Kyouka," *Sankei Shimbun*, May 12, 2015.
43. Reiko Suzuki, "Chutai Shunou Kaidan 'Kounichi Rekishisho' Kyouryoku he," *Mainichi Shimbun*, Nov. 11, 2015.
44. Reiko Suzuki, "Ianfu Mondai Taiwan Nihon ni Shazai Youkyuu he," *Mainichi Shimbun*, Jan. 6, 2016.
45. Yang Xiangjun, "Fabiao 'Nanhai Heping Chengyi Lujingtu'," *Lianhe Bao*, Jan. 29, 2016.
46. Tsai Peifang, "Renqi Sheng 40 Tian Ma Deng Pengjiayu Wu Zhuqian," *Lianhe Bao*, Apr. 10, 2016.
47. Satoshi Ukai, "Taiwan Soutou 'Okinotorishima wa Iwa'," *Asahi Shimbun*, Apr. 28, 2016.
48. Yoshiyuki Ogasawara, "Okinotorishima Oki Taiwan Gyosen Daho Jiken," Ogasawara Yoshiyuki's homepage, http://www.tufs.ac.jp/ts/personal/ogasawara/analysis/okinotorishimadispute.html.

49. Satoshi Ukai, "Abe Shusho to Taiwan Yatou Shuseki ga Kaidan?" *Asahi Shimbun*, Oct. 9, 2015.
50. "The foreign minister's comments on the presidential election in Taiwan," MOFA of Japan, http://www.mofa.go.jp/mofaj/press/danwa/page3_001538.html.
51. "Dai 190 Kai Kokkai, Shugiin Yosaniinkai Kaigiroku Dai 3 Gou" Jan. 18, 2016, Kokkai Kaigiroku Kensaku Shisutemu, http://kokkai.ndl.go.jp.
52. Tadahiro Ishihara, "Taiwan Naisei oyobi Nittai Kankei wo meguru Doukou," *Koryu* 904 (2016.7): 20–23.
53. Tadahiro Ishihara, "Taiwan Naisei oyobi Nittai Kankei wo meguru Doukou," *Koryu* 910 (2017.1): 24–25.
54. Lin Jingyin, "Nanhai Zhongzai Jin Xuanban Fu Jianchi Zhuqian 3 Yuanze," *Lianhe Bao*, July 12, 2016.
55. Lin Heming, "Hanwei U xingxian Tsai Zongtong Buying Huibi," *Lianhe Bao*, Jul. 13, 2016.
56. Tadahiro Ishihara, "Taiwan Naisei oyobi Nittai Kankei wo meguru Doukou," *Koryu* 910 (2017.1): 25–27.

BIBLIOGRAPHY

Asano, Kazuo. 2010. *Taiwan no Rekishi to Nittai Kankei*. Tokyo: Waseda University Press.
———. 2008. The Taiwan–Japan Special Partnership (October 2008). *Mondai to Kenkyu* 37: 171–176.
———. 2012. Ba Eikyu Soutou, Nihon no Shinnin Cyutai Daihyo to Kaiken. *CNA Taiwan Today*, May 17. http://jp.taiwantoday.tw/news.php?unit=149&post=69623
Chen Lo-wei, and Hsiao Hsu-tsen. 2008. Qianghua Tairi Fu She Kuabuhui Xiaozu. *Zhongguo Shibao*, July 24.
Chou Yongjie. 2008. Jiang Bingkun Min Lutan Fangri. *Zhongyang Tongxun*, August 24.
Fukuda, Madoka. 2008. Shindankai wo mukaeru Chutai Kankei. *Toa* 488: 30–39.
———. 2014. Posuto Minshuka Taiwan to Nihon. *Toyo Bunka*, 94. pp.89–120.
Hakuhodo Global HABIT. 2011. Comparative Statistics About People's Preferences for Contents of Japan, Korea, and Western Countries in 10 Cities in Asia. *Hakuhodo*, July 5. http://www.hakuhodo.co.jp/uploads/2011/07/20110705.pdf. Accessed 24 Sep 2017.
———. 2013. Comparative Statistics About People's Preferences for Contents of Japan, Korea and Western Countries in 10 Cities in Asia. *Hakuhodo*, May 22. http://www.hakuhodo.co.jp/archives/newsrelease/10642. Accessed 24 Sep 2017.
Hirakawa, Sachiko. 2009. Ajia Chiikitougou to Chutai Mondai. *Kokusai Seiji* 158: 150–164.

Huang Juei-hung. 2009. Ma Zongtong; Jinnian Shi Tai-Ri Tebie Huoban Guanxi Cujin Nian. *Zhongyang Tongxun*, January 7.

Interchange Association. 2016. *Taiwan no Keizai Data Book 2016*. Tokyo: The Interchange Association.

———. *Agreement on the Establishment of a New Order in the Fishing Industry between the Interchange Association, Japan and the Association of East Asian Relations*. http://www.koryu.or.jp/ez3_contents.nsf/0/2CD490BD755BB CC649257B4900248AAD?OpenDocument. Accessed 24 Sep 2017.

———. *Donations from Taiwan*. http://www.koryu.or.jp/ez3_contents.nsf/0/6 be18444c925ce364925785c00299f24?OpenDocument. Accessed 24 Sep 2017.

———. *The Foreign Minister Genba's Message to Taiwanese Friends*. http://www.koryu.or.jp/taipei/ez3_contents.nsf/Top/8595D637B3D1966C49257A8E 000E39D9. Accessed 24 Sep 2017.

———. *The Japan-Taiwan 'Kizuna' Initiative*. http://www.koryu.or.jp/ez3_ contents.nsf/15aef977a6d6761f49256de4002084ae/f1252464ed57604749 25787d000a8b87/$FILE/07-01.pdf. Accessed 24 Sep 2017.

Ishihara, Tadahiro. 2016. Taiwan Naisei oyobi Nittai Kankei wo meguru Doukou. *Koryu* 904 (7): 18–25.

———. 2017. Taiwan Naisei oyobi Nittai Kankei wo meguru Doukou. *Koryu* 910 (1): 24–30.

Ishii, Toshinao. 2008. Ba Eikyu seiken no tainichi seisaku. *Yomiuri Shimbun*, June 25.

Ito, Shingo. 2013. Taiwan Keizai ga Kakaeru Kadai to Nittai Keizai Kanke no Yukue. *Toa* 557, November: 10–17

Japan and World Database. http://www.ioc.u-tokyo.ac.jp/~worldjpn/. Accessed 24 Sep 2017.

Japan External Trade Organization (JETRO). *The Relationship Between Japan and Taiwan*. http://www.jetro.go.jp/world/asia/tw/.

Japan-Taiwan Exchange Association. 2015. *Dai 5 kai Taiwan ni okeru Tainichi Yoron Chosa*. https://www.koryu.or.jp/taipei/ez3_contents.nsf/Top/7B4C7 6E0FC259BAF49257FF400394934?OpenDocument. Accessed 24 Sep 2017.

Kobayashi, Yoshinori. 2000. *Taiwan Ron*. Tokyo: Shogakukan.

Kokkai Kaigiroku Kensaku Shisutemu. http://kokkai.ndl.go.jp. Accessed 24 Sep 24 2017.

Li, Jia-fei. 2010. Ma Zongtong Duiri Xinxiwang. *Zhongyang Tongxun*, February 4.

Lin, Heming. 2016a. Hanwei U xingxian Tsai Zongtong Buying Huibi. *Lianhe Bao*, July 13.

Lin, Jingyin. 2016b. Nanhai Zhongzai Jin Xuanban Fu Jianchi Zhuqian 3 Yuanze. *Lianhe Bao*, July 12.

Lin Shu-yuan, and Maubo Chang. 2014. Taiwan Ranks 21st in World Human Development Index. *CNA Focus Taiwan*, September 18. http://focustaiwan.tw/news/asoc/201409180039.aspx. Accessed 24 Sep 2017.
Matsuda, Yasuhiro. 2009a. Nittai Kankei no Anteika to Henka e no Taidou. In *Nittai Kankei Shi*, ed. Shin Kawashima, Urara Shimizu, Yasuhiro Matsuda, and Yongming Yang, 129–151. Tokyo: Tokyo University Press.
———. 2009b. Taiwan no Minshuka to Aratana Nittai Kankei no Mosaku. In *Nittai Kankei Shi*, ed. Shin Kawashima, Urara Shimizu, Yasuhiro Matsuda, and Yongming Yang, 153–171. Tokyo: Tokyo University Press.
Minamoto, Kazuhide, and Satoshi Saeki. 2010. 'Senkaku Kougi' Chutai ni Rentaikan. *Yomiuri Shimbun*, September 15.
MOFA of Japan. About the Japan-US Security Consultative Committee (2+2) on Feb. 19, 2005. http://www.mofa.go.jp/mofaj/area/usa/hosho/2plus2.html. Accessed 24 Sep 2017.
———. Japan-China Relations (Archives). http://www.mofa.go.jp/region/asia-paci/china/archives.html. Accessed 24 Sep 2017.
———. The Foreign Minister's Comments on Mar. 22, 2008. http://www.mofa.go.jp/mofaj/press/danwa/20/dkm_0322.html,. Accessed 24 Sep 2017.
———. The Foreign Minister's Comments on the Presidential Election in Taiwan. http://www.mofa.go.jp/mofaj/press/danwa/page3_001538.html. Accessed 24 Sep 2017.
———. The Spokesperson's Talks of the MOFA of Japan on Feb. 28, 2006. http://www.mofa.go.jp/mofaj/press/danwa/18/dga_0228.html Accessed 24 Sep 2017.
———. The Spokesperson's Talks of the MOFA of Japan on Mar. 14, 2005. http://www.mofa.go.jp/mofaj/press/danwa/17/dga_0314.html. Accessed 24 Sep 2017.
MOFA of ROC (Taiwan). Zai Diaoyutai Lieyu Zhengduan, Woguo buyu Zhongguo Dalu Hezuo zhi Lichang. http://www.mofa.gov.tw/News_Content.aspx?n=C641B6979A7897C0&sms=F9719E988D8675CC&s=56A84BD617A31604. Accessed 24 Sep 2017.
National Policy Foundation. *Ma-Hsiao Waijiao Zhengce*. http://www.npf.org.tw/printfriendly/4114. Accessed 24 Sep 2017.
Mainland Affairs Council, ROC (Taiwan). Ma Zongtong Zhuchi Zhonghua Minguo Jianguo 97nian Guoqing Dianli Zhici Quanwen (October 10, 2008). https://www.mac.gov.tw/News_Content.aspx?n=8940E5C0456177C3&sms=2A725F666F2160C6&s=662E1A9DF8898172. Accessed 24 Sep 2017.
———. Ma Zongtong Jieshou Riben 'Dumai xinwen' ji 'Riben Jingji xinwen' Lianhe Xinfang (Jul. 22, 2011). https://www.mac.gov.tw/News_Content.aspx?n=8940E5C0456177C3&sms=2A725F666F2160C6&s=13F919E0D70A5C1C. Accessed 24 Sep 2017.

———. Ma Zongtong Chuxi 'Zhongri Heyue Liushi Zhounian Jinian Huodong (Aug. 15, 2012). https://www.mac.gov.tw/News_Content.aspx?n=21595FA41A9EE70A&sms=DFBE7BE3EE0DB6AE&s=2275E2B118E6B06D. Accessed 24 Sep 2017.

Ogasawara, Yoshiyuki. *Okinotorishima Oki Taiwan Gyosen Daho Jiken*. Ogasawara Yoshiyuki's homepage. http://www.tufs.ac.jp/ts/personal/ogasawara/analysis/okinotorishimadispute.html. Accessed 24 Sep 2017.

Shima, Ryotaro. 1997. *Taiwan Kiko*. Tokyo: Asahishimbunbunko.

Suzuki, Reiko. 2015. Chutai Shunou Kaidan 'Kounichi Rekishisho' Kyouryoku he. *Mainichi Shimbun*, November. 11.

———. 2016. Ianfu Mondai Taiwan Nihon ni Shazai Youkyuu he. *Mainichi Shimbun*, January 6.

Taipei Economic and Cultural Representative Office in Japan. *Nihonjin no Taiwan ni Taisuru Yoron Chosa*. http://www.roc-taiwan.org/jp_ja/post/42473.html. Accessed 24 Sep 2017.

Takeuchi, Takayuki. 2011. *Taiwan Honkon to Higashiajia Chiikisyugi*. Chiba: IDE-JETRO.

Tanaka, Yasuto. 2015. Taiwan, Jyugonichi kara Nihon Shokuhin no Yunyuu Kisei Kyouka. *Sankei Shimbun*, May 12.

Tsai, Peifang. 2016. Renqi Sheng 40 Tian Ma Deng Pengjiayu Wu Zhuqian. *Lianhe Bao*, April 10.

Uchida, Katsuhisa. 2006. *Daijyoubu ka Nittai Kankei*. Tokyo: Sankei Shimbunsha.

Ukai, Satoshi. 2015. Abe Shusho to Taiwan Yatou Shuseki ga Kaidan? *Asahi Shimbun*, October 9.

———. 2016. Taiwan Soutou 'Okinotorishima wa Iwa'. *Asahi Shimbun*, April 28.

United Nations Development Programme. *Human Development Report 2016*. http://hdr.undp.org/sites/default/files/2016_human_development_report.pdf. Accessed 24 Sep 2017.

Wang, Kuang-Tze, and Lee Chih-Te. 2008. Duiri Gongzuo Jiang Chengri Zhuanze Xiaozu. *Lianhe Bao*, July 6.

Wu, Mingshang. 2009. Tairi Guohui Waijiao de Xingcheng yu Fazhan. In *"Qiernian Tizhi" Xia Tairi Guanxi de Huigu yu Zhanwang*, ed. He Sishen and Cai Zengjia. Taipei: Yanjing Jijinhui.

Yabunaka, Mitoji. 2013. Ajiataiheiyo ni Okeru Chiiki Togo Koso de Omoukoto. *Kokusai Mondai* 622: 1–4.

Yang Xiangjun. 2016. Fabiao 'Nanhai Heping Chengyi Lujingtu'. *Lianhe Bao*, January 29.

Yen Anlin. 2009. Lun MaYingjiu Waijiao Linian yu Zhuzhang, Tedian ji Qi Yingxiang. *Taiwan Yenjiu Qikan* No. 2: 15–23.

Author unknown. 1997. Chutai Funsouji Nihon ga Beigun Shien. *Asahi Shimbun*. August 18.

Index[1]

NUMBERS AND SYMBOLS
19th Party Congress, 3, 24
311 earthquakes, Japan, 309
1992 Consensus, 3, 8–10, 17, 22–24,
   101, 107, 108, 112n20, 113n32,
   145–167, 181–186, 190, 192,
   193, 213, 214, 229, 277, 284,
   287, 288, 304, 313
1992 Meeting, 149
1992 Spirit, 149, 182
2012 presidential election, 5, 7, 37,
   39, 41, 52, 54, 64, 97, 98,
   152, 219
2016 presidential election, 1, 3–5, 7,
   49–52, 58, 97, 98, 149,
   157–159, 162, 167, 186,
   200n15, 211, 234, 235

A
Abandonment, 13, 147, 262
Abe, Shinzo, 16, 309–311
Accommodation, 9, 12, 13, 85, 92,
   120, 160, 210, 212–214, 227,
   232, 237, 245–252, 254–257,
   260, 263, 264n7
Alliance, 13, 147, 190, 223, 228, 247,
   256, 287, 301, 305
Alliance cohesion, 14
Anti-access area denial (A2/AD), 248
Anti-China, 9, 19, 154, 159, 167, 194
Anti-establishment, 17, 74, 78–80, 87
Anti-Secession Law (China),
   149, 169n12, 301
Appeasement, 248, 254, 255
Arbitral Tribunal, 16, 218, 230,
   232, 235
Arms sales, 236, 246, 247,
   254, 260, 261
ASEAN Plus One, 272, 289
ASEAN Plus Six, 272
ASEAN Plus Three, 272
Asian Financial Crisis, 1997, 121, 129,
   274, 302

---

[1] Note: Page numbers followed by 'n' refer to notes.

© The Author(s) 2019
W.-c. Lee (Ed.), *Taiwan's Political Re-Alignment and Diplomatic Challenges*, Politics and Development of Contemporary China,
https://doi.org/10.1007/978-3-319-77125-0

Asian Infrastructure Investment Bank
  (AIIB), 280, 293n27
Asian MICE Forum, 274
Asia Pacific Economic Cooperation
  (APEC), 302
Asia-Pacific Industrial Cooperation
  (APIC), 274
Association for Relations Across the
  Taiwan Straits (ARATS), China,
  120, 148, 169n10
Association of Southeast Asian Nations
  (ASEAN), 15, 222, 273, 279,
  280, 292n21
Asymmetric framework, 22
Australia, 186, 217, 218, 229, 230,
  232, 279, 292n21

B
Bandwagoner, 79, 88
Beacon-fire or torching diplomacy, 12
Beijing, 12, 14, 23, 100–102, 107,
  108, 110, 112n20, 113n32, 127,
  128, 130, 131, 166, 167,
  178–184, 186, 187, 192, 195,
  201n22, 210–214, 218–221,
  228–230, 232, 233, 235, 236,
  239n14, 249, 252–255,
  258–261, 285, 306
Bertelsmann Transformation Index
  (BTI), 5, 35, 42
Blue-collar class, 89
Boao Forum, 280
Brexit, 8, 120, 124, 125, 138
Brunei, 279, 286

C
Cambodia, 286
Canada, 282
Century of humiliation, 14, 251

Chen Shui-bian, 1, 11, 12, 14, 21, 23,
  34, 36, 42, 101, 127, 128, 148,
  150, 152, 158, 165, 181, 182,
  191, 194, 200n15, 212, 213,
  278, 285, 293n40, 297, 300,
  304, 314
Chile, 43, 279
China-centered social constructs,
  18, 23, 146, 148, 150
China factor, 8, 19, 22, 119–139
China-friendly policy, 91, 153, 155
Chinese Chamber of Commerce, 282
Chinese identity, 9, 133, 135, 151,
  154, 163, 169n14
Chineseness, 18, 23
Chi-square test, 80
Chu, Eric (KMT politician), 49, 51,
  60, 62, 104, 154, 190
Civil Awareness and Multiple Value,
  81, 87, 93n2
Civil–military relations, 2
Civil society, 4, 17, 18, 23, 126, 303
Closer Economic Partnership
  Arrangement (CEPA), 8, 121,
  129, 130
Cold War, 124, 125, 215, 227,
  258, 282, 289
Communicative manner, 76, 80,
  90, 93
Connective action, 76, 80
Connective logic, 90
Constitutional amendment, 73, 80, 181
Credibility, 3, 14, 18, 155, 224, 246,
  247, 254–257, 262
Cross-Strait relations, 3, 5, 7–9, 11, 14,
  17, 20–23, 36, 54–58, 75, 77, 80,
  82, 101–105, 107–110, 145–167,
  177–196, 209–211, 213, 260,
  261, 284, 288, 305, 313, 315
Cross-Strait Service Trade Agreement
  (CSSTA), 37, 71, 75, 130, 155

Cross-Strait Summit meeting, 309, 310
Cube law, 5, 51, 65n9
Customs Administrative Cooperation Agreement, 272

D
Da-pu Incident, 103, 112n23
Dashed line, 16
De-alignment, 74
Defensive realism, 246, 249, 250, 264n17, 265n18
De jure independence, 60, 101, 107, 158, 165, 199n14, 214
Democratic Progressive Party (DPP), 1, 33, 49, 72, 98, 127, 128, 132, 145, 146, 158–162, 177, 179, 212–214, 217, 229, 233, 278, 304
Democratization, 33–36, 46, 97, 121, 126, 128, 146, 167, 289, 290, 297–304, 314, 315n5
Deng Xiaoping, 166, 180, 181
Deterrence, 14, 148, 161, 163, 246, 247, 254, 256, 259–261
Diaoyu or Diaoyutai Islands (Senkaku Islands), 15, 27n27, 255
Diplomatic privileges and immunities, 282, 283
Disintegration, 120–122, 131, 132, 137, 139, 140n12, 140n22
Duverger's Law, 5, 50, 76, 77, 81

E
East China Sea, 15, 23, 218, 253, 255, 257, 258, 301, 308, 310
Economic Cooperation Framework Agreement (ECFA), 8, 37, 101, 121, 128–130, 133, 142n35, 153, 280, 306

Economic development, 5, 7, 56, 57, 100, 101, 104, 105, 109, 167, 271, 273, 275, 280, 289, 290, 303
Economic globalization, 80, 85, 92
Economic integration, 8, 9, 101, 119–132, 134, 137, 138, 142n40, 262, 279, 289
Economist Intelligence Unit (EIU), 5, 35, 43, 45
Effective numbers of the party, 80, 81
Election Study Center of National Chengchi University, 82
Electoral cycle theory, 11, 178, 179
Electoral period, 177–179, 185, 187, 189, 194
Electoral system
  mixed-member majoritarian (MMM) system, 5, 6, 50, 73, 74, 76, 80, 81, 91
  proportional representation (PR), 5, 41, 42, 49–51, 53, 61, 65n7, 73, 75, 81, 121
  single-member district (SMD) plurality system, 5, 6, 41, 49–51, 61, 63, 65n7, 73, 76, 77, 81, 91
  single nontransferable vote (SNTV), 4, 41, 50, 51, 65n5, 73, 81
Ethnic identity, 35–38, 42, 45
Ethno-nationalism, 4, 147
European Union (EU), 120, 124, 125, 225
Executive Yuan, 37, 39, 71, 112n19, 281

F
Farmer, 80, 89, 276
Finlandization, 249, 263n4
First Island Chain, 220, 254, 258
Floating voter, 78, 88, 92

Freedom House, 34, 290
Free Economic Pilot Zones (FEPZ), 278
Free trade, 7, 85–87, 92, 120–124, 132, 137, 222, 223, 279
Free trade agreement (FTA), 15, 123, 129, 221, 227, 262, 279, 280, 303, 305–307
Fukushima, 16, 309, 312

G
Galvanizing strategy, 11, 178, 194
Green Silicon Island, 278

H
Ha-Ri-Zu (Japan mania), 303
Heterogeneity cost, 121, 122, 120
Homosexual marriage, 91
Hong Kong, 8, 9, 119, 148, 180, 234, 286, 303, 304
Hong Kong Election Study (HKES), 8, 122, 131, 133
Hong Konger, 133, 135, 136
Huei-ming Chen, 90
Humanitarian assistance and disaster relief (HA/DR), 277
Hung Chung-chiu Incident, 103
Hung Hsiu-chu (KMT), 60, 91, 154, 190

I
Identity, 9, 10, 13, 18–20, 22, 24, 35–38, 42, 45, 110n1, 126, 131, 133, 137, 139, 145–148, 150–158, 161–167, 169n14, 179–184, 186, 189, 193–196, 309
Identity polarization, 4, 20, 24
Ideological distance, 73, 77, 80, 86

Independence, 3, 6, 7, 10, 22–24, 34, 36, 37, 60, 61, 64, 79, 82–83, 93n5, 101, 102, 107, 108, 124, 127, 131, 132, 147–149, 151, 154, 156, 158, 160, 161, 164–166, 179, 182–187, 192–194, 200n18, 211, 212, 214, 259, 301
India, 43, 217, 218, 221, 229, 274, 279, 292n21
Indonesia, 274, 276, 277, 282, 284–286, 290, 291n1, 293n33, 293n36, 293n42, 294n44
Information technology (IT), 74–76, 217, 302
Institutional setting, 123, 125, 126, 138
Inter-electoral period, 178, 179, 184, 185, 187–189, 194
International Civil Aviation Organization (ICAO), 157, 287
International Cooperation and Development Fund (ICDF), 276
International Criminal Police Organization (Interpol), 157
International spillover, 123–125
Issue competence, 97–110
Issue ownership, 7, 18, 98–101, 105, 108–110
Issue position, 11, 78, 79, 93n7, 142n42
iVoter project, 80, 93n7, 93n10

J
Japan, 2, 42, 156, 216, 255
Japanese colonial era, 299, 304
Japan-Taiwan Exchange Association, 312
Japan-Taiwan fisheries agreement, 307–309
Japan-Taiwan relations, 16

Japan-US alliance, 301, 305
Justice, 6, 23, 35, 37, 52, 72, 80, 84, 85, 88, 103

K
Ko Wen-je, Taipei Mayor, 11, 191–193, 195
KMT, *see* Kuomintang
Korean War, 253, 256
Kuo-chang Huang, 72, 90
Kuomintang (KMT), 1, 33, 49, 71, 97, 127, 132, 145, 152–157, 179, 212, 229, 277, 298

L
Labor rights, 91
Labor Standards Act, 2
Lai Ching-te, 11, 192, 193, 195, 203n41
Laos, 277, 286
Law of the Sea, 16, 232
Leadership style, 80
Lee Kuan Yew, 285
Lee Teng-hui, 14, 21, 37, 149, 150, 156, 179–182, 200n15, 200n16, 209, 211–213, 259, 260, 284, 299, 304, 309, 315n3
Left-independence political party, 91
Left-wing party, 6, 72, 80, 84, 85, 90, 92
Legislative Yuan, 5, 33, 35, 47n10, 49–51, 53, 54, 59, 61, 63, 64, 65n5, 71, 72, 78, 80, 91, 92, 127, 130, 155, 303, 312
Lesbian, gay, bisexual, transgender, and queer (LGBTQ), 2
Lianhe Hao incident, 305, 306
Lien Chan, 155, 156, 181, 189, 190, 195, 200n18

Li-Luan Chu, 86, 93n11
Localism, 131, 132, 136
Logic of connective action, 18, 76

M
Ma Ying-jeou, 1, 34, 53, 72, 101, 128, 151, 168n9, 180, 210, 261, 277, 297, 304–310
Mainland Affairs Council (MAC), Taiwan, 148, 192
Malaysia, 274, 286, 294n44
Marriage equality, 2
Median approach, 11, 178, 194
Median voter, 11, 73, 74, 77, 80, 82, 84, 85, 178, 185, 194
Melian Dialogue, 22, 27n26
Military injustice, 91
Ministry of Agriculture, 276
Ministry of Economics, 277, 281
Morotai Island, 284
Myanmar, 275, 277, 291n11

N
National identity, 4, 5, 36, 60–64, 77, 79, 80, 82, 84, 86, 137, 160, 162, 163, 168n3
Nationalist Party, 1, 33, 49, 97, 145
Neil Peng, 90, 93
New Power Party (NPP), 6, 36, 50, 71–82, 84–93, 93n2, 93n8, 132, 133, 162
New Southbound Policy (NSP), 15, 21, 108, 186, 187, 194, 274, 275, 277, 278, 281, 288, 291n7, 291n10
New Zealand, 186, 279, 280, 292n21
No unification, no independence, and no use of force, 10, 154, 164

O

Obama administration, 12, 210, 211, 213–216, 218–221, 224, 225, 232, 233, 254
Obama, Barack, 210, 213, 215, 216, 218, 219, 221, 223, 225, 227, 229, 233, 235, 236, 279
Offensive realism, 13, 246, 250, 251
Okinotori Island, 310, 311
Okinotori Reef, 15, 16
One China, one Taiwan, 11, 179, 183–186, 193, 194, 259
"One China" principle, 3, 11, 23, 60, 101, 107, 108, 112n20, 148, 149, 154, 156, 160, 161, 164–167, 179, 180, 182, 186, 193, 199n14, 233, 235, 299, 300, 304
Organizational boundary, 80, 90

P

Pacific Three Closer Economic Partnership (P3 CEP), 279
Panama, 113n32, 186, 288, 294n43
Pan-Blue, 37, 42, 155, 156, 162
Pan-DPP parties, 52, 60, 64
Pan-Green, 11, 83, 156, 158, 160, 162, 195
Pan-KMT parties, 52, 60, 64
Partisan realignment, 50
Party-list proportional representation, 5, 41, 50, 61, 75, 81
Party polarization, 35, 45
Party realignment, 3, 52
People First Party (PFP), 37, 49–52, 65n7, 72, 82, 113n26, 190
Philippines, 216–218, 229, 230, 256, 258, 272, 274, 276, 277, 282–284, 290, 291n1, 294n44
Pivoting, 12
Polarization, 4, 20, 24, 35, 36, 45, 74, 77
Political party, 11, 51, 61, 71–83, 86, 88, 90–92, 93n5, 98, 100, 108, 109, 131, 151, 177, 178, 189, 191, 194
Political reform, 128
Polity IV, 34
Poll boosting, 20
Position mismatch, 7, 78–81, 86–88
Pragmatic diplomacy, 12, 299

Q

Quality of Democracy, 4, 5, 33–35, 37–43, 45
Quasi-alliance, 13, 246

R

Rapprochement policy, 2, 10, 101, 102, 151, 160, 181, 183
Rebalancing, 12, 216, 221, 223, 225
Regional Comprehensive Economic Partnership (RCEP), 15, 272, 279, 280, 292n21
Representative deficit, 7, 77–81, 86–88, 92
ROC agricultural and technical mission, 276

S

Secretary of State, 226, 227, 236, 256, 289
Semi-democracy, 127
Semi-presidential system, 4, 38–39
Sen, Amartya, 4, 25n5
Senkaku Islands (Diaoyu or Diaoyutai Islands), 304–308
Separate Customs Territory, Penghu, Kinmen and Mastu, 280, 283
Separatism, 8, 120, 123–125, 131–133

Severe Acute Respiratory Syndrome (SARS), 129
Singapore, 154, 181, 184, 279, 280, 283, 285, 286, 293n41, 294n44, 310
Sino-British Joint Declaration, 121, 128
The Sino-Japanese communiqué in 1972, 298, 299, 301, 314, 315, 315n1
Social welfare, 5–7, 35, 56, 57, 100, 102, 104, 105, 109, 303
Southbound policy, 14, 21
South China Sea, 3, 16, 23, 217–219, 227, 229–232, 235, 236, 250, 251, 253, 255–258, 301, 310, 312
Southeast Asia, 14, 15, 21, 186, 229, 232, 257, 271–290
Sovereignty, 5, 7, 15, 56, 100, 102, 104, 105, 107, 109, 121, 125, 128, 129, 137, 138, 165, 179, 180, 182, 187, 190, 210, 230
Status quo maintenance, 8, 9, 22–24, 158–160, 164, 166
Straits Exchange Foundation (SEF), Taiwan, 120, 147, 169n10, 180, 181, 186, 201n21
Strategic ambiguity, 155, 247, 260
Structural transition, 13
Summer Universiade Game, 2, 191
Sunflower Movement, 37, 54, 57, 72, 74, 102, 130–131
Sunflower Student Movement, 54, 57, 59, 71, 77

T
Taipei Economic and Cultural Office (TECO), 281, 282
Taiping Island, 16, 232, 310, 312
Taiwan Affairs Office, China, 288

Taiwan Election and Democratization Study (TEDS), 5, 8, 50, 55, 57, 61, 64, 64n2, 66n19, 67n27, 110n4, 122, 131, 133
Taiwan independence, 3, 10, 23, 79, 160, 179, 182, 183, 186, 187, 192–194, 200n18, 211, 259
Taiwan issue, 12–14, 210–212, 214–221, 233–235, 248, 262, 263n1, 299–302
Taiwan Relations Act, 1979, 13, 247, 261
Taiwan Strait Crisis (1995–1996), 259, 300
Taiwan Strait missile crisis (1995–1996), 299
Taiwanese democratization, 297–304, 314, 315n5
Taiwanese identifiers, 10, 151, 152
Thailand, 274–277, 281, 282, 284, 286, 290, 291n1, 291n11, 292n12, 294n44
Third Force, 131, 132, 136, 137
Thucydides Trap, 13, 247
Tiananmen Square incident, 1989, 180, 299
Tianran du (natural supporters of Taiwan independence), 24, 160
Timor-Leste, 286
Trade liberalization, 8, 119, 139
Trade peace, 8
Trans-Pacific Partnership Agreement (TPP), 12, 15, 159, 219, 221–223, 225, 227, 235, 262, 272, 279, 280
Trans-Pacific Strategic Economic Partnership Agreement (TPSEPA or P4), 279
Trump administration, 13, 214, 217, 232, 236, 261, 262

Trump, Donald, 3, 211, 222–224, 228–231, 234–237, 241n37, 279, 287
Tsai Ing-wen, 2, 3, 6, 8–12, 14, 16, 17, 19, 21–24, 34, 37, 40, 41, 45, 49, 86, 101, 137, 148, 185, 200n15, 201n21, 213, 261, 274
Two Chinas, 11, 179, 181, 182, 185, 186, 193, 194, 259

U
Umbrella Movement, 130
Unification, 12, 13, 20, 60, 61, 63, 120, 127, 130, 139n3, 147, 151, 159, 161, 214, 249, 260, 301
United Kingdom Independence Party (UKIP), 124, 138
United Nations (UN), 146, 183, 217, 271, 277, 288, 291n11, 312
United States of America (USA), 2, 36, 99, 128, 146, 178, 209, 245–263, 273, 300
US-China relations, 12, 13, 22, 167, 210, 211, 214, 215, 218, 219, 228, 232, 235, 236, 246, 248, 252, 262
US election debates, 221–228, 230–231, 233–234
US-Taiwan relations, 12, 237, 260–262

V
Vacation diplomacy, 285
Varieties of Democracy (V-Dem), 5, 35, 42
Vienna Convention on Diplomatic Relations, 1961, 282
Vietnam, 216, 230, 272, 274, 276, 277, 282, 291n1, 293n31, 293n33, 294n44
Visa waiver, 14, 281, 286, 287

W
World Health Assembly (WHA), 108, 113n33, 157, 186

X
Xi Jinping, 3, 24, 26n16, 154, 155, 157, 165, 166, 184, 186, 201n25, 202n30, 210, 213–218, 220, 221, 225, 233, 235–237, 247, 285, 293n41, 310

Y
Yizhong Gebiao (one China with different interpretations), 148

Z
Zhang Zhijun, 288